D1244537

States in the Global Economy

Bringing Domestic Institutions Back In

The growing interconnectedness of national economies and an expanding awareness of global interdependence in the 1990s have generated lively debate over the future of national governance. In a world of highly mobile capital, are states still vital to the social and economic wellbeing of their citizens? A number of changes in the state's domestic and international environment – ranging from regulatory reforms and welfare state restructuring to the proliferation of intergovernmental agreements – have promoted the view that globalisation has a negative impact, compromising state capacities to govern domestically. This book challenges the 'constraints thesis'. Covering vital areas of state activity (welfare, taxation, industrial strategy, and regulatory reform), the contributors focus on a range of issues (finance, investment, trade, technology) faced by both developed and developing countries. The contributors argue that globalisation can enable as well as constrain, and they seek to specify the institutional conditions which sharpen or neutralise the pressures of interdependence.

LINDA WEISS is Professor in Government and International Relations at the University of Sydney, Australia. Her previous publications include *The Myth of the Powerless State* (1998), *States and Economic Development* (1995), and *Creating Capitalism* (1988).

CAMBRIDGE STUDIES IN INTERNATIONAL RELATIONS

States in the Global Economy

Bringing domestic institutions back in

Edited by
Linda Weiss

University of Sydney, Australia

CAMBRIDGE
UNIVERSITY PRESS

b25084963

PUBLISHED BY THE PRESS SYNDICATE OF THE UNIVERSITY OF CAMBRIDGE
The Pitt Building, Trumpington Street, Cambridge CB2 1RP, United Kingdom

CAMBRIDGE UNIVERSITY PRESS
The Edinburgh Building, Cambridge, CB2 2RU, UK
40 West 20th Street, New York, NY 10011-4211, USA
477 Williamstown Road, Port Melbourne, VIC 3207, Australia
Ruiz de Alarcón 13, 28014 Madrid, Spain
Dock House, The Waterfront, Cape Town 8001, South Africa

http://www.cambridge.org

First published 2003

Printed in the United Kingdom at the University Press, Cambridge

Typeface Palatino 10/12.5 pt   *System* LATEX 2$_\varepsilon$ [TB]

A catalogue record for this book is available from the British Library

Library of Congress cataloguing in publication data

States in the global economy: bringing domestic institutions
back in / edited by Linda Weiss.
    p.   cm. – (Cambridge studies in international relations; 86)
Includes bibliographical references and index.
ISBN 0 521 81913 X – ISBN 0 521 52538 1 (pb.)
1. International economic relations.   2. Globalisation – Economic aspects.
3. Globalisation – Political aspects.   4. Globalisation – Social aspects.
5. State, The.   I. Weiss, Linda (Linda M.)   II. Series.
HF 1359 .S736   2002
337 – dc21   2002025901

ISBN 0 521 81913 X hardback
ISBN 0 521 52538 1 paperback

HF
1359
·S7345
2003

Contents

Contents

Figures

Tables

Contributors

JALAL ALAMGIR is Visiting Fellow at the Watson Institute of International Studies, Brown University, and Associate Editor of the *International Studies Review*. He is also a strategy consultant at Braun Consulting, Boston, currently researching competition in e-commerce and its narrative and political implications for international organizations.

WILLIAM COLEMAN holds the Canada Research Chair on Global Governance and Public Policy and is Director of the Institute on Globalization and the Human Condition at McMaster University in Canada. His publications include *Financial Services, Globalization, and Domestic Policy Change* (1996); *Business and Politics* (1988) and *The State, Business, and Industrial Change in Canada* (co-authored 1989).

RICHARD DONER is Associate Professor of Political Science at Emory University. He is author of *Driving a Bargain* (1991) and co-author of *From Silicon Valley to Singapore: Location and Competitive Advantage in the Hard Disk Industry* (2001). He is currently working (with Ansil Ramsay) on an institutional analysis of industrial upgrading in Thailand.

JOHN HOBSON is Senior Lecturer in Government and International Relations at the University of Sydney. His major publications include *Historical Sociology of International Relations* (co-edited, Cambridge 2002); *The State and International Relations* (Cambridge 2000); *The Wealth of States* (Cambridge 1997); and *States and Economic Development* (co-authored, 1995).

DAVID LEVI-FAUR is Lecturer in Political Science at the University of Haifa and Visiting Fellow at Nuffield College, Oxford (2000–02). His publications include *Israel: The Dynamics of Change and Continuity* (co-edited 1999) and *The Visible Hand: The State and the Industrialisation of Israel* (2001).

MICHAEL LORIAUX is Associate Professor of Political Science at Northwestern University. He is author of *France After Hegemony* (1991) and *Capital Ungoverned* (ed. 1997).

M. RAMESH is Associate Professor in Government and International Relations at the University of Sydney. His books include *Welfare Capitalism in Southeast Asia* (2000), *Studying Public Policy* (co-authored 1995) and *The Political Economy of Canada* (co-authored 1999).

ANSIL RAMSAY is the D. Charles, Sarah A. and John D. Munsil Professor of Government at St Lawrence University. His publications include *Thailand–US Relations* (co-authored 1988).

DUANE SWANK is Professor of Political Science at Marquette University. He specialises in the comparative political economy of capitalist democracies. His new book is *Global Capital, Political Institutions, and Policy Change in Developed Welfare States* (Cambridge 2002).

MARK TILTON is Associate Professor of Political Science at Purdue University. His publications include *Restrained Trade* (1996) and *Is Japan Really Changing its Ways? Regulatory Reform and the Japanese Economy* (co-edited 1998).

LINDA WEISS is Professor in Government and International Relations at the University of Sydney. Her publications include *The Myth of the Powerless State* (1998); *States and Economic Development* (co-authored, 1995); and *Creating Capitalism* (1988).

MEREDITH WOO-CUMINGS is Professor of Political Science at the University of Michigan. Her publications include *Race to the Swift* (1991), *Financial Liberalization in Interventionist States* (co-authored 1997), and *The Developmental State* (ed. 1999).

TIANBIAO ZHU is a Postdoctoral Fellow in the Department of International Relations, Research School of Pacific and Asian Studies, at the Australian National University. He also teaches political science at Tsingua University, Beijing. His main research interest is international and comparative political economy, and he is currently undertaking research on the political economy of development in Taiwan, South Korea, and China.

Preface

It is often said that comparative and international political economy are sister disciplines which would benefit from greater cross-fertilisation. This volume takes a step in that direction by arguing the case for understanding the impact of globalisation on the state as being tightly connected with the character of domestic institutions (understood broadly as the embedded norms and organisational arrangements that shape interests and outcomes).

The idea for this volume grew out of a talk given at UCLA's Center for Social Theory and Comparative History in 1999. My talk took issue with the 'top–down', overly deductive nature of much of the globalisation literature and the way it rarely seemed to engage with what was happening to states 'on the ground', as it were. While many contributors to the globalisation–state debate have acknowledged that 'institutions matter', surprisingly few have given substance to that aphorism. Encouraged by the responses, I drew up an 'A' list of authors noted for work that was both well grounded in domestic institutions analysis and at the same time able to engage with the concerns of international relations scholars. Prospective co-authors were provided with an outline of the project's aims and rationale, along with key questions. In the interests of producing a tight volume, proposed collaborators were asked to indicate, if they intended to join the project, how their chapter would contribute to the aims of the book. It has been my good fortune to have a generous and talented team, which has certainly made the job of editor a less onerous one than I had been led to anticipate.

The feedback from two anonymous referees was very important in helping to shape the final product. Peter Katzenstein's comments, given in the context of a symposium at Gothenburg to mark the fifteenth anniversary of his study of small states, helped me to shape the conclusion.

Reversing the 'inside-out' argument, it acknowledges that the character of globalisation over the long haul can also be institution shaping, though in ways that globalist analysis does not anticipate. It would be remiss of me not to mention how much I owe as well to colleagues whose invitations to speak at various gatherings – namely, UCLA, Purdue, Simon Fraser, Aarhus, Roskilde, Gothenburg, the ANU, Griffith, and Macquarie – allowed me to try out some of the key arguments of this volume. In addition to the participants at these colloquia, I would like to thank Robert Brenner, John Degnbol-Martinusson, Mette Kjaer, Laurids Lauridsen, Michael Mann, John Mathews, Stephen McBride, Ole Nørgaard, Ulf Olsson, Jonas Pontusson, Tim Rowse, Georg Sørensen, and Urban Strandberg. I am grateful to John Haslam, my editor at Cambridge University Press, and Steve Smith for their support for the project. Sheila Kane's assistance with copy-editing was much appreciated. Elizabeth Thurbon, a much treasured research assistant and young academic *extraordinaire* in the making, gave her usual best in helping to turn the typescript into a book.

Finally, the research for parts of this project was generously supported by a grant from the Australia Research Council.

1 Introduction: bringing domestic institutions back in

Linda Weiss

An issue of central importance in the globalisation debate today concerns the impact of increasing economic openness upon the state's capacity to govern the national economy. As participants in that debate, we seek answers to the big questions, such as whether, in a world of highly mobile capital, states – as territorially centred authorities – are still vital to the social and economic well-being of their citizens. We want to know what, if anything, states can do to promote wealth creation and social protection in an era of economic interdependence. And we want to know whether countries which travel the path of international economic openness must necessarily abandon their distinctive institutions (and embrace the norms, arrangements, and policies of competitive liberalism).

These are not idle questions. The reason we are asking such questions so insistently at the turn of the century has much to do with the widespread changes going on both inside and outside the nation-state – ranging from welfare reforms, through financial liberalisation, to the proliferation of intergovernmental agreements.

These organisational and regulatory reforms appear to be coinciding with other changes taking place in the structure of the international political economy – in particular, the multinationalisation of production and the growth of so-called 'footloose' business corporations, as well as the astonishing increase and speed of cross-border capital flows. So the assumption frequently made is that these two sets of changes must be intimately related, that the state's actions (or inactions) – from fiscal conservatism and deregulation to welfare restructuring – can be explained readily as a response of besieged or hapless governments to global flows and similar pressures of openness and interdependence.

This is why much of the discussion being conducted today about globalisation's alleged impact on the state evokes that well-told tale about a drunken fellow who loses his keys in a dark place and then goes over by the light in order to search for them. 'What are you doing?' asks a passing stranger. 'Well', replies the inebriate, 'I won't get very far searching for my keys in the dark place, so I'm looking over here where the light is brighter.'

Domestic institutions are a bit like the 'dark place' in the globalisation debate. Challenges coming from the global arena are well illuminated. But there is correspondingly little sense of how national authorities are managing the challenges of openness. Indeed, a good many of the participants in the globalisation–national governance debate, somewhat like the drunken figure, have been reeling from the many changes to the domestic and international environments and, like that figure, they have been searching over by the light of globalisation for clues as to what it all means.

The result is a story that is being told largely in terms of one-way traffic. That is to say that most thinking about the changes going on at the domestic level has been oriented towards the global arena because that is where most light is directed, with global actors and markets always seen to be 'constraining' national governance, and states either responding ineffectually, or else retreating more and more from economic management.

In the standard tale, then, globalisation is very much a 'top-down' affair, understood as a series of constraints that economic openness places on the viability and effectiveness of particular national policies – macroeconomic, fiscal, social, and industrial. Globalisation is seen to be intrinsically constraining because openness involves the fall of national barriers to trade, investment, and financial flows, exposure to increasing capital mobility (via the multinationalisation of production and growth of global financial markets), and also conformity with intergovernmental agreements requiring, for example, that governments open their markets to foreign trade and financial institutions as well as eliminating certain subsidies to industry.

Openness is therefore seen to constrain and limit severely what governments can do across a range of policy areas. Globalisation analysts propose that economic openness not only drastically reduces scope for expansionary fiscal and social protection strategies, but that it also renders unviable a host of trade, financial, and industrial policies supporting national wealth creation, since these would conflict with international agreements. Such are the conclusions of the more 'moderate' globalists[1] who differentiate themselves from those who posit the end of the nation-state (Ohmae 1990; Horsman and Marshall 1994), the so-called 'hyper-globalists'. Since few scholars of the international political economy seriously hold to the minority view of the hyper-globalisers, we waste little time in that direction, turning our attention instead to the claims of the more moderate majority (hereafter, the 'constraints school').

In the language deployed by the constraints school, the state is changing and the changes are not generally reinforcing or strengthening its capacities, its autonomy, or control. On the contrary, according to this influential view, state powers are being severely 'constrained', and ultimately 'transformed'. To 'constrain', according to the dictionary, means 'to compel'; 'to force or produce in an unnatural or strained manner'; 'to confine'; 'to hold back by force'. This constraints view of globalisation has many adherents, and although they disagree about many things, they are united in the view that changes in the international political economy have radically restricted policy choice and forced policy shifts that play to the preferences of global investors and mobile corporations, rather than to the needs of the domestic political economy and its citizenry.[2]

Proponents of the constrained state thesis thus advance strong claims about how much political autonomy states have lost (compared with some usually unspecified previous era); about how restricted are their policy choices; and ultimately about how little states can do to provide decent social protection and promote wealth creation. From this perspective, managing the national economy to promote growth, industrial upgrading, and employment – whether by maintaining or raising taxation and spending levels, coordinating an investment strategy, encouraging industrial upgrading, or supporting technological innovation, and so on – are nowadays seen to be increasingly beyond the capacities of territorially centred states.

Moreover, this view of the 'constrained state' is often accompanied by another claim about the 'erosion of national capitalisms'. This is the contention that – from East Asia to continental Europe – we are witnessing the end of an era of 'coordinated market economies' (read also 'organised' and 'managed capitalism') and moving towards a world more consistently 'liberal market' in orientation. In such a world, government's role is restricted to providing rule of law, basic regulation, and minimum social safety nets.

There is clearly something to these claims. It is not hard to recognise that national governments are at times constrained by various pressures beyond their borders and that some of these pressures can be ascribed to international interdependence and economic openness. After all, who could fail to be impressed by the 'electronic herd' which – as Thomas Friedman (1999) and many others endlessly point out – can readily move vast amounts of capital in and out of countries in accordance with the herd's perceptions of their political and economic merit?

In short, the idea of 'globalisation' can certainly help to shed *some light* on national governance issues. But the general point should be clear: before we abandon the *darker place* and go heading off in the general direction of the light, we need to strain our eyes and look more care-fully at what is going on *inside* nation-states – particularly as national authorities set about responding to the global economy.

That is the starting point for this volume. The issue to be explored in this book is the extent to which the global economy has the poten-tial not only to *constrain* but also to *enable* governments to pursue their policy objectives. It asks: 'To what extent does the outcome depend on the character of the domestic institutional context (including its nor-mative and organisational aspects)?' It is the central contention of this volume that if we wish to account for impacts of globalisation in any particular national setting, we must start with the domestic institutions of governance, which mediate the challenges of openness. Such insti-tutions embody regnant ideas and normative orientations (especially ideas about the state's economic role and public purpose) as well as organisational structures (in particular, arrangements which produce cohesive or disunified elites, structure policy networks linking state and society, and more generally aggregate and represent interests in the political and policy process). This book proposes that rather than national states being generally constrained, hollowed out, and trans-formed by global markets, domestic institutions – especially, *but not only*, political ones – are key to understanding the effects of openness and where interdependence may be heading. In general, one cannot de-duce the impacts of global markets – whether constraining or enabling – because these are mediated by domestic institutions, which in turn shape the ways in which national authorities choose to deal with the challenges of openness.[3]

In this introductory chapter I analyse in the first section the key claims of the constraints hypothesis at the core of the standard account along with its strengths and weaknesses; the main critical response – the so-called 'measurement critique' of globalisation – and its limitations are detailed in the second section. Subsequent sections (three and four) then outline the approach developed in this book, which is represented in Figure 1.1 below. Section three sets out the case for studying globalisation as a process with *enabling* – not just constraining – effects on policy. Section four explains why institutions are important and how they matter to an analysis of globalisation's impacts, and summarises aspects of existing research on domestic institutions of relevance to this volume. I conclude with an outline of the main propositions of the present study.

Globalisation as constraint: the standard view

The standard view of globalisation conceives the process as a constraining force that limits what governments can do and ultimately transforms the state into a weaker, meaner, or leaner version of its former self. The globalisation thesis is a two-pronged claim which combines both descriptive and causal statements. It asserts:

(a) that the world is becoming more interconnected through increasing economic openness and the growth of transborder networks that accompany that process, and

(b) that this interconnectedness is increasing the power of global (economic and political) networks of interaction *at the expense of* national (economic and political) networks.

The first is a descriptive claim, the second a claim as to impact or causation. Both are frequently bundled together in various definitions of globalisation. Thus many conceptualisations elide the nature of globalisation (*what it is*) with its effects (*how it impacts*) in the domestic arena. From this confusion stem two features which have framed much of the debate to date. One is the tendency towards 'circularity of argument', whereby globalisation's effects become true by definition.[4] This explains in part the importance attached to measuring interconnectedness through foreign direct investment (FDI), trade, and other such indicators – often seen implicitly at least as a proxy for gauging consequences or impacts, a point taken up in the next section.

The other feature is the embodiment of a 'win–lose logic' in discussions of the global–national relationship. This logic has been expressed in more or less nuanced ways: from the more extreme views positing the extinction of the nation-state or its demise as a sovereign power (Ohmae 1995; Camilleri and Falk 1992), to those of the more 'moderate'

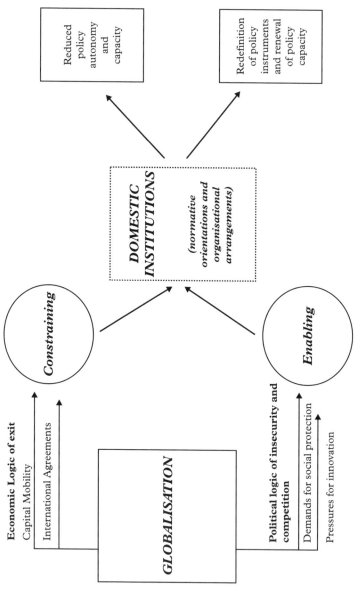

Figure 1.1 The logics of globalisation, domestic institutions, and state responses

majority anticipating erosion of the state's policymaking capacities and virtual retreat from national economic management (e.g., Reich 1991; Cerny 1996; Schmidt 1995; Strange 1996; Held and McGrew 2000; Cox 1997) to the recent transmogrification of this idea into that of the state's 'transformation' or 'reconstitution' (e.g., Scholte 1997; Held *et al.*, 1999; Rosenau 2000).

The 'globalisation-as-constraint' school

While sometimes referring to themselves as 'transformationalists' (globalisation is real but it has 'changed', not 'displaced' the state) in order to distinguish their position from the so-called 'sceptics' (those who question the very existence of a strong globalisation tendency itself), it is none the less reasonable to refer to this moderate globalist majority as the 'constraints' school. This is necessary in order to distinguish the latter from other analysts of globalisation who have also posited or analysed state power changes – as do a number of chapters in this book (Coleman; Levi-Faur; Loriaux; Weiss; Woo-Cumings; Zhu) – but who find unconvincing the negative-sum conclusions more typical of the constraints school. These so-called sceptics (or more appropriately, 'institutional adaptationists'), while often acknowledging important *changes* in the structure of the international political economy, none the less question the *impact* claims proffered by the 'constraints transformationalists'. Among the more prominent sceptics regarding the 'constrained state' and convergence claims of the constraints school are the scholars of comparative politics and comparative political economy whose analyses are informed by a domestic institutions perspective.[5]

In short, while many constraints theorists – like domestic institutionalists – posit state 'transformation' as a major impact of economic openness, the nature of the changes they identify, while not always clearly drawn, are generally taken to imply the emergence of a different kind of beast whose powers, if not eroded, are substantially pared back. In this respect, as we shall see, 'constraints transformationalists' differ markedly from 'institutional adaptationists'.

The propositions

The impact of the international political economy on the state, as espoused by the constraints school, can be encapsulated in two principal propositions. Both focus on the state's policymaking capacities and the ability to pursue its desired goals. The first claims that these capacities are shrinking (or have already eroded) very significantly under globalisation; that in most cases states are being forced into donning the straitjacket of fiscal conservatism, cutting budgets, taxes, and spending. Capital mobility is seen as the key to this outcome, wreaking constraining effects on fiscal, welfare, and industrial-technology policies. While these effects may sometimes occur through direct political pressure as corporate employers, investors, and even foreign governments may seek to influence the policies of a particular state, such 'strategic' pressures are generally held to be less important than 'structural' ones.[6] For the latter are presumed to hold sway, with or without the existence of strategic pressure.

The structural pressures of openness are supposed to work their effects on policy in the following way: economic openness creates a new capitalism of 'entry' and 'exit'. As barriers to trade, investment, and finance fall, governments increasingly compete to attract and retain mobile capital; they must therefore pursue policies that complement the preferences of multinational corporations (MNCs) and financial markets lest these highly mobile investors exercise the exit option and take flight to lower-tax and welfare-conservative environments. As a result, financial openness and corporate mobility are expected to exert downward pressure on fiscal and social policy, forcing welfare retrenchment, corporate tax cuts, and shifts in the tax burden from capital to labour. This is the effect popularly known as a 'race to the bottom'.

The second proposition about globalisation's impact holds that the rise of intergovernmental agreements and international organisations like the World Trade Organisation (WTO) have substantially stripped states of their autonomy and control over the domestic economy, removing the scope for pursuing trade, industry, and financial policies to strengthen the economy.

So policy choices are deemed to be 'straitjacketed' by the pressures of trade competition, the preferences of MNCs and financial markets, and the rules of multilateralism. As a result of these and other developments, states virtually everywhere have been 'reduced to the role of adjusting national economies to the dynamics of an unregulated global economy' (Cox 1996: 528).

From this perspective, then, the overarching conclusion is that it is not just the state's policymaking capacities but the state itself as an institution which is being transformed, downsizing its powers and capacities, and distributing authority to other political and economic actors at local, national, and international levels (Strange 1996: 4; Hirst and Thompson 1996: 183–94; Scholte 2000: 238–9; Held *et al.* 1999: 50).

Although constraints theorists often contend that globalisation has impacted on the sovereignty and autonomy (read also 'capacity') of the state in a radical way,[7] they seek to differentiate their position from the 'hardliner' radical globalists who posit demise or retreat of the nation-state. Yet even as 'moderate' globalists, these analysts none the less maintain that the changes they are at pains to identify lead inevitably to a reduced policymaking capacity. In particular, a number of constraints theorists contend that financial globalisation has had a 'radical impact' on the ability of states to decide and pursue their own policy preferences (Held *et al.* 1999: 442–3). More generally, they assert that globalisation is impacting on the power, functions, and authority of the nation-state in a negative-sum way, producing a marked shift towards a 'divided authority system' in which states share the tasks of governance with a multiplicity of public and private institutions at local, regional, transnational, and global levels (Held and McGrew 1998: 221; Rosenau 2000: 186).

It is significant that for these observers authority is not deemed to be 'delegated' but 'divided'. And when you divide something and redistribute the portions to others, you end up with a smaller share for yourself. This is why constraints theorists conclude that national governments are 'no longer... the locus of effective political power' (Held and McGrew 1998: 242); that their 'capacities for governance... [are] lessening' (Rosenau 2000: 186); and that the state has now lost its centrality, becoming instead just one among many contending rule-making powers, with quite restricted policymaking capacities (Held *et al.* 1999: 50, 442–4), if sometimes heightened rule-making functions in more narrowly defined areas.[8]

Constraints theorists make a number of uncontentious claims about the state's changing context. But the conclusion of most interest to the studies in this volume boils down to the contentious claim that states are losing their independence or autonomy for social goal-setting and that their rule-making authority, decisionmaking powers, and ability to control domestic outcomes – in short, their room to manoeuvre and capacity to govern – are becoming increasingly restricted and specialised over a far narrower terrain than ever before.

However plausible such conclusions seem in the light of so many readily observable changes in the international and domestic political economies, they need to be grounded in systematic empirical research. At the very least, before rushing to easy conclusions, we need to untangle theoretical assumptions: Why, for example, should new forms of cooperation between states and other power actors – whether public or private, domestic or international – be, in principle, more restricting or less enabling than before; and how, in practice, are we to measure 'more' and 'less' capacity to govern?

We can only make progress on these issues when we stop conceptualising states and their powers in static and negative-sum ways. As discussed in later sections, far from curtailing the state's capacity for independent goal-setting, a number of recent studies have found that the new power-sharing arrangements – public and private, intergovernmental, multilateral, and so on – may well extend the state's infrastructural reach and implementation effectiveness, especially where domestic structures are so oriented.

If this observation conflicts with the conclusions of the governance literature (the source of much 'transformationalist-cum-constraints' thinking), this is because the latter operates with a strictly negative-sum conception of power – if A has power, then B does not. But this distributive view of state power (as 'power over') seems in many respects more suited to the pre-industrial state; it has more limited value as a *standard* from which to appraise *changes* in state powers in modern times. The biggest state transformation came with the leap into industrialism as states gained in penetrative reach and extractive capacity what they forfeited in despotic power over their subjects. These newly acquired 'infrastructural powers' of industrial (read 'modern') states implied, increasingly, 'power through' collaboration or negotiation with other power actors in society (Mann 1984). It is fruitful to view the power-sharing changes both inside and outside the nation-state currently being discussed in the governance and globalisation literatures as more recent extensions of this 'collective' notion of power, a point we return to later in this chapter.[9]

Critical responses (I): delimiting the constraints

In spite of these conceptual weaknesses, there is unquestionably some basis to the constraints hypothesis. The hypothesis is at its most compelling in the financial realm, appearing most accurate on monetary policy and least accurate on social, trade, and industry and innovation policies. In particular, the loss of monetary policy autonomy – for example, under the standard trilemma[10] or as a result of European Monetary Union (EMU) – is probably the area of economic policy where conventional 'globalisation' (qua 'interdependence') theory is most on the ball.

But even here there is no need to overstate. The loss of monetary policy control under conditions of capital mobility and floating exchange rates is neither complete nor generalised. It is far from *complete* in that it applies most clearly to loss of control over the price of money (in particular, the exchange rate). However, with regard to levels and types of private debt, governments are still able to regulate domestic credit expansion, if they so choose (Shaberg 1999: 209–10). While this ability is to some degree offset by the access of domestic players to international credit, even here regulatory authorities can, in principle, and sometimes in practice do set rules to define the nature and limits of access (for example, so as to favour long- or short-term debt, or to limit consumer credit). So the loss of control over monetary policy is by no means complete.

Loss of monetary policy control is also far from *generalised*, in that it tends to apply rather more to the small, highly open economies and rather less to the larger ones like the United States, Japan, or Germany. (Although even with regard to smaller states, the evidence on causal sequencing in the relationship between state size, policy choice, and currency stability remains ambiguous).[11] While the nation-states of EMU are also clearly constrained in their monetary policy autonomy, the primary dynamic at work here is one of *regional* interdependence and political choice, not the more abstract, structural pressure of global markets.

With regard to fiscal (and, by implication, social) policy, the major financial constraint has typically been specified in the following way: globalisation limits a government's ability to run fiscal deficits and pursue inflationary monetary policy because financial markets react severely to policies which would lead them to anticipate inflationary outcomes. While this claim is not in contention, the implication that such a policy constraint would disappear in the absence of global financial markets is unsustainable. Macroeconomic policy has *always* been vulnerable to private sector reaction, irrespective of capital market integration. Whether or not capital markets are integrated, high deficit spending in the presence of high government debt is expected to trigger inflationary outcomes and thus a rise in long-term interest rates, partly to insure the bond holders against inflation risk, and partly to hedge against the possibility that governments will inflate in the future to reduce the real costs of the debt (Glyn 1998a: 397; Garrett 1998a: 804).

A corollary of this point is that business is concerned much less with the *level* of government spending than with *how* it is financed. Recent findings based on interviews with fund managers and other financial market players offer strong support for this conclusion (Mosley 2000:

747–50). They confirm that such investors remain largely indifferent to the level or composition of government spending and that their most important concern is inflation. Financial market actors, however, do worry about the total amount of spending if this is financed by borrowing, for reasons noted above. So market players concede that it is the size of the deficit that matters rather than simply *how* the government finances its spending. Thus, as Layna Mosley puts it, 'If domestic constituents prefer and are willing to fund larger public sectors, financial markets do not punish governments for acceding to this demand' (Mosley 2000: 749).

So capital flight is a more likely outcome when governments opt to pay for higher spending by borrowing rather than by raising new taxes. But this too requires qualification, since the evidence indicates that government debt must be very high before a negative impact on policy is felt (see Swank 2000: 23). This would indicate significant room for expansionary fiscal policy before constraints set in, a conclusion that meshes well with the actual taxation and spending patterns reported in Chapters 2 (Hobson) and 3 (Swank).[12]

All in all then, macroeconomic constraints exist, but not to the point of constituting a 'straitjacket'. Most important, where governments do appear to concede to financial market pressures, this applies to a limited number of well-defined areas – chiefly, big deficit spending funded by big borrowing – and with greater consequence for smaller, highly open economies. By the same token, governments retain autonomy in many other significant areas. Indeed, in view of the evidence on investor preferences (real rather than imputed), one might conclude with Mosley that in the developed democracies, at least, the influence of global financial markets on governments is 'somewhat strong, but somewhat narrow' (2000: 766). Constraints theory therefore requires significant modification to tailor its claims to more modest (empirically justifiable) proportions.

Critical responses (II): measuring interdependence

Although the constraints on government policy have been often overstated, there is no disputing that economic interdependence has grown very significantly over the past four decades. The facts concerning globalisation are familiar. Reflecting a reduction in the transaction costs of international economic exchange, trade in goods and services and especially capital flows have increased notably in the last thirty years.[13]

For the average developed democracy, trade in goods and services as a share of Gross Domestic Product (GDP) has expanded from approximately 45 per cent to 65 per cent between the mid-1960s and mid-1990s (United Nations 1996). In 2000, the value of world merchandise trade reached $6,180 billion, and experienced its fastest annual growth rate in over a decade of 12.5 per cent (WTO 2001). Inward and outward flows of foreign direct investment, portfolio investment, and bank lending have increased from a 1960s national average of roughly 5 per cent of GDP to approximately 50 per cent in the mid-1990s. In 1999 alone, global FDI inflows totalled $865 billion and constituted 14 per cent of capital formation around the world, compared with 2 per cent twenty years ago (UNCTAD 2000). In the OECD, cross-border trade in bonds and equities increased from an average of 10 per cent of GDP in 1980 to between 150 per cent and 250 per cent of GDP in 1995 (Petit and Soete 1998). The averages for Germany, Japan, and the United States grew from 6.9, 2.8, and 5.9 per cent of GDP respectively between 1975–79, to a total of 334.5, 85.1, and 178.9 per cent in 1999 (BIS 2000). Total borrowing on international capital markets rose to more than $830 billion in 1995, from less than $360 billion just five years before (OECD 1996). Declines in covered interest rate differentials and liberalisation of controls on movements of goods, services, and finance have proceeded apace. While observers have noted distinct limits to globalisation (e.g., Berger and Dore 1996; Keohane and Milner 1996; Weiss 1998), there is little question that internationalisation has significantly expanded during the post-Bretton Woods era.

While these figures show that national economies are far more interdependent today than in the recent past (though not necessarily more than a century ago), the implied conclusion that they support the existence of a strong globalisation tendency which in turn constrains state capacity has been widely challenged. Indeed, the main critical response to the idea of globalisation as constraint has been a quantitative one, which consists in showing that globalisation is far less advanced than its proponents have claimed.[14] Many scholars sceptical of such a tendency have sought to counter the idea of an all-powerful, border-erasing force at work by setting these quantitative changes within a larger perspective, assessing their overall weight as a proportion of national economic activity. Through rigorous measurement, *inter alia*, of trade, capital, and investment flows, sceptics have shown that economies are still primarily national in scope: around 90 per cent of production is still carried out for the domestic market and about 90 per cent of consumption is locally produced. Moreover, domestic investment by domestic capital is financed mostly by domestic savings and far exceeds the size of FDI flows in all major markets, while companies generally continue to concentrate most of their production, assets, and strategic decisionmaking in their home country (and trade in their 'home' region). Finance on the other hand is a different story – one in which genuinely global markets (especially in foreign exchange, bonds, and derivatives) are central characters. Even so, on most other dimensions, globalisation sceptics leave little doubt that economic enmeshment through trade, investment, and finance has not displaced the preponderance of 'national' networks. If anything, it has simply produced a more complex system in which both international and transnational networks have developed in parallel with, and complementary to, national systems of production and finance.

Sceptics therefore conclude that the reach of globalisation is limited (Wade 1996; Hirst and Thompson 1996; Boyer and Drache 1996), that it has important historical parallels which belie notions of state power depletion (Bairoch 1996), and that borders and national states still matter very much (Helliwell 1998).

Beyond measurement

Accounts focusing on how far globalisation has advanced are valuable for infusing quantitative analysis with a historical perspective that ably clarifies the real extent of globalisation. But, as a critical response, the measurement approach remains limited and inconclusive. For one thing, it has produced a stalemate: if globalists are not impressed with these findings, it is because they can always counter with the claim that even if globalisation has not yet gone far, it is surely only a matter of time.

Moreover, a focus on the extent of globalisation may set us on a false trail. For it assumes that the fate of national governance rests on the outcome and thereby implicitly endorses the win–lose premise that 'more globalisation must equal less scope for state capacity'. The presumption is that if one can show that economic integration has advanced very far, then it must follow that a major power shift is under way – one that restricts the scope for national institutions, actors, and policies, while elevating the interests and preferences of non-national actors in a negative-sum form of logic (Weiss 1999a: 64).

However, the extent of globalisation may tell us little about national responses to, or capacities for managing, the challenges of openness. For, as the next section argues and as the studies in this volume demonstrate, the pressures of interdependence set up both enabling and constraining dynamics, which are approached and 'resolved' in ways that depend to a significant degree on the existing institutional environment.

The enabling face of globalisation

In addition to the structural pressures implied by the growth of capital mobility and international agreements, there is another aspect to interdependence, which has been largely overlooked by the constraints school. I refer to this as the 'enabling' face of globalisation. Unlike the constraining aspect with its economic logic of exit, the enabling dimension of globalisation reveals a political logic of competition and insecurity, which generates incentives for governments to take initiatives that will strengthen the national system of innovation and social protection.

The case for an enabling view of globalisation was first made in a rigorous way by Dennis Quinn (1997) in a correlational analysis of the impact of financial openness on fiscal, social protection, and a range of other policies. Quinn found that financial openness is correlated with *increases* in taxation and spending and that capital mobility had only one negative impact of any significance – increasing income inequality. His conclusion that financial integration is generally enabling runs counter to the conventional wisdom and thus cries out for explanation, a task which correlational analysis, however, cannot meet.

The larger message is the need for a new research agenda, which focuses on the enabling face of globalisation. This book is a contribution to that endeavour. It adds to a small but substantial literature covering a variety of topics – from financial liberalisation to industrial relations – which presents compelling arguments for an enabling view of globalisation. I extract from this literature two theoretical arguments, adding a third of my own, as to why globalisation does not produce a 'race to the bottom' in government taxation and spending policies, and why it does not *in principle* prevent governments from pursuing desired economic and social objectives.

The first argument can be summarised in the following way. Strong exposure to world markets (qua globalisation) has a tendency to heighten insecurity among broad segments of the population, which in turn generates demand for social protection. So rather than implementing generalised cuts, governments will often have strong political incentives either to sustain or to increase domestic compensation. This is the widely overlooked 'political logic' of voice that acts as a counter-tendency to the 'economic logic' of exit, as argued by Geoffrey Garrett (1998a: 791). This view of interdependence – as a process that encourages governments to balance openness with social protection – has a distin-guished pedigree, linking back to Peter Katzenstein's (1985) pioneering work on the small states of northern Europe where he found trade open-ness strongly associated with well-developed measures aimed at pro-viding 'domestic compensation' for labour and industry.[15] In the small states context, Katzenstein found that the strength of economic openness correlates with a heightened perception of vulnerability, giving rise to an ideology of social partnership and complementary (corporatist) in-stitutional arrangements. Thus 'small states' in the Katzensteinian sense can be seen as the forerunners of globalisation's 'enabling' dynamic in the developed democracies.

From this body of work one may generate the following hypothesis: the greater the level of (trade) interdependence, the stronger the elite perception of vulnerability, and the greater the likelihood of compen-satory and inclusionary domestic structures which blunt rather than exacerbate the pressures of openness.

The main point, then, is that against the expectation that mobile capital in the form of multinational corporations and financial market investors will generally depress social spending and drive down corporate taxes via threat of exit, one must set the less noted (politically) *enabling impact of openness*. By heightening perceptions of vulnerability among different social groups, the latter has the potential to encourage compensatory responses from government.

The stress on 'potential' is important because the responses vary with institutional setting. As Duane Swank shows in Chapter 3, the 'political logic' of enablement impacts differently according to the prevailing nor-mative and organisational conditions – hence explaining, for example, the more fiscally restrained patterns of welfare reform in liberal-market economies like Britain, compared with the more fiscally accommodating or moderately expansive patterns respectively in sectorally or centrally coordinated-market systems like Germany and Sweden, all nowadays highly interdependent economies. In a parallel manner for East Asia, Ramesh argues in Chapter 4 that the more competitive the political sys-tem (as a result of democratisation), the more governments have become responsive to welfare constituencies in a period of growing economic openness, even in the absence of any real political commitment to a welfare system.

The second theoretical argument about enablement concerns the conditions of global competition, which serve to valorise business access to national innovation structures, to a constant supply of skilled labour, and to various other infrastructural resources that firms depend on. However potentially mobile the modern corporation may be, increased exposure to world markets heightens the firm's need for continuous innovation, industrial upgrading, and competent workers. So instead of generalised slashing of corporate taxes and shifting the tax burden from capital to labour, governments will often have strong incentives to provide services to capital in exchange for maintaining tax revenue. As a number of scholars have observed, for all the neoclassical strictures about the harm wrought by state intervention, internationally oriented firms are still prone to welcome the benefits offered by a host of government programmes (Boix 1998; Garrett 1998a).[16]

At the very least, this offers a plausible way of explaining why, in many national settings, internationally mobile firms may be willing to sustain relatively high tax (and spending) levels, contrary to the standard expectations of capital exit. For this is where the overall evidence points, as John Hobson demonstrates in Chapter 2, subjecting 'race-to-the-bottom' claims to the test in a compelling analysis of the state's fiscal profile in the current golden period of globalisation. Overturning conventional expectations, Hobson's findings leave little room for doubting the general trend: notwithstanding limited oscillations and country particularities over time, it is clear that the tax burden on corporations in the OECD has generally *increased* rather than declined in the period of rising economic interdependence, that governments have *not* shifted the tax burden from capital to labour and, moreover, that they have generally *increased* taxes.

To these two arguments, we can add a third as to why globalisation has enabling rather than simply constraining effects on national governance. This concerns the way in which intensified competitive pressures may threaten to destabilise key sectors of the economy – from agriculture to telecommunications and finance. The effect of such competitive challenges is to urge governments to devise new policy responses, new regulatory regimes, and similar restructuring reforms. Most critically, responding to these new challenges creates incentives for governments to develop new or strengthen existing policy networks. For some purposes, this entails the expansion of *intergovernmental* cooperation in more or less permanent fora (e.g., the EU, WTO, BIS, G8). For others, it involves the extension of links *between government and business* in order to increase or improve policy input from the private sector. In both domestic and international settings, the capacity for economic governance may be enhanced by more effective information sharing and policy implementation. In each case, neither government nor business autonomy is thereby negated. Rather, it is 'enmeshed' in a network of interdependencies, the rules for which are established by government – hence 'governed interdependence'. Its recent flourishing in unexpected places is discussed in the chapters by Weiss and Coleman. The overall effect of such changes is a transformation in the state's *relational* enmeshment with other power actors.

Staying with the domestic setting, the more general point to emphasise is that openness can create strong pressures for maintaining or extending cooperative ties between government and industry, as well as for information sharing, for coordinated responses to collective action problems, and more generally for the state to act as provider of collective goods. Of course the transformation of public–private sector relations is not the only possible outcome of globalisation's enabling dynamic. In some cases – the Chinese response to WTO-induced reforms being the exemplary one, analysed by Tianbiao Zhu in Chapter 7 – preparing for increased competitive pressures has led to the restructuring of central–local government relations rather than of public–private sector ones. As a result of new power-sharing arrangements between the different units of government, the capacity of the Chinese state has been transformed from one based on the closed-economy model of central planning to one based on selective intervention at both national and local levels.

But outside the somewhat special case of China, in the developed democracies the more general principle applies, whereby increasing policy input from encompassing economic groups in the private sector tends to strengthen the state's transformative capacity. This principle is nicely illustrated in a number of existing studies, in particular, William Coleman's study of agricultural reform in France (2000), Mark Lehrer's analysis of the growth of high-technology entrepreneurship in Germany (2000), as well as my own account of industrial upgrading in European and East Asian countries (1998: especially ch. 3). In a pioneering study of the highly globalised derivatives markets in Chapter 13, Coleman offers further evidence of a similar dynamic at work in this most unexpected quarter. Also running contrary to expectations about the demise of transformative capacity in East Asia is the Korean state's recent partnering with organised industry groups to create, *inter alia*, a domestic software industry, highlighted by Weiss in Chapter 12.

Such examples add flesh to a larger theoretical point advanced in this study: namely, that globalisation does indeed impact on national governance and its domestic structures, but the impact is not *only*, or even *generally*, constraining. For globalisation also contributes to the expansion of governing capacities through both the transformation of public–private sector relations and the growth of policy networks. In Chapter 14 (Weiss) to this volume we consider the implications of this finding for the constraints–transformationalist thesis.

So much then for the third aspect of enablement. The important point to reiterate is that the extent to which these enabling conditions (of international competition) and the political incentives for intervention that they generate are likely to be actualised and to inform policymaking will depend heavily on institutional features of the domestic environment. As Richard Doner and Ansil Ramsay show in Chapter 6, although the economic incentives for particular kinds of intervention may be extremely strong and the national political rewards high – as would certainly be the case for a national strategy to upgrade Thailand's low-technology industries, an issue of critical importance since the Asian crisis – the political and economic institutional capacities may none the less be lacking or inadequate to the new developmental tasks. In this context, globalisation's enabling qualities turn into constraints.

There is then a plausible case for studying globalisation as a process with enabling effects. This case is established in a systematic way in the opening chapters on taxation by Hobson and welfare spending by Swank. But, as indicated in Figure 1.1, just how those enabling conditions will translate into policy responses will depend to an important extent on specific features of the institutional set-up, which mediate those outcomes. The main objective of the discussion thus far has not been to deny the existence of constraints but to offer a more realistic picture of them and to restore analytical balance by turning the spotlight on the enabling face of globalisation.

A domestic institutions approach

As argued in previous sections, the win–lose framework of globalisation analysis offers a limited way of grasping how national authorities are actually managing the challenges of openness. We need to think outside that framework and, to do that, there is no more appropriate place to turn than to the domestic institutions literature. This is of course a large literature and it would serve little purpose here to engage in an extensive review, especially since that task has been so ably undertaken by others.[17] The task of this section is to present a succinct outline of some aspects of domestic institutions analysis relevant to our concerns. In particular, we ask: What do we mean by institutions? Why are they important (what do they do)? And how are they created and changed? These are also issues central to contemporary institutional analysis.

The nature of institutions

Much ink has been spilled on the definitional side, specifically, over whether institutions should be defined as bundles of rules, norms, or organisational arrangements. Disciplinary background has much to do with these different usages. As an economist, for instance, you would be most likely to give primacy to the rule-bound, law-like notion of institutions (North 1990). Sociologists, on the other hand, have tended to emphasise the normative features of institutions, which extend beyond legal norms to define not only what is socially 'acceptable' but also what is 'appropriate' in particular contexts (e.g., Powell and DiMaggio 1991);[18] while political scientists have been drawn to highlight the importance of organisational arrangements, ranging from the structure of policymaking networks and the financing of industry, to the forms of collective bargaining (e.g., Katzenstein 1978; Johnson 1982, 1984; Zysman 1983; Hall 1986; Pempel 1998; Thelen and Kume 1999).

While this schema necessarily simplifies a complex and often highly nuanced literature, it serves as a reasonable statement of tendency. It also makes sense when one recognises that the different usages are typically driven by quite different analytical concerns. For economists, famous for their methodological individualism – which posits the interests and actions of individuals as cornerstone of the economy and unit of analysis – institutions (as rules) set important *constraints* on individual behaviour.[19] For sociologists, who see 'society' or social structure as prior to the individual, institutions (as norms) are *constitutive* of interests and identity. While there is no shortage of political scientists who lean towards either the sociological (e.g., March and Olsen 1989; Katzenstein 1996a, 1996b; Sikkink 1991) or the rationalist understanding of institutions (e.g., Milner 1997),[20] more generally, emphasis has been given to institutions as organisational arrangements. In many of these analyses such arrangements may not simply constrain; they may also *enable* desired outcomes.[21]

Institutional consequences

Thus institutions may be constraining, constitutive, or enabling. But the objective is not to engage in taxonomy. None of these emphases are wrong; nor are they in conflict. They simply address different concerns and thereby offer different pieces of the puzzle. Analytically, as soon as we begin to take institutions apart, we can see that, generally speaking, they are made up of all three components: rules defining appropriate behaviour and sanctions against transgression (the *constraints*), norms espousing or upholding particular values and standards (elements *constitutive* of interests and identity), and organisational arrangements (both *enabling* and constraining certain kinds of outcome, depending on the particular objective).

While political scientists may continue to debate whether institutions should be conceived narrowly or broadly, organisationally or normatively, and while there are compelling precedents for combinative approaches (e.g., Katzenstein 1996a; Ziegler 1997; Vogel 1996, 2001; Evans and Chang 2000), this is not an issue that concerns us here. Although one could reasonably argue that excluding normative orientations from one's conceptualisation of institutions often comes at the cost of explanatory weakness,[22] the task is not to promote the advantages of one specific institutional approach over others.[23] Rather, the larger purpose is to show how institutions – whether by shaping interests and identity, impeding certain outcomes, or favouring others – mediate the impact of economic openness at the national level.[24] A secondary aim is to show whether and to what extent, in performing that mediating role, institutions themselves are transformed.

This volume therefore takes a deliberately eclectic approach, sometimes prioritising the 'hardware' of organisational arrangements (e.g., chapters by Swank, Doner and Ramsay, Zhu, Coleman, Ramesh, Woo-Cumings, Levi-Faur), sometimes highlighting the 'software' of normative and other orienting ideas (in particular, chapters by Loriaux, Alamgir). At other times still, we find a mix of both norms and organisational configurations underpinning the outcomes in question (Tilton, Weiss, Loriaux, Woo-Cumings, Doner and Ramsay). Though it explores a diversity of topics and issue areas, this body of scholarship is unified by its attention to the role of domestic institutions in defining and structuring responses to the challenges of openness and, consequently, in mediating their impact.

Recognition of the importance of institutions in shaping policy responses to common problems has a lengthy pedigree in political science (Katzenstein 1978; Zysman 1983; Hall 1986; Garrett and Lange 1995; Vogel 1996; Risse-Kappen 1998). In trying to pinpoint the relevant properties of political institutions that explain the specific policy responses in question, analysts over the years have lined up a host of likely contenders. On the organisational side lie such factors as the extent to which the political system is centralised or decentralised, pluralist or corporatist, the degree of bureaucratic expertise and coherence, the encompassing or fragmented character of producer organisations, the extent and nature of policy interaction between government and business, and the degree of cooperation between state and industry in coordinating financial, product, and labour markets.[25] On the normative side, institutional analysis has highlighted the dominant orientations and legal norms regarding such things as the primacy of producers versus consumers in competition policy, the state's role in the economy and society, the nature of the government–business relationship, and ideas about the overarching purpose of the economy.

In the abstract, of course, the question of 'which' institutions matter is unfruitful since the answer will depend on the particular issue in question. Take, for example, the welfare state. As indicated in the previous section, explaining why pressures for welfare retrenchment have produced divergent responses in liberal and coordinated market economies involves not only analysis of programmatic structures (e.g., universalist *vs.* means tested) which shape or reproduce different normative orientations towards the welfare state, but also analysis of the organisation of the political economy which aggregates interests and structures access to the political arena (hence moderating or intensifying resistance to reforms). However, when the explanatory focus shifts to differences in competitive strategies for trade and industry, to divergent state responses to the pressures of foreign competition, the relevant institutional configurations will clearly be of a different kind, for the most part centring on legal norms, state structures, producer organisations, and public–private sector linkages. Of course it should also be clear that in a debate preoccupied with globalisation's impact on national governance, political institutions will have analytical centrality. *But the remit of a domestic institutions approach to globalisation impacts must be broader than 'the state' as such, if for no other reason than the 'relational' one.*

For, at the very least, states must interact with (relate to) their societies. So the manner and extent to which power actors on each side of the state–society divide are cohesive, organised, and interconnected through policy networks will make a substantial difference to policy outcomes.

The conditions and outcomes of institutional change

We turn finally to the question of institutional change, which goes to the heart of contemporary debate on globalisation and national governance. Although much of the writing on globalisation expects economic openness to bring about institutional change on a broad scale, including transformation of the state in particular, the conditions under which existing institutions might undergo significant change or new ones be created remain, for the most part, taken for granted.

Existing studies of such matters tend to point on balance to the inertia, 'stickiness', or 'path dependency' of institutions (see, e.g., Berger and Dore 1996; Steinmo *et al.*, 1992). Indeed, there is now a substantial body of scholarship which concludes that – excepting watershed events like revolution, war, and severe and extended economic depression – institutional continuity is the norm, not change. A number of studies have offered forceful arguments as to why institutions (whether the 'microinstitutions' of capitalism or the 'macroinstitutions' of political authority) will not adjust spontaneously to heightened global pressures. One reason is because the policies, laws, and regulatory machinery of governments are the 'major shapers' of the institutional set-up; without political will to adjust, the impetus for change will be lacking (Berger and Dore 1996).

But institutions may remain in place for reasons other than the conventional ones of inertia and stickiness. The role of 'feedback mechanisms' offers a major insight into why institutions persist in the face of pressures for change (see Thelen 1999: 392–6). One broad type of feedback mechanism is the 'power-distributional effect', which underlines the idea that institutions are not so much neutral coordinating mechanisms as structures that are biased towards particular patterns of power distribution in society (Ikenberry 1993). Some of the best work in this area relates to welfare states and social policy; its authors have examined the ways in which different institutional arrangements feed into the construction of identity, the conception and aggregation of interests, and the capacity to construct political alliances and gain access to the political arena.[26] In this volume, Duane Swank (Chapter 3) emphasises similar issues of power distribution to explain the divergent behaviour of different types of welfare states and their persistence under conditions of interdependence. A similar power perspective underlies Mark Tilton's comparison of different reform outcomes in the Japanese and American telecommunications sectors (Chapter 9). But as Tilton's analysis also shows, the power distribution emphasis is quite compatible with a second type of feedback mechanism.

The second major type of feedback mechanism is the 'advantages effect'. Thus, for example, attempts to dismantle the old and install the new may be thwarted or delayed because both potential winners and losers from particular reforms are bound together in arrangements from which each benefit, as Vogel (2001) has argued for the microinstitutions of Japan and Germany. Thelen and Kume's (1999) explanation for the persistence of cooperative industrial relations systems in Germany emphasises similar feedback effects at work, as does Hall and Soskice's (2000) lucid account of why different production systems are unlikely to converge in response to global competition. Like Vogel, they focus on the complementarity of institutional arrangements in particular national settings, arguing that these confer quite distinctive competitive advantages – thus explaining in the economic sphere the propensity to respond to interdependence pressures by strengthening rather than unwinding existing arrangements.

This idea of (political and economic) advantages offers a persuasive account of institutional continuity and change. In the Korean case, analysed by Weiss in Chapter 12, the diminishing benefits to each party from the close financial ties between the Korean state and the chaebol (industrial conglomerates) underscores their increasingly contradictory relationship throughout the turbulent 1980s, leading to a significant rolling back of developmental structures. But the search for new solutions to new problems arising since the Asian crisis has revived developmental forms of governance, not only by drawing on existing institutions (Woo-Cumings, Chapter 10), but also by recombining and redirecting public–private relations in new ways (Weiss, Chapter 12).

Thus, the picture of change that emerges from this perspective is not one of institutional stasis, but one of *constant evolution and change*. None the less, in so far as change is structured by the prevailing norms and arrangements, it should be seen as 'adaptive' change: institutional innovations that none the less follow well-worn paths rather than branching out in entirely different directions, an idea which some refer to as institutional 'bricolage' (see Thelen 1999: 383 for references).

This takes us beyond issues involving conditions of institutional change and enduring stability to the more neglected question of outcomes. For even when reforms do take place under intense external pressure, it would be naïve to expect the marginalisation of pre-existing arrangements. The Korean and Taiwanese approaches to increasing openness in finance, trade, and investment, analysed by Weiss in Chapter 12, offer instructive examples of this adaptive response. It can be seen even more strikingly in Meredith Woo-Cumings's chapter analysing different legal traditions and their consequences for economic development. Woo-Cumings takes issue with the regnant orthodoxy of international bodies like the World Bank and the IMF, which preach the superiority of (a vaguely defined) 'rule of law'. What her analysis of the Korean case conveys so effectively is the deeply ironic outcome whereby *new* institutions (embodying 'rule of law' in the economic arena) have been created only by virtue of the power of the *old* (continuing 'administrative guidance' in the political arena).

The essays in this volume suggest that the challenges of openness do not negate the significance of domestic institutions. Quite the contrary; they tend to make existing normative and organisational structures more important – for it is these which condition the ability (or inability) of states to rise to the globalisation challenge. Over time, however, the pressures of interdependence can also help to redefine an institution's character. In particular, organisational arrangements may be altered in the process of meeting the external challenge. For example, William Coleman (Chapter 13) finds that in the most globalised of financial markets – derivatives – the legalistic, arm's-length regulatory style of US authorities has been set aside in favour of the more informal, public–private cooperation institutionalised by the British. Public–private cooperation in one sphere may recede, only to reappear in another (as in the Korean case where diminishing cooperation between the state and the industrial conglomerates has been supplemented by increasing ties with smaller firm networks essential to the development of new growth areas). In other cases, greater interstate cooperation may ensue (as has occurred in Europe) – an outcome which not only depends upon the strength of national institutions but also impacts on their autonomy of operation (Schmidt, in press).

David Levi-Faur advances this argument in his chapter on the state's evolving role in the telecommunications industry across two regions over more than a century. He examines the contrasting approaches taken historically to nationalisation, then more recently to liberalisation in

Europe and to privatisation in Latin America, which gave rise to a relatively vibrant industry and competitive markets in the European setting but failed to do so in the latter case. Levi-Faur attributes the differential outcomes to raw differences in 'state capacity'. He rejects the influential view that the state's role in telecommunications has shifted authority from governments to corporations, resulting in so-called 'state retreat'. Rather, liberalisation of telecommunications represents 'the most ambitious effort ever' to use the sector 'as a tool for economic development'. This conclusion dovetails with the more broadly based arguments of John Zysman (1996: 159) and Herman Schwartz (2000a: 318) for whom national states compete intensely to secure advantage in shifting markets and in the process proliferate strategies that bring about pervasive market expansion. From such accounts it would appear that states in the developed world are changing as they interact with the global economy, but not generally in ways anticipated by radical globalists. So let us turn to the main propositions to be developed.

Propositions of this study

Three fundamental propositions underpin and give coherence to the chapters in this book.

1. States have significantly more room to manoeuvre in the global political economy than globalisation theory allows.

While there is no need to belabour the obvious point that states nowadays operate in a changed economic and political environment, this volume contests the claim that globalisation has significantly reduced the state's room to move in the fiscal, social, industrial, and financial policy arenas. It proposes that states have a good deal more margin for manoeuvre than anticipated by the constraints school, *especially where this matters for social protection and wealth creation*. In support of this argument, many of the chapters in this volume offer evidence from three broad areas, which include: taxation, welfare spending, and competitive trade and industry strategies.

2. States have room to move because globalisation enables as well as constrains economic governance.

This book does not reject, rather, it substantially modifies the constraints view by proposing that globalisation is (politically) enabling, not merely (structurally) constraining. Enablement implies that, in the face of

26

so-called 'globalisation' pressures (e.g., the logic of capital exit; competition for trade, investment, and technology; the systemic risks posed by financial markets), there are countervailing pressures on governments (as well as political incentives) to intervene. In short, the international political economy generates pressures which, in principle, encourage states to pursue policies that would in some way compensate for the uncertainties, instability, and systemic risks that interdependence creates.

Three theoretical reasons for enablement were adduced earlier and need not be repeated here. What does need emphasising is that state size is not the issue, nor whether the states are traditionally 'interventionist' or 'liberal', though their respective modes of handling enablement will tend to be consistent with their own traditions and institutions (as elaborated below in the third proposition).

There are, however, two important qualifications. First, and somewhat obviously, the enabling features of globalisation are less applicable to countries struggling either to build states (e.g., sub-Saharan Africa) or to reconstruct them (e.g., Russia). Indeed, in all such cases, institution building should precede economic opening. Second, outside the limitations of weak state structures, the strongest and most meaningful constraint on state behaviour in the domestic policy arena is the financial one, as elaborated earlier with regard to financial market reaction to deficit spending.

3.   In conditioning the way states seek to move in the room that they have, the character of domestic institutions (as constellations of normative orientations and organisational arrangements) is decisive.

Domestic institutions mediate both the enabling and constraining logics of global markets, defining their impacts and generating distinctive policy patterns. The proposition is that the pattern of policy responses will vary according to the prevailing normative orientations and organisational structures. (Although at a deeper historical level, both the institutions and the policies, in turn, tend to vary with degrees of international vulnerability or levels of interdependence, as established by Katzenstein (1985)).

This proposition has two related ideas. The first posits that domestic institutions, depending on their characteristics, can hinder or enable states to respond to new challenges and accomplish new tasks, thus softening, neutralising, or exaggerating the potentially constraining effects of global markets. Thus, for example, Thailand's clientelistic institutions, once developmentally effective, now leave the state ill-equipped to manage the urgent upgrading challenge essential to its continued participation in export markets (Doner and Ramsay, Chapter 6). But 'weaknesses' are not the same thing as 'differences', as Japanese and US approaches to telecommunications reform make clear, since both in their own way are achieving nationally desired outcomes with different tradeoffs (Tilton, Chapter 9). Not only is there little need for converging on one best institutional form, but also there is no one best form to encompass both short and long-term economic goals, as has been argued convincingly by Hall and Soskice (2000).

This relates to the second idea, which posits that the enabling logic of globalisation tends to generate different policy patterns, consistent with the normative-organisational (institutional) context. The case of social policy and its relation to different clusters of welfare states, analysed by Swank in Chapter 3, offers an instructive illustration. Swank explains the institutional conditions under which (what I have called here) the enabling logic of globalisation may lend itself to different realisations, giving rise to different patterns of policy choice and policy outcomes. Thus, for example, if the insecurity generated by trade openness serves to increase political incentives for governments to provide domestic compensation, whether and in what ways those incentives translate into either fiscal tightening or sustained social protection will depend on both the norms underlying existing programmatic structures and the political and economic organisation of affected actors, which condition both the aggregation and representation of interests. Hence the typically different patterns of response that one finds, say, in Britain, Germany, and Sweden: in short, relatively leaner-meaner outcomes in liberal conservative states which are organisationally and normatively poised for that result, compared with sustained social spending in states with corporatist arrangements and robust traditions of domestic compensation.

If we switch focus from social protection to promotion of wealth creation strategies in industry, technology, and finance, whether the enabling features of globalisation lead to more market-competitive or more public-private cooperation will once again depend largely upon the character of the prevailing norms and arrangements. In liberal-market contexts, characterised by arms-length approaches, norms of competitive liberalism, and non-interventionist traditions, economic openness has generally enabled governments to deepen market mechanisms in line with pro-competitive norms and pro-consumer preferences (chapters by Levi-Faur and Tilton). On the other hand, in coordinated market contexts, characterised by traditions of statecraft, coordinated or state-guided approaches to economic change, and strong policy networks linking state and business, globalisation has generally enabled both governments and business to manage openness in line with pro-producer preferences and the goals of strengthening the national economy (chapters by Loriaux, Tilton, Weiss, Zhu).

As further substantive research casts light on the mediating role of domestic institutions, we may learn more about the triangular relationship sketched in Figure 1.1 concerning the logics of constraint, enablement, and institutional response. In the meantime, we propose to make some headway with this volume. Globalisation, we posit, has a strong enabling side, which over the long haul is likely to prove at least as significant as, if not more important than, its constraining aspects, depending on the institutional environment.[27]

On one point we can be more certain. We can only make progress on these issues when we stop reducing state power to a particular set of policy instruments or conceptualising such power as something fixed and finite and, hence, cease assessing 'transformation' against an imagined static past.[28] Change is not the issue as the studies in this volume make clear. So we do not need to argue on these grounds. What remains debatable is not whether changes have occurred, but rather which changes are the significant ones and what they imply for the capacity of the state to promote social protection and wealth creation strategies. This draws our attention back to the 'darker place' of our earlier analogy: to domestic institutions, to state capacities and orientations, and more generally to the prevailing norms and arrangements that enable, encourage, or advantage particular patterns of response to the challenges of openness. This is the task for the chapters ahead.

The chapters that follow develop most of the themes raised in this introduction. They are not constrained by the imposition of a rigid framework since the purpose of this volume is to open a fresh research agenda, rather than to close one. That agenda seeks not to deny the existence, but to offer a more realistic picture, of constraints on the policy options of national states, to restore analytical balance by shifting attention somewhat more towards the neglected, 'enabling' face of globalisation, and to come to a clearer understanding of the conditions under which the pressures of interdependence may be intensified or softened by domestic institutions. In contributing to that picture, each chapter relates well to the basic approach outlined here in order to analyse a more specific set of issues. Although there is inevitably some overlap, these issues are grouped under three broad areas of policy activity. The chapters in Part I focus on the taxing and spending capacities of states over the recent period of globalisation. Examining fiscal and social patterns, they take on 'race to the bottom' arguments and associated debates about the impact of globalisation on welfare states. Part II focuses on the state's capacity for economy-strengthening interventions in the areas of trade, investment, and technology – as well as through the legal and regulatory framework – as countries become more integrated in the international political economy. The chapters in this section offer particular insights on the implications of different aspects of globalisation for domestic policy and institutional change. In Part III, the focus broadens to encompass issues of global governance, including the ability of states to mediate the impacts of different intergovernmental agreements not only through regulatory and industrial policy measures, but also through ideologically constructed appeals to shared values. In particular, these chapters (along with several others in Part II), highlight the conditions under which globalisation may promote or fortify the state's transformative capacity.

Though they encompass a wide range of countries, cases, issue areas, and methods, the essays in this volume converge in their concern with the scope for national authorities, bolstered or blocked by domestic institutions, to respond to specific challenges of openness in distinctive ways.

Notes

1. Moderate globalists – those who continue to see some sort of role for the state, however reduced – represent the dominant thinking among globalisers. Although they differ on a number of points, at times even using different language ('interdependence', 'internationalisation'), they are unanimous in viewing openness as a strong constraint (akin to a straitjacket, but not necessarily a golden one – as Thomas Friedman (1999) would claim – on the state's policymaking capacities). Many also posit state 'transformation' – hence the end of the state as we know it and the emergence of a new kind of beast (see below).
2. Among the more influential works in this vein – from the left and the right – see Cerny (1994), Strange (1996), Keohane and Milner (1996), Cox (1997), Friedman (1999), Scholte (2000).
3. For a perspective in some respects complementary to the one presented here, see Thomas Risse-Kappen (1995). That study has a somewhat narrower explanatory target, focusing less on the impact of global markets and various challenges of economic openness and more on the impact of transnational

actors as they seek to gain access to the policy process. Both domestic and international institutions are presented as explanatory variables.

4. Representative of this tendency towards tautology is the recent work by David Held and his co-authors. Their statement outlining what 'a satisfactory definition of globalisation must capture' makes no bones about including 'impact' as one of the four elements (1999: 15). Robert Holton (1998: 10–11) discusses a similar problem with regard to the erosion of territorial borders.

5. There is now a sizeable comparative politics literature which systematically challenges the 'convergence' claims of globalisation theory, showing how, even when re-formed, the microinstitutions of capitalism continue to diverge. Among the important collections, see Berger and Dore (1996), Kitschelt *et al.* (1999), and Hall and Soskice (2000). However, to date, very little of this literature has taken on the 'constrained state' claims which dominate contemporary understanding of interdependence impacts. For an important exception, see Vogel (1996). As this book was going to press, some other studies came to light. See the fine collection by Prakash and Hart (2002).

6. For the distinction between strategic and structural pressures on policy options, see Bhagwati (2000: 336).

7. Many discussions simply elide 'sovereignty', 'autonomy', and 'capacity'. For a brief yet effective discussion of the way in which the different usages of the term, 'sovereignty', have led to conflicting conclusions as to its 'continuity' or 'change', see Georg Sorenson (1999). For an historically based argument that powerfully challenges the 'erosion of sovereignty' thesis, see Krasner (1999).

8. It is noteworthy that Susan Strange, widely cited as the exponent of the more extreme view that states were 'in retreat', was at one with the negative-sum thinking of the constraints school (outlined in this section) when she wrote 'the declining authority of states is reflected in a growing diffusion of authority to other institutions and associations, and to local and regional bodies ...' (1996: 4).

9. For a theoretical discussion of public–private linkages (*A* and *B* cooperating in a relationship of 'governed interdependence') as the basis of the state's transformative capacity, see chapter 2 of Weiss (1998); for an empirical application to European and East Asian cases of industrial upgrading, see especially chapters 3 and 5 of the same work. For an important application to developing countries of the idea of public–private cooperation for a transformative project, see Peter Evans (1995). For an application to global financial market regulation, see Coleman, this volume. It is important to emphasise that where states enter into cooperative relations with private actors or with other states, such cooperation implies neither power symmetry nor absence of conflict. Moreover, the condition of interdependence may be seen as one in which the interdependent entities retain their autonomy in setting their goals yet depend for the realisation of their goals on the choices made by other actors. For a similar view expounded in a different context (aimed at realism's overemphasis on anarchy), see Helen Milner (1993: 162–5).

10. This refers to the so-called 'impossible trinity', the argument that countries cannot simultaneously maintain independent monetary policies, an open capital account, and fixed exchange rates. If it wants any two of these combinations, e.g., monetary autonomy and capital mobility, it must give up the third – in this example, fixed exchange rates (Rodrik 2000a: 180).

11. Compare, for example, the conflicting conclusions of Martin (1997) with Dungey (1999). I am grateful to Dr Stephen Grenville, Deputy Governor of the Reserve Bank of Australia, for his views on this issue and for advice on the relevant literature.

12. While the French Socialists' abandonment of expansionary policies in the face of foreign exchange and balance of payments crises in the early 1980s is widely cited as evidence of external constraints (Petit 1989), the extent to which those constraints derived primarily from 'global' financial markets is contested (e.g., Glyn 1998b: 49–50).

13. For more details on internationalisation, see McKeown (1999) on trade, Simmons (1999) and Quinn and Inclan (1997) on capital mobility. On the causes of the internationalisation of markets, see Helleiner (1995), Cohen (1996), Garrett (2000a), and Schwartz (2000a).

14. Among the leading accounts using quantitative data to refute the existence of a globalisation tendency is the work by Paul Hirst and Grahame Thompson (1996) and Robert Wade (1996). Another less common response is to maintain that there is scope for resistance, however shortlived and costly this may be. Keohane and Milner (1996: 20–1), for example, propose that 'preexisting domestic institutions may allow actors to resist the pressures generated by internationalisation'. This also accords with their tendency to conceptualise the role of domestic institutions as primarily a blocking or constraining one. These authors emphasise the way institutions may enable particular interests to pursue protectionist policies and thus block openness. This, however, has little in common with the approach taken in the present volume.

15. Earlier and more recent works which establish similar arguments include Cameron (1978), Stephens (1979), and Rodrik (1998).

16. In particular, Carles Boix (1998) develops the most sustained argument that increasing globalisation of the economy, far from constraining government delivery of production-enhancing policies, has magnified the role of competing supply-side strategies for growth and distribution. Also telling in this regard is that even the ideologically 'non-interventionist' United States provides handsomely for its national corporations and high-technology sectors through multibillion dollar export promotions schemes for national champions like Boeing and Microsoft (running to *c.* $2 billion each year), through public–private partnerships for advancing high technology and, thanks to a massive defence budget, through a substantial procurement policy that benefits high-technology suppliers in Silicon Valley (*Economist*, 11 December 1999: 18).

17. Among a number of outstanding reviews see Peter Hall (1997); Hall and Taylor (1996); and Guy Peters (1998).

18. There are of course prominent examples of sociologists who examine institutions in organisational terms (e.g., Theda Skocpol *et al.*, 1985).

19. This is not to say that economists would view rules *only* as constraints since they clearly have an enabling dimension as well. Thus the freedom to engage in market-based activities requires certain rules, such as property rights, a key institutional precondition for economic development that historical sociologists have long understood, and that economic historian Douglas North (1990) subsequently made the centrepiece of his historical account. None the less, the main tendency of economists seems clear: entrepreneurial enablement is viewed fundamentally as a consequence of the constraints that property rights impose on the predatory actions of the state and other power actors.

20. For a discussion of the three streams of 'rational choice' institutionalism see Guy Peters (1998).

21. This 'enabling' list is long. For a sample, I include Garrett and Lange (1991), Evans (1995), Vogel (1996), Weiss (1998), Evans and Chang (2000).

22. Scharpf (2000a: 784ff.) for example argues that different trade union responses to monetarism in countries with similarly centralised wage-setting arrangements and incentive structures cannot be explained without an understanding of normative orientations.

23. See, for example, Paul Pierson (2001) on the alleged virtues of historical institutionalism *vis-à-vis* rationalism.

24. For an earlier distinguished effort along these lines, see the studies of foreign policy in Katzenstein (1978). Vogel's (1996) comparative study of regulatory reform, and Risse-Kappen's (1995) collection on the domestic impact of transnational actors offer more recent efforts in this direction.

25. Risse-Kappen (1998), for example, highlights three key variables as constitutive of domestic structures: state structure; societal structure; and policy networks.

26. See Thelen (1999: 394–5) for a succinct overview.

27. Some prominent globalists have begun to point in this direction. After a lengthy exposition of the many big changes in the world political economy, Keohane and Nye (2000: 117) end on a note that is very much in tune with the argument of this book, stating that 'the filters provided by domestic politics and political institutions play a major role in determining what effects globalisation really has and how well various countries adapt to it'.

28. Steven Krasner (1999) makes this point in a historical analysis of different aspects of sovereignty. He notes that observers have conflated two different concepts – Westphalian and international legal sovereignty – and concludes that both principles 'have always been violated' when it suited rulers' interest, being best understood as examples of 'organized hypocrisy' (1999: 24).

Part I
The resilience of welfare states

2 Disappearing taxes or the 'race to the middle'? Fiscal policy in the OECD

John M. Hobson

At least in the Anglo-Saxon countries – Australia, Britain, and the United States – we have grown accustomed to the all too familiar refrain, almost always proclaimed by right-wing governments – that under globalisation, taxes are 'disappearing' and that 'there is no alternative' but to slash spending on education and welfare. Ironically, many academics – especially radicals and Marxists – endorse this proposition; 'ironically' that is, because they have not sought to critically appraise this opportunistic right-wing rhetoric and have effectively fallen for it 'hook, line and sinker'. This chapter examines the evolution of taxation policy since 1965, and reveals this as but empty rhetoric, pointing to the clear fact that states have room for fiscal manoeuvre under globalisation (even if, in turn, this should not be exaggerated). This leads to the robust conclusion that 'reports of the death of taxation and the welfare state remain greatly exaggerated'. Among other things, this chapter calls for a 'middle-ground' position in the politics of globalisation: between the 'politics of helplessness' (right-wing liberalism) and the 'politics of despair' (radical critiques). I argue that there are in fact some grounds for optimism and some grounds for political re-empowerment in terms of the cause for social democracy: that under globalisation 'there *is* an alternative' to the niggardly politics of neoliberalism.

Outside of mainstream politics and within the Academy, the discussion of globalisation is often conducted in the form of a debate, which is marked by two extreme polarities. At one extreme is the reified 'structuralist' position – mainly advocated by Liberals, Marxists and radicals – that I refer to as the mainstream 'conventional' account, which asserts that there is a global capitalist structure that constrains the policy options of states (e.g., Cerny 1990; Cox 1996), the net effect of which is a pronounced 'retreat of the state' (Strange 1996). At the other extreme is the reified 'agential' perspective – mainly advocated by statists and neo-realists – which asserts that states are insulated from global pressures and that they are free to make policy in the absence of global capitalist constraint (e.g., Waltz 1979; Krasner 1995; Hirst and Thompson 1996).[1] This position usually posits that the sovereign state remains the primary actor in world politics and, that in relation to global capital, states 'set the terms of the intercourse, whether by passively permitting informal rules to develop or . . . [w]hen the crunch comes [by remaking] the rules by which other actors [e.g., Multinational Corporations (MNCs)] operate. Indeed, one may be struck by the ability of weak states to impede the operation of strong international corporations and by the attention the latter pay to the wishes of the former' (Waltz 1979: 94–5). Thus, agentialists insist that states hold the upper hand, no less than structuralists argue that global capital 'rules OK'.

Here, I argue, it is time to move beyond the polarities and rigid strictures that have hitherto confined the effectiveness of this debate. In particular, it is limited by its 'either/or' framework: either globalisation is all-powerful and states are impotent; or globalisation is weak and states are dominant (cf. Clark 1999). This chapter proposes an alternative 'both/and' framework for the analysis of states and globalisation. As I have argued elsewhere, globalisation affords states *both* constraints *and* opportunities, as much as states both constrain and enable global capital (Hobson 2000: ch. 7; Hobson and Ramesh 2002). And neither can dictate terms to the other. Here I show that the relationship is often marked in 'win–win' terms, as both global capital and states have entered into a symbiotic relationship, even if both sides have had to accept various constraints. Conventional analyses assume that global capital can dictate government policy, and that the interests of global capital and states are *irreconcilable*. Accordingly, their central claim is that governments must conciliate global capitalist demands by engaging in a 'race to the bottom' in terms of welfare policy or taxation.

My alternative approach begins with the assumption that states and global capital are engaged in what I call the 'race to the middle'. This presupposes that states and global capital share broadly *similar* interests, even though there are often moments of tension. Most fundamentally, the 'race to the middle' presupposes that global capital and national governments *both* have 'negotiative power', such that they constantly negotiate a *middle ground* or equilibrium point. This equilibrium point can be defined as one where 'governments maintain revenue yields and national economic competitiveness, while global capital preserves its profit-making interests'. It is the constant negotiation of this equilibrium point which defines the 'race to the middle' – a process which, as I show in this chapter, fundamentally informs the evolution of tax policy since 1965. This claim in turn suggests that the standard quest for an 'ultimate victor' between *either* the state (as in agentialism) *or* global capital (as in structuralism) is futile.

The mainstream conventional argument concerning fiscal policy comprises at least five core propositions – that increasing capital mobility:

(1)   forces governments to cut the overall tax burden and, therefore, to cut aggregate expenditures (especially on welfare);

(2)   forces governments to shift the tax mix away from progressive and relatively mobile direct taxes, and towards regressive and immobile indirect (consumption) taxes;

(3)   forces governments to reduce and minimise the tax burden on capital (especially mobile capital) and shift the burden on to immobile labour;

(4)   forces governments to slash corporation tax rates (i.e., the 'race to the bottom'), as governments enter into 'tax competition' to attract global capital, leading to the fiscal crisis of the state;

(5)   leads both to a lowering and growing convergence of national tax rates and overall tax/expenditure burden profiles on the one hand, and pronounced fiscal crisis in the future on the other hand, as income tax revenues are squeezed out.

Thus under high global capital mobility we should expect to find a scenario of 'disappearing taxes', in which global capital effectively sucks the very life-blood out of the modern state.

This chapter deals critically with each of the core propositions in five separate parts by analysing the evolution of tax policy across twenty-three OECD countries (listed in the notes to Table 2.2), for 1965–97 and, where possible, to 1999. Here, I follow the preferred approach of public finance economists who point out that we can only make sense of tax changes over time by examining the *real* tax burden (e.g., Andersen 1998; Messere 1998; Tanzi and Schuknecht 2000), which is derived by calculating the ratio of taxes (and expenditures) to national income (i.e., the tax/GDP ratio). Looking at nominal taxes (expressed in national currencies or one universal currency) is problematic because their movements over time are heavily distorted by inflation and economic growth. The tax/GDP ratio necessarily eradicates these distortions. The tables and graphs below are based on these ratios but are presented as index

Table 2.1. *Aggregate tax and expenditure burdens*

	1965–9	1970–4	1975–9	1980–4	1985–9	1990–4	1995–9
Aggregate tax burdens							
Avg. OECD	100	107	113	113	114	117	120
Avg. EU	100	106	114	118	119	122	125
Aggregate expenditure burdens							
Avg. OECD	100	107	120	122	121	126	123
Avg. EU	100	106	121	125	126	129	128

Sources: OECD, *Economic Outlook*, vols. 29, 59, 67 (Paris: OECD, 1981, 1996, 2000). Note that the 'Avg. OECD' covers *all* member countries.

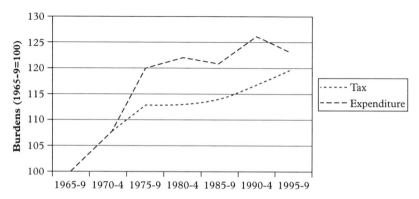

Figure 2.1 Aggregate tax and expenditure burdens (OECD average), 1965–99

numbers (where 1965/9 = 100), in order to more clearly discern the long-term trends.

Disappearing national taxes and declining government expenditures?

Conventional expectations predict that aggregate tax and expenditure burdens should trend downwards from 1965 onwards, in line with the long-term trend in rising global capital flows.

Table 2.1 reveals that aggregate tax revenue burdens trend very clearly *upwards* not downwards for the whole period. The same is true for the expenditure data, though the very marginal reduction for 1995/9 is clearly far too little and far too late to validate conventional expectations. In sum, what *is* striking in an era of intensifying capital mobility, is the degree to which these broad fiscal indicators have *increased*, thereby suggesting a broadly positive rather than negative relationship between globalisation and state fiscal capacity (thereby confirming the scenario of a 'race to the middle').

Disappearing direct taxes and a shifting of the tax burden from direct to indirect taxation?

Conventional expectations claim that governments are forced to reduce direct taxes (which impact on *mobile* capital) and shift the burden onto *immobile* tax bases, most notably labour and consumption – which simultaneously effects a shift from progressive to increasingly regressive tax regimes. I reserve the discussion of labour taxation for the next section, and focus here on the impact of globalisation on regressive indirect taxes. This is a very popular claim and seems to have particular resonance among American and British social scientists, given that Thatcher and Reagan were famous for cutting the top nominal rate of income tax and, in Thatcher's case, for more than compensating the income tax reductions by increasing indirect taxes (specifically the VAT). Moreover, we do know that top-rate marginal income taxes (as well as the nominal tax rates of corporations – see below) have dropped in all countries. In the G7 for example, the 1985 average *top* rate of 57 per cent had dropped to 46 per cent by 1995, and is projected to drop further to about 40 per cent by 2004 (Ganghof 2001). Does the direct tax base shrink in line with conventional expectations, and if so, is it made partially good by rises in indirect taxes?

Looking at Figure 2.2, one could be entirely forgiven for assuming that the lower curve represents direct taxes and the higher curve that of indirect taxes – such is the pervasive influence that the conventional argument imposes upon our imagination. But a closer look at the graph shows that it is, in fact, the other way round: that overall direct taxes have risen steadily on trend by some 49 per cent in real terms, while indirect taxes stood only 9 per cent higher in 1995/7 compared with 1965/9. The personal income tax (PIT) and corporation tax data tell a similar story, though with a few twists. I will discuss the corporation tax data later. The PIT data reveal that for the twenty-three countries surveyed, the burden has increased on trend down to the 1985/9 period, remained static thereafter but dropped slightly in the 1995/7 years. Even

Table 2.2. *Direct and indirect tax burdens*

	1965–9	1970–4	1975–9	1980–4	1985–9	1990–4	1995–7
Avg. indirect	100	101	97	106	112	108	109
Avg. direct	100	112	123	142	147	145	149
Personal income tax (PIT)							
Our avg.	100	121	142	146	147	145	139
EU avg.	100	125	148	137	138	142	140
Corporation income tax (CIT)	100	105	108	116	126	117	135

Sources and notes: All averages (bar EU) are derived from the following 23 OECD countries: Australia, Austria, Belgium, Canada, Denmark, Finland, France, Germany, Greece, Ireland, Italy, Japan, Luxembourg, The Netherlands, New Zealand, Norway, Portugal, Spain, Sweden, Switzerland, Turkey, UK and USA. Average direct and indirect burdens from: OECD, *National Accounts* (Paris: OECD, 1979, 1992, 1997, 2000). Average personal and corporate income tax data from OECD, *Revenue Statistics* (Paris: OECD, 1980, 1989, 1995, 1999, 2000). GDP data: IMF, *International Financial Statistics Yearbook* (Washington: IMF, 1996, 2000).

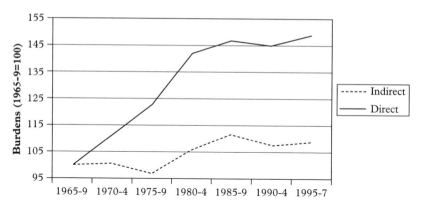

Figure 2.2 Direct and indirect tax burdens, 1965–97

so, this reduction is far too little and comes far too late to confirm the conventional argument.

Moreover, it is vital to keep in mind the proposition under review here. Recall that the conventional proposition asserts that under high capital mobility governments are forced to cut back on direct taxes and compensate for at least some of the loss by raising regressive indirect taxes, thereby shifting the tax burden from rich and more mobile factors to poor, more immobile factors. But my data reveal that the increases in direct taxes far outpace the increments in indirect taxes. This leads to the robust conclusion that the overall *increases* in government taxation since 1965/9 (see Table 2.1 above) have been almost wholly funded by increases in direct and personal income taxes – as well as social security contributions (see also, Tanzi and Schuknecht 2000: 58–9). Put simply, this scenario is precisely the inverse to that predicted by the conventional argument, because it unambiguously reveals that increments in direct taxes have in fact substituted for indirect taxes in order to fund rising expenditures, thereby once more confirming my claim about a 'race to the middle'.

This of course begs the question: how have PIT yields increased as top marginal rates have come down? First, the conventional theorists have been all too easily seduced by the reductions in the top marginal tax rates – which have of course grabbed the headlines – and which have led many governments to disingenuously claim that income tax burdens have come down (a favourite claim made by successive post-1979 British Conservative governments, for example). Beyond the headlines, though, is a largely hidden and less melodramatic story, which reveals that while top rates have indeed been cut, nevertheless this was offset by *broadening* the PIT base, in which all manner of tax exemptions were closed down (see also, Ganghof 2001). *Inter alia*, this reveals that states have 'negotiative power' and can reach an accommodationist equilibrium point with global capital with respect to PIT policy.

Second, such increases were enabled by the combined impact of inflation and 'bracket creep'. Thus, in many countries, rate schedules were not indexed, which meant that nominal annual wage increases pushed tax payers into higher brackets – even if they enjoyed no or small real wage increases (Messere 1998; Tanzi and Schuknecht 2000: 59). This means that while nominal PIT rates often remained unchanged, the *real* rate had surreptitiously crept up. Third, rising domestic discontent among taxpayers – partly because of bracket creep – has led to demands for lower PIT rates, especially, of course, at the higher end, resulting in the slashing of top rates in many countries. This also led to demands for indexation (OECD 1990; Owens 1990). Finally, both these latter explanations also help in part to account for why income tax yields have slowed in the 1990s. For with indexation, as well as low inflation, bracket creep has been both intentionally and unintentionally mitigated.

Table 2.3. *The tax burdens of capital and labour*

	1965–9	1970–4	1975–9	1980–4	1985–9	1990–4	1995–7
Avg. labour							
OECD avg.	100	120	140	145	147	143	131
Our avg. 1	100	121	142	147	149	150	144
Our avg. 2	100	108	115	120	124	124	121
Avg. capital							
OECD Avg.	100	117	143	141	148	148	152
Our avg.	100	119	144	149	157	155	156

Notes: 'Our avg. 1' is taken from the 23 countries listed in the notes to Table 2.2. *Labour tax burdens*: Our avg. 1 – personal income taxes and employees' social security contributions; Our avg. 2: Our avg. 1 plus indirect taxes.
Capital tax burdens: Corporate income taxes plus employers' social security contributions. Note that these definitions are the standard minimal definitions used in the literature.
Sources: OECD, *Revenue Statistics* (Paris: OECD, 1980, 1989, 1995, 1999); OECD, *National Accounts* (Paris: OECD, 1979, 1992, 1997, 2000).

In sum, as I argue in detail later on, while global pressures *do* have an impact in terms of constraining governments with respect to their income tax regimes, we should not lose sight of the fact that domestic pressures have also played an important part (cf. Garrett 1998a; Ganghoff 2001).

Disappearing capital taxes and a shifting of the tax burden from capital to labour?

As already noted, it is conventionally stated that under rising capital mobility, governments in the post-1960s era have increasingly effected a shift in the tax burden away from (mobile) capital towards (immobile) labour (Rodrik 1997a: ch. 4; Wachtel 2000).

Looking at Table 2.3 and Figure 2.3, one could be entirely forgiven for assuming that the top line represents labour taxes, while the bottom line or even the middle line – which tapers off radically after 1985–9 – represents capital taxes. But in fact it is the other way round. Capital tax burdens have risen both considerably and consistently – a proposition which is reinforced by various studies which show that effective capital tax rates have increased since the 1970s (Swank 1998; Ganghof 2001: 629). Moreover, labour taxes either dropped off in the 1990s (the 'minimal'

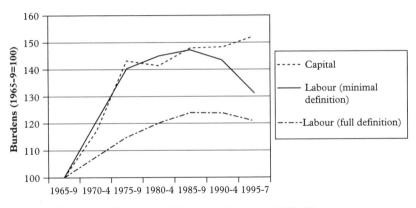

Figure 2.3 Capital and labour tax burdens, 1965–97

definition) or remained far lower than capital tax increases throughout the period (the 'full' definition). The main conclusion drawn here is that at a time when global capital flows are at their highest point, *we see a substitution of capital taxes for labour taxes* which, of course, is precisely the inverse scenario to that of conventional expectations (see also Garrett 2000b: 131). Once again, this confirms the scenario of the 'race to the middle'.

Disappearing corporate income taxes?

For the conventional account, it is especially here that we should expect to find a strong correlation or association between *rising* global capital flows (globalisation) and *declining* corporate income tax burdens.

Table 2.4 (and Figure 2.4) reveals that for each of the aggregate corporate income tax burden (CIT) averages, there is a very clear *upward* trend from 1965/9 through 1995/7, Moreover 'our avg. CIT 2' data (which looks only at central government revenues), confirms that the average CIT tax burden has risen sharply through the *whole* of the 1995/9 period. Thus corporate income taxes are far from disappearing and, more importantly, their movements demonstrate a broadly positive relationship with rising global capital flows – a conclusion which is most fundamentally at odds with conventional expectations.

These conclusions will of course seem counterintuitive given the uncontentious fact that nominal CIT rates have been lowered throughout the OECD. Britain began the process in 1984. In 1986, average OECD nominal CIT rates were roughly 41 per cent dropping to 36 per cent

Table 2.4. *Corporate income tax burdens*

	1965–9	1970–4	1975–9	1980–4	1985–9	1990–4	1995–7	1995–9
Our avg. (*CIT 1*)	100	105	108	116	126	117	135	
Our avg. (*CIT 2*)	N/A	100	108	119	138	115		140
OECD Avg. (*CIT 1*)	100	105	109	116	126	117	131	
Avg. EU (*CIT 1*)	100	115	125	113	131	123	136	

Sources and notes: Our avg. CIT 1 represents total CIT burdens at *all* levels of government for the 23 OECD countries listed at the bottom of Table 2.2, derived from OECD, *Revenue Statistics* (Paris: OECD, 1980, 1989, 1995, 1999, 2000).
Our avg. CIT 2 represents *central* government corporation tax burdens of the 23 countries, derived from IMF, *Government Finance Statistics Yearbook* (Washington: IMF, 1981, 1990, 2000).

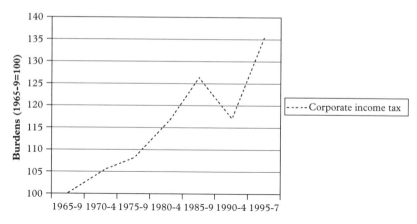

Figure 2.4 Corporate income tax, 1965–97

by 1990/1 and to just over 34 per cent by 1997. Given this, how do we explain the fact that CIT burdens have *increased* at a time when nominal tax rates have clearly declined for all OECD countries?

First, the nominal rate constitutes only one aspect of the CIT structure. Governments also take into account fiscal incentives, concessions and reliefs when choosing their preferred nominal CIT rate. Prior to

1984, governments put in place a CIT structure that had relatively high nominal rates but compensated for these by providing a raft of fiscal concessions and incentives. In other words, a relatively high nominal rate went hand-in-hand with a *narrow* base. While governments have progressively lowered the nominal rate since 1984, they have simultaneously broadened the base (i.e., cut back on concessions and incentives for investment) in order to protect or 'defend the treasury' – to use Duane Swank's phrase (Swank 1998). In general, therefore, reductions in the nominal rate have led either to revenue-neutral or revenue-enhancing compensatory reductions in fiscal reliefs and incentives.

These changes were motivated mainly by global capitalist pressures, which led governments to rationalise the CIT structure, not least to iron out economic distortions that negatively affected investment decisions (Owens 1990; Swank 1998: 678–9; Ganghoff 2001). Nevertheless, governments have not ceded revenues in the process, thereby once more confirming the scenario of the 'race to the middle'. This means that the conventional account errs by confusing the nominal rate with the effective burden, which leads it to the wrong conclusions regarding the corporate income tax burden on business (even if it correctly notes that governments have had to restructure their CIT regimes in order to court global capital). In short, I conclude that that CIT burdens have increased significantly across the 1965/9–1995/9 period, which suggests a *positive* relationship between rising global capital flows and CIT burdens (see also Quinn 1997; Swank 1998; Ganghoff 2001).

National convergence, tax competition, and the 'race to the bottom', or national divergence, 'negotiated accommodations', and the 'race to the middle'?

It is here that we finally confront the crux of the conventional argument. Conventional scholars make three broad fiscal arguments. First, they predict a *growing convergence* in national tax regimes and especially tax rates, as all countries allegedly enter into 'tax competition' or 'tax nationalism', leading to a fiscal 'race to the bottom' so as to attract mobile capital (*The Economist* 29 January 2000: S20–21). Second, they predict that ever-lowering income tax rates will undermine governmental tax takes, leading inevitably to pronounced fiscal crisis (what might be called the 'fiscal doomsday scenario'). Moreover, this proposition

Table 2.5. *National differentials in tax regimes*[a]

	1965–9	1970–4	1975–9	1980–4	1985–9	1990–4	1995–7
Total Tax	7.1	8.4	9.2	9.0	8.7	8.0	7.7
Labour tax	4.5	5.3	5.2	4.9	4.9	5.0	4.8
Capital tax	2.9	3.4	4.4	4.3	4.4	4.4	4.1
Social security contributions	3.8	4.3	5.3	5.6	5.7	5.8	5.6
Direct Tax							
Personal Income tax	4.1	5.1	5.2	5.0	5.1	4.8	4.9
Corporate income tax	1.1	1.3	1.6	1.7	1.7	1.5	1.5

[a] expressed as standard deviations
Source: See Table 2.2. All figures are average standard deviations, derived from the 23 countries listed at the bottom of Table 2.2.

expects that fiscal crisis should already have clearly emerged. But a third supplementary claim is made here, developed in a most sophisticated form by Steffen Ganghoff: that under globalisation the pressure to lower CIT (and PIT) rates *in the future* will intensify further, thereby inevitably leading to pronounced fiscal crisis in the long run. In turn, these three claims rest on the most fundamental of conventional assumptions: that states have no agency and must conciliate, or conform to the requirements, or dictates of, global capital. Here I argue that while these three propositions are problematic, there is a grain of truth in the more general claim that global pressures have pushed states to adjust their income tax regimes. Let's reply to each of these propositions in turn.

What then of the first claim, that under globalisation tax regimes are converging across states? Table 2.5 and Figure 2.5 present the standard deviations of the average OECD's country tax structures. A standard deviation (SD) of zero connotes perfect convergence of tax structures or profiles. Strikingly, in all categories bar CIT, the actual size of the SDs between OECD countries is considerable – which connotes *major* differences between national tax regimes. And while there is *some* indication that *aggregate* tax burden differentials have declined, it is also clear that national differences remain *highly pronounced* even for 1995/7. Most significantly, all other tax indicators remain highly differentiated and demonstrate no signs of convergence.

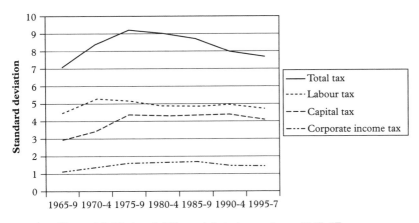

Figure 2.5 National differentials in tax regimes, 1965–97

One possible exception to this lies with the CIT burdens, for although they show no signs of *increased* convergence across the whole period, they do, however, demonstrate the *least* overall divergence of all the tax categories (whose standard deviation averaged only 1.5 for the whole period under review). And it is of course fitting for the conventional argument that this should be so, for it is here that the positive association between rising capital mobility and convergent CIT burdens should perhaps be strongest, given the (questionable) assumption that high tax rates constitute the biggest obstacle to all forms of global business (a point elaborated in the introduction to this volume on the 'enabling' face of globalisation). The major sign of the 'race to the bottom', at least from the conventional perspective, lies in the uncontentious fact that nominal CIT rates have been significantly reduced across the board throughout the OECD. Surprisingly though, while there has been *some* degree of convergence of *nominal* CIT rates, they remain highly differentiated (with a standard deviation as high as 8.9 as of 1997).

But what of the second conventional claim: that declining nominal CIT rates has led to lower tax yields and prolonged fiscal crisis? Here the conventional argument emphasises that states are caught on the scissors: between on the one hand needing foreign investment to maintain or enhance national economic growth rates and, on the other hand, 'having to accept' that the 'price' of such investment is a lower CIT yield. But this is falsified by the simple fact that governments have been able to successfully attract increased foreign investment while *simultaneously*

Table 2.6. *Corporate income tax burdens in countries with very high dependence on FDI inflows*

Countries	1980–4 all govt. CIT	1985–9 all govt. CIT	1990–4 all govt. CIT	1995–7 all govt. CIT	1995–9 central govt. CIT
Australia	100	103	131	141	157
Canada	100	96	74	111	N/A
Netherlands	100	116	113	131	137
UK	100	111	79	100	103
Avg. of above countries	*100*	*107*	*99*	*121*	*132*
OECD Avg.	100	109	101	113	117

Source: 'All govt.' CIT revenues from OECD, *Revenue Statistics* (Paris: OECD, 1989, 2000); 'Central govt.' CIT revenues from IMF, *Government Finance Statistics Yearbook* (Washington: IMF, 1990, 2000). GDP data: See Table 2.2.

maintaining, if not increasing, the CIT yield. This conclusion is supported in a recent OECD survey (OECD 1995: 93), and by the 1992 Ruding Committee, which surveyed MNCs and concluded that the evidence for tax competition between European countries to attract investment via corporate tax reductions was unconvincing, not least because the corporate tax base remained buoyant (Ruding Committee 1992). Thus the conventional assumption that there is an inherent 'trade-off' between national economic growth and national fiscal capacity is not borne out; rather, the two have in fact gone hand-in-hand in a positive-sum game.

However, it might be objected that measuring the *average* CIT burden fails to do full justice to the conventional claim, given that some states might be less dependent on global capital flows than others. Table 2.6 selects four OECD countries that are subject to the highest penetration of FDI inward flows covering the 1980s to mid-1990s, and examines the shifts in their CIT burdens in this period.

Table 2.6 confirms the argument already made. And, interestingly, the average increases across the four countries end up higher for the 1995/7 period when compared to the overall OECD average. The far right-hand column has been generated because it covers the whole of the 1995/9 period (though it is problematic in that it covers only central government revenues), and provides reinforcing evidence for my claim.

In short, even under the very best-case scenario, it seems reasonable to conclude that changes in government CIT burdens have generally performed inversely to conventional expectations – thereby once again suggesting a positive relationship between global capital flows and tax revenues. This means that the conventional dilemma discussed above is problematic, and once more confirms the alternative picture of a 'race to the middle' in the absence of fiscal crisis.

What then of the third conventional claim: that declining CIT rates *will* lead to fiscal crisis *in the future*? Here I argue that this scenario is highly unlikely, though I do argue that there *is* a fiscal dilemma under globalisation – even if it lies down a side-alley that has not been fully explored by conventional analysts. The real dilemma is both more complex and more circumscribed in its impact on states than envisaged by the conventional account. First, tax competition would seem to explain the reduction in the nominal CIT rate. That this has been more than compensated for by various fiscal adjustments, has meant that thus far revenue yields have not been adversely affected. Interestingly, Steffen Ganghof confirms my point that such compensations have been made through base-broadening initiatives, though he goes on to argue that such initiatives cannot go on indefinitely. As he puts it: 'The constraining effect of tax competition is likely to increase in the future. Tax competition will continue to exert downward pressure on some income tax rates, especially corporation tax rates, and governments will find it increasingly difficult to compensate the resulting revenue losses by broadening the corporate income tax base' (Ganghof 2001). There are two points that flow from this: first, the potential loss of CIT revenues *in the future* (i.e., long-term fiscal crisis); and second, declining CIT rates have led to unintended distortions in income tax regimes, in which governments have had to make various compromises or trade-offs. I argue that the first point is overblown, though I endorse the second – Ganghof's thesis – that governments have been constrained in various ways and have had to make compromises with respect to the making of income tax policy.

Both these problems are in fact linked by what might be called the 'income tax gap'. This refers to the situation where in some though not all countries, CIT rates are lower than top rates of PIT. The example of Australia is pertinent here. Because the top rate PIT stands at 47 per cent while the CIT rate presently stands at 30 per cent, the gap has provided a major incentive for high-income earners to *incorporate*. Thus in establishing a business, and declaring their personal income through it, they manage to escape the top rate PIT and have thereby succeeded in lowering their personal tax burden. This has also meant that the middle-income earners have seen an effective ratcheting up of their tax burden, in turn leading to middle-income taxpayer revolts (which led the Liberal–National Coalition government to successfully lower the rates on the middle-income earners in the late 1990s). Following Ganghof, I agree that globalisation *has* constrained the form that income tax regimes have taken, where the dealignment of the top rate PIT and CIT rate leads to significant distortions, which in turn have a negative spill-over effect for the PIT regime (Ganghof 2001). In order to close this gap, and given that many – though by no means all governments – are seeking to reduce CIT rates, so they will also need to lower top rates on PIT, so as to prevent fiscal leakage (as has already occurred). This has, for example, been a central electoral strategy of the present Australian government. This in turn means that the ultimate effect of tax competition as it affects CIT rates lies in the *negative spill-over* effects on the PIT regime, requiring similar reductions in the top rate there.

The worst-case or 'fiscal doomsday' scenario – that would confirm the conventional argument – would be one in which there is a continually decreasing CIT rate, which flows on to a continually decreasing top rate of PIT. Crucially, assuming a future scenario where base-broadening initiatives had reached their limit, this would at some future point inevitably entail a loss of income tax revenue (i.e., fiscal crisis). Under this scenario the conventional prediction of a trade-off between maintaining global competitiveness and reduced taxes (and hence fiscal crisis) would be realised. This leads on to three central and inter-related questions:

(1) What likelihood is there of this future fiscal doomsday scenario?
(2) Can governments negotiate with global capital to maintain future revenue requirements?
(3) And, if the doomsday scenario is unlikely, to what extent have global constraints impacted on income tax regimes?

First, it is important to note that the fiscal doomsday scenario rests on the strict assumption of an almost indefinite 'race to the *very* bottom'. But there are, however, two major problems here. First, it seems a highly unlikely proposition that CIT rates will *indefinitely* decline. Paradoxically this seems unlikely even under the logic of the conventional account; for most conventional writers argue that while states are diminished by globalisation and that their tax regimes are similarly constrained, nevertheless global capital *cannot* function in the absence of a sovereign multistate system, which in turn presupposes the maintenance of taxation, even if only at lower levels than those enjoyed in the past (e.g., Cox 1996; Cerny 1990).

Perhaps the most realistic scenario would be that governments would seek – unilaterally, bilaterally, and multilaterally – to negotiate with global capital their own type of trade-off, in which they might be prepared to lower CIT rates further, but not beyond the point at which this would impact in a negative way on income tax yields. In other words, while governments might be prepared to accept lower CIT rates in the future, as they have done in the past, and would at some point bring top PIT rates into line, nevertheless they would *not* be prepared to allow the PIT rate to drop to a level that would threaten income tax revenues. This claim rests on the assumption that governments *always* seek to 'defend the treasury', and that governments have 'negotiative-agency' with respect to global capital.

This returns us to the fiscal trade-off situation which I have characterised as a 'race to the middle' – a middle that is *negotiated* between states and global capital, and defined by an equilibrium point that enables governments to maintain revenue yields and national economic competitiveness while allowing global capital to preserve its profit-making interests. In addition to the evidence already presented, there is further evidence we can point to here which is indicative of this negotiative power. By the late 1990s many OECD countries had begun to clamp down on MNC tax-avoidance policies. For example, fourteen OECD countries adopted what is known as Controlled Foreign Corporation (CFC) rules, and a growing number have instigated Foreign Investment Fund (FIF) rules, all of which prevent tax avoidance by resident shareholders (OECD 1998: 41–3). And most countries have provisions for 'related party transactions', which seek to prevent the practice of 'transfer pricing' (one means of tax avoidance) by MNCs. The flip-side of this, of course, is that such *enhanced* regulation initiatives have made many OECD countries potentially vulnerable to capital flight. But again, governments have responded through their negotiative power to mitigate this.

Thus in 1996 the OECD finance ministers called upon the OECD to 'develop measures to counter the distorting effects of harmful tax competition' (OECD 1998: 3). The OECD's recommendations prescribed a variety of measures that governments can take both individually and collectively – for example, that *all* EU governments should adopt CFC and FIF rules, thereby reducing the fiscal incentives for MNCs to locate in countries which do not have these regulations (OECD 1998: 41–55). The OECD also set up a whole series of institutional initiatives including, for example, the Forum on Harmful Tax Competition, which prescribed that OECD members should eliminate their harmful tax regimes by 2003, and has also begun to implement measures to clamp down on the problem of tax havens. Furthermore, in December 1997, EU finance ministers *agreed to implement* a package of measures to tackle harmful tax competition, including cracking down on tax havens, sharing of information between tax jurisdictions, and various other measures – most of which complement the OECD's 1998 recommendations.

It is worth noting here too, that while conventional analysts make much of the revenues lost through tax havens, this chapter produces an implicit response. For while some revenues *are* lost through tax havens, it seems that this should not be overplayed, for two main reasons: first, because it seems as though revenues lost are marginal (less than 10 per cent of US income taxes are lost in this way and no more than 3 per cent of total receipts). Second, this has not yet become a problem for governments precisely because they are still *increasing* their aggregate tax (and direct tax) yields. And I speculate that even if a fiscal crunch were to materialise – leading to a desire to 'get tough' – it would *not* be hard for OECD governments to clamp down on tax havens should they so desire (most of which are particularly small third world 'states', many of which are found in the South Pacific and Caribbean). Moreover, the authorities in the tax havens receive perhaps around 10 per cent of the total lost tax revenues from the OECD countries (Sharman 2001). Thus were a fiscal crunch to eventuate, OECD countries could 'at worst' buy out these tax havens for a cost of a mere 10 per cent of the net revenues that they would gain (a 'bargain' by any definition), or simply outlaw them 'at best'.

But the major conclusion here is that the conventional prediction of a 'fiscal race to the bottom', or a Hobbesian fiscal 'war of all against all', has not transpired. Thus while most OECD countries have put into place significant fiscal regulations on MNCs so as to preserve their tax take from mobile capital, the key point is that rather than drop these and engage in all-out tax competition, OECD countries are attempting to do the opposite. That is, they are pressing other governments with more lax regulations to follow suit and tighten these up, thereby preventing MNCs and resident shareholders from minimising their tax bills by playing off different countries. Clearly, global capital is finding that the avenue of the 'exit strategy' is becoming increasingly difficult to access.

So what is the final upshot of all of this? Thus far I have responded to the first two questions posted above by rejecting the likelihood of a future fiscal doomsday scenario, in large part because states have negotiative power that has been ignored by conventional analysts. What then of the third question concerning the impact of globalisation on the construction of income tax regimes? Here I argue that while states do have room for manoeuvre, we should not however, overstate this. Here I follow Ganghof (2001), and agree that global capital *has* posed various constraints on the progressivity of the PIT and CIT regimes, even if this has been the 'price' of maintaining revenue yields. New Zealand is an excellent case in point. This country has one of the lowest top rates of PIT, but simultaneously has the third highest PIT yield in the OECD (Ganghof 2001). This fiscal paradox is explained by the fact that the government has maintained revenues by making compromises in terms of the progressivity of the income tax regime. This suggests more generally that while PIT revenues can indeed be maintained with lower top rates, nevertheless governments have to make some trade-off. This means that we need to qualify the scenario painted by conventional scholars who claim that globalisation forces governments to make a *fundamental* shift to regressive tax regimes (namely by replacing lost income tax revenues by increased regressive indirect taxes). Given the earlier evidence which shows that most states have managed to *increase* direct tax yields (well in excess of indirect tax increases), I conclude that this has come at a certain price: that governments have been forced to effect a *partial* shift to less progressivity *within* the PIT regime and have, also under global pressures, sought to reformulate the *structure* of their CIT regimes (i.e., lower the nominal rate and broaden the base). That is, under globalisation, governments have been pressed to produce flatter income tax regimes in order to maintain revenues (for a detailed discussion of this, see Ganghof 2001). This, I believe, *is* a significant constraint posed by globalisation, though this is not to endorse the conventional fiscal doomsday scenario, given my assertion that direct tax yields have risen significantly through the post-1965 period, and are unlikely to diminish in the future to the levels predicted by conventional scholars, not least because they themselves have underestimated states' negotiative power, and have simultaneously exaggerated the power of global capital to dictate government policy. This rests in turn on my most fundamental claim: that states and global capital are engaged in an accommodationist 'race to the middle'.

Conclusion: the twin myths of capital's victory over state fiscal capacity, and the state's victory over global capital

In direct contrast to the conventional wisdom, this chapter has produced evidence which demonstrates that under high levels of global capital mobility, states' revenue yields have in fact been *enhanced* across the period. Accordingly, it is premature, if not facile, to assume that globalisation signifies the end of the state, or even the 'retreat of the state'. It thus seems clear that 'reports of the death of state fiscal capacity are greatly exaggerated', and that the much heralded prediction of the victory of mobile global capital over state fiscal capacity turns out to be a myth (cf. Weiss 1998). Nevertheless, in contrast to the pure 'agential' alternative to the conventional account, I have also argued that we need to recognise that globalisation *has* posed various constraints on states' fiscal policymaking (mainly with respect to the shape of their income tax regimes), and that states cannot make policy in the absence of global constraint. This leads me to reject the traditional 'either/or' model, in favour of a 'both/and' approach, which recognises that globalisation both constrains and enables states in their fiscal policymaking.

Thus while states are not simply 'passive agents' or 'passive bearers' of global structural requirements – they have a degree of agency – nevertheless, so too does global capital. Both states and global capital have a degree of 'room for manoeuvre', even if neither side has the ultimate advantage – captured in my assertion of the 'race to the middle', where both seek to find an accommodationist equilibrium point which enables them to maintain their interests (taxation and national investment rates for states; investment and profits for global capital). And in crucial contrast to the conventional account, these interests are often more complementary than antagonistic. Both want a secure investment environment, which meets with states' requirements to enhance national economic growth rates (as well as revenue extraction), while simultaneously enabling the enhancement of global capital's profits. And global companies accept (albeit grudgingly) that the price of this is the payment of taxes in order to maintain states. Thus, while the relationship sometimes goes into disequilibrium, nevertheless negotiations resume to restore this back to equilibrium, even if this takes longer for some issues than others (compare states' base-broadening initiatives and the clamping down on MNC tax-minimisation strategies, with the longer-term problem of tax havens).

The point here is that conventional accounts have mistaken the various tensions between states' fiscal needs on the one hand, and global capital's profit requirements on the other, as the sign of an 'antagonistic' relationship, which simultaneously assumes that their interests are *irreconcilable*. Similarly, in terms of my argument about the 'race to the middle', conventional analysts have confused the moments of disequilibrium as signs of irreconcilable antagonism. This chapter reveals evidence that not only have *both* been able to accommodate and re-accommodate each other's needs in a mutually beneficial way through time, but, more importantly, that such tensions are in fact the sign of a *functionally interdependent* rather than an irreconcilable, dysfunctional relationship. This notion complements the recent argument made by Linda Weiss (1999b), who also characterises the relationship as one of interdependence. And as in any close functional interdependent relationship, there are always tensions and moments of disequilibrium, which are restored back to equilibrium at some point in time. This chapter has produced substantial evidence to support this claim for the 1965–2000 period, and I see no reason why this should change in the future.

Finally, I return to where the chapter began. For under the pervasive influence of the conventional imagination, we generally picture a world in which states are increasingly squeezed by global capital, such that they have less and less room for fiscal manoeuvre, in turn leading to the inevitable retreat of the welfare state. This chapter has shown that this popular picture does *not* square with the evidence. It is especially here that the rhetoric of right-wing governments and conventional left-wing critiques of globalisation join hands and paint a picture of the politically impotent state (the 'politics of despair and helplessness'). The evidence presented here reveals this as but empty rhetoric, and in turn presents a more optimistic vision: that states *can* make a difference and that the battle for public welfare and education has by no means been lost to the forces of globalisation.

Notes

I am very grateful to Lutz Hoff for his help in collecting the data, and to Ian Roxan, Linda Weiss, Jason Sharman, and especially Steffen Ganghof, for their advice. Naturally I remain responsible for the final product.
1. Though in fairness, Hirst and Thompson recognise that states are constrained by 'internationalisation' (rather than globalisation).

3 Withering welfare? Globalisation, political economic institutions, and contemporary welfare states

Duane Swank

Globalisation theory suggests that internationalisation creates strong pressure on policymakers in democratic polities to retrench the welfare state. The exit option accorded mobile asset holders by capital mobility purportedly encourages policymakers to compete for transnational investment; in the strongest versions of the theory, potentially costly social expenditures are reduced to the 'lowest common denominator'. The exit option may also enhance the conventional political resources of mobile enterprises as well as strengthen arguments for neoliberal welfare reforms. Trade openness supposedly generates similar pressures: policymakers in open economies encounter demands for reductions in welfare-related labour costs to promote the price competitiveness of exports and otherwise enhance efficiency.

Here, I advance an alternative view. My recent work (e.g., Swank 2001, 2002) argues that institutional features of the polity and welfare state influence the relative capacity of pro-welfare-state interests to defend social protection. I extend these arguments in the present context by exploring how the 'production regimes' of coordinated and uncoordinated market economies are related to, and reinforce the political consequences of, national political and welfare state institutions. My central argument is that globalisation has not led to significant welfare retrenchment in coordinated market economies; coordinated market institutions shape the interests, strategic choices, and capacities of labour, capital, and the state in ways favourable to the maintenance of social protection. Alternatively, globalisation has contributed to welfare state retrenchment in uncoordinated market economies.

I organise the chapter as follows. First, I review globalisation theory and the counterclaim that the postwar system of international liberalisation and significant social protection is still relevant for understanding globalisation–welfare state linkages today. Second, I document the inter-relationships among welfare state, political, and economic institutions and outline their political consequences for defence of social protection. The third section offers an analysis of the roles of coordinated and un-coordinated market institutions in mediating the welfare state effects of globalisation. I conclude with an assessment of the importance of na-tional institutions to the domestic policy impacts of internationalisation.

Globalisation and the welfare state

The facts concerning internationalisation of markets for goods, services, and capital are familiar (Weiss, this volume). With regard to the cen-tral questions of this book, both classic and contemporary political economists have argued that internationalisation, especially rises in capital mobility, diminish the capacity of governments to maintain generous social protection and requisite taxes.[1] The impact of global-isation on domestic welfare policy may be channelled through three mechanisms (see Swank 2001, 2002). The first linkage rests on the 'economic logic' of internationalisation; the second and third mecha-nisms link globalisation and domestic policy through politics. In brief, with regard to capital mobility, the economic logic argues that capital mobility affects social policymakers through markets; in the presence of high capital mobility, mobile asset holders seek the most profitable rate of return on investment. In the context of extensive international fi-nancial integration and little international policy coordination, national policymakers face a prisoner's dilemma: individual governments face strong incentives to engage in competition for investment through re-ductions in social benefits and associated taxes. Rising trade openness supposedly reinforces these pressures: increases in trade may lead gov-ernments to cut social outlays in order to reduce public debt and interest rates, disincentives to work and invest, and labour costs.

In the 'political logic' of globalisation, capital mobility may contribute to welfare state retrenchment through routine democratic politics. Mobile businesses and their interest associations often pressure gov-ernments for cuts in generous social protection and supporting taxes by arguing that the welfare state negatively affects profits, investment, and jobs and by pointing to the benefits of foreign investment locales. Furthermore, internationalisation reinforces neoliberal economic ortho-doxy: business spokespersons and economists as well as centre-right governments frequently use the 'economic logic' of globalisation when arguing for neoliberal restructuring of the welfare state (Swank 2002, chs. 4–6).

Embedded liberalism and the welfare state

In a seminal article, David Cameron (1978) outlined the antithesis to contemporary globalisation theory. In Cameron's 'openness thesis', trade is systematically associated with the expansion of the public economy and income maintenance in capitalist democracies (also see Stephens 1979; Katzenstein 1985). Structurally, Cameron emphasised that open economies have concentrated industrial sectors and, consequentially, strong trade unions, centralised collective bargaining, and powerful left parties. These forces, in turn, increase social welfare effort and overall government intervention. A large public sector and welfare state also enables governments in open economies to lessen insecurities and risks, manage business cycles, and otherwise adjust to openness. Complementing Cameron's analysis, John Ruggie (1982) argued that a multilateral international regime of 'embedded liberalism' emerged after World War II in which trade liberalisation was supported by significant government interventionism and social insurance.

More recently, Geoffrey Garrett (1998a, 1998b) and Dani Rodrik (1997a, 1998) have argued that governments maintain significant social insurance against risks attendant on internationalisation. For instance, Rodrik (1998) presents evidence that high levels of trade with terms-of-trade volatility remain positively associated with generous income maintenance in both developing and developed political economies. Garrett and Mitchell (2001) also present a variety of evidence consistent with their 'compensation hypothesis'. However, Rodrik (1997a) argues that the combination of high capital mobility and trade openness may undercut the ability of governments to finance generous social protection; thus, the joint efficiency and equity gains of embedded liberalism are threatened (also see Pauly 1995; Ruggie 1994).

Welfare regimes and political economic institutions

In contrast to these theories, I argue that the relationship between the international economy and welfare state is cross-nationally varied. Welfare policy change, whether in response to international or domestic forces, takes place in the context of programmatic structures and related political economic institutions. As such, policy reform is fundamentally shaped by the institutions in which social protection is embedded.

Table 3.1 displays data on welfare state structures, political institutions, and economic models during the 1980s and 1990s. First, as demonstrated by Esping-Andersen (1990), welfare states may be ranked by the degree of 'universalism', 'conservatism', and 'liberalism' in programme structure. The universal (or social democratic) welfare state is characterised by comprehensive, universal, and egalitarian income maintenance programmes as well as by universally and publically provided social services (e.g., Stephens 1996). Corporatist conservative welfare states, historically embedded in conservative statist traditions, Catholic political mobilisation, and communal corporatism (e.g., skilled craft guilds), are distinguished by a mix of nationally unified, generous, and employment-based social insurance programmes that cover most employees and their families (e.g., Esping-Andersen 1990). Social protection is dominated by public cash benefits and underdeveloped public social services. On the other hand, liberal welfare states are characterised by a mixture of moderate to low flat-rate, social insurance, and extensively means-tested benefits as well as relatively well-developed private social insurance and low levels of government social services.

The scores for fifteen nations on universalism, conservatism, and liberalism as well as on measures of the social wage, public social services, means testing, and private social insurance are given in Table 3.2.[2] The social democratic welfare state cluster consists of Denmark, Finland, the Netherlands, Norway and Sweden while the conservative welfare state group is composed of Austria, Belgium, France, Germany, and Italy. The liberal group includes Australia, Canada, Japan, the United Kingdom, and the United States. Classifications of the Netherlands, Japan, and Britain, which mix programmatic attributes of welfare state types, were based on the extensive literature on these systems (see Swank 2002: chs. 2, 6). In addition, Australia departs partially from the liberal model: relatively high social benefit equality with progressive financing and labour-friendly wage-setting institutions form a 'wage-earners welfare state' (Castles 1996).

With respect to institutional structures of the polity, one can see that clusters of welfare states are also distinguished by their relative rankings on measures of electoral and collective interest representation: the 'universalism of welfare protection' in the social democratic welfare states is matched by a 'universalism of interest representation'. First, social

Table 3.1. *Welfare state, political, and economic institutions: annual country averages, 1980–95*

	Programme Structure				Programme Generosity		Programme Stratification	Inclusive Electoral Institutions	National Coordination-Corporatism	Sector-Group Coordination
Nation	Univ	Cons	Lib	Soc Wage	Services	Means	Private			
Sweden	8	0	0	82	6.5	7	7	.33	.92	.34
Norway	8	4	0	57	3.8	4	3	.32	.99	.32
Denmark	8	2	6	62	5.7	8	4	.76	.40	.19
Finland	6	6	4	46	3.5	9	4	.83	.52	.50
Netherlands	6	4	8	68	2.0	11	16	.43	.02	−.60
Austria	2	8	4	34	0.9	5	NA	.04	.30	.38
Belgium	4	8	4	43	1.1	4	2	1.58	.23	.19
France	2	8	8	56	1.8	2	NA	−.29	−.41	−.28
Germany	4	8	6	37	1.8	7	8	.25	−.02	.51
Italy	0	8	6	43	1.1	9	7	.59	.39	.63
United States	0	0	12	25	0.5	40	33	−1.23	−1.03	−.76
Canada	4	2	12	55	0.6	19	20	−1.20	−.88	−.90
Japan	2	4	10	28	0.4	4	23/30	−.40	−.31	1.08
Australia	4	0	10	19	0.8	90	15	−.58	.17	−.90
Britain	4	0	6	20	1.6	33	17	−1.20	−.46	−.80

Matrix of Correlation Coefficients:

Variable	I	II	III	IV	V	VI
I Universalism	1.00	–	–	–	–	–
II Conservatism	-.29**	1.00	–	–	–	–
III Liberalism	-.48**	-.23**	1.00	–	–	–
IV Inclusive Electoral Institutions	.37**	.56**	-.62**	1.00	–	–
V National Coordination–Corporatism	.58**	.18	-.82**	.67**	1.00	–
VI Sector-Group Coordination	.05	.51**	-.47**	.54**	.48**	1.00

** Significant at .01 level (N = 240).

Source: See Appendix A.

Note: Definitions of measures.

Universalism: Esping Anderson's (1990) score for universalism and benefit equality in social welfare programmes, *c.* 1980.

Conservatism: Esping-Andersen's (1990) score for degree welfare is occupationally stratified and public employees have special programmes, *c.* 1980.

Liberalism: Esping-Andersen's (1990) score for welfare state reliance on means-testing and private pensions and health care, *c.* 1980.

Soc Wage: Social wage, defined as the percentage of the average production worker's gross income replaced by unemployment compensation/insurance and social supports during the first year of unemployment.

Services: Public Expenditure on Social Services, including government services for families, the disabled, the elderly, and workers (e.g., active labor market programmes).

Means: Reliance on Means-Tested Programmes, defined as the percentage of social security spending composed of outlays for means-tested programmes.

Private: Reliance on Private Social Spending, defined as the private mandatory and voluntary spending as a percentage of total social welfare spending.

Electoral Representation: Weighted standard score index of degree of proportional representation and number of effective legislative parties, annual average, 1980–94.

National Coordination–Corporatism: See Table 3.2 and text.

Sectoral Coordination: See Table 3.2 and text.

Table 3.2. *Principal components analysis for national political economic institutions, 1973–94*

	I	II
Level of Collective Bargaining	.8847	−.0021
Union Organisation	.7894	.1587
Employer Organisation	.6184	.5049
Labour–Management Cooperation	.5620	.5700
Investor–Production Enterprise Linkages	.4492	.7172
Purchaser–Supplier Relationships	.0923	.9173
Cooperative Arrangements–Competitive Firms	.0464	.9244

Sources: See Appendix.
Notes: Principal Components is executed with varimax rotation. Component Indicators: Level of Collective Bargaining: bargaining scale where 0 is plant level, 1 is industry level, 2 is sectoral level without sanctions, and 3 is sectoral level with sanctions.
Union Organisation: Standard score index of the percentage of employed wage and salary workers who are members of unions, and centralisation of confederal power, or the largest confederation's power of appointment, veto over wage agreements, veto over strikes, and maintenance of strike funds.
Employer Organisation: Standard score index of the presence of a peak national association and powers of that association (i.e., power of appointment, power over industrial actions and collective bargains, and industrial conflict funds).
Labor Management Cooperation: Cooperation between management and labour over employment security.
Investor–Production Enterprise Linkage: the strength of long-term cooperative relations between financial institutions and the enterprises they lend to.
Purchaser–Supplier Relations: strength of long-term supplier–purchaser relationships.
Cooperative Arrangements–Competitive Firms: cooperation between competitive firms in training, research and development/technology sharing, export promotion, standard setting, and related activities.

democratic welfare states are characterised by moderately strong electoral inclusiveness (i.e., proportional representation and multipartism). Furthermore, they are characterised by relatively strong social corporatist systems of interest representation. Although Table 3.2 presents an operationalisation of corporatism that is designed to capture national coordination of the economy (see below), the measure is closely related to labour organisation, incorporation of collective actors in the national policy process, and, in turn, the degree to which the interest representation system is corporatist or pluralist (Swank 2001, 2002). While corporatism is modest in the Netherlands (and while Sweden has experienced decentralisation since the mid-1980s), Sweden, Norway, Denmark, and

Finland rank high on the corporatist scale (see Wallerstein, Golden, and Lange 1997).

On the other hand, liberal welfare states are typically pluralist (with the exception of post-1983 Australia) and have relatively majoritarian or 'exclusive' electoral institutions (i.e., single-member districts, plurality electoral rules). Conservative welfare states tend to have moderate to high levels of social corporatism and electoral inclusiveness (although France is moderately low on both). Overall, institutional structures of the welfare state and polity cohere in predictable ways: comprehensive and generous welfare states are embedded in polities with encompassing interest representational systems while the means-tested and private-oriented liberal welfare states are nested in 'exclusive' electoral institutions and pluralist interest representational systems.

Welfare states and production regimes

Welfare state types also share complementarities with divergent 'production regimes' (Ebbinghaus and Manow 2001; Hall and Soskice 2000; Huber and Stephens 2001: ch. 4). With respect to these regimes, Soskice (1990, 1999) argues that employers are central to the organisation of markets. First, countries will be differentiated along a continuum of national coordination through economy-wide collective bargaining among highly centralised employer and union associations. Second, nations will vary by degree of sector or group coordination of the economy, or the degree of cooperation among subnational employers in organising financial, product, and labour markets.

Pursuant to this work, I analysed the relationships between seven key characteristics of market coordination: the level of collective bargaining; employer organisation; union organisation; labour–management cooperation in employment security; finance–industry linkages; long-term purchaser–supplier relations; and cooperation among competitive firms in training, R&D and technology sharing, product standard setting, and export marketing strategy. In theory, the first three factors should cohere and form the core institutional configuration of national coordination. The last four features of economic organisation should also cohere and form the central dimension of sector coordination (continental Europe) or business group coordination (Japan, Asian growth economies). Nationally coordinated economies, especially the Nordic social democracies, are also characterised by finance–industry linkages and some forward and backward integration of enterprises (Huber and Stephens 1998). Nations that are low on both national and sector-group coordination constitute the set of uncoordinated or liberal market economies.[3]

Using new data on the seven focal characteristics (see Table 3.2 and Appendix), I conducted a principal components analysis of underlying dimensions. As predicted, the level of collective bargaining and employer and union organisation strongly 'load' on one dimension: national coordination–corporatism. Investor–producer linkages, purchaser–supplier relations, and cooperation among competitive firms strongly 'load' on a second: sector-group coordination. Labour–management cooperation is statistically related to both, although marginally more so with sector-group coordination. In addition, as theory suggests, employer organisation is also associated with sector-group economic coordination; investor–producer linkages also 'loads' on national coordination–corporatism. Thus, on the basis of these results, I weighted a country's standard scores on the seven dimensions by the respective factor loadings, added a nation's weighted scores for the first three variables to compute country scores for national coordination, and added a nation's weighted scores for the last four variables to compute country scores for sector-group coordination.

The factor loadings for each dimension are displayed in Table 3.2 and the country scores for national coordination-corporatism and sector-group coordination are displayed in Table 3.1. The table illustrates that with the exception of the Netherlands, social democratic welfare states tend to have high national (and moderate sector-group) coordination. To expand, social democratic welfare states support, and are reinforced by, the institutions and policies of nationally coordinated market economies. With regard to national policy frameworks, universal welfare programmes and supply-side oriented economic policy both emphasise work. Active labour market policies provide ample resources for training, placement, and other employment services; income maintenance programmes contain strong work incentives. Until recently, with the exception of Denmark, macroeconomic and supply-side policies have prioritised full employment. With the exception of (pre-1980s) Finland, governments in social democratic systems have utilised Keynesian demand management to manage business cycles. Social democratic governments have also employed tax-based incentives for productive investment, mechanisms which substantially reduce corporate profit taxes on reinvested earnings. They have also used extensive control of banking and credit (especially in Norway and Finland) to direct the flow of resources to job-creating investments. These demand and supply-side policies have been supported by corporatist institutions and universal social welfare programmes; labour has commonly traded wage restraint for full employment commitments and increases in social protection (e.g., Katzenstein 1985; Swank 2002). Wage restraint, coupled with 1970s and 1980s selective currency devaluations, has been particularly important to the social democratic effort to maintain jobs and growth in export-oriented sectors (e.g., Huber and Stephens 1998).

Corporatist conservative welfare states tend to have relatively strong sector-coordinated market institutions and moderate to strong corporatist institutions. France's statist policy framework of indicative planning and selective credit control (and moderately low national and sectoral coordination) is distinct within the corporatist conservative welfare states (see Note 3). To elaborate, these systems exhibit at least moderate levels of centralisation of their labour and industrial relations systems. In this respect, Austrian sectoral bargaining, coordinated by highly centralised national associations of labour and business, rivals corporatist practices of the social democratic cases (Huber and Stephens 1998). Moreover, relatively centralised collective bargaining is supported by cooperative arrangements between business and labour at the enterprise level (e.g., works councils). Second, the economy is structured by high levels of coordination of essential activities within industrial sectors geared to the long-term development and production of high-quality, diversified consumer and industrial goods (e.g., Soskice 1999). Business, in the form of trade associations, industry–financial networks, and other cooperative groups, typically coordinates research and development, export and marketing strategy, vocational training, production standards, and some aspects of competition and pricing. Economic coordination by business is, in turn, supported by legal and public regulatory policies.

Corporatist conservative welfare states facilitate the operation of the coordinated market economy (Manow 1998). Most centrally, the structure of the welfare state integrates labour and capital and promotes long-term stable employer–employee relations. Specifically, the welfare state provides generous employment-based social protection for labour without fundamentally altering class and status distinctions and market incentives. As Manow emphasises, the conservative welfare state offers significant social protection for workers, social stability for capital, and promotes the cooperative relations necessary for long-term development strategies that are impossible in uncoordinated economies dominated by short-term, competitive market exchanges. Furthermore, the occupational basis of the welfare state fosters the acquisition of firm-specific skills by workers and, in turn, enhances the long-term employment commitments valued by workers and employers (Ebbinghaus and Manow in press).

In turn, the Anglo-liberal welfare states are generally uncoordinated market economies. Modest to low means-tested benefits, small social service bureaucracies, and relatively high reliance on private social insurance ease market adaptation to economic change (e.g., through labour market flexibility) and the low-wage production strategies of contemporary liberal market systems (e.g., King and Wood 1999; Swank 2002: ch. 6). In the Anglo group, Australia is a notable exception in that it has experienced relatively centralised wage negotiations between government and labour from 1984 through the early 1990s (e.g., Schwartz 2000b). Japan, on the other hand, stands out among predominantly liberal welfare states given that it has a high level of group-coordination of the economy. However, Japan does not depart completely from the pattern of welfare state-production regime linkage. As Esping-Andersen (1997) has argued, while Japanese social policy has distinct liberal elements (e.g., reliance on private insurance), basic features of social policy such as occupationally based public social insurance closely approximate the 'Bismarckian' model.

In summary, Table 3.1 provides the correlations for the relationships between dimensions of welfare state, polity, and economy. Universal and conservative programmatic structures are positively correlated with inclusive electoral institutions; universalism and national coordination-corporatism are strongly and positively related as are conservatism and sector-group coordination of the economy. Liberalism in welfare programme structure is strongly and negatively related to inclusive electoral institutions, national coordination-corporatism, and sector-group coordination.

The political consequences of national institutions for welfare reform

The institutional structures of welfare states and their polities and economies are complementary if not fully interdependent. It is also arguably the case that the political consequences of welfare state, political, and economic institutions for the interests, strategies, and capacities of political agents are mutually reinforcing. I develop this argument here, first, by surveying welfare reforms in the era of globalisation and, in turn, offering an explanation of the divergent trajectories of national social policies by reference to the institutions in which they are embedded.

A casual observer of post-1970 social policy change would note that all developed democracies have experienced some reductions in benefits, restrictions on programme eligibility, and neoliberal reforms of health and social services (e.g., privatisation, internal markets). Furthermore, neoliberal restructuring has occurred during a period when internationalisation has rapidly accelerated. However, it would also be clear that welfare retrenchment has been generally less severe and temporally disconnected from internationalisation in social democratic and corporatist conservative welfare states. In liberal welfare states, retrenchment has been deeper and temporally linked with globalisation (Swank 2002: chs. 4–6).

Table 3.3 displays data for representative social democratic, corporatist conservative, and liberal political economies: Sweden, Germany, and Britain, respectively.[4] With respect to Sweden, 1976–82 centre-right governments initiated moderate cost controls in response to fiscal stress. These efforts to restrain social welfare expenses were continued in the 1983–91 period by Social Democratic governments; efficiency-oriented policies in health and social services as well as long-term policy planning for pension reform were initiated. However, these cost controls were coupled with extensions in family and unemployment benefits; significant reductions in Swedish social protection did not occur until the 1990s (Stephens 1996). In the early 1990s, severe economic downturn and concomitant rises in unemployment pressured policymakers to cut unemployment, social assistance, and sickness benefits, among other programmes (Huber and Stephens 1998). However, resources for active labour market programmes were increased substantially at the same time. As Table 3.3 suggests, the social wage for Swedish workers did not actually decline during the 1980–95 period; in fact, despite early 1990s reductions, there was a small increase for the period. Continued commitments, needs, and modest extensions to social services and active labour market programmes resulted in an increase of total social service spending equivalent to nearly 2 per cent of GDP.

In the case of Germany, initiation of welfare cost controls began in the late 1970s under the Social Democratic-led government and continued in the early 1980s under both left-centre and centre-right Christian

Table 3.3. *Change and continuity in developed welfare states, 1980–95*

	Sweden	Germany	Britain
Unemployment Gross Earnings Replacement Rate for Production Worker at:			
100 Percent Average: 1981	71.5	38.0	27.8
1995	74.5	35.0	17.4
66 Percent Average: 1981	90.2	40.7	38.3
1995	90.0	37.0	26.1
Social Services for Families, Elderly, Disabled, and Workers (outlays as a percentage of GDP)			
1980	5.3	.8	1.6
1995	7.1	2.7	1.6
Percent of Social Security Benefits Means-Tested, 1992	6.7	11.9	33.0
Private Social Welfare (as percent of total) 1995	6.9	8.4	16.8
Total Social Welfare Effort			
1980	30.4	25.3	18.3
1995	34.0	28.7	22.5

Note: Total Social Welfare Effort is total public social expenditure as a percentage of GDP. Other variables are defined in Table 3.1. Data sources are given in the Appendix.

Democratic-led governments. These programmes of fiscal consolidation, motivated largely by inflationary and deficit pressures, consisted of moderate reductions in benefits and tightening of eligibility standards primarily in unemployment and social assistance programmes as well as cost controls in health care (Swank 2002, ch. 5). During the mid- and late 1980s, policies were targeted at controlling health care costs, offsetting impacts of demographics on the pension system, and holding down contribution rates in order to alleviate tax-wedge effects on employment. However, during this period of internationalisation of the German economy, several expansions of social protection occurred, including extensions of early retirement and unemployment coverage for older workers and increases in programme resources to address new social problems (e.g., social exclusion). In addition, several of these reforms appear to be direct compensations for the dislocations of 1980s export-oriented modernisation of the German economy (Manow and Seils 1999; Swank 2002: ch. 5).

In the 1990s, Christian Democratic-led governments pursued welfare retrenchment with benefit reductions and tighter eligibility for most forms of social insurance as well as efficiency-oriented reforms of health care and social services. However, German unification, rises in unemployment, and the new sociodemographic problems (e.g., the growth of the frail elderly) led to a notable extension of the German *Sozialstaat*. As Table 3.3 suggests, in the context of these contradictory pressures, the German welfare state exhibits stability. The social wage for average and low-income production workers declines modestly while outlays for social and labour market services increases substantially; comparable, modest declines for pension and other benefits have also occurred (Swank 2002, ch. 5). Overall, total social spending rose by roughly three and a half percentage points of GDP.

In contrast to Sweden and Germany, moderate welfare state retrenchment began in the late 1970s and intensified in the 1980s and 1990s in the Anglo-liberal cases (Swank 2002: ch. 6).[5] In Britain, the 1974 to 1979 Labour government initiated broad cost control policies in the wake of capital flight in 1975 and of 1976 International Monetary Fund pressures for fiscal retrenchment. The post-1979 Conservative party governments led by Margaret Thatcher and then John Major accelerated welfare state retrenchment: significant rollbacks in social protection occurred in old-age pensions, income support for the working-age population, and health care and social services (Swank 2002: ch. 6). For instance, with regard to pensions, the Thatcher government in effect substantially reduced the relative value of the basic pension in 1980 by shifting the indexing method from changes in wages to changes in prices. The 1986 Social Security Act significantly reformed the earnings-related tier of public pensions (SERPS) by reducing income replacement rates and by introducing significant tax incentives to encourage workers to opt out of SERPS and establish personal pensions. The 1995 pension reforms further reduced the benefits and importance of SERPS (Williamson 2000). Overall, changes in the British welfare state have been notable. Beyond pension reforms, the social wage has declined by roughly one-third for average and low-income workers. In the face of substantial increases in unemployment, poverty, and adverse sociodemographic trends (e.g., aging) – forces nearly entirely responsible for the 1980s and 1990s growth in aggregate welfare outlays as shares of GDP (King and Wood 1999) – social services held constant in the range of 1.5 per cent of GDP. Significant neoliberal reforms have also occurred in housing and health policy (e.g., Pierson 1994; Swank 2002: ch. 6).

Comparing changes and the programmatic character of the Swedish, German, and British welfare states, data presented in Table 3.3 indicate that general properties – and the distinction between welfare states – have remained roughly similar across the 1980s and 1990s. Mid-1990s differences in the social wage and public social service commitments are notably similar to differences in the early 1980s. Although comparable early 1980s data do not exist, Table 3.3 information on means testing of social benefits and reliance on private social insurance in the mid-1990s suggests a continuation of relatively substantial divergence in programmatic profiles of welfare states. Finally, levels and differences in mid-1990s public commitments of national resources to welfare provision across the three welfare states are generally similar to those in the early 1980s.

Globalisation, political institutions, and welfare state structures

An important part of the explanation for these divergent welfare state trajectories rests with national institutions and their impact on the relative ability of pro-welfare state interests to defend social protection. In recent work (Swank 2001, 2002), I have argued that the political institutions and programmatic structures of social democratic and corporatist conservative welfare states are likely to blunt the pressures of internationalisation; the political institutions and programmatic structures of liberal welfare states are likely to promote retrenchment. To summarise, the system of interest group representation, particularly the extent to which the polity is social corporatist and not pluralist, and the system of electoral representation, especially the degree to which it consists of inclusive institutions and not majoritarian institutions, is important. So too is the degree to which the welfare state is characterised by universalism and conservatism, and not liberalism, in programme structure.

Specifically, political institutions structure the opportunities for representation for those who are harmed by internationalisation and oppose the common neoliberal responses to globalisation. Institutions that offer encompassing interest representation to pro-welfare state interests – social corporatism and inclusive electoral institutions – blunt neoliberal reforms. Second, institutions affect the conventional political capacities of pro-welfare state interests (e.g., the size, unity, coherence, and conventional political resources of actors and alliances). Social corporatist interest representation and inclusive electoral institutions tend to significantly increase the capacities of pro-welfare state interests (e.g., votes and seats of social democratic parties). Moreover, universal and conservative welfare structures promote the creation of cohesive national electoral coalitions of working- and middle-class constituencies while liberal programme structures fragment populations by class. Third, national political institutions shape values important to social welfare policymaking. Social corporatism, inclusive electoral institutions, and universalism promote cooperation, consensus, and welfare state legitimacy. Liberal welfare states tend to foster competition, conflict, and anti-statist orientations. As a result, globalisation pressures for retrenchment of social provision are likely to be greater in liberal welfare state contexts.

To test these arguments, I have examined through extensive quantitative and case study analyses the impacts of multiple dimensions of international capital mobility on multiple programmatic features of welfare states (Swank 2001, 2002). In this work, I find that liberalisation, capital flows, and international market integration have no systematic relationship with, or a small positive influence on, welfare provision in the context of social corporatism, inclusive electoral institutions, and universal and conservative programme structures. On the other hand, I find strong evidence that internationalisation is systematically and negatively related to features of welfare provision in majoritarian electoral systems, pluralist polities, and liberal welfare states.

Globalisation, social welfare reform, and varieties of capitalism

National and sector-group coordination will reinforce the pro-welfare state consequences of complementary welfare state and political institutions (as liberal market institutions will reinforce biases towards welfare retrenchment). Specifically, the production regime is important because it is likely to play a foundational role in shaping the interests, strategic choices, and political capacities of labour, government policymakers, and (especially) capital.

With regard to labour, while conditions may on occasion create anti-welfare-state orientations, labour has been the most consistently pro-welfare-state interest in the development and defence of the welfare state in the developed capitalist democracies (Hicks 1999; Huber and Stephens 2001). The consequences of 'varieties of capitalism' for labour are relatively straightforward. As suggested above, both national and sector-group coordination will be positively associated with representation opportunities and the general political capacities of unions. Both production regimes have, by definition, moderate to high corporatist interest representation where labour is formally or informally incorporated into tripartite policymaking. In addition, integration of labour in national policymaking as well as other key features of coordinated capitalism (e.g., enterprise-level labour–management cooperation) will, in turn, contribute to greater union organisation (Western 1997). In liberal market economies, decentralised industrial relations systems and the centrality accorded to labour market flexibility inherently produce weaker trade union movements.

With respect to the interests and policy choices of incumbent governments, the implications of diverse production regimes seem equally clear. As King and Wood (1999) forcefully argue, the Thatcher and Reagan governments' policies of international and domestic liberalisation and welfare state retrenchment constitute a neoliberal response to stagflation and problems attendant on globalisation. King and Wood note that within the context of a liberal market economy, American and British policymakers could not successfully pursue social corporatist management of wage costs or industrial policy strategies that depend on high levels of state–business cooperation and employer organisation characteristic of coordinated market economies. Alternatively, American and British policymakers initiated substantial liberalisation as well as welfare retrenchment in order to enhance overall market flexibility and to reduce the social wage that undermines the low-cost production strategy of liberal systems.[6]

With respect to capital, both national and sector-group coordination depend, in large part, on the presence of moderately to highly organised employers' associations; sector-group coordinated market economies also rely on formal and informal modes of firm coordination (Soskice 1990; 1999). With respect to welfare state interests of capital, nationally and sector-group coordinated economies will influence the social policy interests and strategic choices of employers in two ways. First, as Cathie Martin and I have argued (Swank and Martin 2001), high levels of employer organisation are conducive to employer support for social welfare policy. Specifically, collective organisation is important for preference formation; highly organised business associations cultivate constituent firms' recognition and acceptance of their shared interest including, for example, a collective interest in social policies that contribute to human capital. Second, moderate to high levels of corporatist industrial relations systems and tripartite bargaining promote norms of cooperation, trust, and 'social partnership' that influence business's behaviour and the nature of policymaking. The encompassing organisation of functional economic interests in corporatist systems internalises 'externalities' and, in combination with sustained interaction and consensus formation between labour and capital, facilitates a search for the public good (Visser and Hemerijck 1997). As Martin and I point out (2001: 895): 'Norms of reciprocity, trust, and public-regarding behavior tend to be reinforced at multiple levels of social corporatist systems: centralised collective bargaining over wages and conditions of work, explicitly tripartite policymaking forums (commissions, boards, committees), and subnational networks of business–labour exchange such as works councils.'

Furthermore, employers have a general interest in preserving extant political economic institutions. As Soskice (1999) notes, while globalisation theory posits that employers will increasingly work to decentralise industrial relations and otherwise pursue liberal market reforms, business elites have a strong interest in maintaining existing institutions in order to promote their social status and job security as well as the roles of their expertise and networks. Thus, while Swedish employers mobilised to decentralise bargaining (Pontusson 1992), other coordinated systems have largely maintained their centralised character (e.g., Wallerstein, Golden, and Lange 1997). In Germany, Thelen (1999) argues that despite significant international and domestic pressures for market-oriented reform, the interests of German employers in preserving the extant system of bargaining and their uncertainty about the feasibility of alternatives have led to reluctance by employers to support decentralisation.

More centrally, business has specific interests in social policy reforms; for the most part, these interests are defined by the incentives and constraints faced by employers within the extant production regime. As I have noted (Swank 2002: ch. 5), policymakers in coordinated market economies during the post-1970s era have regularly expanded early retirement and other programmes for the support of workers displaced by internationally oriented restructuring (e.g., active labour market programmes). As Esping-Andersen (1996), Scharpf (2000b), and others have observed, in the context of impediments to the generation of service sector jobs, the corporatist conservative welfare states of continental Europe have chosen to absorb labour through the welfare state, creating what some call the syndrome of 'welfare without work'. And, as Ebbinghaus (in press) argues in his comparative analysis of early retirement programmes, these policies should not be interpreted simply as mechanisms to ease mass employment. Alternatively, they have been developed on the basis of consensus where capital has typically cooperated with the state and labour in order to promote labour peace and economic restructuring. Overall, the interests and political behaviour of employers in specific reforms are shaped in significant ways by the institutional features of divergent production regimes.

In sum, theory on the impacts of economic institutions on the interests, strategic choices, and capacities of labour, capital, and state policymakers leads to the hypothesis that national and sector-group coordination should reinforce the pro-welfare state biases of complementary welfare state and political institutions; pressures associated with internationalisation should not produce significant welfare retrenchment in these institutional contexts. In fact, net of welfare state cost controls and other restrictive reforms that address social policy pressures (e.g., the aging crisis), globalisation may be positively associated with modest extensions of social compensation in coordinated economies. However, internationalisation should be negatively associated with social welfare provision in liberal market economies.

Globalisation, varieties of capitalism, and welfare state reform: a test

To test my central contentions, I estimated a model of welfare effort in which I assess the welfare effects of two central dimensions of international capital mobility – foreign direct investment (FDI) and borrowing on international capital markets (ICM) – across divergent institutional contexts. This model controls for socioeconomic influences on social welfare provision as well as political forces (partisan control of government, political institutions). Data sources for the measurement of explanatory variables are given in the Appendix; details on model specification and statistical estimation are given in the note to Table 3.4. I present my estimates of the welfare effects of levels of FDI and ICM in different institutional contexts in Table 3.4. Specifically, the table reports the change in total social welfare effort (total welfare spending as a percentage of GDP) associated with an increase in FDI and ICM equivalent to 1 per cent of GDP in six institutional contexts: low, medium, and high national coordination of markets and low, medium, and high sector-group

Table 3.4. *The social welfare effects of international capital mobility across nationally coordinated, sector-coordinated, and uncoordinated market economic institutions, 1973–95*

The Social Welfare Effect of Global Capital in Specific National Political Economic Institutional Context:	I Foreign Direct Investment	II Borrowing on International Markets
Nationally Coordinated-Corporatist Institutions		
Low (United States)	−.5365**	−.3360**
Medium (Netherlands)	.0906	−.0725
High (Norway, Sweden)	.6282**	.1534*
Sector-Coordinated Institutions:		
Low (Canada, United Kingdom)	−.1870*	−.2149**
Medium (Denmark)	.1510	.0979
High (Germany)	.3423**	.1898**

* significant at the .10 level.
** significant at the .05 level.
Note: Reported estimates are derived from interactions between capital mobility and institutions variables. Models control for the welfare state effects of percentage of population over 64, unemployment, inflation, per capita GDP in international prices, left and Christian Democratic cabinet portfolios as percentages of total portfolios, trade flows as a percentage of GDP, inclusive electoral institutions, and decentralisation of policymaking power (index of federalism and bicameralism). For details on statistical estimation, see the discussion for similar models in Swank (2001, 2002).

coordination of markets. Representative examples of specific countries are also provided.

As Table 3.4 indicates, there is a notable pattern of welfare effects of capital mobility across institutional contexts. Where national and sector-group coordination is low – that is, in liberal market economic contexts – rises in FDI and ICM are significantly related to lower welfare effort. Specifically, net of central political and socioeconomic determinants of welfare provision, a rise in FDI of 1 per cent of national GDP, for example, is associated with a decline in welfare effort equal to about 0.5 percentage points of GDP. Given that FDI increased by about three percentage points of GDP in liberal market economies from the early 1970s to mid-1990s, increases in the level of direct investment are associated on average with a reduction in social welfare spending of about 1.5 per cent of GDP. Comparable relationships were found for the impact of FDI (or ICM) on programmatic measures of welfare provision such as the social wage (not reported).

In addition, in contexts of high national or sector-group coordination, rises in FDI and ICM are associated with moderate increases in social welfare effort. For instance, in nationally coordinated economies (e.g., Norway and Sweden) and in sector-coordinated economies (e.g., Germany), an increase in ICM of 1 per cent of GDP is associated with an expansion of welfare state effort of roughly 0.2 per cent of GDP. Given that ICM rose on average from about 1 to 5 per cent of GDP between the mid-1970s and mid-1990s in these systems, ICM is associated (net of other welfare determinants) with an increase in social welfare spending of just under 1 per cent of GDP. In liberal market economies, comparable increases in ICM are associated with declines in welfare outlays equivalent to roughly 1.00 to 1.5 per cent of GDP (see Table 3.4 estimates of −0.33 and −0.21 for ICM effects in nations ranked as low on coordination). Recalling the nation-specific analysis of welfare policy change, these quantitative estimates are quite consistent with the empirical record of expansions of social compensation in co-ordinated economies and retrenchments of welfare provision in liberal market systems. Finally, in institutional contexts characterised by moderate levels of national and sector-group coordination, my estimates indicate that rises in capital mobility had little effect on trajectories of welfare provision.

Conclusion

The preceding analysis gives rise to several conclusions. Most important, the relationship between contemporary internationalisation and the welfare state is fundamentally shaped by national political economic institutions. Specifically, strong associations exist between institutional structures of welfare state, polity, and economy in advanced capitalist democracies. Functional complementarities among components within nationally coordinated, sector-group coordinated, and liberal political economies constrain and shape reforms of any one dimension. More important, policy reforms such as the neoliberal restructuring of welfare states are political acts and are fundamentally grounded in the interests, strategic choices, and political capacities of labour, capital, and the state. As I have demonstrated, welfare state and political institutions in social democratic and corporatist conservative systems systematically favour pro-welfare state actors. Moreover, the institutional structures of coordinated market economies reinforce the political bias of universal and social insurance-based programme structures and the encompassing interest representational systems that accompany them. In contrast to liberal market economies, the institutions of national and sector-group coordination promote pro-welfare interests, behaviours, and capacities. The pro-welfare state impact of coordinated economic institutions on capital is centrally important. Employers in coordinated market economies have simply been less likely than their liberal system counterparts to perceive that aggressive neoliberal reform programmes are in their interests; alternatively, they have participated in, or acquiesced to, maintenance and even expansion of social protection in the wake of internationalisation. Both case study and quantitative analyses provide support for these arguments.

In addition, it is important to note that the analysis has implications for trends in income inequality in capitalist democracies. Recent studies have shown that globalisation has made at least moderate contributions to the general trend towards greater income inequality in the post-1970s era (e.g., Alderson and Nielson in press). However, the present work and associated studies emphasise that institutions may condition these trends. For instance, Wallerstein (1999) has shown that the centralisation of bargaining mitigates trends towards higher inequality in wages. Rueda and Pontusson (2000) have illustrated that coordinated market institutions, generally, tend to weaken the negative effects of various socioeconomic and political forces on wage inequality. Furthermore, social welfare spending has significantly ameliorated the trend towards inequality in final (as opposed to market) income distribution. Thus, the present study suggests that the pro-welfare state bias in coordinated market economies has, in all likelihood, also retarded the growth of inequality in these systems.

At the same time, it is important to note that both internationalisation and domestic political economic changes continue to place stress on coordinated market economies. While recent works have consistently concluded that there is no substantial internationally induced convergence towards common neoliberal policies and institutions (e.g., Kitschelt *et al.* 1999), some trends in coordinated market economies indicate future reform pressures will be strong. With respect to the welfare state and broader institutional change, scholars such as Fritz Scharpf (2000b) have suggested that the 'welfare without work' syndrome, common across the corporatist conservative welfare states, continues to raise questions about the sustainability of the coordinated market model. That is, continuation of generous social insurance and welfare state supports for both young and older workers, in the face of high unemployment and the absence of job creation, adds weight to neoliberal calls for market reforms (e.g., the proposals of the OECD 'Jobs Study'). With the persistence of 'welfare without work', reforms of basic elements of the (sector-)coordinated model – neoliberal reform of governmental and private employment protections, market regulatory structures, a generous social wage, and the high social insurance contributions – may be increasingly likely.

Appendix

Data sources

Foreign direct investment, portfolio investment, and bank lending: IMF, *Balance of Payments Statistics*, Washington, DC: IMF; OECD, *Foreign Direct Investment in OECD Countries*. Paris: OECD.

Borrowing on international capital markets: OECD, *International Capital Market Statistics: 1950–1995*, Paris: OECD, 1996.

Exports and imports of goods and services: OECD, *National Accounts*, Paris: OECD.

Total and disaggregated social welfare outlays: OECD, *Social Expenditure Statistics of OECD Member Countries*, Labour Market and Social Policy Occasional Papers, No. 17, Paris: OECD, 1996; OECD, *Social Expenditure Database, 1980–1996*, Paris: OECD, 1999.

Programmatic characteristics: means-testing data are from Gough *et al.* (1997); private social insurance is from Adema (1999).

Social wage: OECD, *Database on Unemployment Benefit Entitlements and Replacement Rates*, Paris: OECD, forthcoming.

Cabinet portfolios: Eric Browne and John Dreijmanis, *Government Coalitions in Western Democracies*, New York: Longman, 1982; *Keesings Contemporary Archives*. For party classification: (1) Francis Castles and Peter Mair, 'Left–right political scales: some "expert" judgments', *European Journal of Political Research* 12 (1984): 73–88. (2) Country-specific sources.

Political economic institutions: Union membership: Jelle Visser, 'Trade union membership database', 'Unionisation trends revisited', Type-scripts, Department of Sociology, University of Amsterdam, 1992 and 1996; *Confederal Power, Level of Wage Bargaining, and Related Union and*

Employer Measures: Miriam Golden, Michael Wallerstein, and Peter Lange, 'Union centralisation among advanced industrial societies', Typescript, Department of Political Science, UCLA. *Political institutions data*: Huber, Ragin, and Stephens (1993) and country-specific sources. *Legislative seats and votes*: Mackie and Rose, *The International Almanac of Electoral History* and 'political data handbooks' in *European Journal of Political Research*. *Components of Sector-Coordinated Economic model*: Hicks and Kenworthy database (see Hicks and Kenworthy 1998).

Welfare state institutions: Esping-Andersen (1990). Percentage unemployed, population 65 and older: OECD, *Labor Force Statistics*, Paris: OECD.

Gross Domestic Product, consumer price index: OECD, *National Accounts*, Paris: OECD, various years.

Real Per Capita GDP in constant (1985) international prices: The Penn World Table (Mark 5.6). National Bureau of Economic Research (http://www.nber.org).

Notes

I thank the German Marshall Fund of the United States and the Marquette University Committee on Research for support of portions of this research. I thank participants in the 2001 Northwestern University conference, 'Renegotiating the Welfare State', Sarah Brooks, Alex Hicks, and Linda Weiss for comments.
1. The notion dates to at least Adam Smith (1976 [1776]). Bates and Lien (1985), Gill and Law (1988), McKenzie and Lee (1991), and Strange (1996) represent contemporary scholars who argue that globalisation undercuts national policy autonomy.
2. Ireland, New Zealand, and Switzerland as well as Iceland and Luxembourg are excluded from Table 3.2 and subsequent analysis because of data unavailability on one or more crucial factors.
3. As Soskice (1990; 1999) and others have noted, the position of France is somewhat unique: the dimensions of national and sector coordination do not capture state–business cooperation in economic planning and market regulation extant in France for much of the postwar era (e.g., Loriaux 1991).
4. While different sets of cases might reduce differences across models, extensive analysis of social welfare reforms in a large majority of cases produces the same conclusions as outlined above (Swank 2002).
5. Australia is a notable exception: post-1983 corporatism enabled trade unions to limit neoliberal welfare retrenchment and extract social compensation (e.g., new national health care and superannuation programmes) for wage restraint and cooperation with Labour government-led liberalisation (e.g., Schwartz 2000b; Castles 1996).

4 Globalisation and social security expansion in East Asia

M. Ramesh

Contrary to what is explicitly or implicitly suggested by much of the literature on globalisation, some newly industrialising economies (NICs) in Asia have recently expanded their social security systems in significant ways. First it was Korea that established a comprehensive health insurance scheme followed by a generous pension scheme. Not far behind was Taiwan, which also started with health insurance and is now in the throes of establishing a national pension plan. Singapore offers a contrasting example: it has not established any new social security programme involving significant additional public expenditure since the 1960s. Since the constraints of global competition faced by the three states have been similar, there is a strong *prima facie* case that it is the domestic factors that explain their different approaches to social security. This chapter is an exploration of the thesis that domestic factors continue to be salient determinants of policy choices and that globalisation merely establishes the outer parameters within which states operate.

This chapter is about how Korea and Taiwan have expanded statutory social security – defined here to include income maintenance and health – in the last fifteen years or so while Singapore continues to avoid it. I will begin by briefly reviewing the globalisation literature pertinent to social welfare and indicating what it suggests for social policy development in East Asia. I will then briefly discuss the globalisation of the three economies and outline their social security programmes. Next, I will show that the similarities and differences among them can be explained not by some international systemic force but local political institutional arrangements, especially the extent to which they encourage competitive politics and offer governments incentives for redistributive policies. The conclusion will reiterate one of the central themes of this book: there is no basis for writing off the state's ability to choose its own destiny in the face of pressures unleashed by economic openness.

Globalisation and social security

Much of the writing on globalisation and social policy from a variety of perspectives is structuralist in orientation, suggesting that liberalised international trade and investment rules make it difficult for states to pursue policies – such as high taxes, strict labour laws, or rigorous environmental standards – that raise production costs. This is said to be a consequence of internationally mobile capital's ability and willingness to move to countries where costs are lower due to the absence of such policies. The result is competition among states – a 'race to the bottom' – to move towards the lowest common denominator in social policies in order to attract foreign investment and enable national firms to compete internationally (McKenzie and Lee 1991; Rodrik 1997a).

A key reason posited for the state's inability to sustain the welfare state is the multinationalisation of production which allows firms to shift their activities to locations with lower costs. Given the states' limited policy options with respect to labour and capital costs, which depend on a complex range of macroeconomic variables, states are allegedly under pressure to maintain taxes lower than in competing locations. The competition makes it difficult to sustain non-productive public expenditures, of which social security is usually the largest component (see Rodrik 1997a; Steinmo 1993). Globalisation is also said to pressure states not to resort to budget deficit because they otherwise must pay higher interest rates on their borrowing. Huber and Stephens (1998) argue that the reluctance to incur budget deficit makes it difficult to maintain low unemployment, which is essential to keep social programmes affordable and the tax burden manageable. Trade openness is claimed to have a similar effect, in that states are pressured to reduce social welfare expenses in order to lower labour costs essential for promoting domestic firms' export competitiveness. The only social policy sectors to escape the pressure are those, such as education, that contribute to nations' and firms' global competitiveness.

Forceful as these claims may appear, they are not supported by empirical evidence. Earlier studies show that growth in government spending, the size of public sector deficit, and corporate tax rates vary substantially across OECD countries and there is no evidence of policy convergence towards minimal state provision of social security (Garrett 1998b; Swank

1998; Webb 1998). John Hobson and Duane Swank add powerful evidence which extends these findings in Chapters 2 and 3 of this volume. Their data shows not simply variation but growth – both of corporate tax rates generally and of social protection expenditures outside the lands of competitive liberalisation.

It is beyond doubt that Korea, Singapore, and Taiwan have been integrating rapidly with the world economy. More significantly, the three economies have globalised in ways that make them more vulnerable to actors and forces outside their borders. However, there is no evidence to suggest that this has stymied the growth of their social security programme.

Korea has had a current account deficit in most years for the past two decades, suggesting *prima facie* that it is vulnerable to the wrath of international financial markets. Its financial accounts picture is complex and very worrying from the conventional globalisation theorists' point of view. In addition to its large current account deficit, foreign direct investment (FDI) flowing into Korea grew more than thirteen fold between 1985 and 1997, from $532 million to $6,971 billion in 1997 (Asian Development Bank 1999). The outflow of FDI was even larger and increased yet more rapidly, yielding a net deficit of $1.6 billion in 1997 on the FDI account in 1996. What would seem to really highlight Korea's vulnerability is its huge and increasing foreign debt, which rose from $46.97 billion in 1990 to $115.03 billion in 1995 and $143.37 billion in 1997. Particularly disconcerting would appear to be the fact that around half of its debt in the mid-1990s was of short-term variety. The value of Korea's foreign trade was equivalent to 74 per cent of GDP in 1980, falling to 67 per cent in 1995. Exports accounted for about one-third of its GDP throughout the period. If the conventional globalisation theorists were correct, then Korean social security would have at best frozen some time in the 1970s.

Taiwan, unlike Korea, enjoyed a large current account surplus throughout the 1980s and 1990s, although the size of the surplus has shrunk gradually. However, it has had huge deficits on capital and financial accounts, leading to an overall deficit in a number of years recently. The outflow of FDI increased from $65 million in 1986 to $3.84 billion in 1996 and of portfolio investment from zero to $4.37 billion over the same period. Inflow of direct investment grew more slowly, from $326 million to $1.86 billion over the period while inflow of portfolio investment increased from $75 million to $3.26 billion. Thus, while Taiwan is a large recipient of foreign investment, it is an even larger exporter of investment, and the trends have accentuated in recent years. The value of Taiwan's foreign trade was equivalent to 95 per cent of GDP in 1980, falling to 83 per cent in 1995. Exports accounted for about one-half of its GDP throughout the period (DGBAS 2000). Taiwan's large exposure to international trade and investment is an ominous trend for social policy if the conventional globalisation theorists are correct.

The nature of Singapore's economic globalisation is different from the other two countries and its magnitude simply staggering. Its current account has been in surplus every year since the mid-1980s and in some years has been as large as 17 per cent of the GDP. The small island is one of the largest recipients of foreign investment in the world, with average annual net inflow of FDI of $4.7 billion during the 1985–97 period. The stock of FDI in Singapore increased from S$65 billion in 1992 to S$139 billion in 1997. In recent years Singapore has become a major investor abroad, with the stock of its outgoing FDI increasing from S$23 billion in 1992 to S$67 billion in 1997 (Singapore Department of Statistics 2001). Singapore is, of course, the most trade-dependent nation on earth: the size of its foreign trade has been three to four times the size of its GDP for decades, with exports alone averaging 185 per cent of its GDP since 1985.

The governments' budgetary position would appear to constrain policy options in Korea and Taiwan but not in Singapore. The deficit in Taiwan is particularly large, accounting for on average 2.9 per cent of annual GDP in the 1991–5 period and 1.5 per cent in 1996–7 (DGBAS 1999). In comparison, Korea's average annual deficit was only 0.1 per cent of GDP in the 1986–90 period and 0.5 per cent in 1996–7 (Asian Development Bank 1999). In contrast, Singapore has enjoyed huge budget surpluses for a long time, amounting to as much as 15–16 per cent of GDP in the mid-1990s. We would expect Korea and Taiwan to be relatively cautious making large public expenditure commitments while Singapore is free from any such constraint.

The large current account deficit in Korea and, to a lesser extent, Taiwan and the large surplus in Singapore is not reflected in their government expenditures on social security outlined in Table 4.1. Nor do the expenditures parallel the large budget deficit in Taiwan and Korea and the huge surplus in Singapore.

Table 4.1 shows a small difference between Korea[1] and Taiwan: the former spends 5.3 per cent of its GDP on social security while the latter spends 5.8 per cent. Moreover, the share grew by 145 per cent in Korea

Table 4.1. *Government expenditure*[a] *on health and income maintenance as per cent of GDP*

	Korea	Singapore	Taiwan
1986	2.15	1.64	2.92
1990	3.15	1.40	4.00
1997	5.28[b]	1.42	5.84

[a]Includes expenditures from the government's general accounts as well as social insurance.
[b]1996
Sources: DGBAS, *Statistical Yearbook of the Republic of China 1999* (2000); IMF, *Government Finance Statistics Yearbook 1999*; Shin, Dong-myeon, 'Financial crisis and social security: the paradox of South Korea', *International Security Review*, 53: 3 (2000), 83–107.

and 100 per cent in Taiwan over the period 1986–97. Singapore, on the other hand, spends only 1.4 per cent of its GDP on social security, perhaps the smallest in the world. Moreover, the share actually shrank by 13 per cent during the 1986–97 period, which is highly unusual.

We now turn to reviewing the social security programmes in the three countries. As we shall see, the programmes have proliferated in Korea and Taiwan but not in Singapore. While Singapore's reticence would seem to confirm globalist expectations – given its intense exposure to global markets – that would be the wrong conclusion to draw because its huge surpluses on foreign and budget accounts allow it more policy options than are available to most countries in the world.

Social security programmes

Korea

Korea has gradually established the entire range of social security programmes found in welfare states. Health insurance became compulsory for firms employing 500 or more employees in 1976 and for government employees and school teachers in 1977. Coverage was expanded to other workers in phases, with the largest expansion taking place in the late 1980s, and nearly the entire population was covered by 1989. The scheme pays for the full range of inpatient and outpatient services and medication, though there are substantial co-payment requirements at each point of service.

The beginning of the statutory pension goes back to 1960 when a scheme was established for government employees, followed by a scheme for military personnel in 1963, private school teachers in 1975. The programme reached the general population with the establishment of a scheme for employees in firms with ten or more in 1988 and its expansion to employees in smaller firms and the self-employed in the 1990s. The schemes provide a comprehensive range of retirement, disability, and survivors' benefits. The maximum monthly retirement benefit is 60 per cent of one's last income after twenty years of contribution, except for civil servants who receive 76 per cent of the final monthly salary after thirty-three years of contribution. These are generous benefits by international standards, but are yet to show up in expenditure statistics because the scheme will start paying full benefits in 2008, when the first cohort of private sector workers will have contributed for twenty years.

There is also a compulsory unemployment insurance scheme, which was established in 1995 and expanded in a major way in 1998. The benefit is 70 per cent of the worker's earnings during the month immediately preceding unemployment, to the maximum of 35,000 won ($28) per day. The maximum duration of unemployment benefit ranges from two to seven months, depending on the length of the insured period and on the person's age.

Public assistance schemes provide a range of cash and in-kind benefits to the low-income, aged, and sick indigent. The eligibility conditions for the various programmes have been relaxed and benefit levels improved over the years, especially since the mid-1990s. In addition, the Medical Aid programme pays for health care of the poor who are not covered by the health insurance programme.

What we now have in Korea is an embryonic welfare state which will, on present trends, continue to expand, even if no new programmes are established, due to ageing of the population and maturing of the programmes. Its broad orientation will eventually be a paler and less decommodifying version of the conservative welfare state found in Europe: occupational stratification with special benefits for government employees, close linkage between contribution and benefits, and low public assistance benefits (Esping-Andersen 1990).

Taiwan

Notwithstanding the 1947 Constitution committing the government to establishing social insurance and public assistance programmes, the government did little to assist those who needed protection. The social insurance schemes it did establish together covered only 22 per cent of the population in 1985.

The situation changed with the launch of the National Health Insurance (NHI) scheme in March 1995. It is a compulsory health insurance scheme for the entire population paying for almost all inpatient and outpatient services and drugs, but beneficiaries still pay a substantial amount in the form of co-payment. The government subsidises the premium to different degrees, ranging from nil for the high-income professionals and self-employed (except farmers and fishermen) to 100 per cent for low-income families and retired veterans.

There exist separate social insurance schemes which together cover less than half the population and provide varying levels of old age, disability, and death benefits to different occupational groups. The government began to consider fundamental overhaul of the old age social security system in the mid-1990s and published a detailed planning document in 1998 which recommended the establishment of a National Pension Plan (NPP). The proposed launch of the scheme at the end of 2000 was thrown off-rail when the ruling party lost the presidential election and a new president sought a different scheme. While the exact form and date is in doubt, all the main parties agree on establishing a pension scheme in the very near future.

Public assistance programmes providing income support for various contingencies were expanded greatly in the 1990s. The benefits are roughly equivalent to 22 per cent of the national per capita income. In addition, aged farmers and fishermen have received a monthly stipend of NT$3000 ($93) without means test since 1998.

There are indications that Taiwan is in the early stages of transforming into a welfare state, although it is still some distance behind Korea. Its orientation will also in all likelihood be conservative with a large dose of liberal values introduced in the form of financial solvency and co-payment requirements.

Singapore

Almost all social security programmes that exist in Singapore were established during the period of British rule. The most prominent of these is the Central Provident Fund (CPF) established in 1955. Participation in CPF is compulsory, except for foreign, casual, and part-time workers. It is financed entirely by employees and their employers, who each normally contribute 20 per cent of the wages to the employee's personal account. Withdrawal of the balance in one's account is permitted at the age of fifty-five years. Since the amount is really one's personal fund, it is not counted as 'public' expenditure. It would be, in any event, difficult to calculate the annual equivalent of a lump sum amount intended to last through the entire retirement period.

There exists a modest public assistance scheme which was originally established by the British and has gone through little improvement since. The aged, disabled, and chronically ill with no means of subsistence and no one to depend on are eligible for financial support under the scheme. Those able to meet its stringent criteria are eligible for S$200 per month ($116) for single adult households and S$530 for households consisting of two adults and two children.

The government has been heavily involved in providing, but not financing, health care, again since the days of colonial rule. Public hospitals contain 81 per cent of all hospital beds which operate on a full or partial cost-recovery basis depending on the type of accommodation chosen. Health care financing has gone through a series of reforms since the mid-1980s with the purpose of increasing the share of costs borne by the patients themselves and their families. In addition, the government has implemented a range of measures to maintain a downward pressure on medical costs which has enabled the island republic to maintain one of the most inexpensive health care systems in the world (see Ramesh with Asher 2000).

Singapore has, and will continue to have in the near future, a markedly liberal social security system which provides benefits strictly according to one's contribution with no scope for redistribution, except for the subsidised public hospital beds and paltry public assistance. The only exception is that of senior government officials who enjoy generous pension benefits.

Domestic politics and social security

In the previous section we saw that Korea and Taiwan have laid the foundations for what may eventually turn out to be some sort of a welfare state, whereas Singapore continues to stick with the system established almost half a century ago. The difference cannot be the result of shifts in their broader development strategy, which continues to prioritise economic growth. If social security were underemphasised to promote economic growth, as is purportedly the case (see Deyo 1992; Goodman and White 1998; Holliday 2000), then the recent policy shift in Korea and Taiwan would have to have been a difficult choice because of its allegedly damaging effects on their international competitiveness. Why the two Northeast Asian countries decided to go down this route while Singapore did not is the question to which we now turn.

When and why states initiate major policy change depends on the particular circumstances they face, whereas the substance of the change and its implementation depends on the configuration of key socio-economic institutions. But these are empirical questions and one must be cautious arriving at cross-national generalisations. While the literature on Western welfare states no doubt sheds some valuable light on developments in East Asia, its direct relevance is rather limited (see Ramesh with Asher 2000).

There is no particular social, economic, or political condition which makes the establishment of a welfare state inevitable. The widely held position that welfare state development is a function of industrialisation, economic development, and urbanisation has only a slim basis in reality. Singapore ranks very high on all these criteria but they are not reflected in its social security policies. Moreover, the programmes hardly grew in Korea and Taiwan in the 1960s and 1970s despite rapid industrialisation, economic growth, and urbanisation at the time.

If domestic socioeconomic imperatives do not elicit a predictable and uniform policy response across nations, neither do international economic factors. The conclusion that there is a positive relationship between small open economies and welfare state expenditures (Cameron 1978; Katzenstein 1983; Rodrik 1998) may well be true for Western Europe but has no parallel in East Asia, or else Singapore would have one of the world's most developed welfare states. Nor do highly internationalised economies necessarily cut back on social security, as confirmed by the existence of a range of different levels and types of welfare efforts across the Western world (Berger and Dore 1996; Garrett 1998; Kitschelt *et al.* 1999; Swank 1998 and this volume).

Major policy decisions are explicitly political acts and this is how social security development must be approached (see Amenta and Carruthers 1988; Flora and Heidenheimer 1981). Of all contingencies facing governments, the prospect of being thrown out of office is the most worrying and ruling politicians do whatever it takes to avert it within the limits set by existing institutions. How international investors react to their policies is also an important concern for them, and certainly the prospect of an economic downturn triggered by the investment exodus and voter disenchantment this might cause is not something they take lightly, but it is one they can dispense with, at least in the short run (Garrett and Lange 1996: 51–2). Life is somewhat easier for non-democratic states, but only slightly, as they too must enjoy public support if they are to remain in office for long and rule effectively.

But political contingencies determine only the timing of the response and why governments are moved to act. To understand the substance of the policy, we need to understand the organisation of the state and its relationship with key socioeconomic groups (Keohane and Milner 1996; Garrett 1998; Swank 1998). Policy change occurs in the context of existing programmes and socioeconomic institutions which condition how policy problems are viewed and the solutions assessed. But, again, we must be wary of extending generalisations based on Western experience to other parts of the world. The notion that the coexistence of centralised states with encompassing business and labour organisations leads to Social Democratic or Conservative welfare states and their absence to Liberal welfare states (Esping-Anderson 1990; Huber and Stephens 2000; Soskice 1999) has little relevance for East Asia. Nor is there evidence that the nature of the electoral system has had a decisive impact on policies (Garrett and Lange 1996; Swank 1998), as all three countries studied here have majoritarian and exclusive electoral systems but have not yielded the sort of result suggested in the literature. The single transferable vote system that the three have in common has been manipulated by the ruling parties to further their electoral prospects and has had little independent impact of its own (Grofman *et al.* 1999)

Political-economic institutions' effects on policies are most manifest in normal times when the rules and norms underlying them are widely accepted. They have relatively less impact in non-normal times – such as during economic or political crises or fundamental reorganisation of the polity or economy – when established institutions lose legitimacy and conditions become propitious for measures that would not normally be possible (see Starling 1975; Meyer 1982). Crises may foster new 'policy windows' for 'policy entrepreneurs' (Kingdon 1984), undermine path dependence (Weir 1992; Wilsford 1994), and open up closed policy networks (Baumgartner and Jones 1991). The result is often policies which diverge significantly from established policy 'styles' (Howlett and Ramesh 1998).

Korea and Taiwan have hardly had normal times since the mid-1980s. The democratisation of the polity and the opening up of the economy that they have experienced has torn apart authoritarian structures but the changes have yet to congeal in political institutions. In Korea and

Taiwan we thus now have states which are still relatively autonomous, but at the same time elected politicians must respond to conflicting public pressures in ways in which they have little experience or for which there are few precedents to which they can refer (Chan *et al.* 1998; Mo and Moon 1998). The corporatist mechanisms for aggregating interests that worked well in the past stand discredited due to their association with authoritarian rule, but are yet to be replaced with alternatives acceptable to the key players. As a result, governments often respond willy-nilly to immediate public pressures, actual or perceived. As we shall see in the following discussion, Korea and Taiwan launched social security initiatives to shore up their fledgling democratic regimes in ways which do not necessarily bear the imprint of the pre-existing institutional context. Singapore, in contrast, has had stable and generally prosperous conditions since the 1970s and the government has seen little need for departing from existing practices.

Korea

It is well recognised in the literature that major policy reforms in Korea were precipitated by the government's need to strengthen its hold on office in the face of some political crisis (for e.g., see Joo 1999; Kim 1997; Kwon 1998; Lee 1997). Indeed there is a remarkable correspondence between the announcement of major social policy initiatives and political unrest or election campaigns (Park 1990).

The democratisation of the polity in the 1980s brought those previously excluded by the authoritarian regime – unions, farmers, and small businesses – into the policy process and transformed the policy outputs accordingly (Mo and Moon 1999: xvi). The intense political competition which accompanied democratisation afforded opportunities for newly empowered groups to press demands which the government could not always ignore. At other times, however, the government supplied policies even when there was no demand for them in the hope that the measure would prove popular with voters.

After nearly losing the 1971 election despite a booming economy and various restrictions on opposition parties, President Park began to pay greater attention to social policy issues (Ramesh 1995). The hurried introduction of the NHI was to compensate for the government's back-tracking on its commitment to establish a pension programme and intended to marginalise the radical critics of the regime (Joo 1999; Park 1997). However, the pressure to do yet more for non-business interests continued unabated. While the ruling party won all presidential and general elections until 1997, it won less than 40 per cent of the votes in every election held between 1973 and 1996 (Shin 1999: 47). The introduction of the national pension in 1988 and its expansion in the 1990s took place in the context of the governing party's uncertainty about its electoral future and struggle to remain in office. What is remarkable is that the government expanded social security despite lack of commitment to it, as pre-emptive measures to contain labour unrest and voter disenchantment (Kwon 1997; Lee 1997).

The politicians' inclination to pander to voters was, however, offset by the reluctance of the peak economic agencies to implement any social programme that could divert funds away from economic development. To ensure that this did not happen, they successfully insisted that the programmes be based on social insurance and funded from contributions by employers and employees rather than the public exchequer (Lee 1997). While social insurance expenditures are also public expenditures, their appeal lies in the fact that they do not compete with other policy sectors for funds. However, even the economic agencies could not prevent some premium subsidy for those on low incomes, though they did succeed in delaying the expansion of the scheme to the low-income self-employed by almost a decade. For the same reason, public assistance programmes, which rely on the government's general budget, have been kept to the minimum.

Business and labour played hardly any role in the launch or expansion of the social security programmes because of their organisational fragmentation. While the trade unions have considerable capacity to disrupt economic activity, they lack the capacity to propose coherent alternatives (Hyug 1992; Watson 1998). Business similarly was too fragmented to come up with anything more than knee-jerk opposition to any scheme that might increase cost.

Taiwan

Studies of Taiwan have also shown how political crises have been followed by expansion of social security programmes (Ku 1997; Lee 1997; Tang 1997). However, unlike Korea where the government has faced the possibility of losing elections since at least the early 1970s, the Kuomintang (KMT) faced no such uncertainty until martial law was lifted in 1987. It is therefore not entirely surprising that the development of social security remained frozen in Taiwan until the mid-1980s.

The KMT experienced its first setback when it lost the election for the two seats reserved for labour in the legislature in 1986. It responded by establishing the Council for Labour Affairs and by paying closer attention to labour grievances (Ku 1997). In the face of widespread anxiety about rising medical costs in the mid-1980s, the KMT seized the opportunity to launch the NHI before the opposition party could capitalise on it (Lee 1997).

The shift in the Democratic Progressive Party's (DPP) electoral strategy also had an effect on the government's attitude. Given the KMT's excellent record in managing the economy, the DPP began to focus increasingly on social policy to win voter support. The KMT responded by announcing similar or yet more generous measures of its own in order to counter the opposition's rapid rise in popularity. In the 1993 local election, the DPP offered non-contributory pensions for the aged and within days the KMT promised a similar scheme. In the course of the 1994 legislative election campaign, the KMT committed itself to an earlier than planned introduction of the NHI, a pension scheme for farmers in 1995, an unemployment insurance programme in 1996–7, and a national pension programme is promised in the near future (*Business Taiwan* 11 October 1993). Similarly, in preparation for the 1996 presidential election, the government issued 'The Guiding Principles of Social Welfare Policy', which promised major improvements in the social security system and public housing for low-income families. The bidding contest over social security was repeated in the 1997 local election and the 1998 legislative elections (Pei 1998). The competition between the two parties led to a continuous ratcheting up of social security programmes (Liu 1994).

Similar to Korea, business and labour play only a marginal role in the policy process, but for somewhat different reasons. Organised labour in Taiwan is dominated by small craft unions which are not only conservative but find collective action difficult to mount. The preponderance of small and medium-sized firms – who together employ more than 78 per cent of the labour force – and the organisational difficulty this involves has similarly weakened business's capacity to oppose the government's social security proposals.

As a result of business's and labour's organisational weaknesses, the ruling party has had a relatively free hand in designing social security. The only constraint has come from the Ministry of Economic Affairs and the Council for Economic Planning and Development (CEPD) which have insisted that social security schemes be funded from contributions by employers and employees rather than the general budget. Their position was largely adhered to in the design of NHI, albeit one which involved significant premium subsidy for various segments of the population, but became difficult to maintain after the DPP began to promise schemes funded from general revenues and the KMT was forced to match it with similar promises of its own.

Singapore

Almost all the social security programmes that exist in Singapore were established by the British in the 1950s when nationalist and communist movements posed a real threat of ending colonial rule. When the People's Action Party (PAP) came to office in 1959, it too was faced with massive social and political unrest, with the added difficulty of having to face popular elections. To neutralise the appeal of radical opposition parties and trade unions, it adopted some of the key elements of the opposition's policy offerings in conjunction with measures to attract foreign investment (Rodan 1996). Although public housing was the centrepiece of its social policy strategy, it also emphasised health and education – a policy orientation which continues to this day.

The dual strategy of promoting export-led and foreign-capital-based economic development while providing education, health, and housing yielded handsome political benefits for the government. Elections have shown a remarkably solid support for the ruling People's Action Party, even after discounting for the various handicaps put in the way of the opposition parties. It has won every election with an impressive majority, polling between 69 per cent and 84 per cent of all votes cast. Indeed it won all seats in elections held between 1968 and 1980 and it was not until 1981 that an opposition member was elected to Parliament.

Once it felt secure in office, by the early 1970s, the PAP became less enthusiastic about social security. The realisation in the mid-1980s that the population was ageing rapidly, which would eventually involve huge income maintenance costs, reinforced the government's determination to resist the establishment of state-funded social security. However, it was forced to fine-tune its strategy somewhat following the loss of four seats in the 1991 election which it interpreted as a reflection of dissatisfaction with its priorities among low-income voters. It responded by offering welfare benefits on a piecemeal basis delivered in the form of *ad hoc* cash grants and tax rebates (Ramesh 2000).

The Singapore government, unlike its Northeast Asian counterparts, has been able to successfully maintain its opposition to state-funded social security due to its unique organisational capacity. The statist-corporatist (Schmitter 1982) nature of its political system and the overwhelming dominance of the state *vis-à-vis* civil society enables it to contain and shape the political demands placed upon it. There is a complex range of supportive and coercive measures in place which ensure that organised labour does not challenge government policies (Anantaraman 1990; Deyo 1989). The state also enjoys instrumental autonomy from business (Chalmers 1992). Employers would prefer a lower CPF contribution rate, but the government has ignored the demand, except during economic slumps when the contribution rate for employers (but not employees) was temporarily reduced. The government also maintains a dense network of links with the civil society, which it uses to spread its message and shape public opinion. State corporatist institutions in Singapore thus have been used to contain the demand for welfare state responses rather than to expand them, as is arguably the case under social corporatist arrangements in continental Europe.

Thus Singapore has had a rock solid political system since the late 1960s with few of the uncertainties and predicaments found in its Northeast Asian counterparts and few political reasons to expand social security. To the extent that social welfare funding was necessary to secure political support, it was accomplished through spending on public housing, education and, to a much lesser extent, health, rather than via transfer payments.

Conclusion

This chapter has shown that social security programmes have gone through major expansion in recent years in Korea and Taiwan but not Singapore. Indeed the two Northeast Asian countries expanded the programmes at a period when they were integrating rapidly with the international economy. I explained the shift with reference to the domestic political threats faced by the two regimes and their absence in Singapore. The intense political competition which emerged in Korea and Taiwan following their democratisation in the late 1980s fostered attempts on the part of the ruling parties to win public support by expanding social security, whereas the continuation of the one-party dominant system in Singapore has kept the PAP largely exempt from such pressures. There are parallels to be found in other countries in the region. The advent of democracy led to expansion of social security in Thailand in the early 1990s and government policies in the Philippines too have begun to focus more on social development issues (Ramesh with Asher 2000). Malaysia is similar to Singapore in that it stopped expanding social security programmes in the early 1970s after it was firmly ensconced in office and faced little fear of losing elections.

The social security programmes put in place in Korea and Taiwan suggest they are on their way to transforming into conservative welfare states, albeit a lot less decommodifying than is the case in Europe. Singapore, in contrast, will remain a hyper-liberal welfare state with minimal public spending until such time as the ruling party faces a real possibility of losing office to an opposition party with strong commitment to expanding social security. It is too early to confirm Swank's conclusion (this volume) that Conservative welfare states are more resilient to adverse international pressures than their Liberal counterparts. It is unlikely that typologies developed to describe social policies in advanced welfare states would apply easily to countries which have just begun to establish social security schemes.

The point at which globalisation will cut in and inhibit further expansion of public spending on social security in Korea and Taiwan is very far indeed. They have room to increase their social security spending many times and yet not reach a position where they will appear high spenders compared to Western welfare states. Even then, they will not be without choices as is sometimes claimed, as they will still have the ability to choose the policy sectors for cut-back. What governments spend, or do not spend, money on depends on their and their voters' preferences, mediated by the institutional context within which their preferences are defined and responded to. International competitiveness is a significant but not the only consideration for either the government or the public. In any case, there is more than one way to win voter support. Just as policymakers in Korea and Taiwan have chosen to expand social security to boost electoral support, Singapore has emphasised housing. States were not entirely unencumbered in their policy choices before, and they are not so now, with or without globalisation (Hobson and Ramesh 2002).

Note

1. Note that the data say nothing about the pension scheme which has been put in place in Korea but is not yet paying benefits because of the minimum years of contribution required to receive benefit.

Part II

New economic challenges, changing state capacities

5   France: a new 'capitalism of voice'?

Michael Loriaux

Recent scholarship has documented the resistance of national economic institutions to the forces of globalisation (see, e.g., Berger and Dore 1996). But resistance has not always been appreciable among national financial institutions. Several Western European countries have experienced some form of 'Big Bang' financial liberalisation. France, once the European representative of state-led developmentalism, has shown greater liberalising zeal than other European countries, and looks today like the poster child of global financial capitalism. But French liberalisation has had its limits. I focus on those limits here, not to contest the obvious, but to inform discussion regarding the room to move accorded to states under conditions of globalisation.

I articulate the examination of financial reform in France around three themes, a structural one, a more sociological one, and finally, a speculative one. The structural theme inquires into the usefulness of the opposition between state power and market power. The structural constraint that contributed most significantly to reform in France did not oppose a Colbertist state and a global market. Rather it opposed a large country, the United States, and a smaller (small, that is, in the sense of price-taker), more trade-dependent country, France. French vulnerability to the vagaries of US policy supplied the principal motivation behind French reforms. France's interest in European integration today is fed to a considerable degree by the desire to diminish the force of that structural constraint. Because I develop this theme elsewhere, I offer only a summary here, and a response to critics.

The sociological theme inquires into the usefulness of the distinction between state and society. Elsewhere, I characterise French *étatisme* as more than a set of institutions, rather as a kind of culture, composed of language games and norms, which institutions can 'house' in a variety of ways. Developmentalism, understood as a kind of culture, informs and constrains the way the French think about investment strategy, both inside and outside the formal institutions of the state. I focus on the fate of the *noyaux durs* that arose as a way to safeguard French control of privatised French firms. The *noyaux durs* did not resist the efforts of French core financial institutions to diversify and rationalise their portfolios. But continuity in strategy before and after privatisation suggests the existence of a cultural approach to the enterprise that does not depend on financial institutional links with the state.

The third theme is speculative. It inquires into the impact of institutional investing on French firms. Institutional investors, principally American, account today for a significant share of equity in major French firms. They have affected firm strategies by generating pressure to produce capital gains over the short term, at the expense of long-range industrial planning. Yet one wonders whether one can explain that pressure in purely structural terms. Could it not result from US financial habit (or culture), and could that habit not be adapted to European practices in a way that advances the interests of the investors themselves?

The exploration of these themes generates a speculative conclusion: the French political economy will remain recognisably 'nationalist' despite globalisation. The source of French economic nationalism, however, will not be located in the institutions of state intervention in the economy. It will be located, rather, in habits of thought and speech that incline privatised French firms to think about investment in a particular way, more focused on long-term development and more sensitive to national economic interests than is the case of American firms.

French developmentalism

Prior to the reforms of 1983–5, France pursued a developmentalist industrial policy supported by subsidies, credit controls, indicative planning, and direct intervention in state-owned industries. The principal source of subsidies was the Fund for Economic and Social Development (*Fonds de Développement Économique et Social*, or FDES), which was financed directly by the budget. The FDES was the workhorse of industrial policy under the Fourth Republic (1945–8). Its importance shrank under the impact of Charles de Gaulle's (1958–9) fiscal conservatism, but the oil and monetary crises of the mid-1970s, and the subsequent need to reform finances and reorganise industry (discussed below), gave the Fund new life. In 1974–5, for example, the Fund was still funnelling billions of francs to key industries, especially automobiles and steel.

The Fund for Economic and Social Development contributed to other subsidy programmes created in the wake of the oil crisis, such as the Interministerial Committee for Industrial Restructuring (CIRI), established in 1974 to help small and medium-sized firms in which jobs were at risk. It also contributes to the Interministerial Orientation Committee for the Development of Strategic Industries (CODIS), which subsidises investment in innovative technologies, and favours large firms. The Interministerial Committee for the Development of Investment and Defense of Employment (CIDISE) supports investment in medium-sized firms. The Institute for Industrial Development (IDI) was created to aid adaptation in declining industries. The Special Fund for Industrial Adaptation (FSAI), created in 1978, was designed to promote investment in regions of high unemployment. Most of its aid went to heavy industry: shipbuilding and automobiles. Finally, the National Agency for the Promotion of Research (ANVAR), whose role has grown considerably in recent years, directs its aid to small and medium-sized firms that invest in innovative products or techniques.

Most of these subsidy programmes survived the liberalisation of the mid-1980s, though significantly diminished. Inversely, liberalisation all but eliminated what had served as the principal tool of state intervention for almost three decades: state control over the allocation of credit by banks and other financial institutions. France has a dozen or more public and para-public financial institutions that are or have been either state owned or operating under a state charter. They include the Caisse des Dépôts et Consignations (CDC), which acts as the 'bank' for local administrations, the Crédit National, which specialises in industrial loans, and the Crédit Foncier, which once specialised in home mortgages. The law requires that state and para-state financial institutions, including the post office (which, as in most European countries, manages checking accounts), deposit a part of their resources with the Treasury. The Treasury, in turn, keeps an account of its own with the post office to pay government fees and salaries and to facilitate the collection of revenues. The banking system was partially integrated into this 'Treasury circuit' in fulfilment of the requirement that banks retain a certain fraction of their reserves in Treasury bonds. This criss-crossing of liabilities between the Treasury, the post office, the banks, and the semi-public financial institutions allowed Treasury officials in the 1950s to draw on multiple accounts to finance public spending without issuing bonds or relying on deficit spending, transforming short-term deposits into long-term loans and subsidies. The Treasury used money deposited in post office accounts in much the same way that a bank uses its reserve assets to create more money, that is, by inscribing transfers onto the post office accounts of households (the salaries of civil servants, for example) and firms (subsidies and grants). But because the money borrowed by the Treasury from one of these institutions to pay off the state's creditors ultimately found its way back to the banks, the post office, or one of the financial institutions that composed the Treasury circuit, a fraction of the money that was created made its way *ipso facto* back to the Treasury. Thus the Treasury had the unusual capacity to feed its 'reserves' with money of its own creation (see Loriaux 1991: 65–72, 150–3). Properly handled, the Treasury circuit offered policymakers a tool that they could use to redistribute money while avoiding the dangers of inflationary financing as well as the political liability of increasing state income through higher taxes (Patat and Lutfalla 1986: 140–1).

De Gaulle's fiscal conservatism made it impossible for the Treasury in the 1960s to continue to serve as the French economy's principal source of capital. But bank reforms in 1966–7 allowed the French to disengage the Treasury from industrial policy while keeping intact the interventionist logic of the Treasury circuit (Patat and Lutfalla 1986: 163). The reforms moved the principal site of 'transformation' (of short-term capital into long-term loans) to the banks. They encouraged the banks to extend medium-term loans to certain types of activity by extending the eligibility of such loans for rediscounting at the central bank. Simultaneously, the state discouraged the banks from making other types of loans by placing quantitative restrictions on the overall growth of credit. Those restrictions were referred to as *encadrement du crédit*. *Encadrement du crédit* supplied the state with a powerful interventionist tool. In effect, the state had only to exonerate a particular sector from *encadrement* to direct credit to it. The attractiveness of exonerated sectors was enhanced by declaring medium-term loans to such sectors eligible for discount at the central bank.

France, unlike other states that have been characterised as developmental, has used some form of 'indicative' (as opposed to imperative) planning since World War II (Hall 1986: ch. 6). The first three plans promoted overall expansion of the economy by funnelling investment to basic industries. When trade liberalisation stripped away such safeguards, the French redirected the plan to promote competitiveness on newly internationalised markets. The plan fostered contractual agreements with firms, according to which the state provided financial support in exchange for firm-specific strategies approved by the state. Such agreements produced a series of mergers in the 1960s and 1970s designed to develop 'national champion' firms.

Businessmen have never felt any real compunction to refer to the plan except as a statement of the medium-term intentions of the state with regard to public procurement and subsidies (McArthur and Scott 1969; Caron 1981: 247–9). In the estimate of Pierre Rosanvallon (1992: 247–50), the 'latent functions' of the plan – the promotion of alliances between industrial sectors and the state to reform industrial structures, and the promotion of a certain 'apprenticeship' in social change – were more important than economic coordination. Planning proved ineffectual in achieving more abstract macroeconomic objectives, such as price stability, demand management, and employment. These were all more sensitive to short-term pressures. Planning lost much of its attractiveness in the 1970s when France confronted problems that required radical change in the thrust of fiscal and monetary policy. Industrial policy turned its back on the plan and focused on more immediate problems of preserving employment and propping up firms threatened by bankruptcy (Berger 1981). The Socialists, in power from 1981 to 1986, resurrected planning. Priority programmes (*programmes prioritaires d'exécution*) committed the state to support projects on a multiyear basis. Planning contracts (*contrats de plan*), signed between the state and chosen industrial firms, provided financial support to pursue state goals while leaving firm management largely autonomous in determining how those goals might be achieved.

The plan remains the emblem, but not the vehicle, of industrial policy in France. Industrial policy was, in reality, more *ad hoc* and more tightly focused on the development of sectors that were, however arbitrarily, designated as being of national interest, such as steel and computer technology in the 1960s, nuclear power and telecommunications in the 1970s, and electronics in the 1980s. In the post-OPEC period, industrial policy was often driven as much by the desire to avoid bankruptcy and unemployment as by the enlightened vision of economic development. Critics have shown that industrial policy was frequently 'captured' by the economic sectors it was designed to serve and develop, with the result that the state became the provider of sectoral rents rather than the instrument of national economic modernisation. Nevertheless, industrial policy did exist and function, and did provide the French state with outcomes that it desired.

Between 1981 and 1986, the principal tool of developmentalism was direct 'stock-holder' intervention by the state. The electoral platform of the Socialist–Communist alliance called for the nationalisation of banks and large industrial firms. Nearly all large banks and industrial firms became state property. Because nationalisation occurred at a time of low business profitability, the state used the leverage of ownership to restructure French industrial firms. Low profitability had two sources, one in the structure of the French political economy, and the other in the international business conjuncture. High levels of business indebtedness to banks were the structural source. The two oil shocks that accompanied first the Iranian revolution then the high Reagan dollar were the conjunctural source. The effects of low profitability were aggravated by the impact of the reflationary economic programme of the Socialist–Communist alliance and by a world recession. Inflation priced French goods out of range in a depressed international (especially European) market.

State ownership made possible structural adjustments that the traditional tool of credit policy could no longer achieve because of the high level of business indebtedness. The state reduced firm debt and funded industrial restructuring programmes that lowered production and operating costs. Between 1981 and 1985, the state invested 5 billion francs in nationalised firms, a level of investment that Vivienne Schmidt (1996) estimates at roughly twenty times the level of private investment between 1965 and 1980 (Hancke and Amable 2001: 11). Many of these programmes came at the expense of employment. Restructuring and rationalisation eliminated about one fourth of the work force in automobiles and about half of that in steel. Socialist reforms also induced state firms to turn to subcontractors for components, thus cutting the cost of managing large inventories and of investing in the research and development of components (Hancke and Amable 2001: 11). Finally, French firms, both public and private, adopted a strategy of merger and acquisition in radical innovation markets, particularly through the acquisition of non-French – especially American – firms. The stock market value of American firms acquired by French companies between 1985 and 1995 was double the value acquired by their German counterparts. American subsidiaries became an important element in the strategic thinking of French firms.

In sum, the French redesigned institutional support for state-led developmentalist policy several times. That support changed from one of budget-funded subsidies to credit controls to nationalisation of the most important banks and industrial firms.

One set of institutions that did not change in this period, however, was that of the Grands Corps de l'État, the corporations of high civil servants.[1] France's administrative elite is powerful and pervasive. It is recruited from France's *grandes écoles*, specialised professional schools that function independently of the French university system. Highly selective competitive examinations guard access to the *grandes écoles*.[2] The Grands Corps co-opt the top students of the *grandes ecoles*, especially the École Nationale d'Administration (ENA).[3] Co-optation means a job with tenure and the possibility of extended leave from the administration without loss of tenure. The high civil servant is free to move about, from administration to politics to business, without professional risk. Thus one finds the administrative elite not only in the state but also throughout the world of business and politics. They dominate ministerial cabinets and abound on the boards of large firms, both public and private, and in the inner circles of France's principal political parties. The pervasiveness and power of France's civil service elite creates a political economy in which the boundary between public and private is extraordinarily porous.

If we look at the various manifestations of developmentalism in France – budget-based, bank-based, state-ownership-based – the common thread that ties them together is the presence of this state elite. Developmentalism in France is rooted not only in organisational structures, but also in the pervasive presence of an elite that shares a common education, language, socialisation, and self-confidence. French thinking about industrial strategy is informed by the cultural fact of this elite's existence, of its socialisation into a system of values that thinks in terms of national interest, of France's place in the world and in the world economy.

Structural change in the international political economy as cause of liberalisation in france

France has changed remarkably since 1986. First, France assigned monetary policy instruments, especially interest rate policy, to the defence of the exchange rate of the French franc. Concern for the franc traditionally took a back seat to concern for industrial development. Second, the state cut back significantly on direct and indirect subsidies to business.

Third, the state implemented reforms that strengthened French financial markets. Fourth, institutional investors, especially American, began to invest heavily in French business. One also encounters change in the instruments of policy implementation, for example, in the laws regulating the banking industry, on which the state relied to guide bank lending to priority borrowers. There has been significant change in the very institutional structure of the French political economy. For example, the central bank was, until the 1990s, the 'executive' of the Treasury, which held 'legislative power' over monetary affairs. The bank was made independent in 1994, and given essential control over monetary policy, which it then surrendered to the European Central Bank in 2000. France no longer has a monetary policy. To take another example: the money market, as in the United States and Great Britain, became the principal locus of central bank efforts to control interest rates. Before the mid-1980s, however, there was no money market in France in the usual sense of the term.

Do such changes in the instruments of policymaking mean that globalisation has 'americanised' the institutions and conduct of capitalist political economies? Care must be taken in answering this question. Change in the instrumental mechanics of developmentalism is not new, and whatever instrumental change we observe must be weighed against the permanence of a developmentalist culture and the strength of representation of that culture at centres of economic and political decision-making.

The first step in answering this question consists in situating the cause of change in French policy. I argue elsewhere (Loriaux 1991) that the cause is structural. Change in the hegemonically structured international political economy occasioned reform in France, as in other trade-dependent, developmental political economies. American monetary and fiscal policy in the 1950s supported new, post-war international trade and monetary arrangements that sought to make Keynesian policy possible under free trade. But American policy began to turn more nationalist in the 1960s in response to international and domestic conflict. Nationalism in monetary affairs – refusal to address inflation in the key international currency – brought down the Bretton Woods system of fixed but adjustable exchange rates in 1973. The demise of fixed rates left the French political economy in a difficult situation. French developmentalism arose within the framework of a forgiving international monetary environment. The possibility of multilateral ratification of change in fixed monetary parities internationalised the inflation that developmentalism tended to produce, in France as in other developmentalist economies. But the post-1973 non-system of floating rates made that kind of internationalisation impossible. The cost of price inflation was borne entirely by the inflationary country's balance of payments. For a trade-dependent country like France the cost was high. Floating rates generated the threat of vicious circles of inflation and currency depreciation. Inflation depressed the demand for French exports. But the demand for certain imports, notably petroleum and other raw materials brought in dollars, proved insensitive to price hikes occasioned by depreciation. Imported price hikes aggravated inflation as they percolated through the economy, further sapping market confidence in the currency. To combat such vicious circles French authorities were, by 1974, assigning a high priority to stabilising the currency. The French strengthened their commitment to currency strength in the mid-1980s following three devaluations (within the European Monetary System).

The shift of emphasis in monetary policy brought reform to French finances. Under fixed rates, French statism had given rise to what French economists called an *économie d'endettement* or overdraft economy, according to which hikes in interest rates had little or no impact on business demand for credit. Businesses, operating under the policy-induced expectation of assured borrowing power (or other financial support), responded to increases in the cost of credit simply by asking for more credit (higher interest rates produced cash-flow problems that firms addressed by borrowing more). The expectation of assured borrowing power vitiated the government's efforts to use interest rate policy to slow monetary supply growth and thus regulate the supply of money to currency markets. In the mid-1980s, under a Socialist government, France implemented deep-reaching liberalising reforms in order, first, to wean business off state-controlled bank credit and direct it to the market for stocks and bonds and to international lenders, and, second, to make the French economy attractive to foreign capital so that foreign investment might compensate for the reduction in state-sponsored or supplied funds.

'Reaganomics' reinforced structural pressure on French policy. The peculiar combination of monetary rigour and deficit spending caused the United States, a powerful economy with a sound financial reputation, to address a high level of demand for money in the world's markets. That policy raised interest rates globally, as well as the exchange value of the dollar (which was still the currency of choice in international transactions). In response, France (and other nations) multiplied liberalising reforms to make its economy more appealing to – and better able to compete for – international capital.

Identifying the structural origins of French reformism clarifies the weaknesses in two widespread interpretations. According to the first, ideological shift away from statism produced reform. It is true that support for liberal policy in France grew in the 1970s and 1980s, but the link between ideological argument and policy is tenuous and indirect at best. Socialists, after resorting heavily to statist interventionism in the form of nationalisations and planning agreements, soon abandoned interventionism and implemented the liberalising reforms. Moreover, there have always been strong pro-liberalisation voices in French debate. That such voices should prevail at this particular moment, rather than in, say, 1959, when Charles de Gaulle brought in the very orthodox Jacques Rueff to reform public finances, suggests that there was a 'right time' for liberalisers. The second widespread misconstruction emphasises the role of 'globalisation' in French reform. Setting aside the fact that the term is ill defined, it suffices to observe that French reformism antedated, and indeed contributed to the emergence of an open, global financial market, which is the principal characteristic of the 'globalised economy'. In the same vein, it is important to note that French reformism antedated and contributed to monetary integration in Europe, which culminated in the single European currency in January 2000.

Some scholars have disputed this structural interpretation of French reformism. Jonah Levy, for example, identifies three problems. First, it does not account for timing. Why did French governments wait until 1983 to submit to constraints that had been in evidence for the previous ten years? Second, the constraints the structural argument emphasises are not always in evidence. Levy cites fiscal policy during the early 1990s, in which budget deficits varied between 4 per cent and 6 per cent of GDP, far above the 3 per cent deficit that helped precipitate the move to liberalisation in 1983. High deficits, Levy points out, did not prevent the French from bringing inflation below 2 per cent. Finally, reforms that were 'unnecessary or unrelated to the task of balancing the budget and controlling inflation' went beyond what Levy esteems were necessary to deal with the structural constraint. 'It is very hard to believe', Levy writes, 'that balanced budgets and the defence of the franc somehow necessitated the deregulation of labour markets or the elimination of price and exchange controls' (Levy, 1999: 30).

Levy addresses his objections to a variety of efforts to link French reform to developments in the international political economy. They therefore do not address in any direct way my claim that change in foreign economic policy by a hegemonic United States set off a chain of events that compelled the French to liberalise their financial system. If that specific claim is taken into account, the objections fail. First, on the issue of timing, I claim that floating rates forced the French to deploy a strong franc. The decisive shift to a policy of currency strength occurs in 1974, in the immediate aftermath of the global currency crisis that sank the Bretton Woods system. The temptation to ignore the exchange constraint, in 1975, and in 1982–3, was short lived. Delay did occur in the reform of finance, the necessary support of the new monetary policy, as the French experimented for several years with less radical solutions. But it is important to note that *encadrement du crédit* became a permanent feature of French policy in response to the currency crises that precipitated the scuttling of Bretton Woods. Second, I explain the allegedly exaggerated character of the reforms with reference to the need to rid the political economy of the moral hazard that characterised the overdraft economy. Moral hazard, in the form of the presumption of assured borrowing power, vitiated the power of interest rates to control money supply growth. That fact made radical reform necessary in order to alter economic expectations regarding the availability of state-sponsored credit. The need to replace inflationary financing with foreign investment and the supplementary impact of Reaganomics provide further explanations of the radical nature of French liberalisation.

The objection that policy leeway remained considerable, as evidenced by the budget deficit of the early 1990s, ignores the most puzzling feature of policy during this period. High deficit spending in the early 1990s reflects the social costs of fielding a currency that varied in lock step with a German mark, which was being bid 'artificially' high because of bond emissions to finance reunification. The puzzle is this: why did France deploy such a costly and apparently unnecessary monetary policy, which aggravated unemployment and, by preventing the mark from rising against the franc, made in effect an appreciable contribution to the cost of German reunification? The solution to the puzzle is in the preceding two observations: the commitment to currency strength and the need to alter monetary and financial expectations.

Sofia Perez (1998), in her comparison of financial policy in France and Spain, underscores the importance of politics in the overdraft economy. The French state was generous with its credit policy because it feared the political costs of parsimony. When fears of currency disorder displaced fears of social disorder, the state altered its thinking. In Spain, in contrast, the more autonomous banking sector's efforts to defend its monopoly informed reform efforts that slowed liberalisation. Perez's analysis complements rather than contests my structural interpretation, but I would amend her argument in a way that places the politics of the overdraft economy within an existing condition of moral hazard. The politics of easy credit did not breed moral hazard. It is, rather, moral hazard that bred the politics of easy credit. Under the impact of moral hazard, developmental and interventionist policy in the 1960s evolved into a kind of defensive, rearguard action against economic rationalisation in the 1970s.

Financial liberalisation is a global phenomenon. It is therefore logical to seek its sources in the international political economy rather than in the peculiarities of French political life. Nevertheless, national specificities inform the way economies experience and address international change. It is useful in this regard to draw comparisons between France and other overdraft economies, such as Japan and Sweden (Loriaux 1991); the parallels with Sweden are particularly intriguing, particularly the bank crises in each country that followed on efforts to deregulate and reorient bank activity.

Liberalisation within the discursive framework of developmentalism

To summarise the argument to this point: the history of developmentalist policy in France reveals frequent change in the policy instruments and even in the underlying institutional structures of the French political economy, such that one wants to identify the 'location' of French developmentalism, not in the instruments and institutions of financial and industrial policy, but rather in the heads of Frenchmen who seem constantly to fiddle with those institutions in order to adapt them to changing conditions. There is one state institution that is invariant, however. It is that of the Grands Corps of the French civil service. The Grands Corps 'house' the 'heads'. They are home to an elitist culture composed of language games and norms. That culture informs and constrains the way the French think about industrial development, both inside and outside the formal institutions of the state. Under the pressure of structural imperatives, the French liberalised their political economy, but did so within the framework of that culture. They liberalised the tools and institutions of financial and industrial policy. But the minds that conceived the liberalisation remained imbued with developmental prejudice (Levy 1999).

The tension, whether creative or destructive, between cultural prejudice and structural constraint, shows up in the privatisation of state-owned industrial firms in the late 1980s and 1990s. The Socialists who assumed power in 1981 nationalised most banks and large industrial firms, and used state ownership to effect structural reform. The legislative elections of 1986 returned the right to power on a platform of privatisation. But privatisation occurred under the cloud of enduring concern that low profitability exposed French firms to buy-outs by foreign capital. The conservative government arranged privatisation in such a way that the 'nationality' of French firms was preserved. They divided shares in five categories, each earmarked for a particular kind of buyer. These included employees of the firms undergoing privatisation, the general public, French institutional investors, and foreign institutional investors. But the fifth category was the most important. It was the hard core or *noyau dur* that enmeshed ownership of controlling stock in a net of cross-shareholdings with other major French firms, private and public. Two such networks emerged, each anchored by a major utility company, a holding company, a major bank, and a large insurance company.[4] Within each network, firms retained direct and indirect controlling stakes in one another. Control of most publicly quoted firms was located within these hard cores.

The hard cores reflected the legacy of economic 'patriotism' under conditions of liberalisation (Hayward 1986). Other aspects of privatisation reveal an enduring developmental prejudice. Under rules set by the government, privatisation gave CEOs the right to appoint most board members. Privatisation concentrated power in top management, where the Grands Corps elite was ensconced (Levy 1999). The power of the French CEO was greater than that found in any European country. Cross-ownership arrangements and CEO power sheltered decision-makers from interference by labour, foreign capital, and even the state.

Thus structured, large firms continued, after privatisation, to pursue radical and generally successful internal reorganisation strategies to adapt themselves to new international markets. Top managers and engineers controlled most decisions regarding product architecture, development, work organisation, and parts specifications. They enjoyed considerable freedom to lay off labour, to subcontract, and to enter into international corporate alliances. Firm autonomy from capital markets made long-term planning possible. The hard cores sheltered them from hostile take-overs and provided them with capital. Management was free to position their firms in new market segments. French firms were particularly successful in the area of complex, high-tech engineering goods – such as nuclear power technology, telecommunications, complex armament systems, high-speed trains and aerospace technology – and in the area of 'flexible mass production' (which combined relatively hierarchical shopfloor and supplier relations with modular product architecture). French firms in this latter category, particularly in automobiles, household appliances, and simple electronics, competed successfully with the Germans and Japanese.

Inversely, one can gauge the source and motivation of liberalisation in the developmental strategies of Électricité de France (EDF), the country's state-owned power company. EDF responded to pressure from Brussels to liberalise by digging in and defending its territorial monopoly. But in 1998 it adopted a strategy of internationalisation and diversification designed to make it one of Europe's, and the world's, leading energy groups. It lobbied a very hesitant government to open up the French market to foreign producers. Under the direction of the Grands Corps engineer, François Roussely, the company has internationalised its Board of Directors. It seeks to earn half its income from activities other than electricity by 2005. It is on target to reach that goal, having increased such earnings from 12 per cent in 1998 to 18 per cent in 1999. Its strategy and performance is consistent with that of a publicly traded firm. Yet there is no plan to privatise EDF, nor is there even talk of such a plan (*The Economist* 4 November 2000: 71).

The power of the Grands Corps elite to imprint its developmentalist ethos on economic life in the absence of direct state intervention is visible in other areas of the French economy. The institutional insertion of Grands Corps engineers in the information technology (IT) sector, for example, still creates a prejudice, anchored in complicities between directors of firms and state officials, for developmentalist missions. In IT, the old strategy of nurturing national champions saddled France with the computer firm Bull, a minor player inextricably entwined in the slow-growth sector of computer mainframes. But the developmentalist, mission-oriented prejudice nevertheless produced movement in French IT that has made it competitive on European markets. French firms established themselves successfully in IT system integration servicing and in the development of applications. That success owes much to prior missions that concentrated high-tech industries in regional 'technopoles' (Grenoble, Toulouse, and Cannes) through the location of public sector research establishments (CNRS, INRIA, CEA, CNET). That policy created a Silicon Valley-like environment in which engineers explored innovative technologies. Certain firms benefited from their proximity to state-nurtured aerospace and nuclear industries to develop and market scientific calculation and other state-of-the-art software. The state also responded to perceived national vulnerability in IT by launching a programme to increase the supply of engineers by the engineering *Grandes Écoles*. France's engineering schools increased the supply of newly minted computer scientists from 4,200 in 1982 to 20,100 in 1997 (in sharp contrast with the 6,600 IT graduates supplied to the German economy by its engineering schools).

In genomics, initiatives by private foundations, the Centre d'Etudes sur le Polymorphisme Humain, and the Association Française contre les Myopathies, attracted state attention. The state created the Bioavenir programme in 1992, which subsidised private research and proposed incentives to public research centres to collaborate with the privatised pharmaceutical firm Rhone-Poulenc. In doing so, the state attempted to overcome the absence of a tradition of cooperation between public and private researchers. That absence has hampered French efforts to promote technological innovation. In 1999, the Socialist government liberalised legislation in order to facilitate genomic start-ups. It also created the Évry Génopole, a mission-style, 'national champion' research and administration centre designed to coordinate research efforts at the national level. Critics complain that the Bioavenir programme, an integrated programme aimed at both fundamental research and industrial development, discourages the creation of smaller, more flexible and dynamic centres of gene therapy research in the teaching hospitals. But after a slow take-off, French genomics has become competitive in Europe. The sector now numbers 140 companies in France, compared to 220 in Germany and 280 in Great Britain.

Successful adaptation to world markets is one factor behind France's good economic performance. French GDP growth has been higher than that of Germany and Italy since 1995, and about the same as that of the European Union as a whole. Industrial growth equals that of Germany and exceeds that of Italy and Great Britain. Labour productivity growth in France exceeds that of Germany and the United States. Capital stock has grown more rapidly in France than in Great Britain or Germany. Profitability, a principal concern of the French since the mid-1980s, has doubled. Finally, foreign trade had gone from protracted deficit to surplus by the end of the 1980s.

A capitalism of voice?

The *noyau-dur*, cross-ownership structure of French capitalism attained its ideal type in 1996 following the merger of two insurance giants, Axa and UAP. The importance of the hard cores has since declined. In 1995, the ownership structure of French firms was relatively concentrated. The average equity stake of the principal shareholder group in these two groups of firms varied between 18 and 43 per cent. Cross shareholdings among CAC 40 corporations was widespread: thirty-three firms had significant cross shareholdings with at least one other firm. The aggregate average value of these cross shareholdings was 5.8 per cent, 'a figure similar to the equity stake held by Japanese main banks'. This pattern of equity ownership 'reproduced the relationships that had prevailed prior to the nationalisations' of 1982 (Hancke and Amable 2001).

Three years later the ownership structure was dramatically different. Firms sold their cross shareholdings. Axa, the rare French firm that owed none of its success to state support, showed no interest in playing the role the state wanted it to play, and sold off its hard core holdings. By 1998, the average equity stake of the core shareholder group in CAC 40 firms had fallen to 20.5 per cent (down from an average of 28 per cent in 1995). For the following blue chip firms, that stake was: Accor, 14.5 per cent; Air Liquide, 7.8 per cent; Danone, 12.9 per cent; Elf, 8.2 per cent; Paribas, 12 per cent; Rhone-Poulenc, 6.5 per cent; Saint-Gobain, 16.9 per cent; and Vivendi, 14.4 per cent (Hancke and Amable 1998).[5] The hard core now represents less than 30 per cent of the capital for half of France's blue chip, CAC 40 enterprises, less than 20 per cent for fifteen of the forty, and less than 10 per cent for five of the forty.

Institutional investors, especially American, are now the principal shareholders in the majority of big French firms. Their assets amounted to 83 per cent of French GNP in 1996, compared to Germany's 50 per cent and the United States' 181 per cent (OECD 1998). The rise of the institutional investor in France has been rapid, climbing from 10 per cent of CAC 40 capital in 1985 to 35 per cent in 1999 to more than 50 per cent today. Neither Germany nor Japan has experienced this kind of structural change. The share of foreign investors in the capital of Japanese firms is 11 per cent, in German firms 10 per cent, in British firms 9 per cent, and in American firms a mere 6 per cent. At 35 per cent, France is, of the major industrial powers, the one most open to foreign capital. Institutional investors accounted for 85 per cent of market transactions in French stocks in 1998, and thus contributed much to the dynamism of the Paris market. As one would expect, the growing stake held by institutional investors has made hostile take-overs easier. Institutional investors sold 85 per cent of their shares when Société Générale launched its hostile bid to take over BNP (also a French bank), and 70 per cent of their shares in (French oil producer) ELF when it came under siege by Total (also a French oil producer).

Institutional investors have brought about important change in French corporate governance. Under their influence, CAC 40 firms increased the proportion of independent (or 'outsider') board of director members from 3 per cent in 1988 to 28 per cent in 1998 (Hancke and Amable 1998). Eighteen of the CAC 40 firms have established specialised committees to oversee auditing, remuneration, and nomination of new directors. German and Japanese firms have resisted the creation of such committees. Thirty-eight of the CAC 40 firms, unlike those of other European countries, have made use of stock options, especially for independent directors and board members sitting on specialised committees. The use of stock options is rare in Europe. In Germany, one encounters their use in only four firms: Daimler-Chrysler, Deutsche Telekom, Hoechst, and Lufthansa (Hancke and Amable 1998).

And yet it is not apparent that this evolution threatens the predominance of developmentalist prejudice (or culture) in French economic life. First, the shares held by institutional investors, though an important percentage of the total stock of individual firms, is nevertheless dispersed among many shareholders. The combined ownership of the top three foreign institutional investors surpasses 5 per cent in the case of only six CAC 40 firms. French capital, moreover, remains highly concentrated. Among all French firms, the principal stockholder possesses, on average, 66 per cent of the firm's capital. That figure falls only to about 50 per cent for quoted enterprises. For the 120 largest firms, the five principal shareholders control almost half the capital. There are, in addition, significant family holdings. These represent 50 per cent of the capital of French firms, and 12 per cent for quoted enterprises.

French practices have not aligned on American norms, particularly as regards the relationship between the executive director and the board president. The French system continues to endow its executives with considerable power and autonomy. The French also deviate in the extent to which they facilitate the accumulation of board positions, making the true 'outsider' a rare commodity in French capitalism. Foreign investors remain under-represented on boards, despite the growing importance of foreign capital. Such deviations from the American model concentrate power and multiply opportunities for collusion between firms, lending institutions, and even the state.

The evolution towards a more Anglo-Saxon-looking capital structure would suggest a movement towards an open market system in which the possibilities of 'exit' create a market for corporate control. Yet, developmentalist habits and a capital structure that remains rather concentrated suggest a kind of capital that privileges 'voice', as in the German or Japanese 'closed bank' system, in which firm strategy is not driven by the market for corporate control, but rather is informed by ongoing conversation between directors and institutional lenders.

A second factor that makes the thesis of convergence problematic is the yet insufficiently understood nature of the institutional investor itself. It is a relative newcomer to capitalism, at least in its present dimensions. Its impact, even in the freewheeling United States, is still largely a matter of speculation. Institutional investors are, like large firms, answerable to their shareholders. But they are also potentially answerable in some way to public opinion, as evidenced by the multiplication of 'social responsibility' and 'environmental' savings plans that they make available. They are not anonymous, as is the private stockholder of capitalist myth, and are quite possibly 'too big to walk'. Exit is not viewed in all circles as a legitimate option, as made plain by the financial crisis in East Asia. One speculates that in the future we will see the rise of a kind of 'capitalism of voice', characterised by dialogue between large firms and large investors. That dialogue may come to resemble that which occurs between firm and bank in closed bank systems. Institutional investors currently exercise 'voice' in shareholders' meetings. They make known their concerns at meetings of Boards of Directors. French management has learned to lobby institutional investors in order to convince them of the promise of their strategic plans. There is no reason to dismiss *a priori* the possibility that cultural prejudice for long-run developmental strategy will inform the conversation. Institutional investors, themselves (particularly retirement funds), have long-range concerns.

Finally, one should factor two other items into speculation regarding the future of French developmentalism. The first is the rather high volume of long-term savings in France. Currently, collective investment programmes exist for such savings, and, in value, represent a sum that exceeds French GNP. But such programmes invest only 10 per cent of their assets in stocks. Life insurance plans now manage about 22 per cent of household financial capital, but place up to 75 per cent of their funds in fixed return assets (especially government bonds), and only about 15 per cent in stocks. Fiscal measures stimulate household investment in stocks, but in a way that favours the medium (five to eight years) term. It is not unreasonable to predict that the French will look for ways to channel household savings towards long-term investment, possibly through reforms in pension funds. But one can also expect that such efforts will assume the form of charters and regulations that enhance voice and loyalty over the long term and discourage speculation.

The construction of the European Union (EU) also affects the evolution of corporate governance in France. France is not the only country experiencing mutation. Germany is under similar pressure to dismantle its cross-ownership structure and shows no clear sign at present of acquiescing. A European model of corporate governance might arise through the integration of non-nationals in management and cross-ownerships that build networks at the European level, and through the creation of European institutional investors who would show greater loyalty over the long term. The sheer economic size of the EU, and its relatively low level of trade dependence (7–8 per cent) render it potentially invulnerable to US pressure to conform to the Anglo-Saxon model. European integration may provide developmental culture with yet another set of structures and institutions that favour its survival in a more open globalised economy.

We thus observe, in conclusion, that changes in the structure of French capital, as in the institutions and norms of corporate governance, have not produced change in firm strategy since the period of public ownership. The strategy of core competence and foreign direct investment, in evidence during the period of state ownership and promoted by state planners, has not been affected by either privatisation or the decline of the hard cores (Loriaux 1999). The absence of a tradition of collaborative research between business and the university in France continues to make that strategy rational. The concentrated ownership structure of French firms protected them from foreign take-over and diminished the risk of direct investment in foreign markets. The absence of Anglo-Saxon monitoring systems sheltered ambitious strategists from second-guessing by shareholders. The power and autonomy of management, infused with Grande École and Grand Corps vision and self-confidence, facilitated bold moves.

Such observations enrich debate about moral possibilities under 'globalisation'. Ten years ago, at the height of the liberalising reform movement, Frenchmen lamented loudly the triumph of a certain *pensée unique* – 'single thought'. Globalisation, they complained, had all but silenced debate over goals and means. Globalisation had ushered in an era of 'totalitarian liberalism', the ideological cover for a kind of American-style cowboy capitalism. But in recent years, the French have found room for policies that aim at greater justice and solidarity in economic life. Their experience suggests that the state's institutional strength is still sufficient to constrain that of the marketplace. But it also invites us to scan widely for the institutions that count. In the French case, it is not the institutions that funnel capital to investment that differ from those found, say, in the United States; rather, it is those that funnel talent to positions of power. It is the institutions that socialise elites. It is the institutions that produce culture rather than those that produce subsidies and credit that safeguard the tradition of developmentalism. It is the institutions that protect the supremacy of that culture in the firm that account for the difference in business behaviour.

Notes

1. The most important and most relevant of these Grands Corps are the Inspection des Finances, the Corps Diplomatique, the Cours des Comptes, the Conseil d'Etat, and the Corps Préfectoral.
2. The works of Ezra Suleiman (1974, 1978) remain the most enlightening and important regarding the French elite.
3. Although the attractiveness of the high civil service has diminished somewhat under globalisation, the number of students competing for a spot in ENA is still a significant multiple, say ten-to-one, of those who are admitted.
4. The first was composed of the Lyonnaise des Eaux, the Banque Suez, the Banque Nationale de Paris, and the Union des Assurances de Paris. The other brought together the Générale des Eaux, Banque Paribas, the Crédit Lyonnais, the Société Générale, and the insurance company Assurances Générales de France.
5. Figures cited appear in *Les Échos*, 8 December 1998.

6 The challenges of economic upgrading in liberalising Thailand

Richard F. Doner and Ansil Ramsay

Thailand's spectacular economic performance until the mid-1990s earned it classification as one of the World Bank's 'High Performing Asian Economies' (World Bank 1993). In 1997, however, the country's financial meltdown triggered the Asian crisis. Analysts may differ as to the precise explanations for Thailand's economic performance, but all would agree that globalisation, in the form of significant and increasing exposure to regional and global markets for goods, services, and capital, has played a significant role in the country's successes as well as its problems.[1] This chapter uses the case of Thailand to explore the impact of domestic institutions on economic upgrading efforts in the face of globalisation, with an emphasis on globalised *product markets*. More specifically, we highlight the necessity of market-conforming, domestic arrangements capable of resolving sector-specific and intersectoral coordination and distributional dilemmas inherent in economic upgrading. In this perspective, recent neoliberal calls for sector-neutral institutional strengthening are useful but insufficient for middle-income developing countries to advance in a more globalised environment.

Our emphasis on the real sector is not meant to minimise the weight of problems in Thailand's financial sector.[2] But the financial crisis was itself in part a function of weaknesses in the real sector – of 'too much foreign money chasing too few sound investments that were capable of earning foreign exchange sufficient to service the principal and interest on the debt' (Jackson 1999: 5). And, as a World Bank report noted at the end of 2000, strength in the real sector will be key to long-term development: 'Thailand's future growth is less likely to come from capital growth, and more from productivity and knowledge-intensive growth' (2000b: 24).

We undertake this examination in the theoretical context of a 'state *vs.* market' debate that has become less polarised and more nuanced than in the early 1990s. On the 'statist' side, extensive empirical research has demonstrated the pitfalls of state interventions (even among the Newly Industrialised Countries – NICs). This research has also recognised the potential contributions of private interests, the developmental benefits of various kinds of networks, and the variety of institutional arrangements among successful industrialisers and even across issues within the same country. As a result, those extolling the benefits of sector-specific, state interventions now talk about states as 'embedded', as catalysts involved in relationships of 'governed interdependence'.[3]

Conversely, free market advocates, typically sceptical of the benefits of state interventions, have begun to pay more explicit attention to non- or extra-market institutions for countries that have opened themselves to external factor and product markets. Evidence of significant weaknesses in first-generation price reforms and the growing prominence of the New Institutional Economics (NIE) have resulted in an emerging, second-generation consensus. The new view is that, even in the presence of neutral prices, smoothly functioning markets can be undermined by factors such as weak property rights, corruption, non-competitive behaviour, and distributional conflicts. The reform challenge has shifted from advising states to stop intervening in markets to urging them to provide pro-market institutions, such as stable property rights, banking regulations, transparent corporate governance rules, better educational institutions, judicial services, conflict management mechanisms, social insurance, and capable public administration (Burki and Perry 1998; World Bank 2002).

This new emphasis on institutions represents an important and useful recognition that markets do not function smoothly without supporting social arrangements. But the second generation pays insufficient attention to issues that are central to developing countries' responses to new challenges of globalisation: the distinction among diverse kinds of economic growth; the shifting challenges of globalised product markets; the potential benefits of competition-based sectoral policies; and the institutional challenges of such policies. All of this leads to an appreciation of arrangements largely neglected if not dismissed by second-generation proponents: cohesive, market-driven state agencies, systematic public–private exchanges, and collective private sector institutions capable of addressing sector-specific and intersectoral upgrading.

Several considerations make Thailand a useful lens through which to assess the value of a sector-specific institutional approach. First, Thailand has clearly been highly 'globalised' in terms of trade, investment, and finance.[4] Second, the country is facing further external pressures in the form of ASEAN Free Trade Area (AFTA) commitments to reducing tariffs on most goods to between 0 and 5 per cent as of 2003; WTO provisions to end local content requirements; General System of Preference (GSP) cuts; and an Information Technology Agreement (ITA) condition to reduce tariffs on electronics to zero. In addition, several of Thailand's key industries, e.g., sugar, textiles, and autos, are facing strong pressure from foreign markets and production networks to improve quality, to reduce prices and, in some cases, to shift away from mass production of standardised goods towards smaller batches of more customised goods.

Third, Thailand ought to be a relatively 'easy' case for second-generation proponents of neutral prices, open markets, and sectorally neutral institutions. The Thai state has not exhibited the autonomy, coherence, and expertise characteristic of the East Asian NICs. And, as a natural-resource-rich country, its growth has been fairly consistent with comparative advantage in agricultural and labour-intensive manufactured goods. Its success prior to 1997 should therefore conform to neoliberal prescriptions. Its recent failures should reflect a departure from those prescriptions, and its ability to contend with new globalisation pressures should depend on its return to them.

The argument of this chapter is that second-generation expectations are far from sufficient to explain past growth, and second-generation prescriptions are insufficient to restart and sustain development. Thailand's successes have reflected a range of institutional arrangements that go well beyond the hands-off and sectorally neutral assumptions of the second generation. Present Thai problems reflect not so much a departure from neoliberal prescriptions but the *obsolescence* of the particular institutional arrangements that proved so useful in the past. Sustained growth in the face of globalisation requires institutional innovation capable of implementing policies that are both market-conforming and attentive to the needs of specific sectors. Our argument, put most simply, is that institutions vary with regard to their capacity to resolve developmental challenges. From this perspective, it is not surprising that Thailand has grown impressively in some areas and time periods but not in others.

In the second section, we critique the second-generation consensus. In the third section we review the strengths and weaknesses of Thai growth prior to the crisis of 1997. In the fourth section we identify the factors promoting and constraining growth. In the fifth section we examine responses to the crisis. We conclude by highlighting useful directions for future research.

Weaknesses of the new Washington consensus

Outcomes/economic transformation

Although the second-generation consensus emphasises that 'institutions matter' for economic growth, its definition of growth tends to be fairly narrow, usually limited to the rate of GDP per capita growth.[5] Although a critical indicator of growth, per capita income fails to distinguish among a range of outcomes indicating different capacities for *sustained* growth in the face of new external challenges. Such capacities involve a country's maintenance or increase of autonomy within the international political economy by adapting to or insulating itself from external shifts.

Countries can grow through some combination of static efficiency, structural change, and upgrading. *Static efficiency* involves maintaining productivity, quality, profitability, and capacity utilisation in an existing product range. Other things being equal, such growth is possible in a context of stable, neutral prices and competitive markets. *Structural change* refers to intra- and intersectoral changes, including shifts from agriculture to manufacturing, diversification within agriculture and/or manufacturing, expansion from downstream products to upstream intermediates and capital goods, and moves from labour-intensive manufacturing to more capital- and technology-intensive production.[6]

By contrast, *upgrading*, the third source of growth, refers to making more efficient use of new investments in order to generate higher value added and thus to capture rents.[7] At one level, upgrading is indicated by the capacity of indigenous firms to move into more sophisticated economic activities (production, design, marketing) and/or to advance from simple assembly, to original equipment manufacturing to original brand manufacturing, and to original design manufacturing (Gereffi and Tam 1998: 8). Upgrading in turn requires the ability to promote human resource development and intersectoral linkages, and to develop technology and advanced infrastructure.

External context

The nature and success of national development efforts will vary with changing pressures in globalised product markets. The second-generation consensus is largely silent on such shifts, one of the most important of which has to do with increasing pressures for more flexible production. Until the 1990s, developing country firms in a range of industries could prosper by producing large volumes of standardised goods for domestic markets based on protectionism or for export based on cheap labour. Such a trajectory is less and less possible with liberalised trade in industries increasingly characterised by at least four more demanding features: reduced importance of cheap labour; final consumer markets that are both more fragmented and more demanding on price, quality, and delivery; shortened product cycles; and increasingly rapid technology change. Under these conditions, sustainable success for developing country firms – even in ostensibly lower-technology industries such as autos and textiles – demands not simply structural shifts, but even more so the capacity for upgrading (e.g., McKendrick, Doner, and Haggard 2000: ch. 11).

Policies

The second-generation consensus highlights the benefits of institutions to support markets operating in a context of neutral and stable prices on the one hand, and openness to foreign capital and products on the other. Recent empirical work suggests that openness is insufficient (Rodrik 2000b; Mody 1998). 'The trick in the successful cases has been to combine the opportunities offered by world markets with a domestic investment and institution-building strategy to stimulate the animal spirits of domestic entrepreneurs' (Mody 1998: 8). Such a policy – variously termed 'competitiveness-oriented' or 'productive development policy' (Gore 2000a: 797) – eschews protection as a core strategy, even if it supports liberalisation as a gradual process. It explicitly positions indigenous producers within multinational companies' (MNCs) global or regional networks. Traditional objectives of capital formation, job growth, and foreign exchange earnings are supplemented by efforts not just to exploit current relative cost advantages but also 'to promote investment and learning in economic activities where comparative advantage can realistically be expected to lie in the immediate future as the economy develops and as other late industrialising countries catch up' (Gore 2000a: 797).

These goals require policy instruments to address issues typically plagued by market failures: human resource development, supplier linkages, technology diffusion, and advanced infrastructure – all in the context of intensifying and shifting competitive pressures (Mody 1998; Peters 1998). The second-generation policies do not address these probems adequately. Their solution requires sector-specific policies and organisational arrangements as well as supportive developmental norms. Moreover, under new globalisation pressures, such tasks must be addressed in ways that go beyond the support for discrete industries to foster the growth of dynamic industrial clusters of complementary assembly, component production, and related producer services and technology support (Felker and Jomo 1999: 4; Gore 2000a: 797).

Institutions

Such problems tend to be 'institution-intensive' (Clague 1997: 3), requiring arrangements that facilitate information sharing, mutual monitoring, implementing collective goals, and compensating losers while empowering winners. Institution-intensive, however, refers not simply to clearer rules and regulations but also to stronger states, public–private consultations, and private *organisations*.[8] Competition-promoting policies require enhanced rather than minimalist states. Only states with expertise, flexibility, and some degree of autonomy can appreciate, much less implement, sector-specific policies that promote private sector efficiency. But states cannot pursue such policies without extensive contact with those most directly involved in the market. Systematic public–private consultation can improve information for public sector decisions, broaden 'ownership' and enhance the credibility of such policies, improve accountability and transparency, and expand resources for policy implementation.[9] And finally, such public–private sector exchanges can benefit from business itself being organised (although bilateral consultations with specific firms may be more suitable for policies involving highly proprietary information). Business associations can help to limit the pursuit of particularistic benefits by individual firms and facilitate the provision of critical industry-specific information from – and among – firms (Doner and Schneider 2000). The second-generation approach to institutions pays little if any attention to the industrial policy role of states, public–private sector linkages, or business associations. This neglect is, we suspect, reinforced by the NIE's tendency to define institutions only as formal and informal rules or norms, to the exclusion of organisations (Doner and Schneider 2000). But as discussed in the next two sections, organisations as well as rules have been key in Thailand to both past successes and more recent problems.

Thai economic growth: sources and constraints

The central features of Thailand's impressive economic development can be summarised briefly. In terms of simple GDP growth, the economy expanded at a 7.6 per cent annual rate during the two decades from 1977 to 1996 (Jansen 1997: 6–8). Structural change has been especially impressive. Thai agriculture not only grew absolutely (around 4 per cent from 1950 to 1994) but underwent significant diversification (Christensen 1993).

Significant structural change was also evident in exports. Agriculture fell from around 85 per cent of total exports in 1960 to 18 per cent in 1990 whereas manufacturing rose from 2.4 per cent to 73.8 per cent during the same thirty-year period (Lauridsen 2000: 50). The growth in manufactured exports after 1980 was especially striking: a 24 per cent annual compound rate from 1980 to 1990 and 22 per cent from 1990 to 1995 meant that Thailand 'had the highest rate of growth of both manufactured and total exports of all the Asian "high performing economies"' (Lall 1998: 2). Within this growth in manufacturing exports was a further shift: from 1985 to 1993, labour-intensive goods (e.g., garments, gems, shoes) dominated manufactured exports. As the growth of these products slowed in the early 1990s, medium-high technology products (computer parts, electronics, electrical appliances) grew rapidly, so that by 1995 the export value of these products was 40 per cent greater than labour-intensive goods (Chalongphob 1997: 7).

In 1996, the value of labour-intensive exports continued to fall. Indeed, total exports stagnated, raising significant questions about the country's exchange rate and contributing to the 1997 meltdown. As the Thai Development Research Institute noted, Thailand was losing its comparative advantage in labour-intensive manufactured goods after only a decade (Chalongphob 1997: 8; Lall 1998: 4). Theoretically, the country could now begin to rely more on medium-high technology products. However, Thailand's export success in these products was misleading: a detailed analysis of Thai exports prompted Lall to conclude that 'Much of technology-intensive production in Thailand comprises relatively simple assembly activity...', and that Thailand is not operating at much higher technological levels than Indonesia or China (1998: 7). Since much of the country's comparative advantage in medium-high-tech products is based on low assembly cost, that advantage is likely to be as transitory as that in labour-intensive goods (Chalongphob 1997: 8).

This hollowness in the Thai production structure highlights the country's weakness in upgrading. First, with the exception of agricultural and agro-industrial products (e.g., rice, canned pineapple, tuna) and isolated firms in other industries, Thai exporters have remained largely as original equipment producers (e.g., Nipon and Fuller 1997: 498). Second, intersectoral linkages are weak at best. For many firms, foreign inputs are either unavailable or quite expensive due to persistently high duties on raw materials and capital goods (indeed, the country's average import tariff as of 1999 was 18.4 per cent, one of the highest in Southeast Asia (World Bank 2000b: 47)). Protests by downstream firms in textiles, auto parts, electronics, and other industries burdened with low quality and high costs of, say, domestic steel, animal feed, or petrochemical products remain a common theme in Thai political economy (e.g., Nipon and Pawadee 1998: 313; Wichit 1998; Doner and Ramsay 2000: 167). It is unclear how, under these conditions, Thai downstream firms will be able to compete with regional imports given AFTA commitments to reduce tariffs noted earlier in this chapter.

Finally, the technological level of indigenous Thai firms remains unimpressive, with a recent World Bank report concluding that 'Thailand is lagging behind other countries in the region in terms of... technology-related capabilities.' Indeed, in 2000, the World Bank concluded that Thailand was nowhere near 'the level of technology system development that Korea reached around the early 1980s' (World Bank 2000b: 43). Although Thai levels have been high relative to the rest of the region (Rodrik 1997b: 4, 32), growth rates have been falling since the late 1980s (2000a: 42–3; Colaco 1998).

These weaknesses have contributed to a highly *dualistic* structure in key industries, including automobiles, textiles, and electronics: Thai incentives (e.g., protectionism) have contributed to a relatively inefficient, domestically owned local supply base largely isolated from technologically advanced, export-oriented producers. Under these conditions, 'Thai firms have still not developed the capability to make major changes in products, processes or organisation techniques...' (Nipon and Pawadee 1998: 310). Indigenisation is thus *becoming* a problem as looming trade liberalisation threatens the very existence of locally owned firms in protected industries. In autos, for example, a recent report concluded that liberalisation and the end of local content requirements could well result in nearly all of the 300 Thai-owned OEM firms going under (Crispin 2000a: 46). In garments, local firms do export but have been penalised, as noted earlier, by the high cost of protected inputs. In textiles, the Thai Melon group, one of Thailand's largest and most diversified fibre producers, went out of business after being touted as a case of local success (Rock 2000; Doner and Ramsay 1993; Busaba and Cholada 1998). In electronics, local firms are largely absent from the higher-technology export sectors (Nipon and Pawadee 1998). All of this suggests that 'while production diversified during the period of rapid industrial expansion, no significant industrial deepening occurred' (Nattapong *et al.* 1994, cited in Sevilla and Kusol 2000: 7).

Explaining Thai performance

Thailand has done well in static efficiency and structural change, but it has been much less successful at upgrading. In this section we advance two arguments regarding this mixed performance. First, although factor endowments and external opportunities were of central importance in Thai success, so were domestic institutional factors. Second, the institutions which contributed to Thai success served largely to obtain and shift resources into new areas, not to facilitate the more efficient utilisation of such resources.

Sources of growth – static efficiency and structural change

The sources of Thai growth can be divided into external and internal factors. The former have loomed large throughout the postwar period, with foreign markets and external finance playing central roles. Several observers have concluded that the external environment was the primary source of Thai growth (e.g., Westphal *et al.* 1990). But since other countries in the region (e.g., the Philippines, Indonesia) did not fare as well as Thailand, we need to identify domestic factors that helped the Thais to take advantage of favourable external opportunities. In addition to natural resource endowments and low wages, these factors included sociopolitical and institutional arrangements that helped to create competitive markets, to construct a stable environment in which to do business, and to encourage resource shifts into new productive activities.[10]

Creating competitive markets through clientelism: Clientelism in Thailand was characterised by competition and insecurity among numerous political patrons through the 1970s. The absence of a landed aristocracy and an inability to tap into government budgets (see below) meant that these patrons relied for funds on private interests attempting to gain access to lucrative market opportunities. Such private efforts often took the form of bribes, but competition among patrons for bribes weakened tendencies towards monopoly cronyism and encouraged new entrants. The result, as reflected in industries such as rice, textiles, sugar, and autos, was a tendency towards competitive market structures on the one hand, and *de facto* property rights, as clients could rely on patrons for protection from expropriation.

Stable macroeconomic environment through an insulated technocracy: Thailand's post-World War II economy has been characterised by macroeconomic prudence. Fiscal policy has been notably conservative, and the emphasis on exchange rate policy has been stability and realism. The institutional strength of key agencies – the Budget Bureau, the Finance Ministry, and the Bank of Thailand – was key to this cautious and realistic approach to macroeconomic policy. These agencies were not only staffed by highly trained and well-paid officials; they were also protected from political pressure since members of parliament had no power to allocate budgets or to propose budget increases. This insulation had two further virtues. First, as noted above, was budget constraints on political leaders, who were then forced to seek financial support from private firms. These hard budget constraints also discouraged public bailouts of weak firms (e.g., Doner and Ramsay 2000: 161). Second, insulation allowed Thai technocrats to open the economy to foreign investors whose linkages to domestic Thai firms served to further strengthen private property rights.

This combination of a favourable external environment, competitive market structures, and macroeconomic stability was clearly necessary for Thailand's growth and structural change. However, it is doubtful that such conditions would have been sufficient for the impressive diversification of the Thai economy. More specifically, studies of growth in several key sectors including rice, sugar, agribusiness, tourism, and automobiles show that state agencies, private sector institutions, and public–private sector linkages played critical roles in successful structural change.[11] The textile and garment industry, a key source of Thailand's manufactured export growth, illustrates well the role of institutions.

From modest beginnings, this industry grew to become one of Thailand's leading export industries, accounting for some 14 per cent of total export earnings, around 23 per cent of industrial GDP, and over a million workers by 1994.[12] In addition to the factors noted above (e.g., low wages, macroeconomic stability, and competitive clientelism), this industry grew through a constellation of state and private sector institutional efforts. State officials have provided consistently high levels of protection while trade associations and commercial banks, especially the Bangkok Bank, have been key to resolving a range of problems. The Bangkok Bank was the key mechanism for coordinating the initial shift of funds from agriculture to manufacturing, especially textiles and fibres. The Bank also established its own textile centre to recruit engineering graduates for the textile industry and, with the help of industry associations, to help in resolving the industry's overcapacity problems through coordination of production limits and export promotion initiatives. Trade associations have also helped to identify new markets and to coordinate export quota allocations. Finally, associations have been part of attempts to reconcile tariff-related differences among various subsectors of the textile/garment complex and to provide technical training. But, as discussed below, efforts regarding the trade regime and technical training have been recent and only moderately successful.

Constraints to growth – upgrading problems

As Thailand succeeded in diversifying its economy, it began to encounter the limits of simple structural change. Labour became more expensive, pressure for trade liberalisation was growing, new competitors were emerging, and foreign markets were becoming both more volatile and more demanding. All of these contributed to the 1997 crisis. But the crisis also highlighted factors impeding Thailand's ability to go beyond structural change: weaknesses in technical training, supplier development, technology diffusion and absorption, and advanced infrastructure.

The country's lack of investment in technical training has meant that the country's human resources are more suited to low-wage assembly than to 'the emergence of a knowledge economy' (World Bank 2000b: 40). The weak local supplier base has contributed to the country's persistent trade deficit and to its lack of industrial deepening (Sevilla and Kusol 2000). New technologies (e.g., computer numerical controlled machines) have been diffused in Thailand, but quite unevenly and without much R&D support (Brimble 1995). Weaknesses in this area are reflected in the fact that only 3–5 per cent of industrial firms have actually drawn on the services of a wide range of science and technology programmes (World Bank 2000b: 44). Finally, Thailand suffers from important weaknesses in advanced infrastructure, such as logistics and e-commerce (Peters 1998; Crispin 2000b).

These weaknesses are in part a function of policy constraints. The country's trade and tax regimes have discouraged the foreign–local

131

subcontracting relationships and 'dynamic complementarities' that can strengthen local suppliers; they have also inhibited the use of imported equipment critical to the diffusion of new technologies. Development of an indigenous supply base is discouraged by investment incentives and financial structures favouring large firms over the small and medium-sized enterprises (SMEs) that constitute potential suppliers (Sevilla and Kusol 2000). Furthermore, human resource policies have been short lived and largely without connection to the needs of competitive firms (Felker 1997).

What accounts for these policy weaknesses? Part of the story has to do with normative preferences of the Thai technocratic elite. The macro-economic agencies that were traditionally the most expert and cohesive part of the Thai state – the Finance Ministry, the Budget Bureau, and the Bank of Thailand – have viewed macroeconomic stability as necessary and sufficient for Thai growth. Measures to promote efficiency through more sectoral interventions were suspect at best (McKendrick, Doner, and Haggard 2000: 243–4). And if, as we have argued, sectoral interventions were in fact quite important for Thai growth, these interventions were never part of a cohesive approach to economic governance. Instead, they occurred through 'pockets of efficiency' that did not contribute to an institutional ethos or improve the country's broader capacity for market-based interventions.

In many ways, such a capacity became even weaker in the 1990s with a deterioration in key components of the country's institutional make-up. To begin with, the bureaucracy in all areas has lost expertise, cohesion, and stability. These weaknesses are a function of downsizing, the departure of experienced officials to better-paying jobs in the private sector and, perhaps most importantly, political factors – Cabinet instability and the tendency of politicians to seek ministerial positions largely to gain resources in support of rural electoral networks. Such problems have even extended into the traditionally 'clean' macroeconomic agencies (e.g., Ockey 1994; Handley 1997). Frequent changes of ministers make it very difficult to sustain policies because the payoffs are too far in the future. Ministers need results quickly so that they can take credit for them while they are still in office and pay off supporters. The problem would not be so severe if well-qualified, politically insulated civil servants had incentives to engage with and monitor the industry. Civil servants who get in the way of politicians' goals cannot be fired, but they can be transferred, sometimes to very demeaning jobs.

Fragmentation within the state gives rise to a second problem: the fragility of public–private sector linkages. Historically, coordination between state officials and organised business has intensified during periods of economic crisis. This was especially notable during the 1980s when the corporatist Joint Public–Private Sector Consultative Committee (JPPCC) was established and became quite active in resolving problems such as those facing the gem and jewelry industry (Anek 1988). But, since 1988, the JPPCC has met sporadically. The key point here is that state officials have not provided consistent incentives for business to engage with the state systematically and collectively (Lauridsen 2000: 35).

Still a third problem has to do with the end of Thai commercial banks as investment coordinators. Despite post-1997 allegations of cronyism, Thai commercial banks had been 'phenomenally successful' in gathering Thai savings and investing them productively.[13] Typically, banks developed close ties of trust with clients, acquiring equity in many of them, and thus engaging in insider lending. These linkages, and the banks' diversified interests, led them to coordinate clients' investments in sectors such as sugar and textiles. In this coordination function, the commercial banks' importance *'substantially overshadowed that of government agencies'* (Lauridsen 2000: 14; emphasis added). This relatively opaque arrangement worked well from the 1960s until the early 1990s. But with financial liberalisation, large volumes of foreign money poured in and weakened the link between lenders and borrowers. The good news was that new sources of credit, especially short-term loans, freed corporate clients from reliance on a small number of commercial banks. The bad news was the loss of a previously effective mechanism of investment coordination.

Together, these weaknesses have predisposed Thai public agencies towards projects whose large investments, small number of actors, and low rate of technological change made them easier to understand and control. Thus, Thai irrigation officials have traditionally favoured the lumpy and easily monitored construction of large-scale dams over the disaggregated and demanding challenge of diffusing new agricultural technologies (Pasuk and Baker 1998: 327). When Thai officials have attempted a project characterised by high levels of complexity, shifting costs and information, and intense distributional conflicts, as in the case of efforts to create a petrochemical and infrastructural complex in the Eastern Seaboard, the result was what Unger terms 'incredible commitments and policy chaos' (1998: ch. 6).

These domestic political and institutional weaknesses have combined with new external pressures to generate new upgrading-related challenges. Again, textiles and garments constitute an important, illustrative case. By 1995 Thailand was one of the world's top garment exporting countries (Dicken 1998: 291). However, the external environment posed new challenges in the 1990s. First, the industry was being undercut in low-end production of textiles and garments by lower wage countries, some of whom, such as Indonesia, China, and Vietnam were getting close to Thailand in terms of product quality (*Nation* 6 June 1997). Second, global textile production networks were becoming much more demanding: continued success, Thai garment firms were told by foreign buyers, now meant being able to cut the time between order and delivery from at least three months to six weeks, to reduce inventory significantly, to produce in small batches, and to do so at a lower price (author interview, Thai Garment Manufacturers' Association, summer 1999). Third, Thai producers were confronting an increasingly open and transparent global industry: the Multi-Fibre Agreement (MFA) is scheduled to end in 2004. The termination of the MFA will open all markets up to fierce competition, especially to China, whose entry into the WTO will enhance its competitiveness in world textile markets. In addition to these changes, Thai textile and garment producers face growing competition from other, less-protected and lower-cost Southeast Asian producers as a consequence of commitments under AFTA. Lastly, new 'social accountability' standards and corporate codes of conduct will deprive Thai firms of the ability to cut costs through poor working conditions and the use of child labour (author interviews, Thai Garment Manufacturers' Association, summer 1999).

Contending with these pressures requires addressing several challenges. One is improving links in the textile–garment supply chain: A 1998 Bangkok Bank study concluded that 'upstream products cannot sufficiently satisfy the demand of the downstream industries both in quality and variety' (Sombat 1998: 1). A second involves updating equipment: as of 1997, most local factories in both upstream and downstream industries still used old and outdated machinery. Some 80 per cent of Thai weaving firms still used shuttle looms, despite the global industry standard of more efficient shuttleless machines (Somporn 1997). Third, the industry suffers from severe shortages of engineers, textile chemists, textile technicians, designers, and international marketing experts (Somporn 1997: 9). And finally, Thai textile producers suffered from tariffs on raw materials significantly higher than regional competitors (Sombat 1998: 9).

The matrix of state agencies, private sector institutions, and public–private sector linkages that played critical roles in successful structural change in the past have been only moderately successful in meeting these new challenges. Fragmentation of responsibility among state agencies makes upgrading of the textile and garment industry difficult. The Ministry of Industry, the Ministry of Commerce, and the Ministry of Finance all make decisions that affect the industry, yet policy coordination among these agencies is poor. After several years of planning, a Textile Institute was created in 1996 to help overcome this fragmentation, and to link the efforts of the public and private sectors to improve competitiveness in world textile and garment markets, but the institute has only recently begun to make any progress along these lines (*Textile Digest* (Thailand) 1998: 26–9).

The lack of strong cooperative relations among business associations in the industry further hampers upgrading efforts in Thailand. The main federation coordinating efforts in the industry is the National Federation of Textile Industries (NFTTI), but it tends to be only as strong as its current leader, and leadership rotates among the associations every two years (author interviews, Bangkok, July 1999). There are considerable differences among the associations in their levels of organisation, goals, and capabilities. The Thai Garment Manufacturers' Association (TGMA) has a large staff, sophisticated strategies for upgrading, and close links with government agencies such as the Department of Export Promotion. Other associations are much weaker in all of these respects.

Distributional conflicts also hamper cooperative efforts among the associations. Highly protected upstream producers of petrochemicals and midstream producers of dyestuffs have been reluctant to give up their protection, yet upgrading the industry as a whole requires the removal of protection from these sectors. The struggle among potential winners and losers delayed improvements in the dyestuff sector for years and is still a problem in the case of petrochemicals.

Progress towards upgrading has depended mainly on the efforts of individual firms and on the efforts of particular business associations in the industry working with state agencies to address problems. These efforts have led to moderate success in some areas. The TGMA has worked very effectively with the Department of Export Promotion to stage the Bangkok International Fashion Fair each year and to bring foreign experts to Thailand to advise Thai garment makers on design and fashions (Somporn 2001). Some improvements have begun to take place in strengthening connections in the domestic supply chain as a result of meetings among the major business associations coordinated by the Thai Textile Institute. The Textile Institute has also organised seminars led by Hong Kong garment manufacturers to discuss ways of improving quick responses by strengthening links in the supply chain (Achara 1999). Steps have been taken also to improve the supply of engineers, technicians, managers, and skilled workers. The TGMA has established a fund for training managers and skilled workers and the Thai Textile Institute has worked with the Ministry of Commerce to improve the supply of skilled personnel (Busrin 1999; Achara 1999). Despite these improvements, the industry still has a substantial way to go in addressing its major challenges.

Responses to the crisis

The 1997 crisis provoked extensive discussion and research on Thailand's declining competitiveness. The World Bank itself highlighted the challenges, asserting that to reach Korea's 1980s level in technology, the Thais would have to raise total R&D expenditures as a share of GDP fivefold; the share of business-funded R&D over twenty fold; the number of researchers per 10,000 population fourfold; and the number of international patents around sixfold (World Bank 2000: 43).

The government responded with a range of industrial and institutional modernisation efforts. The Ministry of Industry initiated a wide-ranging industrial restructuring effort that involved an extensive set of public–private discussions with representatives of almost all sectors of the economy. In terms of process, this was a real effort to promote bottom-up exchanges and to reach consensus on both problems and solutions. These discussions highlighted new external challenges and explicitly noted Thai producers' general lack of attention to productivity issues. The discussions resulted in a comprehensive plan that explicitly recognised the need to move out of low-wage, mass-production activities through measures such as skills upgrading and SME support. To these ends, it proposed specific productivity-enhancing measures for thirteen of Thailand's most important industries. In terms of process, the plan called for more systematic public–private consultation.

In line with these proposals, the crisis prompted significant efforts at institution building. These included measures to strengthen the state's effort to screen foreign investment for technology spillovers; to increase bureaucratic cohesion; and even to create a Ministry of International Trade and Industry (MITI) (*Bangkok Post* 26 May 2000). Although immediately opposed by the Foreign Affairs Ministry as an out-of-date, Japanese-style institution (Yuwadee 2000), the MITI proposal was significant because it highlighted government awareness of the need to respond to market pressures by consolidating responsibilities for manufacturing excellence and export promotion. Indeed, throughout the Thai bureaucracy officials are actively investigating the relevance for Thailand of other countries' productivity efforts (e.g., Singapore's skills development programme, Brazil's shoe production clusters, and Italy's success in flexible production) (author interviews, Summer 1999). Finally, the government created eight public–private institutes designed to address productivity issues in key sectors such as food, textiles, autos, and electronics. Most of these institutes were headed not by bureaucrats but by individuals with extensive private-sector experience in both firms and associations (author interviews, Summer 1999).

In the past, Thailand has historically shown impressive capacities at institutional innovation when confronted with significant economic threats. An intensification of public–private sector coordination during difficult times has been a critical component in the establishment of quality standards in rice, the promotion of textile and garment exports, and the development of the gem and jewelry industry. Further, under the pressure of tariff liberalisation, there is evidence of serious upgrading efforts by specific firms in a range of industries as noted above (e.g., Deyo and Doner 2001).

Unfortunately, there is reason to think that such innovative efforts will remain isolated enclaves rather than industry standards (Deyo and Doner 2001). Some argue that the Ministry of Industry's industrial restructuring plan was simply a package of proposals representing bureaucratic efforts to secure resources (author interviews, summer 1999). A senior Ministry of Industry official stated outright that, owing to 'red tape and lack of cooperation from the private sector', the Industrial Restructuring Programme 'was a failure in terms of boosting efficiency and cooperation' (*Bangkok Post/Mid-year Economic Review* July 2000).

Underlying this gloomy assessment are persistent institutional weaknesses. Fragmentation remains common among key state agencies, thus undermining efforts in areas such as technical training efforts (Ritchie 2000). Public–private sector linkages have intensified but have not resulted in the resolution of sticky problems such as tariff-related tensions between upstream producers in areas such as steel and petrochemicals, and downstream users of these products in the textile and auto industries (author interviews, Thai Synthetic Fibre Manufacturers' Association, Summer 1999; *Nation* 9 June 2000).

Finally, there remains the gap between savers and investors and the related weakness in investment coordination. Financial liberalisation opened up new sources of short-term funds and thus freed corporate clients from dependence on Thai commercial banks. But the crash ended the illusion of corporate growth based on short-term financing. The natural alternative is the equities market, however weaknesses in corporate governance have made it difficult for individual investors to monitor corporate officers. Such problems will eventually be resolved; and there is, of course, no going back to traditional Thai-style capitalism. But new processes of financial intermediation will take time to develop. Meanwhile, argues a respected Thai economist, 'the savings-investment nexus will remain frayed and this is yet another reason why growth will be stunted' (Siamwalla 2000: 14).

Conclusion

We have argued that the second-generation consensus does not account for key mechanisms of pre-1997 Thai economic growth. Contrary to second-generation expectations, the Thais constructed competitive markets through a particular type of clientelism and by using varying combinations of state, private, and public–private sector institutions to not only address a range of collective action problems, such as standards, over-capacity, and market development, but to also encourage and to support private-sector initiation of new activities. This pattern comes close to Robert Wade's conception of 'big followership' (1990).

We have also argued that this traditional combination of arrangements is ill-suited to confront the new challenges of globalisation. As Linda Weiss notes (Chapter 1 this volume), while states are not straitjacketed by globalisation, their ability to respond to the challenges of globalisation is conditioned by prevailing normative orientations and organisational arrangements. The norms and organisations that led to rapid economic growth are inadequate for the current challenges of human resource development, promotion of intersectoral linkages, technology diffusion, and development of advanced infrastructure. Nor do neoliberal prescriptions address these challenges. Effective participation in more globalised production structures probably demands more, rather than less, developed *local and sectoral* institutional strengths. Ironically, if globalisation imposes pressure for 'convergence', it is towards enhanced local capacities that go beyond the second-generation consensus.

The evidence to back this claim is, of course, far from conclusive. It is too early in the game to assess how Thailand fares with or without new institutional arrangements. But we can suggest several avenues of research through which to deepen our understanding of our claims. One is to test the second-generation argument by identifying an 'easy case', i.e., an industry that most approximates the second-generation approach. Thailand's hard disk drive industry – Thailand's largest single export product in the late 1990s – is useful in this regard. In this industry, second-generation prescriptions, such as open markets, stable property rights, transparent corporate governance, and relatively reliable public-sector management are clearly in evidence, but more ambitious institutional initiatives in training, supplier, and technical diffusion are absent. The result has been a highly successful, very high-technology export industry. But this technology is imported and unrelated to local producers. In fact, research on the hard drive industry identified *no* Thai suppliers or assemblers (McKendrick, Doner, and Haggard 2000: ch. 8).

A second avenue of research involves specifying, *ex ante*, the kinds of difficulties inherent in developing the technical skills, supplier base, advanced infrastructure, and technology diffusion mechanisms necessary for industries to improve their positions within global production chains.[14] As resolving these difficulties will inevitably require some combination of mediation, information provision, side payments, and, in some cases, coercion, a third avenue of research involves identifying the kinds of institutions possessing such capacities. We have pointed to the benefits of more cohesive public sector agencies, more systematic and transparent public–private engagement, and greater interaction within the private sector. But what would efficiency-promoting institutions look like in the Thai context? And what role is the Thai state currently capable of playing in the development and support of such institutions? Following in this vein, a final line of inquiry may involve exploring the lessons for 'weaker states' such as Thailand that can be drawn from an analysis of the institutional capacities of other 'stronger' and more successful East Asian NICs. An examination of, for example, Taiwan's system of industry associations and Singapore's and Taiwan's growth-oriented bureaucracies are likely to bear fruit in this regard.

Analysis of such institutional capacities must be informed by a final line of inquiry involving institutional origins and change. Institutional reforms to promote upgrading have been weakened in Thailand. Thailand's recent (January 2000) election, for example, raises important doubts as to the political basis for sustained and extensive reform (Nareerat 2000; Crispin 2001). An understanding of Thailand's (or any other country's) capacity to confront the challenges of globalisation will thus, in the last analysis, depend on a grasp of the interaction among external contexts, institutional legacies, and more immediate political pressures.

Notes

1. This concise definition of globalisation is drawn from Garrett (2000).
2. For one of many thoughtful analyses of the financial crisis, see Siamwalla (2000).
3. On embeddedness, see Evans (1995). On governed interdependence, see Weiss (1998). For an early discussion of the role of business, see Haggard (1994). On importance of networks, see Moon and Prasad (1998). On public–private sector interactions, see Maxfield and Schneider (1997). For an especially thoughtful comparative sectoral and cross-national analysis on Japan, Taiwan, and South Korea, see Noble (1998).
4. For an overall discussion, see Jansen (1997: 22). Thailand's trade ratios, especially its export/GDP ratio, have been high relative to countries of similar sizes and development strategies since the mid-1960s (Jansen 1997: 38). Foreign capital flows have been critical in compensating for Thailand's persistent savings/investment gap (which reached 5–6 per cent of GDP in the early 1990s) (Jansen 1997: 55–65). On the diversity of Thai export markets, see World Bank (2000b: 15).
5. This is the case for both the World Bank's *Institutions Matter* (Burki and Perry 1998: 16) and Aron's (2000) recent, extensive review of the evidence regarding the impact of institutions on growth.
6. Structural change, along with upgrading (discussed below), is usually referred to as the achievement of dynamic efficiency. On static *vs.* dynamic efficiency, see for example, Pack and Westphal (1986: 103); Westphal *et al.* (1990: 124); Chang (1994); Hall and Taylor (1994).
7. On rents as the result of purposive actions involving the search for new combinations that lead to innovations, see Kaplinsky (1999).
8. This definition of institutions largely follows the World Bank's *Institutions Matter* and North (Burki and Perry 1998: 11; North 1990). However, much of the NIE-influenced second-generation writings emphasises rules and norms while excluding organisations. Because it is difficult to separate rules, say about taxation, from the enforcement mechanisms of a tax bureaucracy, our definition includes organisations as well as rules. For a similar usage of the term 'institution' see Levi (1990).

9. For example, even if external linkages with private technology suppliers are of greater use than publicly provided technical support, public officials have an important role to play in tailoring incentives that encourage firms to avail themselves of private services, such as ISO consultants. See, e.g., Nadvi (1999).
10. This overview draws from Doner and Ramsay (1997; 2000).
11. For the importance of such linkages in rice and agri-business see Christensen (1993: 192–200). For sugar, see Ramsay (1987). For autos, see Doner (1991); and Nipon and Fuller (1997). The growth of the gems and jewelry industry is discussed in Nipon and Fuller (1997: 491–3). See Muscat (1994: 197) on public–private sector coordination in the growth of the tourist industry.
12. Unless noted, information on the textile/garment industry is drawn from Doner and Ramsay (1997; and 2000: 156– 67).
13. Siamwalla (2000: 13), from which, unless otherwise noted, this discussion of commercial banks is drawn.
14. An analytical framework for such a purpose is developed in Doner (2001).

7 Building institutional capacity for China's new economic opening

Tianbiao Zhu

Introduction: is China a neoliberal state in the making?

Few people would deny that China's economic miracle is consistent with its continuing integration into the world economy. According to a survey in *The Economist* (Ziegler 2000: 20), economic growth in China averaged nearly 8 per cent a year from 1979, and exports grew by 15 per cent and imports by 13 per cent a year between 1979 and 1999 – 'a faster rate of growth than Japan managed during its golden period in 1953–73'. China became the tenth biggest exporter in the world in the mid-1990s, and the amount of foreign direct investment (FDI) it has received in recent years is exceeded only by that of the United States.[1] Nicholas Lardy (1994: 110), a US expert on China's foreign economic relations, notes that in many respects, 'China is already somewhat more integrated into the world economy than Japan, Taiwan, or South Korea were at comparable stages of their economic development'. As China has just entered the World Trade Organisation (WTO), the Chinese economy is set to become even more integrated into the world market.[2]

Given China's two-decade experience of rapid growth and increasing openness, it seems a good test case for the main theme of this book: the role of domestic institutions in an era of intensifying economic interdependence. Thomas Moore (1996) argues that there is a 'global' logic behind China's economic opening. That is, the changing nature of economic activity in China is a function of its position in the international division of labour rather than a function of state intervention. A neoliberal view would further suggest that globalisation leads to a decline of state power and a triumph of market forces. Hence, a successful state in the present era of globalisation would be a neoliberal state, which plays a minimum role in the domestic economy. However, as Linda Weiss (1999b: 127) has argued, 'global and national are not necessarily competing principles of organisation, they can be – and indeed in many ways already are – complementary'. She points out that in many countries economic openness is in fact 'managed openness', and domestic purposes, priorities, and institutions continue to play an important role in shaping national economies in this era of globalisation.

This chapter investigates the economic role of the Chinese state by examining the transformation of state capacity under economic openness. State capacity here refers to the state's capacity to govern the domestic economy. First, I argue that the old form of state capacity based on the closed economy model has declined with increasing economic openness. However, both the central and local governments gained new capacities as China integrated more deeply into the world economy. In order to deal with greater openness concomitant with China's entry to the WTO, the state needs to further develop these new capacities. Second, while some of the new capacities are consistent with those of a neoliberal state, such as the capacity to engage in macroeconomic adjustment, others, such as the capacity for microeconomic intervention certainly go beyond this. Thus, the Chinese state continues to play a strong interventionist role as the era of globalisation proceeds. Finally, this chapter gives a particular focus to two new state capacities. The first is the capacity of the central and local governments to engage in selective industrial promotion, and the second is the capacity to reconfigure central–local relations in order to better manage national–global relations. The latter point is particularly worth noting. Instead of emphasising government–business relationships as happens in much existing literature on state transformation under globalisation, this chapter points out that central–local relations are key to China's ability to manage increasing economic openness.

The first part of the chapter discusses China's economic system and state power before 1979, the open policy after 1979, and how openness led to the decline of the old form of state power. The second part explains how the central and local governments are managing economic openness and developing new capacities to govern the Chinese economy. Finally, the conclusion discusses whether China is a developmental state in the making.

Economic openness and the decline of the old form of state power

Economy and state power before 1979

The Chinese economy before 1979 was a closed economy, built on central planning and public ownership. In such an economic model, economic resources are centralised through a particular process of state extraction. First, the government transfers as many resources as possible from the agricultural sector to the industrial sector. In order to do this, the government must extract all grain surplus from the peasants, and keep agricultural procurement prices low. Second, the central government directly collects revenue from industry, which consists entirely of state-owned enterprises (SOEs). The state's monopoly over industry means that there are no new firms entering the industry to compete for its profits, and it therefore ensures the state's revenue. The central planning system then redistributes the state's revenue to the industrial sector and to other sectors in order to promote further economic growth (Naughton 1992).

To complete this closed economy model, foreign investment is prohibited and foreign trade is highly centralised. The government (or more particularly, foreign trade corporations under the Ministry of Foreign Trade) monopolises the operation of foreign trade. The prices of imports and exports are determined according to a central plan, which shelters the domestic economy from international market forces. The price of imports, in particular, is set below the world price in order to promote the development of domestic heavy industry (which was the core of China's closed economy).

This model of the closed economy had three fundamental implications for the Chinese state's capacity to intervene in the economy before 1979. First, the model suggests that state capacity was based on the centralisation of economic resources. The discussion on resource transfer, revenue collection, and foreign-trade control shows that the country's economic resources were highly concentrated in the hands of the central government.

Second, the model suggests that Chinese state capacity was exercised through relatively simple techniques of political control rather than via sophisticated economic instruments. The state relied on administrative order, via the central bureaucracy and local authorities, to extract the grain surplus from peasants at a low and fixed state price. The central government occasionally sent work teams to help extract the surplus. Administrative order also enabled the state to collect revenue directly from the industrial sector. The central bureaucracy then allocated the revenue according to a plan. Consequently, since state intervention was normally exercised through administrative order and political coercion, an extensive taxation system and sophisticated fiscal and monetary instruments were not developed.

Finally, the closed economy model also had a fundamental implication for the strength of state capacity in pre-reform China. State capacity can be evaluated at the level of economic policymaking and at the level of implementation. At the level of policymaking, the closed economy model suggests that the state essentially had a free hand to make policy decisions, with no credible challenge from society. However, the situation was different at the level of policy implementation. Effective policy implementation requires a certain degree of state–society cooperation, but the closed economy model left very little material incentive for local cadres to enforce the government's policy. This is particularly true in the basic rural unit – the village – where cadres relied on the community for their wages.[3]

This does not mean however that state power was directly challenged by society, or that the model of a closed economy did not work before 1979. After all, the Chinese state did exercise strong political coercion over society. However, limited incentive to cooperate and passive resistance at the local level compromised the quality of the state's economic intervention. Thus, state capacity in pre-reform China was less than many have previously assumed.

Open policy and economic decentralisation

Deng Xiaoping and his followers began to change the closed economy model in 1979, initiating an 'open-door' policy (for simplicity, 'the open policy'). Under the policy, Special Economic Zones (SEZs) were established to attract foreign investment by giving foreign investors tax breaks and other benefits. National foreign trade purchasing and allocation plans were abolished. Foreign trade corporations were formed at the local level and were granted power to determine trade operations.[4] The reform improved China's foreign trade immediately – the total value of foreign trade grew by 13.3 per cent annually on average between 1978 and 1989 (Lardy 1992: 14). The reform also led to a rapid inflow of foreign investment. The number of projects for pledged investment in equity joint ventures increased from twenty-six projects worth a total of US$40 million in 1980 to 3,909 projects worth a total of US$3.13 billion in 1988 (Pearson 1991: 118).

Susan Shirk (1994, 1996) uses the concepts of 'gradualism, particularism and decentralisation' to describe the foreign sector reforms. Often, in the beginning, a small number of units were selected for reform 'experiments'. If successful, the reform was then extended to other units. For example, there were just four SEZs in the beginning of the reform, and gradually over more than a decade more areas were incorporated. Decentralisation of economic policymaking was a key feature in the foreign sector reform. During the reform process, local authorities were given more policy tools to deal with foreign investment (such as the ability to grant tax breaks). Because of this, many foreign investors feel that China is more open to FDI than Japan or Korea, where the central governments held tight control over the behaviour of local authorities (Rosen 1999: 234). Local government and locally managed firms were given strong incentives to promote growth through external linkages. For example, the first foreign exchange retention rules were introduced in 1979, which allowed locally managed firms to retain 40 per cent of the above 1978 level export earnings (Shirk 1996: 204).

It should be noted that the open policy was an integral part of a wider reform package that covered the whole economy.[5] The concept used to describe the reform in the foreign sector – gradualism, particularism, and decentralisation – can be used to characterise the wider economic reforms. A main feature of the domestic sector reform is best summarised by the title of Barry Naughton's book – *Growing Out of the Plan* (1996). He argues that the reform was a gradual process during which central planning coexisted with market forces. Only slowly did market forces become strong. Decentralisation also led the way in the reform of the domestic sector.

In the agricultural sector, the system of unified procurement was abolished, and the government began to sign contracts with peasants to purchase their agricultural goods. In the industrial sector, SOEs were allowed to sell above-plan output at negotiated prices directly to other economic agents and to plan their output accordingly. No unit has benefited more from economic decentralisation than local government. In 1980, the central government introduced the centre–local revenue sharing system, under which fixed large shares of financial revenues were given to local governments which were made responsible for their own budgeting. In the following years, as decentralisation deepened, local governments gradually gained some power over material allocation, investment, bank loans, and foreign trade (Chen 1991: 212–14). This increase in local government power also produced the rise of rural collective enterprises (discussed in detail later), which challenged SOE monopoly over the Chinese economy.

The decline of the old form of state capacity

The open policy and economic decentralisation gradually dismantled the closed economy model in China. First, it became harder for the state to transfer resources from the agricultural sector to the industrial sector at low prices. The reform raised agricultural procurement prices in several rounds (Oi 1989: 157), and therefore led to increased production costs in industry. Second, the development of township and village enterprises (TVEs) began to challenge the dominance of SOEs in the Chinese economy. While economic decentralisation provided an incentive for local governments to promote TVEs, the open policy created an extra source of growth for rural industry. By 1991, TVEs accounted for more than 26.6 per cent of China's industrial production, and about 25 per cent of total exports and joint ventures in China (Zweig 1995: 256–8). The share of state ownership in total industrial output fell from nearly 80 per cent in 1978 to 57 per cent in 1988 (SSB 1991: 396). Naughton (1992: 28) argues that the entry of TVEs and urban collectives into the domestic market broke the state monopoly over industry and drove down its profit rate.

The reduction in profitability of SOEs meant a reduction in total resources controlled by the state (before the reform, about 80 per cent of government revenues came from the state sector). Figure 7.1 shows that government revenue, expenditure, and investment all experienced a significant decline in the 1980s. According to Shaoguang Wang and Angang Hu (1994: 36–8), the fiscal situation of China's central government was in particularly bad shape. While its revenue as a percentage of GNP was 6.9 per cent in 1989 – a very low rate by international comparison – the ratio for expenditure decreased sharply from about 20 per cent in 1972 to about 7 per cent in 1989.

The dismantling of the closed economy model led to a serious decline in the old form of state capacity in China. As argued earlier, the old form of state capacity was based on the centralisation of economic resources. The reduction in resources available to the central government (mentioned earlier) clearly weakened capacity in this respect. The old form of state power was also based on the state's complete control

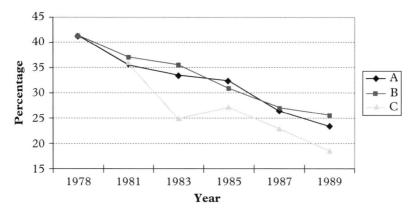

Figure 7.1 Government revenue, expenditure, and investment, 1978–89
Source: Based on data from Hussain and Stern (1991: 156)

over the foreign sector. However, control was largely undermined by the open policy, economic decentralisation, and the ensuing increase in local power.

The decline of state capacity was, in particular, reflected in the state's inability to deal with the new economic situation in the 1980s. Economic decentralisation and the fiscal decline of the central government led to a dramatic increase in investment towards the late 1980s. Between 1984 and 1989, the economy-wide investment ratio averaged around 34 per cent. Athar Hussain and Nicholas Stern (1991: 158) argue that this ratio is exceptionally high by international standards. The substantial increase in investment led to inflation. In 1988, the economy's real growth rate was 11.5 per cent but the inflation rate was 18.5 per cent. In cities, inflation was more than 21 per cent, and food prices rose by more than 25 per cent (Hussain and Stern 1991: 145–6). China was in danger of an economic crisis in 1988, and this triggered social unrest in 1989. However, given that the state lacked sophisticated fiscal and monetary instruments – a legacy of the closed economy – it did not have the capacity to deal with the new economic situation produced by reform in the 1980s. Without other options, the Chinese state again used its strong coercive power to put down unrest.

Thus, both diminishing economic resources and a lack of macroeconomic instruments meant that the old form of capacity faced serious decline under economic openness. However, the decline in the old form of state capacity did not mean that the state had to play a minimal role in China's opening economy. In fact, both the central and local governments developed new capacities to manage economic openness.

Economic openness and the rise of new state capacities

Managing economic openness at local level

As the old form of state power declined, new state capacities were developed and transformed under economic openness. The aim was to turn openness into opportunities for further economic growth. This section starts with the new localised capacity of the state in China.

Under the old economic system, economic resources were concentrated in the hands of the central government and heavy industry was the development priority. After 1979, the open policy and economic decentralisation gradually made the foreign sector, local government, and rural industry alternatives to SOEs and the central planning system as the source of economic growth. Rural industry became the most dynamic part of China's economic growth under the reform. Since 1978, the growth of its gross output value has averaged more than 20 per cent a year. In 1991, TVEs produced 26.6 per cent of China's total industrial output. In 1996, the figure rose to 44 per cent, and TVEs also contributed 26 per cent of China's GDP (Smyth 1998: 784). In the early 1990s, based on the impressive growth of TVEs, the gross value of industrial output in the southern Jiangsu area[6] exceeded that of China's largest industrial city, Shanghai, and this rural-based area became the largest industrial area in China (Xu 1993: 49).

This impressive development of rural industry is partly due to its connection to the international market. As noted earlier, TVEs already commanded about 25 per cent of China's total export earnings and joint ventures by 1991. Their share of total export earnings further increased to 36 per cent in 1996 (Smyth 1998: 784). David Zweig (1995: 254) argues that while rural industries in coastal areas are key contributors to China's remarkable economic growth, 'the areas of deepest foreign penetration are also the areas of highest growth'.

The development of rural industry is due also to the support of local governments. As noted before, economic decentralisation led to the centre–local revenue-sharing system, which enabled localities to keep a large proportion of their revenues. There are also so-called extra-budgetary revenues, which can be kept entirely by local governments. Since TVEs are the main contributors to both types of revenue, local governments naturally have a strong incentive to promote TVEs (Oi 1999).[7] Local governments particularly have a strong incentive to attract FDI and promote export production because under the open policy the state provides an export-oriented firm with subsidies and easy access to inputs and loans.

Many counties have established trade offices under local governments in order to promote exports. Many local governments also give targeted support to export-oriented TVEs by offering them lower taxes, easier access to cheap loans, raw materials at lower planned prices, foreign exchange, and technology (Zweig 1995: 259). Other strong methods of economic intervention include factory management control and investment and credit control. Jean Oi (1992 and 1999) uses the notion of 'local state corporatism' to describe the strong interventionist role of local governments. However, she notes that the key difference between local state corporatism and the former central planning system is that 'the local corporate state selectively targets certain enterprises for development. Subsidies and assistance are no longer given equally or to all. In this sense, China has switched to a strategy similar to the industrial policies of the East Asian NICs' (Oi 1999: 117–18).[8] As noted before, export-oriented TVEs are often targeted for special support.

Since the mid-1990s, local governments have encouraged TVEs to experiment with new forms of management to improve their efficiency and competitiveness. New management practices include leasing, shareholding, and the formation of large/medium enterprises and enterprise groups. Russell Smyth (1998) argues that the rise of large/medium enterprises and enterprise groups in rural areas is a government response to the increasing pressures of globalisation. China's bid for WTO membership means that it has to further reduce tariff barriers and open its domestic market. Large enterprise and enterprise groups can benefit from economies of scale and become more competitive in world markets. However, it is noted that the state continued to play a crucial role in the process of transition at a local level (Smyth 1998; Oi 1999). Extensive field research in Shangdong province shows that even with the adoption of the shareholding cooperative system, local government still maintains its control over management appointments, although it no longer commands a majority share (Vermeer in Smyth 1998: 798).

While the old form of state capacity hinged on the centralisation of economic resources, one new capacity of the state under economic openness is to be found in the hands of local government. This new capacity is reflected in the ability of local government to engage in local industrialisation and selective intervention. It is not hard to ascertain that the new capacity has been the result of China's open policy and economic decentralisation since the late 1970s.

Managing macroeconomy and central–local relations under economic openness

Strong local governments have brought both benefits and problems to the Chinese economy. While successful local industrialisation serves as the engine for China's continuing growth, a lack of central control and competition among local governments also led to the dramatic rise in investment and the concomitant sharp rise in inflation towards the end of the 1980s. Thus, facing the rise of local power and having lost much of its old capacity, the central government had to develop new policy instruments to maintain China's macroeconomic stability and to balance local power under economic openness.

Ironically, the first effort made by the central government between 1989 and 1991 was to reclaim the old form of state capacity through recentralisation of investment and financial powers. This move was, however, strongly resisted by the governor of Guangdong province, Ye Xuanping, and subsequently by other governors (Shirk 1993: 194–5).[9] The central government soon realised that after a decade of economic decentralisation, the price of recentralisation would be very high. In addition, some localities had accumulated large resources in ways that could not be easily confiscated by the central government (Montinola, Qian, and Weingast 1996: 69).

In early 1992, Deng Xiaoping made a trip to southern China and in particular to a number of SEZs. He openly praised the market economy and open policy. This finally put an end to the recentralisation programme. The Chinese economy boomed again, accomplishing double-digit growth from 1993 to 1995. However, the fundamental problem of the power imbalance between the central and local governments was still unsolved. Thus, as the economic growth rate rose, so did the inflation rate, which reached more than 20 per cent in 1994 (see Figure 7.2).

In 1991, Zhu Rongji was put in charge of economic reform. His first target for inflation control was China's banking system, in which all major banks were still owned by the state. Zhu took direct control of the central bank in 1993, and initiated banking reform, recalling much irregular credit, tightening control over lending, and enhancing central supervision over local branches. In 1995, bank laws were implemented

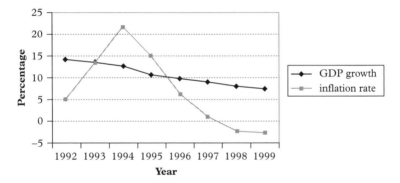

Figure 7.2 Economic growth and inflation, 1992–99
Source: Based on data from SSB (2000: 55, 289)

to strengthen the centralised control of state banks over their branches and to increase the autonomy of local branches from local governments. Zhu also started fiscal reforms in 1994. New taxes were introduced with relatively low, uniform rates applying to all economic actors. The centre–local revenue sharing system was abolished. New tax revenue was divided into central, local, and shared revenue, based on agreement between the central and local governments, which was more favourable than before to the centre in financial terms.

By the late 1990s, the reform had proved successful. As Figure 7.2 shows, inflation was brought under control without high costs to the growth rate. This result should be considered particularly successful when compared with the general economic crisis situation in other parts of East Asia, caused by the Asian financial crisis in 1997. More importantly, Zhu's reform succeeded without returning the Chinese economy and state to the old closed and centralised form. There are three reasons for this.

First, reforms in the foreign sector continued. A dual exchange rate system existed before 1994 in China – there was an official exchange rate and there was also a swap market rate. In 1994 the government devalued Chinese currency and united the foreign exchange rate to the swap market rate. Before 1994 China's foreign trade corporations had to obtain a foreign exchange certificate for each trade transaction in order to purchase foreign exchange. In 1994 the government abolished this requirement. A large trade surplus and capital inflow, as a result of the foreign-sector reforms, helped the banking reform by forcing the central bank to buy up foreign exchange reserves and therefore leaving

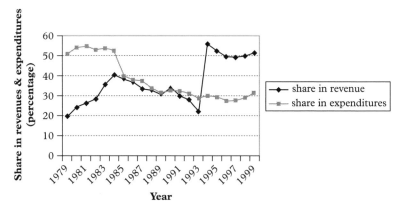

Figure 7.3 Central government's share of total revenue and expenditure
Source: Based on data from SSB (2000: 267–8)

little room for it to create money through lending (Naughton 1999: 212). Second, Zhu made macroeconomic adjustments by implementing a conservative monetary policy via the banking system – very different from the old form of state control over the economy that operated via direct control over investment through the central planning system.

Finally, the fiscal reforms increased the share of the central government's revenue as Figure 7.3 shows, but the state did not return to the old form of economic control. Figure 7.3 also shows that the reforms kept the central government's share of expenditure low; it remains at the lowest level since 1979. The fiscal reforms also gave a number of concessions to local governments. For example, the amount of each province's revenue after 1993 was guaranteed at no less than that of 1993, and the central government also promised to compensate provinces for their revenue losses. The reforms did not touch the extra-budgetary funds of local governments. Furthermore, it is argued that the reforms really introduced a fiscal federal system into the Chinese economy (Montinola, Qian, and Weingast 1996; Bahl 1998), which formalised the central–local financial arrangement, balanced the economic powers of the central and local governments, and legitimised the strong role of local government in the Chinese economy.[10]

Since 1979, the Chinese state, or more particularly, the central government, has struggled to adapt to the new economic situation under openness. The central government initially lost its old form of capacity,

153

and then failed to regain it in the context of China's more open economy. From this process of losing centralised control over economic resources, the central government developed a new capacity to govern the economy by reconfiguring its relationship with local government. This new capacity is reflected in the development of new monetary and fiscal instruments, which emerged under Zhu's reform.

However, behind the new policy instruments is the government's commitment to economic reform and openness (e.g., Deng's 1992 trip), and the decade-long building of a pro-reform coalition (e.g., Ye and others' resistance to the recentralisation programme). It should be noted that China's cadre control system also plays a role. Throughout the reform, cadre management remained centralised and the top party and government organisations continued to control vital aspects of personnel allocations (Lieberthal and Oksenberg 1988: 348; Huang 1996: 119). Thus, while local reformers were able to resist the recentralisation effort made by party conservatives at the centre, the party and government hierarchy were strong enough to carry through the monetary and fiscal reforms initiated by reformers at the centre. Out of this institutional context the new policy instruments emerged, and so did the new state capacity.

Managing economic openness at the centre

The integration of the Chinese economy into the world market increased in the 1990s. Disbursed FDI averaged US$2 billion a year in the 1980s, rising to US$20 billion in the 1990s (*The Economist* 19 June 1999: 69–70). After an economic downturn in 1998 and 1999 due to the impact of the Asian financial crisis, economic growth, exports, and FDI picked up again in 2000. According to reports in *Far Eastern Economic Review* ('Economic Monitor' 19 July and 29 March 2001), GDP grew by 8 per cent in 2000 and is expected to be 7.5 per cent in 2001. Exports grew by 27.8 per cent in 2000, and FDI is expected to have 25 per cent growth in 2001. As the integration of the Chinese economy into the world market deepened, the central government searched for new means to govern the economy. While the policy instruments of macroeconomic adjustment, discussed in the previous section, may be close to what a neoliberal state normally holds, the effort of the Chinese state has certainly gone beyond that.

Up to the early 1990s, China's trade policy was similar to that of the Northeast Asian countries in their early development stage, i.e., promoting exports with subsidies while limiting imports with high tariffs.

Since the early 1990s, many protection measures have been gradually removed or reduced due to mounting international pressure and China's efforts to enter the WTO. Direct subsidies for exports were abolished in 1994. The average tariff rate was reduced from 43 per cent to about 17 per cent, with a promise of further reductions. Despite the changes, significant protection measures remain. There are still indirect subsidies for exports, such as low cost energy and inputs, preferential bank loans, and tax incentives (McKibbin and Tang 1998: 6). The real tariff rate is still regarded by foreign exporters to be close to 40 per cent, given that value added tax is always levied on imports but domestic products are normally exempted from the tax by local governments (Breslin 1999: 1188).

China's financial reform also took place gradually. As discussed before, in 1994 the government united foreign exchange rates and abolished foreign exchange certificates. In 1996, currency convertibility was introduced under the current account to cover payments for foreign trade and services. However, China's financial market is still under considerable state protection. The state continues to control all major banks, and there is still a lack of currency convertibility under capital account. The lack of full currency convertibility is considered to be one of the main factors shielding China from the Asian financial crisis (Lardy 1999: 91).

While some old protection measures remain, the central government also tries to find new means to manage economic openness, since Chinese leaders have realised that entry to the WTO and increased globalisation will further limit the old protection measures. China has committed to a large tariff reduction for agricultural and industrial products after its WTO accession. China also promises to allow foreign banks to operate in China, taking deposits from Chinese companies two years after its WTO accession and from Chinese individuals five years after. This, together with other WTO-related measures, will accelerate China's movement towards full currency convertibility. Clearly, as the old protection measures are gradually removed, the Chinese economy has to become more competitive. A big problem for China's banking and financial reforms was the large number of bad loans made by uncompetitive SOEs – since the mid-1990s about half of SOEs have made losses. Thus, how to make SOEs become more competitive is important for not only the overall competitiveness of the Chinese economy but also the competitiveness of China's banks in their up-coming competition with foreign banks.

The key strategy to deal with SOEs since the mid-1990s has been the so-called 'grasping the large and letting go of the small'. The strategy aims to push small SOEs to embrace market discipline via different ownership experiments, including private ownership. It also aims to reorganise large SOEs into even larger ones and enterprise groups in order to increase their economies of scale and therefore to enhance their international competitiveness. The central government targeted 1,000 SOEs to form the core of China's new SOE system and selected 512 enterprises to form the basis of enterprise groups. At the same time, the government has been reorganising the banking system to support those large SOEs and enterprise groups. Banking and enterprise cooperation agreements were signed between a major bank and 279 such enterprises in 1996 (Smyth 2000: 722). In March 2001, three of the largest steel groups in China – Baoshan Steel, Capital Steel, and Wuhan Steel – formed a strategic alliance.

The strategy of 'grasping the large and letting go of the small' is clearly neither a strategy of the free market nor a strategy of total state control, since on the one hand the market allowed the takeover of a large number of small SOEs, and on the other the state continued to control a small number of large SOEs. The strategy is also that of 'picking winners'. SOE, in general, has been in bad shape – its share of total industrial output has declined sharply, about half of SOEs are making losses, and many of them are tied to bad loan problems. However, large SOEs are a different story.

Although small in number, large SOEs are still important actors in China's industrial economy. Between 1994 and 1998, sales by large SOEs on average comprised more than 40 per cent of the country's total industrial sales. SOEs accounted for more than 50 per cent of total industrial assets and more than 60 per cent of total industrial profits (Lan and Cao 2000: 49). Figure 7.4 shows the profit rate of large and medium enterprises (LMEs). Of these enterprises, about 90 per cent are SOEs (Smyth 2000: 722). This LME profit rate has been consistently better than that of SOEs as a whole, and also better than that of collectively owned enterprises (COEs) before 1996. Large SOEs also dominate the upstream of production processes, which basically consists of petrochemical and heavy industries (Nolan and Wang 1999). Thus, by controlling and supporting large SOEs and enterprise groups, the state can both guide domestic economic development and enhance international competitiveness of the key industries.

While the state is reorganising SOEs, it is also beginning to reorganise the government. In 1993, for the first time in the history of the People's Republic of China, open and competitive recruitment examinations

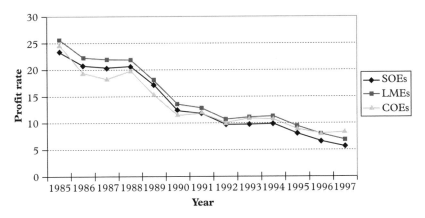

Figure 7.4 Profit rates of SOEs, LMEs, and COEs
Source: Based on data from Smyth (2000: 726)

were introduced as a crucial part of China's civil service system. In 1998, the party adopted Zhu Rongji's proposal of reducing the size of the central government, including abolishing industrial ministries and re-placing them with an economic planning and trade commission, which was regarded as an attempt to create an economic 'superministry' like the Ministry of International Trade and Industry (MITI) in Japan (Unger and Chan 1995: 42).

In summary, the promotion of large SOEs, the reorganisation of the banking system around those SOEs, and the creation of an economic superministry, formed a new system of Chinese state intervention for the twenty-first century. It gave rise to new policy instruments for the central government to use to govern the economy under an intensive trend of globalisation. Continuing commitment of the Chinese leaders to economic openness in combination with strong state intervention, state reorganisation, and the rise of new policy instruments combined to create a new capacity for the central government to manage the new challenges of globalisation.

Conclusion: is China a developmental state in the making?

The Chinese state continues to play a strong interventionist role in the process of globalisation. As the open policy and economic decentrali-sation dismantled the model of the closed economy in the 1980s, the old form of state capacity declined sharply. However, both the central and local governments in China gained new capacities to govern the domestic economy under economic openness. Those capacities were created by the reform process, which gave rise to state and industrial reorganisation and new policy instruments.

Chinese state capacity after 1979 was qualitatively different from that which existed previously. As argued early in this chapter, state power prior to 1979 was not as strong as commonly believed, given the relative weakness of the central government in terms of policy implementation despite its strength at the policymaking level. State capacity after 1979 seems to have been based on a good balance between policymaking and policy implementation. Reform allowed local governments to share a part of the policymaking process with the central government, while the latter developed a new capacity to regulate the central–local relationship. This means that the state continues to have a national-level economic strategy, while the policymaking process has to take into account community-wide interests. This makes policy implementation relatively easy.

By targeting selective sectors and enterprises, state capacity after 1979 is also qualitatively different from that of a neo-liberal state. State practice at the local and central levels in China resembles that of developmental states in Northeast Asia. In particular, China is becoming increasingly similar to Taiwan in its early developmental stage. In the 1960s and 1970s, Taiwan's upstream production process was also dominated by large SOEs, while export-oriented private firms were located in the downstream process. The government in Taiwan also controlled all major banks and gave strong support to the upstream SOEs. In terms of state–society relations, China is also more like Taiwan in its early days of development than it is like other developmental states in Northeast Asia. In early Taiwan, private business tended to be small in size and did not have much political power to influence the policymaking process. In China, despite the two-decade development of private business, its share in China's economy is still not large,[11] and the number of business elites remains small (Pearson 1997: 10–18).

There are of course differences between China and other developmental states in Northeast Asia. First, while central–local relations are not normally a major issue in those countries, they are key to the process of state transformation in China and its future economic development. Central–local relations determine whether state strength can combine the local and central levels in China to promote further economic growth. Regulating central–local relations is an on-going process. The 1994 fiscal settlement was just the beginning. Without an overall political settlement which specifies each party's rights and responsibilities, the central and local governments run the risk of turning against each other, which will surely undermine China's development. In addition, the scale of corruption in China is commonly believed to be larger than that of Northeast Asian countries in their early developmental stage. Controlling corruption is therefore a key issue for the success of state and economic transformation in China. Finally, the international economy is more open now than it was forty years ago, and this requires the Chinese state to become more flexible and adaptable to the changing international economic situation. Thus, state capacity must be further developed. Despite the arguments of this chapter, whether the Chinese state is up to the job remains to be seen.

Notes

I would like to thank Linda Weiss and Gregory Noble for their thoughtful comments. I am also grateful to Jane Ford and Jessica Ellis for their efforts in editing the paper.

1. It should be noted that Hong Kong is the biggest source of FDI for China, and it is suggested that much of its investment is, in fact, Chinese cash reinvested through Hong Kong (*The Economist* 25 September 1999: 71–3).
2. WTO agreements are generally viewed as being tougher on protectionism than previous world trade agreements. The new investment code requires a host country to treat foreign investors the same as it treats domestic entities. The new agreements also prohibit non-tariff barriers and new restrictions on subsidies.
3. Specific discussion on how local cadres encouraged the passive resistance to government policy can be found in Shue (1988), Oi (1989), and Liu (1992).
4. For a detailed discussion on reform in the foreign sector, see Li (1996).
5. Although foreign trade and investment played a key role in China's economic success, the size of China clearly prevents it from becoming another South Korea, and it tends to depend on foreign trade for economic growth. It is estimated that FDI has never exceeded 5 per cent of China's GDP (*The Economist* 19 June 1999: 69–70), and China's trade ratio is only about 13 per cent, which is a little more than that of India and a little less than that of the United States (Findlay and Watson 1997: 110). This means that reform programmes other than the open policy are also important in order for us to understand China's economic success.
6. The southern area of Jiangsu province consists of a few counties (such as Wuxi and Wujin) and county-level cities (such as Changshu and Zhangjiagang).

7. Local cadres also have strong private incentives to promote the development of rural industry. Profits remitted from TVEs and the shared portion of budget revenues comprise a significant proportion of the salaries of township and village cadres (Byrd and Gelb 1990: 105). Furthermore, according to Gore (2000b: 135–6), the reform also makes economic achievement a major criterion for the career advancement of local cadres in the bureaucratic hierarchy.

8. It should be noted that not every local government in China has a similar degree of economic intervention. Scholars have produced different models of local government in relation to intervention (Blecher 1991; Liu 1992; Shue and Blecher 1999). In an entrepreneurial-state model, local government directly engages in business activity and controls day-to-day business decisions of TVEs. In a developmental-state model, local government intervention is much less explicit and mainly takes the form of selective support. There is also a 'Wenzhou' model, in which private business flourishes and local government plays only a minor role, such as in building infrastructure. However, the existing literature tends to suggest that the developmental model is most successful in terms of promoting local industrialisation.

9. Ye was later transferred from his provincial post to a central-level post in 1991, but it was reported that he only agreed to leave on condition that the province (effectively Ye himself) could freely choose his successor. In any case, the successor, Zhu Senlin, continued Ye's policy (Cheung 1994: 225).

10. It should be noted that although the centre's share of total budgetary revenues increased sharply in 1994 (as Figure 7.3 shows), its share of disposable revenues over 1994–98 was still lower than the 1992 and 1993 levels due to the tax refunds from the central government to local governments based on the concessions made by the former during the tax reform (Lee 2000). However, the key point here is that the central government has finally begun to institutionalise its new relations with local governments in the 1990s. The move itself shows that the central government has developed a new capacity to govern the central–local relations under economic openness.

11. According to the most optimistic estimation (*The Economist* 19 June 1999: 69–70), the private share of the whole economy in 2000 is 53 per cent.

8   New regimes, new capacities: the politics of telecommunications nationalisation and liberalisation

David Levi-Faur

One of the most important and influential ideas of globalisation is that the capacity of states to govern is constrained and diminished by increased liberalisation and competitive markets. This chapter examines the validity of this claim through a comparative historical analysis of the role of the state in the telecommunications industry since the invention of the telephone. Telecommunications has been an extreme case of *étatisation* as it has experienced nationalisation almost all over the world. Starting in Europe as early as 1880, nationalisation spread across the globe, leaving the provision of telecommunications under private ownership in only a handful of countries, most notably the United States.[1] Indeed, among the infrastructures of the modern world economy only the delivery of post was more *étatist* than telecommunications. This has changed drastically, however, since the 1980s, when the telecommunications industry experienced radical degrees of liberalisation, Europeanisation, and globalisation. Increasingly telecommunications equipment is traded on competitive rather than protectionist rules. Foreign direct investment in the sector is booming and global alliances have proliferated. Single national networks have been replaced by multiple and competing networks which may operate within traditional technologies (wire telephony) or new and competing technologies (e.g., internet telephony, mobile telephony, and cable telephony). These striking changes are especially evident in the Europeanisation of the telecommunications sector (Schneider *et al.* 1994; Schmidt 1997; Thatcher 1999; Levi-Faur 1999a). They are also manifested in a series of international agreements, such as the WTO agreement on the liberalisation of government procurement (1994), the Information Technology Agreement (1996), the WTO agreement on trade in basic telephony (1997), and the Mutual Recognition Agreements on the testing and certification of telecommunications equipment (1997) (Levi-Faur 1999b).

The long period since the invention of the telephone is divided roughly into two distinct eras, the era of telecommunications nationalisation (1880s–1960s) and the era of telecommunications liberalisation (1980s–).[2] Each of these two eras gave rise to a remarkable political paradox: the paradox of nationalisation and the paradox of liberalisation respectively. These paradoxes are especially visible in the dynamics of nationalisation and liberalisation in Europe and Latin America. While Latin American and southern European countries were very slow to nationalise, western and northern European countries were quick to do so. These findings run counter to the neoliberal assertions about the negative relations between government ownership and higher level of economic development, so we call this the paradox of nationalisation. Yet in the era of liberalisation Latin American countries have been very quick to privatise, while European (including the southern European) countries have been much slower. Moreover, liberalisation in Europe has been manifested primarily in the creation of regulatory institutions for the promotion of competition while in Latin America the emphasis has been on privatisation rather than on the promotion of competition.[3] Indeed, more regulation in Europe has resulted in more competitive markets while less regulation in Latin America seems to have resulted in less competitive markets. We call this puzzling outcome the paradox of liberalisation.[4] This chapter suggests that while these two paradoxes have unique aspects they are best explained by the notions of state capacities and strength of the state.

In a radical break from conventional wisdom, it is argued here that nowadays liberalisation represents the most ambitious effort ever to use telecommunications as a tool for economic development. For almost a century, governments, business, and telecom users failed to understand the critical economic and social importance of telephony, and subjected the development of their nationalised telephone network to the constraints of the state budget. We know better now, and this knowledge serves as one of the most important rationales for liberalisation. Still, this new knowledge is not a sufficient factor for liberalisation. A critical component is the strength of the state and its capacities as it is that strength that allows the creation of new capacities and it is these that allow competition to work. This proposition disputes the globalist argument about the demise of the nation-state in the field of telecommunications – one of their most important cases.[5] The telecommunications sector commonly serves, it is argued, as '[a] classic, extreme example of one process by which authority has shifted massively away from the governments of states to the corporate management of firms'. Furthermore, 'The result of this shift has been to narrow the options open to supposedly sovereign states, and to extend the opportunities – and risk – of those enterprises engaged in the supply of services and the hardware by which the services are offered on the market' (Strange 1996: 100).[6] As competition increases and markets widen, telecommunications may become a paradigmatic case for political and economic change. This makes it a critical case in the debate about the relations between globalisation and state capacity for economic governance.

The following question is therefore raised here: what can we learn about the role of the state in the telecommunications sector from the conflicting approaches to nationalisation and liberalisation across Europe and Latin America? The research design that supports the discussion of this question is broad in two senses. First, it compares two different political periods, namely the era of nationalisation (1880s–1960s) and the era of liberalisation (1980s–). Second, it maximises the range of countries studied by including a variety of states: old and new, economically developed and underdeveloped, liberal and *étatist*. By doing so it follows the logic that variations in a data-set have to be maximised in order to boost the validity of its argument.[7] Variations are maximised within each era and between eras.

The current process of liberalisation includes many components. Particularly important are the policies of privatisation, deregulation, and regulation-for-competition (Levi-Faur 1998). The relative mix of privatisation and regulatory reform and their sequencing have strong implications for the success of the policy. Unfortunately, the globalist literature places too much emphasis on the policies of privatisation and far too little on the content of regulatory reform. Moreover, regulatory reforms are identified mostly with deregulation rather than reregulation.[8] In fact, the reregulation aspects rather than the deregulation aspects of the reforms tell most about the strength of the state and are the most critical aspects for the success of liberalisation. Indeed, it is the strength of the state rather than its retreat that allows effective liberalisation. This last suggestion turns the tables on the neoliberal argument that liberalisation, especially competition in telecommunications, is a product of state retreat.

163

Regional and national trajectories of nationalisation

States all over the world, with only few exceptions, nationalised the provision of their countries' telecommunications services. Cross-national and regional variations are, however, significant. These variations are observable in regard to the timing, the origin, and the scope of nationalisation, as well as the degree to which it was directed against foreign domination. On the basis of these variations, five major trajectories of nationalisation may be identified: *étatist*, timid *étatist*, colonial, communist, and anti-imperialist. While most European countries have followed the trajectories of *étatism* and timid *étatism*, the Latin American and the southern European countries fall into the anti-imperialist trajectory.[9]

The *étatist* trajectory includes countries that nationalised their entire telephone network before World War I and created a highly stable and uncontested *étatist* order for the governance of telephony. In this trajectory, which was highly influential as to the future governance of telephony all over the world, the government became the owner, the regulator, the policymaker, and the service provider of telecommunications services. The *étatist* trajectory includes mostly European countries and their extension to the New World: Germany (nationalisation since 1878), France (1889), Australia (1887), New Zealand (1880), Japan (1889), Luxembourg (1889), Switzerland (1880), Austria (1895), Belgium (1896), and Britain (1912).

The trajectory of timid *étatism* includes all the countries that entered early (before World War I) into the provision of long-distance telephony services but maintained a considerably fragmented structure, compromising private, municipal, regional, and provincial forms of supply in the local networks during the postwar period. The timid trajectory covers a relatively small number of countries from northern Europe, such as Denmark, where a telecommunications act passed by the Danish Parliament in 1897 gave the state a monopoly over the provision of telephony but allowed concessions to private companies. While the Danish government kept private ownership intact, it acted to promote consolidation and reorganisation on a regional basis. The number of telephone providers was first reduced from fifty-seven companies to eleven by the turn of the twentieth century and to four by 1953. Other countries that followed similar policies in that period, and therefore are included in this trajectory, are the Netherlands, Finland, and Norway.

The third trajectory of nationalisation is the anti-imperialist. This trajectory includes all countries that nationalised their telecommunications networks in the postwar period. In all cases they nationalised their telecommunications companies from 'foreign' owners as a declaration of economic nationalism and economic and technological independence. Nationalisation in this trajectory had a mixture of a populist and a nationalist hue. For example, in Argentina Perón nationalised telegraph and telephone in 1946. In his words, they constituted 'the nervous system of the nation'. For him, foreign control of the system was an anachronism 'incompatible with sentiments of national sovereignty and the level of domestic development' (Petrazzini 1995: 56). All the Latin American countries (except Uruguay, where nationalisation occurred in 1915) and many of the southern European countries, notably Spain (1945), Portugal (1969), and Greece (1945), belong to this trajectory. Figure 8.1 presents the cumulative number of nationalisation occurrences for the two groups of countries. While the take-off stage of the process of diffusion started as early as the 1880 for the thirteen northern

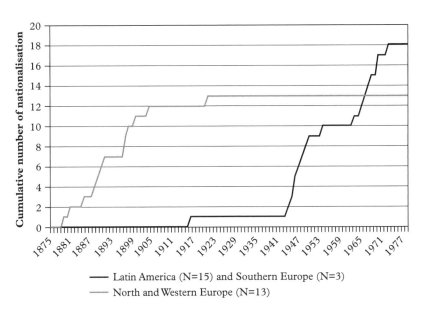

Latin America (N=15) and Southern Europe (N=3)
North and Western Europe (N=13)

Figure 8.1 The diffusion of nationalisation
Source: The author's regulatory database. Based on various accounts of a country's economic developments and online histories by a country's incumbents and by government agencies (Bennett 1895; Holcombe 1911; Noam 1992).

and western European countries that were studied here, it started as late as 1943 for Latin America and southern Europe.

What explains the late nationalisation in Latin America and southern Europe? How was it that those states, wherein telephony spread so poorly and slowly, followed for so long a liberal regime of private foreign ownership, when highly developed capitalist countries in western and northern Europe nationalised the sector so early and so thoroughly? The next section of the chapter shows that the major cause, which will also help us to shed light on the paradox of liberalisation, is the variation in state capacities and in the strength of the state.

Resolving the paradox of nationalisation

The variations in the timing of nationalisation between western and northern Europe on the one hand and Latin America and southern Europe on the other are not unique to telecommunications but represent a more general trend across sectors and policy arenas. Late nationalisation in Latin America and southern Europe is evident in other sectors as well: in water and in electricity, in broadcasting and in the provision of welfare services. Thus, unlike in Europe, telecommunications nationalisation in these countries is not a distinct sectoral process but a reflection of national conditions. This observation leads us to suggest that the origins of telecommunications nationalisation are not to be found only in the sector's special characteristics and particular pattern of interest intermediation. They also lie in the broader political characteristics of the two groups of countries, namely late nationalisation reflects the belated process of state building in Latin America and southern Europe. Accordingly, early nationalisation reflects a more successful process of state building in western and northern Europe. The relations between nationalisation and state strength are however not causal. Nationalisation does not necessarily enhance the strength of the state. In fact, when it finally reached Latin America and southern Europe it created such pressures on the budget and administrative capacities of the state that it might even be argued that the state was weakened in those countries after nationalisation.

Could it be that nationalisation represents an attempt to solve efficiency problems? Indeed, this is how nationalisation is often portrayed: a response by the state to the problem of natural monopoly on the one hand and networks integration on the other.[10] This functionalist interpretation makes sense, but only to a certain extent. If worldwide nationalisation was primarily motivated by a problem-solving logic, it is reasonable to suggest that the slow spread of telephony in Latin America and southern Europe under private ownership made their telecom industries better candidates for nationalisation than in western and northern Europe. Yet, we know that the opposite happened. Thus, the fact that the telephone was not nationalised in these areas points to the limits of the problem-solving approach in policy analysis. Alternatively, nationalisation may be understood as an exercise by European politicians, and later by Latin American politicians, to express their ability to act for their own preferences in respect of business (domestic and foreign). Their purpose was to solve economic problems (natural monopoly rents and incentives and network integration) on the one hand, and to tackle problems of social support (legitimacy) on the other. These two goals of state action are intimately linked to the notions of strong and weak states and may explain many of the variations in the timing of nationalisation in the two groups of countries. However, before doing that, we should first clarify the concept of state strength and its relation to the notions of autonomy and social support. In doing so we rely on Eric Nordlinger's studies of state autonomy and strength of the state (Nordlinger 1981, 1987). According to Nordlinger, states vary according to their ranking on two variables: autonomy and support: 'Strong states are those that enjoy high autonomy and support. They are doubly strong in that they regularly act on their preferences and have societal support in doing so . . . [Weak states] strive to act autonomously despite divergent societal preferences, but failing to do so, they rank low in both autonomy and support' (Nordlinger 1987: 369).

Variations in the autonomy of the state between these two groups of countries serve as our point of departure. A positive decision to nationalise the telecommunications industry requires not only political entrepreneurship, skills that were probably available in Latin America and southern Europe, but also a supportive institutional framework. Such a framework is supplied by strong states that enjoy penetrative policy capacities. These strong states are generally to be found in Europe and their origins are usually related to their capacity to mobilise resources to compete militarily through the development of an extractive state apparatus (Tilly 1975). State formation in Latin America was characterised by comparatively low levels of warfare and by a long period of Spanish and Portuguese patrimonial rule, which was hostile to the creation of *corps intermediaires*. Both factors led to the creation of relatively weak states in Latin America (cf. Anglade and Fortin 1985: 287).

In this regard the Latin American state is similar to the Greek, Spanish and Portuguese states. Nationalisation of telecommunications or of any industry in this weak institutional context required more than the creativity of an individual or even of a committed group. State ownership of the telecommunications industry required policy capacities that were barely at the disposal of Latin American and southern European states at that time. It required a legal framework, financial resources, and technological and managerial capacities, whose absence impeded telecommunications nationalisation. The high costs of nationalisation, due to these difficulties, were not balanced by its benefits in terms of social support. Not that it was impossible to build a coalition in favour of nationalisation or that there was any significant social opposition to such a move. On the contrary, it was possible to carry out this policy and to design a telephone regime that would reward its entrepreneurs with social support. However, the oligarchic regimes in Latin America and southern Europe were not interested in the maximisation of social support and regime legitimacy. Telecommunications nationalisation had to wait until populist politicians such as Vargas in Brazil and Peron in Argentina found it politically beneficial and useful to enhance their legitimacy.

The demand for legitimate political action is greater in societies where social participation is on the rise or where there are changes in social orientations. European state elites in the late nineteenth century and the first decades of the twentieth faced popular demands and pressures for democratic change. These pressures challenged the legitimacy of the state in the sense that they created a new agenda and new criteria for good governance. Specifically, they made economic development and the economic welfare of the population a political matter, hence a legitimate sphere for state action. Evidence of these developments in Europe is widespread. Probably the most notable evidence, but not most widely studied, concerns the *étatisation* of certain social services that later became the basis of the welfare state. While there were significant variations in the timing of these developments within Europe, the widest were between northern and western Europe and Latin America and southern Europe. Political pressures from labour and other groups existed in both regions.[11] While it is difficult to compare the weight of social pressures in these two groups of countries, the way these pressures were accommodated seems to have differed. Western and northern Europe experienced the institutionalisation of a highly competitive party system, a process that occurred only marginally in Latin America and southern Europe. These differences made the state in the latter regions less responsive to social demands because it lacked the means to hear them and to direct them towards constructive political projects.

Trajectories of telecommunications liberalisation

Telecommunications liberalisation reflects a radical change as to what policymakers, professionals, and lay persons perceive as a desirable and efficient governance regime. In contrast to the recent past, private provision of telecommunications is now widely accepted. To some extent it is part of a more general trend of 'hegemony breakdown' (Kalyvas 1994: 316) and 'paradigmatic change' (Hall 1989) that exerts an effect well beyond telecommunications. Yet it has peculiar sectoral characteristics, something that is often understood to reflect policy learning. The argument that much of the change reflects 'learning' is plausible especially since it downplays the origin of liberalisation as an expression of right-wing ideology in highly divided countries (such as Thatcher's Britain and Pinochet's Chile). Instead, liberalisation is embraced and legitimised as a pragmatic step and a 'rational' policy option. It is nowadays advocated by political leaders of the left as well as the right, by engineers as well as economists, in highly economically developed countries as well as in less-developed ones. Indeed, the train of telecommunications liberalisation seems to move up the hills and down the dales at varying speeds – but, in general, with sweeping power. Some evidence of this sweeping power is presented in Figure 8.2, showing the diffusion of privatisation and regulatory authorities around the world. Before the early 1980s the number of these institutions was marginal but after the establishment of Oftel (the British telecommunications regulator) in 1984 they became widespread all over the world. In fact their spread was faster than that of privatisation, the most celebrated component of the liberalisation programme.

As in the case of nationalisation, different trajectories of liberalisation may be distinguished among the world's countries. Three trajectories that have originated since the early 1980s are especially important for our analysis. These are the deregulatory (ideologically driven) trajectory, the privatisation-oriented trajectory, and the market-enforcing trajectory. These distinctions are based on the timing and scope of privatisation and liberalisation, as well as the extent to which they also involved regulatory reform. All three trajectories are part of the liberalisation

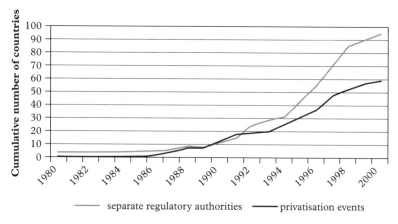

——— separate regulatory authorities   ———— privatisation events

Figure 8.2 The diffusion of liberalisation
Source: The author's regulatory database. Books by Noam (1992;
1998), Petrazzini (1995), Molano (1997) and Manzetti (1999) and
paper by Wellenius (2000). In addition, interviews and e-mail
exchanges with regulatory authorities and ministries were used
such as EU regulatory developments (http://www.ispo.cec.be),
the ITU regulatory database (www.itu.int/ITU-D-TREG/),
OECD (www.oecd.org/subject/regreform/) and World
Bank Papers on Regulatory Reforms
(http://econ.worldbank.org/topic.php?topic = 14).

process, and demonstrate the sweeping nature of change in the way
in which states govern the utilities' sectors in general and telecoms in
particular. Yet, as in the case of nationalisation, the commonalties are
accompanied by considerable variation, which reveals much about the
new role of the state in the economy.

The deregulatory trajectory includes all countries that privatised or
restructured their operators in the first half of the 1980s and made a
sustained effort to eliminate regulatory constraints on the supply of services by business actors. This trajectory carries a particular ideological
(neoliberal) shade, which may be illustrated best by the attitudes of
policymakers to the regulatory design of the regime and especially the
sector's regulatory authority. Major examples in this trajectory of liberalisation are the American divestiture of AT&T (see Tilton, Chapter 9,
this volume), the British privatisation of British Telecom in 1984, as well
as the privatisation of Chile's telecom operators since the end of 1970s.
In all three cases the policy process started considerably earlier than in

other countries, and justifications for privatisation (and, in the American case, divestiture) were legitimised on ideological grounds, namely the preference for private ownership, increased competition, or self-regulated markets.

The privatisation-oriented trajectory covers all countries that directed their efforts to the comprehensive transfer of ownership from public and private hands but turned only limited attention (or effort) to redesigning the regulatory framework governing the supply of services. In short, these countries substituted public monopoly with private monopoly either by delaying the establishment of regulatory authorities for the promotion of competition or simply by explicitly committing themselves to the monopoly provision of telecommunications. The group of countries that fits squarely into this trajectory is that of Latin America, which implemented sweeping and comprehensive privatisation of the telecom industry (more than any other region) but at the same time preserved the old monopolist structure (Manzetti 2000: 1; Wellenius 2000: 191).[12] In doing so this group gave priority to short-term revenue considerations (maximising the revenues from privatisation) over the long-term prospects of their telecom markets (which largely depend on maximising investment opportunities and competition).

The market-enforcing trajectory embraces all countries that followed the logic of privatisation but gave precedence to regulatory reform. The emphasis on regulatory reform was reflected in these countries' moves to ensure the establishment of a strong pro-competitive regulatory framework before privatising, and when privatising, doing so slowly and gradually. The outstanding example of this gradual but steady process of liberalisation is that of the EU member states. Instead of acting unilaterally, like the British, the member states used the institutions of the EU to maximise their gains from liberalisation and to reduce the conflicts and pain involved by taking more than a decade to implement full liberalisation (Levi-Faur 1999a). Telecom liberalisation in some cases was implemented on its own terms but also as part of international deals among the member states, and thus was used to increase their gains from this policy step.[13] Most of the Asian countries also belong to this trajectory, although they are following this road in a very cautious (read 'timid') fashion.[14] In the next section we propose an explanation for the paradox of liberalisation and for the different trajectories followed by Latin America and Europe. We propose that the paradox of liberalisation and the variations in its trajectories can be understood by means of the same framework used to explain the paradox of nationalisation.

The paradox of liberalisation

The different trajectories of change in Latin America and Europe have important implications for economic performance in these regions. Without a reliable mechanism of governance that can promote competition and level the field for new competitors, the gains from privatisation will be limited and most probably will find their way to a limited group of managers and shareholders. They are also important, however, because of the evident paradox of liberalisation: more regulation in Europe seems to have resulted in more competitive markets while less regulation in Latin America seems to have resulted in less competitive markets. This evidence is especially puzzling because win–lose interpretations of state–market relations assert that competitive markets are compatible with the retreat of the state.

Before offering our explanation for the trajectories of liberalisation and for the paradox of positive-sum relations between some regulatory mechanisms and competitive markets, let us examine the explanatory power of some prevalent approaches to the study of telecommunications. Starting with labour power, one may ascribe the sweeping change towards privatisation in telecommunications in Latin America to the weakness of the unions in these regions, compared with the power of unions in western and northern Europe. This seems a valid explanation when liberalisation is narrowed down to the component of privatisation alone, but as already suggested liberalisation also means the promotion of competition. The threat of competition to the power of labour and to the union leaders' position of power is more ominous than the threat of privatisation (layoffs and pay cuts are more extensive under threats of competition). If the power of unions is a critical factor in the explanation for the differences between the Latin American and western European trajectories of liberalisation, the promotion of competition may be expected to face the greatest obstacles in Europe rather than in Latin America. Evidence to the contrary deeply undermines explanations that concentrate on the power of labour. Evidence of the spread of liberalisation around the world suggests that while labour is indeed an important actor in the process of liberalisation it does not have the power of veto nor is it the factor that has shaped the particular governance structures of the sector.

Serious limitations also beset explanations centred on potentially more powerful actors, namely business in general and big telecommunications users in particular. Economic globalisation has made telecommunications on the one hand a growth sector that stands at the centre of the new information economy and on the other a vital source of economic competitiveness for multinationals, which buy, sell, plan, and produce on a global scale. Economic actors that targeted this growth sector and others irritated by the slow, inefficient, and expensive telecommunications services that they got from public providers finally became organised and used their collective power to push towards reform. This explanation is especially attractive because it relates the powerful interests of capital to a seemingly desired policy outcome. In addition, one of the most international business organisations, the International Telecommunications Users Group (INTUG), provides empirical support for this explanation. On international platforms INTUG represents the interest of users, and it actively promoted the idea of telecommunications reform. Its members include national associations mostly from economically developed countries as well as big corporations such as American Express, Bank of America, and Aloca. In a self-evaluation of its role, the association claimed, 'It is not an exaggeration to say that the Green Paper of 1987, which committed member states to deregulation, was largely the work of INTUG and a few other user organisations.'

Indeed, variations in the extent and scope of cross-business cooperation between Europe and Latin America seem to lend additional support to this explanation. The robustness of organised users in Europe as compared with Latin America (INTUG, for example, has no Latin American members) seems to be compatible with a more liberal and competitive environment in telecommunications.

Despite the apparent power of business-centred explanations, their usefulness in explaining the variations between the two regions is still limited in diverse ways (see also Tilton, Chapter 9, this volume). First, to emphasise business power when liberalisation occurs is only partly convincing. Where were business users before the 1980s? True, telecommunications services are more important nowadays, but does this really account for their passive role for almost a century? After all, business was the major user of telephony from the first days of the industry. Second, while INTUG and the national associations were important factors in pushing for liberalisation, any examination of their resources (budgetary and human) reveals their limits. Not only did most users fail actively to support the association (and thus acted like free-riders) but in most countries liberalisation moved forward without any apparent role for business users. Third, business was united in its support for liberalisation. Core members of the old telecommunications community – suppliers of telecommunications equipment for users and operators – generally opposed liberalisation as it threatened their privileged position in their respective markets. So internal divisions in the capitalist camp weaken this explanation. Finally, the role of the state and state agencies in encouraging the formation of business associations is underestimated. In the case of INTUG, the initial trigger for its formation in 1974, came from the European Commission's concerns about the lack of user input in its policy process. Similar evidence exists in the case of the Trans Atlantic Business Dialogue (TABD), a most impressive business association of European and American multinationals that works for the creation of a New Transatlantic Marketplace (NTM) permitting goods, services, and capital to flow more easily across the Atlantic. Here the initial push for the creation of the association came from the European Commission and the US government, and its agenda was closely coordinated with these public bodies.

A more powerful explanation for the variations in the trajectories of liberalisation starts with the variations in the strength of the state in these two regions. Weak states in Latin America emphasised privatisation but failed to promote regulatory structures for the promotion of competitive markets. In doing so they most probably sacrificed the long-term prospects of their telecom industry in favour of short-term revenues that they received from selling their telecom operators. Stronger states in Europe[15] were able to use the institutions of the EU to promote a controlled process of change, which was slower in regard to privatisation, but, on the other hand, much more vibrant in its creation of an institutional design that promoted competition. These propositions are developed, as in the case of nationalisation, by drawing on Nordlinger's two critical variables: social support and state autonomy. Below it is argued that social support for liberalisation and state autonomy in designing and implementing telecom liberalisation was greater in Europe than in Latin America, not least because of the role of the European Union.

While the focus of the discussion of social support for liberalisation in Europe and Latin America usually focuses on ideological preferences for market or social forms of governance of the economy, other sources of social support and legitimacy may be as effective. One of the most important sources of legitimacy for telecom liberalisation lies in the support of professional groups. The critical element in the sphere of social support that was readily available in Europe but missing in Latin America was the existence of a vibrant professional community of telecom specialists and telecom interest associations that could support the implementation of liberalisation in all respects. Professional associations and interest groups supply information and knowledge that are critical for the implementation of complex policies. At the same time they represent an authoritative voice outside the circle of the government and international institutions that may function to increase the legitimacy of liberalisation. Moreover, professional associations and interest groups act as the watchdogs of the policymakers. Their existence makes public policy more efficient and rational because policymakers know that they are being watched and that some members of the public understand what they do and what they do not do. Note that professional information and knowledge are critical whenever complex policies are considered. In direct application to our case, it is reasonable to suggest that the deliberation gap, which expresses the variations in the attention of professional groups to the details of liberalisation, was critical when regulatory institutions had to be designed. It was less important for privatisation, which requires less complex administrative work; to the extent that privatisation required legal and financial expertise, this was readily available for hire from American investment banks.

Variations in the autonomy of the state between Europe and Latin America had their own effects as well on the particular trajectory of liberalisation in the two regions. The creation of institutions for the governance and especially the promotion of telecom competition is a very demanding task and requires an autonomous state machinery. Here again the professional discussion as far as it dealt with autonomy tended to focus its attention on struggles between state and societal actors, particularly the opposition of labour unions to privatisation (e.g., Petrazzini 1995; Molano 1997). Yet this is only part of the story since autonomous states need not only the ability to overcome opposition but also the capability to create the administrative structures and regulatory machinery that will support their quest for more competitive markets.

The apparent similarities between Europe and Latin America in the creation of independent regulatory institutions are less convincing when the evidence of persistent variations in the strength of the state is considered. These institutions represent an innovation in the administrative tradition of the state and there are considerable similarities in their institutional design across countries. For example, they are most often independent of the supervising ministry through financial autonomy and the fixed-term nomination of their managing directors. Yet, these new features, which potentially could eliminate the old distinctions between types of state, are embedded in the old institutional structure and stable traditions of economic governance (see also Mark Tilton, Chapter 9, this volume). Different administrative traditions, different resources, and different ideational, political, and economic contexts may well result in different degrees of administrative capacity and effectiveness. Regulatory reforms will have varied effects depending on the context of their implementation and, in particular, the type of the degree of state strength (autonomy and social support) and its economic orientation (mercantilist, liberal, social-democratic). What thus seems to be a convergence of Latin American and European practices of governance of telecoms may well hide new divergencies, which carry significant implications for policy outcomes.

Conclusions

In his seminal book *Political Order in Changing Societies* Samuel Huntington argued that a major distinction among states lies not in their type of government but in the degree to which the government really governs (Huntington 1968: 1–2). Paraphrasing Huntington, it is possible to suggest that the major distinction among different types of states lies not in their pursuit of nationalisation or liberalisation but in the degree to which they can use their domestic institutions effectively to create and sustain effective markets for telecommunications. The room for manoeuvre of states in the world economy is largely influenced by their ability to coordinate economic responses by political means. In both eras examined here the Latin American states were less capable than the European countries of doing so. The telecommunications markets in Latin America did not suffer from too much state intervention but from the wrong kind of state intervention. It is the strength and autonomy of the state in Europe, not its withdrawal from the market, that makes competition feasible nowadays (despite many problems already clearly visible in the telecommunications sector). Similarly, it is the strength and autonomy of the state that allowed the nationalisation of this industry in Europe so early. The ability of European countries to move slowly and gradually towards privatisation, yet to perform more effectively than the Latin Americans in perfecting regulation-for-competition capacities reinforces observations of a highly autonomous state at the centre and a weak one on the periphery. In this context the differences between

'neomercantilist' and 'liberal' countries at the centre are of less importance than the inequalities in state capacities at the 'centre' and on the
'periphery'.

If one accepts that direct positive relations exist between the strength
of the state and the extent of competition in telecoms, it follows that the
relations between state and markets are not mutually exclusive. There
is wide room for win–win policies, as proposed in the introduction to
this book as well as by several of its contributors. The liberalisation
of telecommunications requires a strong and autonomous state, a conclusion at odds with the view that openness and global competition
equals a retreat of the state from the market. Certainly, some components of liberalisation such as privatisation, when not accompanied by
new regulatory mechanisms, may result in state withdrawal. But the
evidence indicates that the more likely outcome is that strong states will
not be weakened because they constitute a new mechanism for governing the market. Accordingly, weak states will continue to stay weak or
become even weaker as they fail to integrate privatisation and regulation
into one coherent framework. A more optimistic view is grounded in
the expectation that through policy imitation and policy learning many
developing countries are now acquiring the new regulatory capacities.
While many will fail, some have fair chances of success, not least because
international bodies like the World Bank now promote regulation-for-
competition rather than pure privatisation.[16] While they are constrained
by older state structures and patterns of relations between state and
society, success and failure are not preordained. Regulatory effectiveness, however, requires domestic political change as well as external
resources in the form of material aid and policy advice. Without them,
despite liberalisation, there will be no significant change in the welfare
gaps between the centre and periphery of our world.

Notes

I would like to thank Linda Weiss and Elizabeth Thurbon for their comments
and suggestions on an earlier draft of this paper. The research for this study
was conducted through a Marie Curie Fellowship and the hospitality of the
Centre for European Politics, Economics and Society and Nuffield College
at the University of Oxford. I am grateful to Jeremy Richardson for his help
during my stay in Oxford.
1. My accounts of the history of the world telecommunications industry are
   based on Bennett (1895), Holcombe (1911), a series of publications by Noam
   (1992, 1994, 1997, 1998, 1999), as well as a systematic collection of secondary
   sources from various countries.

2. The invention of the telephone in 1876 by Alexander Graham Bell also marked the start of the nationalisation period since some important countries like Germany and Switzerland monopolised the services from its very beginning and thus gave other countries an example to follow (see also the next section of the chapter). The era of nationalisation starts with the divestiture of AT&T (1984), as well as Thatcher's privatisation of Cable and Wireless (1981) and British Telecom (1984). Notable also is the privatisation of Nippon Telegraph and Telephone (1985).

3. These observations are based on my own database of telecommunications governance, and on the regulatory database of ITU (www.itu.org) which deals only with liberalisation.

4. This paradoxical outcome was captured elegantly by Steven Vogel's (1996) title *Freer Markets, More Rules*. Vogel's study includes mainly banking and telecoms, but these features are now common across the entire economy, from electricity to transport, and from finance to water supply.

5. Telecommunications and finance are the archetypal cases in globalist theory building.

6. Similar suggestions were made by Hulsink (1999) and Sandholtz (1998).

7. In Przeworski and Teune's (1970) terminology, we follow a 'most different system' design.

8. A notable exception is Vogel's work (1996).

9. Space constraints limit our discussion to these three trajectories alone. The colonialist trajectory encompasses all the countries that inherited their *étatist* provision of telecommunications services from the colonial government and kept it intact. The communist trajectory includes all countries that nationalised their industry following the rise of communist parties inspired by Russian or Chinese models of socialism. The most notable exception among countries outside these trajectories is the US telecommunications regime, which was based on regulated private ownership. Demands for nationalisation and objections to private ownership are observable also in the US case, but unlike other cases they did not result in public ownership except for about one year during World War I.

10. Network integration allows the subscriber of one telephone provider to contact the subscriber of another telephone provider. Evidence from the early history of telephony demonstrates that competing providers did not allow network integration under reasonable terms. For many subscribers this meant that they had to subscribe to two telephone services in order to achieve maximum benefits from the telephone networks.

11. See Collier and Collier (1991) on labour incorporation in Latin America.

12. For country-by-country data see the ITU regulatory database, http://www.itu.org

13. See, for example, the Franco-German deal in telecoms (Schneider and Vedel 1999).

14. Outside these trajectories are steadily dwindling groups of countries that include mainly Middle Eastern and African countries. But if the current rate

of 'jumping onto the liberalisation bandwagon' continues, one may safely predict that these countries will also liberalise their telecommunications industries in the coming decade.

15. Unlike the era of nationalisation, which saw similar patterns of state–society relations, in the era of liberalisation the southern European states departed from the Latin American pattern. The entry of these states into the European Union represents a critical juncture in their politics. One may speculate that it represents a potential break from their 'Latin' tradition, the full implications of which may be traced through an in-depth study of their new regulatory structures.

16. It seems that in the field of infrastructure regulation, the World Bank embraces more readily the notion of mutual empowerment of state and economy than in other fields, most notably international trade.

9 Ideas, institutions, and interests in the shaping of telecommunications reform: Japan and the US

Mark Tilton

One might think the telecommunications market an obvious place for the state to be swept away by the swift tides of transactions and information washing across borders. Telecommunications firms have become very active internationally and telecommunications services themselves provide instantaneous and rich intercourse among nations. Markets that were until recently dominated by stodgy telecommunications monopolies are now convulsed in international mergers, hostile takeovers, and falling prices. Behind the dizzyingly rapid business changes, however, lies an enormous stock of wires and switches. Since duplicating this infrastructure is extraordinarily expensive, competition takes place in large part because governments have decided to use regulation to force incumbent telecommunications providers to rent their networks to new entrants. Because making rules to decide how and at what prices these networks should be shared is complicated and must change constantly as technologies and costs change, there is great scope for policy differences among states.

The US and the European Union have moved towards converging on strongly pro-competitive telecommunications policies in very recent years, though the process by which they arrived at these policies was quite different (see Levi-Faur, this volume). But Japan has maintained policies that are considerably less pro-competition, and this chapter will consider the reasons why the difference has persisted.

Certainly, both the US and Japan have experienced great change in their telecommunications policies. The biggest change for the US came with a court order to break up AT&T in 1982, opening the way for new firms to enter the market and for a dramatic fall in prices. Japan also has seen important changes in telecommunications policy, principally with the privatisation of Nippon Denshin Denwa Kōsha (NTT) in

1985, and its breakup into subsidiaries of a holding company in 1999. The US was the pioneer in telecommunications deregulation, and US telecommunications policy has largely been driven by domestic concerns, with relatively little reference to foreign pressures or examples. Japanese telecommunications regulatory reform has been influenced by the US, yet Japanese regulators have not been as aggressive at promoting competition as American regulators.

This chapter will consider persisting differences in telecommunications policy in the US and Japan, why these policy differences remain, and how more open markets have affected policies and state capabilities. One might think of a number of ways in which the pressures of open markets could produce responses by national governments. One would be that the pressures of the global marketplace push firms to call on their own states to change policies. This is the most straightforward expression of the materialist thesis that the marketplace forces policy convergence. Market pressures might also directly influence policymakers' assessment of the need for change, even without the mediation of private interest groups. In addition to direct market forces, a second source of pressure to change may be foreign governments. Because of the increasing importance of economic openness, national governments may be forced to bend to political pressure from other states to harmonise policies in order to improve reciprocity of trade and investment access. A third source of change may be ideas that flow more freely along with goods and services as markets become more open. New ideas from abroad may directly cause political leaders to change policy, and they may shape the way economic actors perceive and express their interests. Ideas, of course, may be part and parcel of political pressure and suasion from foreign governments.

There certainly are large financial interests at stake in the telecommunications industry. Telecommunications services produce large revenues, and the companies producing the services have been motivated to use political power to protect them. Yet while the established carrier in Japan has had considerable success in blocking pro-competitive reform, the American dominant carrier was much less successful. Why the difference? The explanation seems to be twofold. First, while American political leaders and bureaucrats became fervent advocates of pro-competitive deregulation, pro-competitive ideas held far less sway in Japan. Second, Japan lacked the independent institutions that applied competition policy to telecommunications in the US, or for that matter in the European Union (EU). In the US, the Department of Justice and the courts played the dominant role in pushing for policy change, while the Japan Fair Trade Commission (JFTC) had no jurisdiction over telecommunications. The power of Japan's Ministry of Posts and Telecommunications (MPT) to intervene was limited. In this institutional context, the vested interests of NTT have played a far greater political role than have the interests of AT&T.

Foreign political pressure on the US government to change its telecommunications policies has had little effect on American telecommunications policy, because the US has generally been at the forefront of reform. Direct foreign pressure on Japan, largely from the US, though in recent years with EU backing, has not been the major force behind Japan's most important reforms. In recent years it has influenced policy, but has hardly brought about convergence.

Telecommunications reform in the US

American telecommunications policy began as *laissez-faire*, but had shifted to regulated monopoly by the 1930s. American policy towards the telecommunications industry is unusual in that its telephone monopoly has not been state owned. State regulation played a role in encouraging the early development of the telephone service, but it was the rather limited role of recognising the Bell patents, thus giving Bell Telephone a monopoly in its early years. As the Bell company's patents lapsed in the early 1900s, Bell-owned local telephone companies encountered competition from new companies, and by 1910 Bell's market share had dropped below 50 per cent. A number of possible policy responses to the new competitive environment were floated, *laissez-faire* competition, nationalisation, antitrust regulation, and regulated private monopoly, but Bell's preference for regulated private monopoly prevailed. Regulation was first created by individual states and then standardised on a national level by the 1927 and 1934 Communications Acts, which protected the telephone monopoly in exchange for standardised universal service (Cohen 1992: 25–46). Under this protected monopoly AT&T-owned local phone companies came to serve 80 per cent of American phone users and provided almost all interstate long-distance service (Crandall and Waverman 1995: 2). Long-distance service subsidised local service and urban areas subsidised service to rural areas. The 1934 Act thus fostered equality of access to telecommunications services, and ensured rates high enough to pay for the creation of a national network. The Act was part of a broader move during the Depression to regulate capitalism and attempt to correct its obvious failures.

The US continued the system of regulated private monopoly for the next fifty years, though in some tension with antitrust law. In 1949 the US Department of Justice brought an antitrust lawsuit, charging the Bell operating companies with illegal exclusion because they only purchased equipment from the Bell affiliate Western Electric. In 1956 the court allowed AT&T to keep Western Electric, on condition that AT&T agreed not to go into the computer market (Economides 1998). The first significant erosion of AT&T's monopoly was the Federal Communications Commission's (FCC) approval in 1959 of the use of microwave by large firms which wanted to establish private networks.

Not just telecommunications, but many American industries were regulated in order to stabilise supply and moderate prices. Beginning in the 1970s, deregulation overturned this system in such industries as transportation, telecommunications, public utilities, and agriculture. The causes of this change were primarily that economists' proposals for deregulation were widely accepted, and that the executive branch of government and the courts were willing and had the power to radically change policy. Interest group pressure played only a minor role in promoting change.

American deregulation has its roots in academic works by economists written in the late 1950s and 1960s, which argued that regulation unnecessarily prevented competition that could improve service and lower prices. This literature exploded in volume in the 1960s and 1970s and led to a solid academic consensus in favour of deregulation (Derthick and Quirk 1985: 35–6). These ideas were brought into the public policy arena by think tanks, which carried out their own studies, and by large numbers of economists who went to work in the government.

In addition to ideas, the other factor that made drastic reform possible was the courts' and the executive's initiative in pushing reform through over the objections of AT&T. Through the 1960s and 1970s the FCC and the courts gradually expanded room for competition in telecommunications. In 1969 the FCC allowed Microwave Communications, Inc. (which later became MCI) to offer private-line circuits to firms which did not want to build networks on their own. In the mid-1970s MCI went beyond what the FCC had allowed and began offering ordinary long-distance service. Steven Vogel points out that the vigour with which private industry challenged the status quo distinguished the US case from Japan and even Britain (Vogel 1996). The FCC tried to prevent MCI from providing this service, but the court allowed MCI to continue. The FCC also forced AT&T to let their customers buy telephones and other equipment from competing equipment providers and connect them to their phone lines, thus breaking AT&T's monopoly over telephone equipment.

Interest group pressure played no significant role in propelling these pro-competitive policy moves by the FCC or the courts. Consumers on the whole were content with the status quo. Even after a decade of public discussions of deregulation, in 1979 80 per cent of consumers judged their telephone rates reasonable and 56 per cent believed that the current system of telephone regulations should be left in place.[1] Business customers eagerly took advantage of lower phone rates from new providers, but were not politically mobilised over telecommunications deregulation until the 1980s (Derthick and Quirk 1985: 25). Once telecommunications deregulation began, general business interests weighed in on the side of greater competition, but the key regulatory reforms continued to be made by the executive branch and the courts. AT&T was powerless to prevent the imposition of a tough new pro-competition regulatory regime. In 1976 it lobbied for passage of the Consumer Communications Reform Act, which would have ensured a place for regulated monopoly. With the political support of independents and local telephone companies, unionised telecommunications workers and many state public utility commissions, AT&T garnered co-sponsorship for the Act from 175 Congressmen and 17 Senators. AT&T's failure to push the Act through Congress was in part due to the blunder of making it so extreme in its protection for incumbents that independents and the Communications Workers of America withdrew their support. Another reason was that consumer advocates led by Ralph Nader, MCI, and other special common carriers, and big business interests opposed the bill (Cohen 1992: 70–1). These pro-competition interest groups helped stem AT&T's counterattack, but they were not the driving force behind reform.

The principal initiative for pro-competition reform came from the executive branch. In 1974 the Department of Justice filed an antitrust suit under the Sherman Act, charging that AT&T was using its monopoly over local phone service to monopolise the markets for equipment and long-distance service. The suit went to trial in 1980 and resulted in a consent decree, called the Modification of Final Judgment of 1982 (MFJ), that AT&T divest itself of the Bell local operating companies. Under this agreement AT&T retained most long-distance services, equipment manufacture, and research operations. The seven regional Bell operating companies were not allowed to manufacture equipment or engage in long-distance services outside their local areas. They were also required to change their switching networks to give equal access to competing long-distance companies (Crandall and Waverman 1995: 3–4). The idea behind the MFJ was 'quarantine theory'. Local companies were considered to have market power and were not allowed to compete in the long-distance, manufacturing or information services industries. The MFJ created competition in the industry and, as Hausman and Sidak put it, began the 'modern era of telecommunications regulation' (Hausman and Sidak 1999: 427).

While it was the executive branch and the courts that were responsible for radically changing telecommunications policy, once the basic changes had taken place interest groups took a more active role, and eventually Congress passed legislation that confirmed and advanced the policies originally implemented by the court. The states also played a significant role in setting new policies. The 1982 MFJ gave the courts responsibility for overseeing telecommunications policy, but the courts had a difficult time keeping up with rapid technological change in the 1980s and 1990s. Many worried that the courts' weak regulatory capabilities were holding back technological innovation. For instance, there were concerns that regulatory problems prevented the US from developing consumer information services that were widely used in France. The MFJ had a process for waivers, but this became bogged down and blocked the development of new technologies such as cellular telephones. Thus the courts, while useful in breaking a political logjam and enabling the US to develop a competitive market, were inefficient at ongoing regulation. Congress finally dealt with this problem by passing the Telecommunications Act of 1996 (Hausman and Sidak 1999: 428–9).

The Clinton–Gore administration was firmly behind internet promotion, and supported telecommunications regulation reform as a means to this end. Proposals to rewrite the 1934 Act prompted intense lobbying, with AT&T being the largest contributor, followed by local, long-distance and cable companies (Aufderheide 1999: 43). The 1996 Act ended the MFJ, introduced the principle of competition in local telephone markets, and made the FCC the sole federal regulator. Although the central goal of the Act was to promote competition, it states explicitly that American innovation and efficiency in telecommunications is necessary in order to compete in world markets (Aufderheide 1999: 33, 62).

The 1996 Act created a thorough system of regulation to promote competition and set the stage for ongoing legal battles over the particulars of this regulation. The Act puts interconnection rates under the jurisdiction of the FCC and the states, but is ambiguous as to who has ultimate authority. Such ambiguities, and the technical complications of making decisions about rates, have sent firms to the courts to appeal regulatory rulings (Aufderheide 1999: 64, 82). The result of three decades of telecommunications deregulation has been an increase in long-distance competition and a sharp drop in long-distance rates. Local telephone prices have risen faster than the consumer price index, because subsidies from long-distance calls have disappeared, and because it has been difficult for new entrants to challenge incumbents. Productivity has increased and large firms have shed workers.

The driving force for the principal policy of telecommunications deregulation, the 1982 MFJ, was ideas rather than interests. Political leaders played an important role in bringing about the MFJ, and did not initially do so at the behest of interest groups. The courts and the Justice Department provided an institutional basis for using antitrust law to bring a radical shift to telecommunications. Given that the US was the first nation to deregulate telecommunications so boldly, it is clear that the move was not due to foreign market pressures, foreign example, or foreign political pressure, but came entirely from within the US. After the initial change to deregulation and the creation of a host of new competing telecommunications firms, regulators have created extensive pro-competitive regulation – 'reregulation' to use Steven Vogel's term (Vogel 1996). Public Utility Commissions (PUCs) and the courts provide a fairly transparent setting for extensive conflict over regulatory details.

Telecommunications reform in Japan

Japan has been deeply influenced by American telecommunications deregulation, most importantly through ideas and examples. US government pressure has also played a modest role in promoting change. Pressure from user business interests because of a desire for lower prices in order to compete in global markets has been modest, and pressure from consumer groups inconsequential. Yet while American ideas and pressure have been influential, the nature of pre-existing Japanese economic thinking and the character of Japanese policymaking institutions has meant Japanese telecommunications policies continue to be quite different from those of America.

The Japanese telecommunications industry started out even more tightly regulated and monopolised than the American telecommunications industry of the mid-twentieth century. Unlike the case in the US, though like northwestern Europe, Japan's telecommunications service was established as a government monopoly in 1890. In 1949 American occupation authorities separated the Ministry of Telecommunications from the Ministry of Communications. In 1952 this new ministry was re-named NTT and international service was split off and provided by KDD (Kokusai Denshin Denwa Kōsha) (Fūke 1999). The shift towards com-petition came in 1985, when NTT was formally privatised. In 1999 NTT was split into four parts. These reforms were inspired by the American breakup of AT&T, and in some sense parallel American telecommuni-cations deregulation. Yet continued Japanese government ownership of 46 per cent of NTT's shares, the continued unity of the post-breakup NTT through a holding company, and the continued overwhelming dom-inance of the Japanese telecommunications market by NTT represent major contrasts to American telecommunications policy.

The original impetus in Japan for telecommunications deregulation is quite different from that in the US. Whereas in the US it is academic pro-posals for reform, translated into policy proposals by think tanks that are the initial basis for reform, in Japan it is bureaucratic politics. From the 1950s until 1985 the Ministry of Posts and Telecommunications had formal regulatory authority over NTT, but only modest power. NTT op-erated as a self-regulating government bureaucracy. In the 1970s MPT officials looked to American deregulation initiatives with an eye to not only increasing efficiency in Japan but also increasing MPT regulatory powers (Vogel 1996; Johnson 1989). Later the Second Provisional Com-mission on Administrative Reform (Rinchō) also promoted the privati-sation of NTT, but again for very different reasons than deregulation had been promoted in the US.

Business at that time was interested in reducing fiscal deficits and forestalling tax increases, and saw the sale of NTT as a way to bring in significant government revenue (Vogel 1996). Rinchō enjoyed a mandate from big business, certain prominent Liberal Democratic Party (LDP) leaders, and the conservative wing of the labour movement to make drastic public policy changes. In 1982 Rinchō recommended privatis-ing and also breaking up NTT (Carlile 1998: 76–83). Unlike the early deregulation movement in the US, Rinchō's goal was not to introduce aggressive competition into markets such as transportation or telecommunications.

The Rinchō movement eventually led to a boom in interest in deregulation, especially after the 1991 economic downturn. However, there were important differences between American and Japanese ideas about regulatory reform. The most important difference has to do with notions of appropriate levels of competition. Based on nearly a century of experience with antitrust policy, American proponents of deregulation assumed that when government restrictions on entry and price were dropped, antitrust authorities or other regulators would continue to regulate markets to ensure competition took place. But in Japan it was assumed that regulation would continue, and that it should play some role in *moderating* competition. Current thinking in Japan about the appropriate place of competition in the economy is more cautious than in the US. An indication of this difference in dominant ideas is the widespread Japanese use of the term, 'excessive competition'. Whereas in American liberal economic thought 'excessive competition' is an oxymoron, under Japanese competition law it has had a precise definition: a condition of excess supply, prices below costs, and producers in danger of being pushed out of business (Iyori and Uesugi 1983: 114). The term is widely and uncritically used in the mainstream Japanese business press to refer to the dangers of competition (Tilton 1998: 186). Thus, ideas and examples from abroad have played a role in shaping Japanese telecommunications policy, but they have combined with pre-existing Japanese ideas about competition to result in a less aggressive approach to promoting competition.

One of the most noticeable differences between the US and Japan is the much greater political power of NTT, even after its breakup, in comparison with AT&T in the 1970s before its breakup. The biggest reason for NTT's greater influence seems to be the difference in level of commitment to pro-competitive regulation, and the lack of independent regulators like the Justice Department, the FCC, or the courts of the United States.

Another reason that NTT is so much more influential and able to resist change is the institutional character of Japanese bureaucracy. Japanese bureaucracy contrasts with the American bureaucracy in some important ways. The top level of the American bureaucracy is composed of thousands of presidential appointees, in contrast to the Japanese bureaucracy, where only the minister is a political appointee. The elite members of the Japanese bureaucracy are hired straight after graduation

from college, and almost without exception remain in their bureaucracies until retirement at around 60, when they move on to a post-
retirement (*amakudari*) job arranged by their bureaucracies. The Japanese
bureaucratic career track gives top bureaucrats a concern with protecting their bureaucracy's power in a way that would make no sense for top
American bureaucrats. Japanese bureaucrats certainly often display
dedication to their bureaucracies' missions, but they have strong disincentives to give up regulatory power. The career structure has led to
an intensity of fighting between bureaucracies over jurisdiction that one
does not find in the US, and makes policy choice hostage to concerns
with preserving bureaucratic power. In the late 1970s MPT and Ministry
for International Trade and Industry (MITI) each sought expanded regulatory powers over telecommunications. MPT argued that it should
regulate NTT but MITI argued against putting broad policy capabilities
in the hands of a 'non-policy ministry'. In the end Prime Minister Suzuki
Zenkō intervened in MPT's favour (Johnson 1989: 195). Lodging NTT so
firmly within MPT's orbit has probably had the effect of making Japan's
telecommunications policy more conservative than it might have been
had a greater role been preserved for MITI, because of MPT's greater
political vulnerability to NTT pressure. With the 1985 NTT Law, MPT became a 'policy' ministry and gained expanded regulatory powers over
NTT, but it is still outgunned by the sheer size of NTT's budget and staff
(Vogel 1996: 141). In 2001 MPT was folded into the larger Ministry of
Public Management, Home Affairs and Posts and Telecommunications
(MPHPT). Many at MPHPT would be happy to see NTT weakened by
greater competition, but MPHPT lacks the political power to take on
NTT aggressively.

NTT's power is based on its influence with the LDP. It makes large
campaign donations and the over 200,000 employees of the NTT conglomerate are readily mobilised for elections. MPHPT has 30,000 post
offices through the nation, which gives it considerable political clout
as well since the officials in the far-flung outposts also campaign for
politicians who support MPHPT (Vogel 1996). But MPHPT is at the
same time beholden to the Diet to maintain its system of postal savings, and worries that if it takes on NTT with tough regulation NTT
might retaliate by mounting an attack from the Diet on the postal savings system. The resources of NTT are parallel to those held by AT&T
before its breakup. What is different is that MPHPT, in contrast to the
FCC, lacks the power to take on the dominant carrier. Although Rinchō
recommended in 1982 that NTT break up, it took seventeen years for

this to come about, because of NTT's political power, its status as a government-owned agency, and bureaucratic politics.

The 1985 NTT Law mandated a review in 1990 of a possible breakup of NTT. When 1990 arrived, MPT favoured a breakup, but MITI, NTT, and the NTT union were opposed. The Ministry of Finance (MOF) was also against breakup, because it feared a fall in the value of NTT stock. The next review in 1995 led to drawn-out wrangling between NTT and MPT. Finally, a compromise was reached, pending a repeal of the Japanese Anti-Monopoly Law's prohibition on holding companies, to break up NTT but allow a holding company to own the resulting fragmented firms. NTT was also allowed to enter the international telephone market (Vogel 2000b). NTT was split up in July 1999. Its local service was taken on by NTT East and NTT West, while long-distance and international telecommunications service was handled by NTT Communications. The 1999 NTT Law places a number of requirements and restrictions on NTT. The Law requires NTT to provide universal service and to promote R&D, and gives MPHPT approval (*ninka*) authority over changes in contracts and enterprise plans. There are also regulations on government ownership of NTT shares, on NTT holding of regional NTT company shares, and on shareholding by foreigners. There are a number of regulations on NTT that are heavier than on other carriers, such as price cap regulations, regulations on interconnections contracts, and requirements to publish financial accounts based on accounting rules. And there is a financial firewall between NTT Communications and the local NTT companies (Seifu Kisei 2000: 9).

The 1985 privatisation of NTT created the opportunity for many new firms to compete in the telecommunications industry. It created a regulatory distinction between Type I carriers, which own their own circuits, and Type II carriers, which lease other companies' circuits and sell telecommunications services. As of April 2000 there were 249 Type I carriers, including cable TV firms and electric power companies, and 7,651 Type II carriers, such as internet service providers. The introduction of competition has brought about sharp price decreases. A 3 minute, 500 km daytime domestic phone call fell from 400 yen in 1985 to 63 yen in July 2000. A daytime phone call to the US had fallen from 1,530 yen for 3 minutes to 132 yen by July 2000 (MPT 2000: 15).

Although there has been great change in Japanese telecommunications policy, inspired in important ways by the American example, Japanese telecommunications policy remains very much shaped by Japanese concerns. The privatisation and breakup of NTT were far more timid than the breakup of AT&T. While there is much more competition in the Japanese telecommunications market today than before 1985, policy reforms – in keeping with Japanese ideas about the dangers of 'excessive competition' – have created less competition than in the US or in Europe. Moreover, Japanese telecommunications services remain expensive by international standards. An OECD survey of the combined charges by telephone service and internet service providers found that 40 hours of internet use in Japan cost $78, compared to the average of $41 in both the OECD and the EU, $49 in Germany, $29 in the UK, and $23 in the US (OECD 2000).

The reason prices are so high is that the Japanese telecommunications market is still dominated by the NTT conglomerate. NTT controls 96 per cent of the so-called 'last mile', which is to say that it is the local service provider of virtually all households and thus potentially has first crack at providing a range of services to those households. Moreover, in 1998 NTT had an 84 per cent market share of all domestic phone calls and NTT-affiliate KDDI had 68 per cent of the international telecommunications market. NTT DoCoMo had 59 per cent of the cellular phone market and 58 per cent of the radio paging market (MPT 2000: 13–14). In comparison, the market share of dominant firms in the US is much smaller. ATT has a 30 per cent share of the long-distance market in the US, and the largest mobile phone companies have a 10 per cent market share.

Given NTT's dominance of the telecommunications market, it is not surprising that prices are so high. But why are other firms unable to break in? The reason is that Japan's regulations still hobble new entrants. A key to opening up telecommunications competition is the requirment that competitors be allowed to interconnect with existing networks. Barring that, they would have to set up duplicate networks and the costs would be prohibitive. In order for new entrants to compete, interconnection rates must be low enough so that they are not paying more for interconnection than the established carrier is paying to replace and maintain the existing network.

Scholars, Japanese firms competing with NTT, and the US and EU governments argue that the MPHPT-affiliated committee that sets interconnection rates is biased in favour of NTT and sets the rates too high (Fransman 1996; USTR 2000). The US government complains that the MPHPT uses data it gets, presumably, from NTT but which is not made public. It points out that in the US, public utility commissions (in New Mexico and Virginia) have rejected cost models provided by established carriers because the cost data was not made public. United States Trade Representative (USTR) also complains that the three-week period provided for comments is too short to make meaningful analysis and comment possible, and that MPHPT uses exaggerated cost data that assumes equipment will cost more and wear out faster than comparative estimates in other countries. USTR complains that this is based on equipment developed by NTT which is not competitive with that of other nations, and that this price structure does not represent the true market cost of the network. NTT interconnect charges in early 2000 were 5.54 yen for 3 minutes, compared with 1.7 yen in the UK, 1.76 yen for Bell Atlantic, 1.98 in France, and 2.77 yen in Germany (USTR 2000). The US and Japan agreed on a 20 per cent reduction in interconnection rates over two years in July 2000, though one foreign telecommunications executive observed that one would expect these rates to come down over time anyway, both in Japan and in other countries, and that Japan's rates would continue to be excessive (personal interview, Tokyo, July 2000). The political reason for the bias towards NTT in the interconnection rate-setting process lies in the dependence of the rate-setters on NTT. The committee which sets rates is appointed by MPHPT, which because of career structure is less independent than the FCC. And there is no role for the courts to adjudicate disputes in Japan.

The JFTC notes that other regulations are also biased against new entrants. For instance, the regulatory distinction between Type I and Type II carriers may hamper the operations of competitors to NTT. These regulations prevent companies from setting up telecommunications infrastructure solely for leasing purposes, and provide a cumbersome barrier for firms that switch back and forth between owning circuits and using other firms' circuits.

There are also competition issues in the field of mobile telephones. MPHPT has divided Japan into blocks and allocates frequencies within them. Three or four companies provide cellular phone services and three provide PHS service in each region, but NTT DoCoMo is the only firm that has a licence for the entire nation. IDO, Seruraa, and J Phone's more restricted licences limit their ability to provide services on a national basis (Seifu Kisei 2000: 6). Another problem is that the original breakup of NTT was too timid to promote tough competition. AT&T was genuinely divided into separate firms in 1984, and local service monopolies were prevented from providing long-distance service. NTT is still held together by a holding company. Although in principle the parts of NTT are to be separated by firewalls so that they cannot cross-subsidise or help each other, the JFTC questions the effectiveness of these firewalls. It notes that NTT firms have considerable scope for personnel exchanges and thus for information flows, and that the NTT regional companies may give unfair advantages to NTT Communications (the long-distance branch of NTT) as compared to new long-distance providers in handling customer information or distributing business. And in terms of advertising there is no firewall (Seifu Kisei 2000).

The JFTC comments: '[t]here can be no doubt that the purpose of the NTT restructuring was to promote competition in Japan's telecommunications sector, but it is essential that there be analysis of market realities after the restructuring, an evaluation of the results, and possibly an indication of problems, if we are to think about policies to promote telecommunications competition' (Seifu Kisei 2000: 11). It is up to MPHPT to make sure regulations encourage competition, but it is timid about challenging NTT. Like all Japanese ministries it appoints deliberation councils to review policy, but the Telecommunications Deliberation Council mirrors the conservatism of its host ministry (Schwartz 1998). The institution charged with reviewing telecommunications policy is the Telecommunications Deliberation Council. Its members are appointed by MPHPT, which it advises. According to one Japanese professor close to the council, although the meetings are more lively than they used to be, policies are decided before the meetings take place and most members echo MPT's cautious approach (Personal interview, 13 July 2000).

Institutionally, it is difficult to have genuinely independent regulation in Japan because the bureaucracy is set up on industry-specific lines and responsibilities for developing industry and for providing for consumer protection are joined in the same ministry. This grows out of Japan's past as a late-developing catch-up economy. A number of Japan's industries, such as electric power, gas, telecommunications, railways, and buses have been regulated by industry laws which authorised monopolies and regulated prices (Tsuruta 1997: 84–5). In the case of telecommunications, regulatory functions and developmental functions were combined in NTT and then partially hived off and transferred to MPT. Finance, manufacturing, and other sectors suffer from a similar conflation of developmental and consumer regulatory functions.

The real problem with this set-up is not so much putting regulation into the hands of dedicated ministries, but the understanding that competition policy authorities have no jurisdiction over the industries. It is this lack of standing of competition policy authorities that sets Japan apart from both the US and the EU. While in the US the Department of Justice used antitrust law to promote regulatory change, the corresponding institution in Japan, the JFTC, has until recently had no role in changing telecommunications policy. A JFTC official involved in writing the above-cited June 2000 JFTC study group report on telecommunications commented to me that prior JFTC reports on telecommunications were 'probably not worth reading because they didn't say much'. The June 2000 report, timed one year after the breakup of NTT, was critical of post-breakup regulatory arrangements. However, the report was simply the product of a 'study group' and was 'not meant to have any direct effect on policy'. According to the official, 'legally the JFTC has no real authority in telecommunications' (Personal interview, July 2000). The official himself regrets this weakness, and notes the contrast to competition policy authorities in the US and Europe. The JFTC's promotion of pro-competitive deregulation is merely advisory and only occurs at the request of the ministry responsible for regulating a particular industry. Thus MITI asked the JFTC for advice on deregulating gas and electricity, but because MPT has asked for no help on telecommunications the JFTC has no authority to step in. The JFTC, which in a formal sense is the guardian of consumer interests, simply has no jurisdiction over industries that are regulated under industry laws like the NTT Law. Industry law takes precedence over the Anti-Monopoly Law.

In terms of personnel resources the JFTC also has little capacity to help shape telecommunications regulation. The authors of the June 2000 JFTC study group report on telecommunications were starting from scratch and had no expertise in telecommunications. Their lack of familiarity with the industry is reflected in their austere and impractical pronouncement that regulators properly should not be involved in setting interconnection rates. This is far from the experience of regulators in Europe and the US, who have found it necessary to regulate these rates closely in order to promote competition.

In the US, political appointees were key to overcoming AT&T opposition and pushing through pro-competitive reforms. Politicians in Japan have been far more willing to protect the interests of NTT. The president of one of the largest Japanese competitors of NTT told me he doesn't bother working with LDP or opposition politicians because there are none who are sympathetic enough to his cause to be helpful. He lamented that the only way to accomplish policy change was with the help of 'black ships', meaning American pressure, a reference to the fleet of Admiral Perry that forced Japan's market opening in 1853 (Personal interview, Tokyo, 11 July 2000). Peak business groups also have not been very helpful. Keidanren, Japan's most influential business organisation, makes bold general statements favouring liberal reforms, yet according to industry insiders the fact that Keidanren chairman Imai Takashi is on the board of directors of NTT prevents Keidanren from pushing hard for tougher regulation. Consumer representatives from Shufuren (the Housewives' Federation) on the Telecommunications Deliberation Council are interested in stabilisation of service and show little interest in regulating measures that would lower prices (Personal interview with a professor close to the industry, 13 July 2000). The lack of political activism on the part of users is not particularly surprising or different from the early days of telecommunications regulatory reform in the US.

The bigger difference from the US is the lack of enthusiasm of Japanese politicians for tougher pro-competitive reforms. During negotiations with the US over interconnection rates, it was widely reported that LDP Secretary-General Nonaka Hiromu, with close ties to NTT, played a major role in preventing larger concessions. This is not to say that top politicians are unconcerned with improving telecommunications service. There is great concern with Japan's slowness to develop internet technology. But instead of the American approach of aggressive attempts to promote competition, the state has chosen to promote information technology through tax breaks and government spending for public investment. This 'Information Technology (IT) Policy' is the brainchild of the late Prime Minister Obuchi, who hoped to pull the nation out of recession and enable it to catch up with the US in an increasingly important field. The core of the policy is investment in high-speed internet infrastructure (*Financial Times* 31 August 2000), although there is suspicion among Western observers that the real goal of the policy is to create old-style public works projects under a new-fangled name (*Financial Times* 2 August 2000).

Prime Minister Koizumi Junichiro has argued for more competition in telecommunications, and both the MPHPT and the JFTC have made some moves in this direction, though it is too early to forecast the significance of the change. MPHPT has put pressure on NTT to rewrite its business plans in ways that pursue cost-cutting measures more aggressively. In December 2000 (before Koizumi) the JFTC had intervened to force NTT to allow its competitors to place equipment in its facilities, and in September 2001 it issued guidelines for telecommunications competition. At the same time, Shogo Itada, Commissioner of the JFTC, continues to argue that intervening to help NTT's competitors by setting interconnection rates is an inappropriate interference with the market mechanism (Itada 2001).

State capabilities

Has a more open market in telecommunications made the American or Japanese states less capable of carrying out desired policies or of promoting economic development? Both the American and Japanese states have retained considerable capabilities, which they use to different ends. The US state has acted as a 'competition state', and carried out a drastic transformation of telecommunications regulations in the face of staunch opposition by AT&T. The federal government has promoted continued reform with the 1996 Act, though local state utilities' boards have not necessarily been successful in realising the possibilities for vigorous local competition.

In the case of Japan, for both structural and ideational reasons, the state is less autonomous of the dominant provider. MPT is jealous of NTT's power, but is worried that tougher regulation would bring reprisals through the LDP. But even if MPT had a free hand, it is doubtful that it would impose tough American-style regulation. Measured in terms of producing inexpensive telecommunications services and widespread use of the internet, Japan has been less successful than the US or most of Western Europe. The Japanese state has been ineffective at creating strongly liberal, pro-competitive policy, but quite effective at finding a compromise between liberal, pro-competitive policies and old-style industrial policy. The state has introduced considerable competition and efficiency and brought down telecommunications prices, even if not as far as in the US or Europe. While the disadvantage of this strategy is that consumers pay high prices, the advantage is that NTT enjoys higher fees from telecommunications services than its Western competitors and is able to invest this money in developing technology, most notably wireless phone service and internet service, at a higher level than US or European firms (*The Economist* 11 March 2000, pp. 97–8).

While consumers in the US and Europe are benefiting from falling telecommunications prices, as of this writing Western telecommunications providers have taken on large debts to fund expansion and are suffering financially as prices fall (Crane 2000). The response of big firms in the most competitive markets, such as AT&T and British Telecom, has been to break themselves up. These firms hope that the new, smaller successor firms will have be more innovative and entrepreneurial, and that they can persuade investors that as smaller, quicker firms they are worth more in share value. In contrast, NTT enjoys a less competitive market and has not been forced to take on high levels of debt because it enjoys high profits in its fixed phone market (Roberts 2000). Large profits have enabled NTT DoCoMo to invest internationally (*Financial Times* 11 November 2000).

Competitive arrangements in telecommunications resemble a broader pattern in the Japanese economy of restrained competition and high prices (Tilton 1996; Lincoln 2001). As in other markets, the pattern hurts downstream user industries (in this case, internet-based services) but helps upstream supplier industries (the telecommunications equipment manufacturing industry). Foreign firms have long contended that NTT overpays for its equipment, and the equipment suppliers obviously benefit from this. The large fees NTT can charge provide valuable funds for investment. As yet, the fruits of this investment, such as wireless technologies, have not so far shown much success in markets outside Japan where regular internet services are cheaper, but they may yet do so.

Conclusion

At the outset we considered three ways in which economic openness might translate into policy change. The first followed the logic of the globalisation model. Firms find that in order to compete in a global marketplace they need policies that match those of competitors in other nations and they pressure their governments to adopt such policies. In the US there is relatively little reference to policies in other nations, because the US has largely been at the forefront of regulatory change. However, even in terms of domestic politics, interest group pressures have had little influence on the dramatic shift from regulated monopoly to deregulation. AT&T was opposed, and user interest groups showed little interest. In the Japanese case users have made only modest efforts to influence policy.

A second way in which more open markets would influence policy would be for political leaders to hold up innovations in other nations as a model to follow. This seems to be a more important way in which 'globalisation' has influenced Japanese telecommunications policy. For instance, most of the section on 'Telecommunications and Innovation', in MITI's 2000 *White Paper* is devoted to a review of the history of deregulation and promotion of competition in the United States, with attention drawn to the US low telecommunications prices and the stimulus they provide to innovation. It concludes, 'Given that globalisation of the market is progressing, it is important to use Europe and the US as a model for moving forward with reform and to show Japan's reform to the world' (MITI 2000: 155). This use of foreign models for domestic economic policy is nothing new in Japanese policymaking, but continues a pattern Japan has followed since the 1870s.

A third way in which more open economies can affect policies is if a state is pressured by other states to change its policies in exchange for access to foreign markets. US pressure on Japan has in fact been important in pushing through logjams and helping make some changes in policy. Nevertheless, when examining actual outcomes American influence is limited, for these are shaped by Japanese ideas and arrangements.

While open economies have influenced policy in both the US and Japan, policy change in each country is shaped powerfully by domestic institutions. Two important institutional differences seem to account for the variation in telecommunications policy between the US and Japan. The US orientation to antitrust policy predisposed political leaders to enthusiastically embrace the new pro-competitive deregulation paradigm in the 1970s, setting the stage for dramatic policy change. Japanese leaders were far less receptive to radical pro-competitive ideas. Second, American regulatory institutions – the courts, the Department of Justice, and the FCC – were more independent of the telecommunications industry and available for a complete about-face on regulatory policy. In contrast, Japan's telecommunications policy follows a previous pattern of combining industrial policy functions and ostensibly pro-competitive regulatory functions in the same bureaucracy and denying the JFTC any power to intervene.

Particular policies, such as telecommunications regulation, are not just isolated sets of rules, but are part of a larger *Gestalt* of ideas and institutions (Jowitt 1978). These ideas and institutions can change, but it is difficult for a particular policy to change in ways that are at odds with the larger pattern. The US maintained regulated private monopoly in telecommunications for over fifty years, but in tension with antitrust policy. Once a coherent academic critique of regulated monopoly was developed, it quickly gained broad support because it fitted with America's orientation towards antitrust policy and liberal economics. The court system provided ample opportunity for challenges to policy. The Justice Department used the courts to break up AT&T, and once new pro-competitive regulations were in place, competing telecommunications companies used the courts extensively to make sure regulators set interconnect fees and other conditions of entry to the market at levels that would favour competition. This process has been contentious, but transparent.

Many in Japan look at America's booming telecommunications sector and its low prices with envy and call for pro-competitive reforms. Yet there is no interest in importing the larger package of institutions that make possible the US's intense telecommunications competition. A Japanese Dietmember told me in 1997 that Dietmembers interested in tougher competition policy number 'two, maybe three' (Personal interview, Tokyo, March 1997). Prime Minister Koizumi has argued for stronger anti-monopoly policy, yet the rank and file of the LDP are not offering much support. New Japanese entrants to the telecommunications field say they find *no* helpful opposition Dietmembers. The Keidanren publishes reams of liberal policy papers, but it opposes giving much power to the JFTC and is not beating down the LDP's door to force tough telecommunications competition. The courts and the JFTC play no role in overseeing or promoting telecommunications policy. Japan's telecommunications policy has been influenced by both the example of the US and pressure from the US, but there are limits as to how far Japanese elites want to go in adopting American-style reforms, and how far Japan can go given its lack of strong courts and independent regulators.

Notes

The author would like to thank Akira Kudo, Toshimasa Tsuruta, Steven Vogel, and Piers Williamson for advice, assistance and criticism, and the Japan – United States Friendship Commission for its support of the research.
1. National Harris poll done for AT&T in 1979 ('Public Attitudes towards Competition in the Telecommunications Industry'), cited in Derthick and Quirk (1985: 24).

10 Diverse paths towards 'the right institutions': law, the state, and economic reform in East Asia

Meredith Woo-Cumings

In the wake of the global financial crisis that began in 1997, an influential body of opinion arose which argued that a primary cause of the crisis in the affected countries was a lack of institutional transparency and accountability, and more generally, an absence of the rule of law. This argument reflected both the nature of the financial crisis itself and the likely policy remedies for it, and a growing international consensus in the 1980s and 1990s that different law traditions had differential effects on economic development. More specifically, the argument was that a common law tradition was more likely to promote economic development because it was the best source of and predictor for the rule of law, transparency, and accountability. By the same token, the civil law tradition was more likely to privilege state intervention in economic processes, and to be less sensitive to concerns about the rule of law and transparency.

In this chapter I will argue that however compelling this argument may be – and I will lay the argument out in some detail – legal traditions and institutions do not determine the nature of the state (although they may be reflected in it) or its likely role in the economy, nor do they critically determine the course of economic development. Therefore the current tendency of pointing to the 'rule of law' as an elixir which will fix various contemporary problems of development may simply be wrong, and it may reverse the causal arrows: instead of common law leading to a minimal state and the broadest extension of the market, or civil law leading to state intervention in the economy and corresponding shrinkage of market activity, there may be no relationship at all between forms of law and the role of the state. I want to make the argument that the current discourse about the rule of law, as well as the long intellectual pedigree behind the argument about law and economic development, may misguide us into thinking that we have unlocked the conundrum of economic growth and reform, when in fact we may be less well off today than when we tried to understand the reasoning behind (and the successes of) state-directed development programmes. This is because of the built-in bias in this literature against the state, which is viewed as *ipso facto* inimical to economic development. And it is the common law background that is assumed to be *ipso facto* conducive to development and to the virtues of transparency and accountability.

I will begin by reviewing the core literature on the rule of law and economic growth; the influential arguments of some institutional economists on the relationship between law, finance, and government; and the current consensus on the part of international development agencies, like the World Bank and the Asian Development Bank, on these issues. In particular, I will examine the influential arguments advanced by Raphael La Porta, Florencio Lopez-de-Silanes, Andrei Shleifer, and Robert W. Vishny (henceforth abbreviated as LLSV), on the superiority of the Anglo-American common law system (*versus* the civil law tradition of continental Europe, Latin America, and much of East Asia) in fostering financial development. I will seek to demonstrate the inadequacy of these arguments on the rule of law and economic development, by flashing them against the backdrop of East Asia.

I will first argue that these mechanisms of state intervention in the economy (*Gyosei shido* in Japanese and its direct transliteration, *Haengjong Chido*, in Korea) were highly *informal* mechanisms which had at best a tangential relationship to formal law or law traditions, and thus this experience contradicts the argument that it is the structure of law that determines the nature of the relationship between the state, economy, and society. Administrative guidance developed both in the 'civil law' countries like Japan and Korea, but also in a 'common law' country like Malaysia – in the latter case an elaborate and sophisticated common law system still posed no barrier to arbitrary decisions by the chief executive.

Second, I will also show that the process of reform itself has developed out of the same pre-existing patterns of state intervention, in particular in the Republic of Korea, one of the success stories of reform since 1997. I will argue that the Korean government has used administrative guidance as an effective policy tool to restructure the corporate sector and to bring about neoliberal reforms – precisely in the direction of accountability and transparency. In other words, administrative guidance remains a powerful tool of state intervention, whether to promote growth or to reform economic practice, in spite of the sense on the part of advocates of the rule of law that such intervention ought to come to an end. It is not a case of the right goal being achieved by the wrong means, so much as the right goals (transparency, accountability) being achieved by means that run in predictable historical grooves, that is, by means that are hard to avoid in any case. More importantly, perhaps, I will argue that administrative guidance bears little relationship to either a civil law or a common law background, and those who think it does are barking up the wrong tree. This experience of state action that was simultaneously heavy-handed and successful, may therefore illustrate that rapid economic reform in a developing society will bear fruit most quickly and effectively in countries already having a more centralised and powerful government, with the trick being to direct that state towards a commitment to reform. This experience may also point the policy community towards considering ways of fostering more effective state institutions, of which the legal institutions are but one aspect, rather than assuming that greater adherence to developing legal institutions and the rule of law, while reigning in the state, constitutes the best path to reform.

Common law and civil law

Nobel laureate Douglas North has been a prolific advocate of the idea that states throughout history more often have been inimical to economic growth than conducive of it, and that the key to economic development is to get states to behave as 'impartial third parties', or to adapt a role sometimes called that of a 'night watchman state' (North 1981, 1990). In his view, the comparative advantage of the state is its capacity for violence, with a typically predatory goal of enhancing state revenue through the power of taxation. Set against this state, rather than alongside it, is North's conception of property rights, and the capacity of property owners to resist the state and to exclude it from involvement with their separate sphere of activity – the (theoretically) free arena of impersonal economic exchange otherwise known as the market. The best state is one that can monitor property rights and enforce contracts, but knows how to step aside or into the background as an impartial enforcer of and advocate for the rights of property holders. A good system of impersonal exchange combined with third-party enforcement of the rules of the game, has been 'the critical underpinning of successful modern economies involved in the complex contracting necessary for modern economic growth' (North 1990: 35). By and large, the most effective of those modern economies have been ones that sprang from the common law tradition.

Another powerful argument for the virtues of a common law tradition comes from Rafael La Porta, Florencio Lopez-de-Silanes, Andrei Shleifer, and Robert Vishney. Through an empirical study of the determinants of quality government in a large cross-section of countries, the authors seek to assess state performance using various measures of government intervention, public sector efficiency, public good provision, size of government, and political freedom (LLSV 1999). They argue that what defines 'good government' is what is 'good for economic development'. Following Montesquieu (1748) and Adam Smith (1776), they focus on the 'security of property rights – lack of intervention by the government, benign regulation, [and] low taxation – as the crucial metric of good performance'.

These authors view legal systems as 'indicators of the relative power of the State *vis-à-vis* property owners', or as 'cruder proxies for the political orientation of governments' (LLSV 1999: 224, 232). Civil law is largely an instrument of the state in expanding its power, the authors write. This type of law focuses on 'discovering a just solution to a dispute (often from the point of view of the State) rather than on following a just procedure that protects individuals against the State', and so the civil law tradition 'can be taken as a proxy for an intent to build institutions to further the power of the State' (pp. 231–2). Common law, by way of contrast, was made by judges who 'put their emphasis on the private rights of individuals and especially on their property rights' (p. 232, quoting Sam Finer). Common law is therefore one's best proxy 'for the intent to limit rather than strengthen the State' (p. 232). More to the point, the authors consider a country's legal system 'as a potential determinant of government performance ... [They] find that the use of a more interventionist legal system, such as socialist or French civil law, predicts inferior government performance ...' (p. 224).

LLSV's 'good government' (1999) and North's 'night watchman' state (1981, 1990) are analogues for the common notion of the rule of law; advocates of the rule of law want an impartial body that is above the fray of day-to-day political and economic conflict, a body that may be composed of human beings, but that owes its allegiance to the law, or to interpreting the law, such that we have a government of laws and not of men, and a final arbiter of right and wrong when political men cannot reach a consensus or remain divided.

Arguments by North and La Porta *et al.* have been important to the contemporary influence of neoliberalism, signified by a concern for applying 'the rule of law' as it is known in Western countries, as a remedy for the defects of developing countries. However, such universal therories of the relationship between legal form and economic performance tend to be so broad that they do not really discriminate between countries and regions. For example, Latin American cases can sensitise us to what a blunt instrument this distinction of civil or common law background may actually be; all the Latin American governments have civil law backgrounds, yet few would compare their record of growth, their financial systems, or their levels of corruption and 'crony capitalism' to the East Asian civil law cases of Japan, Korea, and Taiwan.

In a recent paper, the LLSV authors define corporate governance as 'a set of mechanisms through which outside investors protect themselves against expropriation by the insiders' (LLSV 2000: 1). This expropriation may take the form of transfer pricing, asset stripping, investor dilution, and outright stealing, with the authors finding several practices which may be legal (like investor dilution) having the same effect as stealing. Once again they argue that common law countries offer the strongest protections for outside investors, having judges who base themselves on precedents 'inspired by principles such as fiduciary duty or fairness'. Effective investor protection, according to the LLSV authors, enhances savings and also channels these savings 'into real investment'; the development of strong financial protection 'allows capital to flow towards the more productive uses, and thus improve the efficiency of resource allocation'. Civil law countries, on the other hand, offer much weaker protection to foreign investors, with laws made by legislatures rather than judges looking at precedent.

Raghuram Rajan and Luigi Zingales criticise the work of La Porta *et al.* for giving too much emphasis to legal origin as a key determinant for financial development. Rajan and Zingales's time series empirical data show that paths of financial market development have not been linear, but instead show many fluctuations and departures in countries like the United States, France, Germany, and Britain (2000: 4). The authors argue that it was not legal or cultural factors that determined the level of financial system development in these countries but political factors, such as the support by government and interest groups for financial institution growth, that determined the course of development.

The authors point out that whereas it took over a century and a half for the English common law system to work out something like the limited liability form to its satisfaction, a mere ten years were required for the French civil code to emulate it: 'This explains the almost instant success of continental European Governments in promoting financial development' (Rajan and Zingales 2000: 8). In the end, what is critical is the will of the government to develop the financial market, and in the civil law tradition financial reform may bear fruit more quickly in the more centralised governments of this tradition, than in the weaker governments associated with the common law tradition.

It is also true that civil law countries can learn from common law traditions, and vice versa. Katharina Pistor and Philip A. Wellons (1999: 139–41) argue that classifying countries according to the origin of their legal systems may ignore the fact that 'investor protection developed in most countries only after the period of transplanting major legal systems', and that much of that transplantation involved civil law countries adopting Anglo-American law, as in Japan, the Republic of Korea (ROK), and Taiwan.

Another example along these lines would be the fairly remarkable experience in Latin America, a region made up almost entirely of civil law tradition countries, of governments moving quickly towards market-oriented policies. As Paul Mahoney (1999) puts it, in the light of this experience it is important to recognise that 'legal systems are endowments but not straitjackets'. Indeed, Mahoney thinks that market-oriented policies do not require changes in the legal traditions of given countries, so much as the emergence of new political leadership committed to change; effective leaders not only can implement new market-oriented measures, but also can change public opinion and, over time, the nature of legal practice itself. Mahoney's point here is an important corrective to the historical determinism that lurks in the law-and-economics school: that is, if you have a civil law tradition, should you just give up? What chance do leaders in civil law countries really have to chart a new direction, given the enormous historical advantages (according to the LLSV authors) of a common law tradition? But Mahoney shows that adapting this tradition is much easier and quicker than one might think.

Much of my previous work has been concerned with identifying the specificities of 'late' industrial development, as a way of asking the question, what difference does it make when a country industrialises in the middle of the twentieth century, as opposed to the early nineteenth century (England) or the late nineteenth and early twentieth centuries (Japan)? How do the requirements of industrial strategy, finance, and the role of the state differ, depending on when a country begins to industrialise? (Woo 1991). Without putting too fine a point on it, from this perspective it seems clear that a common law tradition is consonant with early industrial development, in which the private sector is much more active than the state in promoting industrialisation, the time frame for industrialisation is much more lengthy, and leaders do not have to worry so much about competition from countries that have already arrived at an advanced industrial status. This sequencing would also suggest that judges have the luxury of time to develop precedents on a case-by-case basis. The civil law tradition, to the contrary, is much more identified with 'late' industrialisers like Germany and Japan, in which the state became a resource to be deployed to hasten the process of development and to make up or substitute for various disadvantages, such as the modest nature of private sector business or the middle class.

One of the 'advantages of backwardness', in the words of Alexander Gerschenkron, was the ability of late industrialisers to copy the earlier industrialisers, and often the state was the key institution engaged in doing that. But copying a machine is much easier than copying the theory and practice of a law tradition that evolved over centuries, through the establishment and subsequent citation of precedent. It was thus far easier to write a code authorising desired economic behaviour. How much more so would the intense competition for industrial development in recent decades bias countries towards making haste in adapting legal institutions, and those who deplore this process or say that haste makes waste need to tell us how it might have happened otherwise, that is, how a common law tradition based on a long historical evolution could quickly be spliced into effective day-to-day practice in the hot-house conditions of late-twentieth-century development.

Japan: informality, administrative guidance, and 'rule-by-law'

It is a curiosity that Japan endured first an unconditional surrender and then a seven-year occupation (1945–52) by the standard-bearer of the rule of law, the United States, and yet law was more important in Japan before 1945 than it was in the long period of rapid growth that ensued after the Occupation ended. A civil law code modelled on German examples played a significant role in the eighty years of Imperial Japan after the Meiji Restoration in 1868, but with the advent of the postwar democracy came a 'relative shrinkage of the legal sector' (Upham 2001). As Japan became a model of postwar industrial growth, formal legal institutions played at best a back-up role to informal mechanisms, especially the well-known state practice of administrative guidance. Or as Upham puts it, 'economic policy was discussed, formed, and implemented largely through informal mechanisms that were consciously shielded from the interference of the formal legal system...' The courts were relatively inactive, citizens rarely brought actions to them on behalf of individual rights or privileges, and consumer protection was minimal, at least through lawsuits brought to the courts. 'Intervention by the courts in the implementation of economic policy on behalf of private parties', was rare to the point of non-existence. Foreign firms were on the outside looking in on policy formation, of course, and had little recourse to the courts to protect their interests (Upham forthcoming).

Obviously the Japanese system worked to promote economic growth, so how did it do that without following, say, the World Bank criteria of transparency, openness, and arms-length adjudication of disputes, as described by the former General Counsel of the bank, Ibrahim F. I. Shihata (1991)? First, the actors involved in policy implementation were stable institutions staffed by dedicated and competent private and public bureaucrats; second, there were pervasive and institutionalised means of communication between the public and private sectors; third, there was little corruption in the public sector; and last, the legal system did provide distinct outer limits on the flexibility and arrogance of the insiders. But, as Upham lists these qualities, he also notes that Japan cannot be a model for the developing world because these practices are too unique to Japan (Upham forthcoming). But then he also thinks that the World Bank criteria also draw primarily upon the experience of a unique political economy, namely, that of the United States.

As we have seen, a political science deriving from Lockean liberal assumptions never took root in Japan; instead, early Japanese legal and constitutional scholars drew upon the 'state science' of Germany – and not just Germany, but the homeland of conservative reaction, Prussia. The Meiji Constitution of 1889 was modelled on the Prussian example, and constituted 'a compromise between absolute monarchy and modern democracy' (Hashimoto 1963: 239). Japan thus became a country of civil law, with one scholar attributing this largely to 'the historical accident' that common law could not easily be emulated or copied: 'Had Sheldon Amos' civil code for England become a reality, Japan might have had a common-law-inspired civil code, and the subsequent course of her legal development might have been entirely different' (Takayanagi 1963: 37).

207

During the American occupation not only was a new constitution adopted according to Western precedents, but it was also written mostly by Americans; one of its major advances was to abolish the administrative court and introduce the Anglo-American system of judicial review. Did that result in grafting a system of common law onto the Japanese experience of civil law? Some scholars argue that the predictable did indeed happen: that Japanese law thereafter developed in the direction of American law, and that in spite of the vast differences in historical, political, economic, and social backgrounds of Japan and the United States, the postwar system has steadily been 'proving its fitness', with case law and precedent developing rapidly (Hashimoto 1963: 271). Or as another scholar puts it, the old practice of 'rule by law' (*hochishugi*) gave way after 1945 to the 'rule *of* law' (*ho no shihai*) (Takayanagi 1963: 13).

Most others, however, do not think that postwar Japanese legal practice has ever come very close to resembling the Anglo-American system. Indeed, the translation of the above terms is quite revealing. In Japan and Korea *hochishugi* (the phrase is pronounced pobch'ijuui in Korean) is used without carrying the negative connotation that in the West would be attributed to the phrase 'rule by law', and this is not a matter of poor translation. Instead the phrase bespeaks the difficulty of translating or conveying liberal conceptions in a statist society; even the term 'liberal' developed the connotation in Japan and Korea of conservatism (e.g., the ruling Liberal Democratic Party in Japan is neither liberal nor democratic, as these terms are understood in the United States) so the distinction may also be lost between the (liberal) 'rule of law' and the (illiberal) 'rule by law'.

Nor did the Japanese adoption of American-inspired law make people more litigious, as one might expect; instead they were far less litigious than citizens in any other advanced industrial country, and even less litigious than they had been before 1945 (Pistor and Wellons 1999: 230). This experience speaks quite soberly to the travelability of the arguments made by the LLSV scholars and others of the law-and-economics school. That is: have law (but), won't travel.

Instead, postwar Japan preferred administrative action to litigious reaction, and even though the 1946 Constitution required that administration be based on legislation coming out of the Diet, in fact the Diet merely set general guidelines and then authorised the bureaucracy to flesh out the rules, which gave bureaucrats substantial discretion in practice. Constitutional legality receded as administrative guidance (AG) proceeded, a practice that we can usefully define as giving broad discretion to the bureaucracy 'to make, interpret, and enforce detailed rule of economic behaviour'. Or as the most famous analyst of this practice put it, administrative guidance

> ...refers to the authority of the government, contained in the laws establishing the various ministries, to issue directives (*shiji*), requests (*yodo*), warnings (*keikoku*), suggestions (*kankoku*), and encouragements (*kansho*) to the enterprises or clients within a particular ministry's jurisdiction. Administrative guidance is constrained only by the requirement that the 'guidees' must come under a given governmental organ's jurisdiction, and although it is not based on any explicit law, it cannot violate the law (for example, it is not supposed to violate the Antimonopoly Law). (Johnson 1982: 265)

Not only was administrative discretion very broad, but powerful ministries, preeminently the Ministry of Finance (MOF), got away with dusting off interwar laws dealing with financial regulation (especially control of foreign exchange and cross-border financial flows), thus allowing the MOF to change policy by prewar ordinance if not by fiat. The MOF thus based its control over the financial sector on the Banking Act of 1928 and the Foreign Exchange Control Act of 1933 (Pistor and Wellons 1999: 92–3, 98). South Korea likewise often based postwar economic regulation on prewar (Japanese) law.

It is, of course, possible to overemphasise the degree to which AG held sway in postwar Japan. John Haley reminds us that many analysts have missed the degree to which AG reflected the needs and demands of those being 'guided'; often, business firms were in control (Haley 1986: 108). However critical Haley may be of what he sees as the overemphasis on AG by Chalmers Johnson and others, his understanding of the process still reinforces its essential informality, in that AG '(b)y definition it involves neither formal legal action nor direct legal coercion. Compliance is thus voluntary in the narrow legal sense' (1986: 109).

If the role of the MOF, MITI, and the reliance on prewar laws was mitigated by the atmosphere of reform and deregulation in the 1980s, and if AG seems at best vestigial in the year 2000, that probably happened because of the inutility of state direction in an era of information-age industries and technologies, not because someone in Tokyo finally saw the common law light. Indeed, substantial legal scholarship by Michael Young has shown how, even in the atmosphere of change and deregulation in the 1980s, with judges using procedures of judicial review to try to confine AG to carefully defined purposes, the courts were more concerned with bringing AG into line with an informal social consensus than with conforming to legal procedure or abstract legal principle, as might have happened in a common law system. Rather than giving a priority to one side's view, as in an adversarial legal system, the courts have been reluctant to state their position and preferred to rely on societal consensus and informal agreement between the involved parties (Young 1984: 923–5, 965–7, 977). Of course AG was itself an informal system, and so the remedies for the abuses of AG also had to be informal.

Have law, will travel: Korea learns from Japan

One clear case of dramatic international or cross-border learning is the Republic of Korea where administrative guidance remains the primary tool used by the state to intervene in the economy, something that Koreans learned under Japanese imperial tutelage before 1945, but also through emulation of Japan's postwar industrial prowess. In Korea, however, there may have been a kind of *over*-learning, since the use of administrative guidance is far more pervasive than in Japan, and in two important ways goes to unheard-of lengths: first, administrative guidance is not just the province of the state ministries, but can be issued directly by the president through the relevant ministries and agencies, in an executive-dominant political system where the president has far more power than in Japan's parliamentary democracy. Second, the informalities of AG in Japan, limited by formal mechanisms of judicial review and shaped by a prior consensus, give way in Korea to AG almost by fiat; extensive consultations do not necessarily precede administrative guidance, and judicial review was non-existent during the decades of dictatorship and remains weak under the democratic governments of the past decade. Befitting Korea's long authoritarian legacy and its extraordinary history of centralising everything in the capital (far more so than in Japan) and then concentrating that authority in the hands of the chief executive, administrative guidance is far more uneven and abrupt and less consensual, resembling a coercive demand more than an informal guidance (even though on paper Korea's administrative laws clearly call for AG to go through proper legal procedures, and not to involve coercion).

Perhaps because of Korea's authoritarian history and the reams of legalese and formal procedure that powerful executives have made into so much confetti, the literature on law in Korea is extremely slim. While most bookstores have shelves groaning with books on law, these books explain and interpret very narrow forms of law (for example, on export controls and the like), mostly for the consumption of students in legal studies. Perhaps instructive is the fate of one of the few comprehensive books in English to cover varied aspects of Korean law, *Korean Law in the Global Economy* (edited by Song Sang-Hyun, 1996), which went out of print the month it was published. This cuts another sharp contrast with the situation in Japan, where a voluminous literature exists to interpret the place of law in society. Let's have a look at just how weak the judiciary has been in Korea, and just how intrusive and arbitrary the state could be in its interventions in the market.

The well-known legal scholar Song Sang-Hyun likened Korea's judges less to august interpreters of constitutional intent than to dependent factotums; at best they were 'distinguished bureaucrats' and at worst 'expert clerks'. In other words, they were essentially powerless civil servants, mostly incapable of exerting influence on the political system. Given that the administration of justice had virtually no bearing on governmental and political life, their real sphere of influence and action was in civil and commercial matters where their expertise was needed to adjudicate conflicts among private parties and to rule upon the application of criminal laws. Here the power brokers felt no need or interest in interference (unless a friend needed a helping hand), so the judges could have their little realm of autonomy. Given the bureaucratic nature of the judicial system, which exercised its own effect on the basic lack of judicial creativity that all observers noted, and given the judges' lack of power even to interpret (let alone create) the law, the basic requirements for a judge were to be technically competent, inveterately apolitical, risk-averse, and preternaturally quiet (Song 1996a: 300–2).

Real change can come – and has come – to Korea's judiciary only from outside forces. Scholars like Joon-Hyung Hong (1999) argue that with democratisation in the wider society has come the primary impetus for change, and in recent years there has been a lot of it – to the degree that the ideals behind Western conceptions of 'the rule of law' have become widely accepted. Since the national protest mobilisation of June 1987, which ousted dictator Chun Doo Hwan, civil society has advanced rapidly and a proliferation of new laws has done much to democratise the judicial sphere: reform of government fiat under the Administrative Procedure Act (APA), opening of politics through the Freedom of Information Act and the Information Protection Act, devolution of power from the centre under the Local Autonomy Law, and the development of case law through the (finally) vitalised law-finding activities of the courts. Like Lazarus, the Supreme Court and the Constitutional Court sprang to life, trading rigor mortis for habeas corpus and discovering an utterly unaccustomed penchant for judicial review and a theretofore invisible activism in examining the constitutionality of laws.

Dr Hong attributes this new-found judicial determination to the demands and pressures from an invigorated popular sphere, especially for good governance having both a better quality of performance and clear adherence to the principle of the rule of law. Citizen pressures, often in the form of suits filed against public authorities demanding that they do what the letter of the law long had authorised them to do (something unheard of under the dictators, even though all Korean constitutions going back to 1948 look liberal on paper), brought about the court reorganisation of 1994, established the Administrative Court in 1998, along with more recent reform measures that add up to a newly invigorated judicial function in Korea. The significance of these gains cannot be underestimated, since for forty years Korean judges and government officials themselves often felt unconstrained by the very laws that they were called upon to implement, there having been so little force in the concept of 'legal right' in Korean law practice; even when there was evidence of good judicial intervention – or justice in the best sense – it rested upon 'common sense', 'good will', or the judge's 'benevolence' – but not the 'rights' of the individual (Song 1996b: 1246).

Administrative guidance had been ubiquitous in Korea going back to the 1960s, of course, but its very breadth of activity made defining it difficult indeed (Song 1996b). However, while the utility of AG to Korea's rulers was so broad as to complicate its definition, the infamous mid-1980s case of the Kukje conglomerate can at least tell us what Korean-style AG actually felt like through most of its authoritarian tenure.

By the mid-1980s Kukje was a typical Korean diversified megalith, making everything from jogging shoes to aluminium smelting plants, from automobile tyres to farm tools; its subsidiaries engaged in general construction, steel making, paper making, shipbuilding, and if there was no rest for the weary in that extensive tableau, Kukje also built tourist resorts. To keep these far-flung ventures going, Yang Chung Mo, Kukje's founder and owner, had been contributing around $700,000 annually to Chun Doo Hwan's coffers, a yawning maw that subsequently turned out to hold billions of dollars in political funds. Although the owner's son kept telling him that Kukje's political contributions were

212

deemed insufficient to keep Chun happy, the owner refused to increase the payoffs. To make a long story short, in May 1985 the Chun government decided that it had had enough of Mr Yang's insolence and via the intervention of the Finance Minister it instructed Kukje's main bank to initiate and implement the dissolution plan, divvying up its factories among several other firms – and for good measure it also dispossessed Mr Yang of his personal fortune, sending him running for the cover of Los Angeles. As Mark Clifford put it, there was 'no due process, no bidding for assets, only a multimillion-dollar takeover operation shrouded in secrecy' (Clifford 1994: 218–19).

Mr Yang sued in both the United States and in Korea to get his firm and his property back, but nothing could be done until Chun and his successor (and close friend) Roh Tae Woo were finally removed from power. A court finally ruled on the Kukje case in 1993 and as the late legal scholar James West (1998: 321–51) notes in his summary of those rulings, found that:

> The legally groundless exercise of state power in this case not only infringed the requirement of a process based upon law, but also that the person exercising power was lacking in authority contravened the prohibition on arbitrariness, which derives from the guarantee of equal protection of the laws in Article 11 of the Constitution.

The court went on to find that while law required that the legal basis of intervention by the president or other executive organs of the state into the private sphere of civil society and commerce 'must be knowable in advance by the subjects of such regulation', in truth, 'administrative guidance was complex, opaque and often legally irregular. Discipline was imposed through explicit regulations, tacit threats of unfavourable treatment in the future, by intimidating use of punitive tax audits, and sometimes by cynical abuse of the criminal justice system' (1998: 328).

What happens when these provisions are used for the good of the country and to accord with new 1990s concepts of the rule of law, instead of being a mere means to punish and dispossess a political enemy of the president, as in the Kukje case?

Unlike its diminution in Japan, administrative guidance is alive and well in Korea – even if under a democratic government, and even if its uses today are often to correct the abuses of yesterday. Kim Dae Jung came to power in February 1998 as a result of the first truly important political and democratic transition in Korean history (the ruling party in its various transmogrifications having held power since 1961), and proceeded to use this informal mechanism of state interventionism to bring about the rule of law, Korean-style. The 'rules of law' that Kim wants to champion in the economic sphere are: creating transparency in corporate governance, reducing excessive reliance on the banking system for capital, improving the financial structure of the conglomerates (cosy and shady financial arrangements having been both the daily-life norm and the corrupt nexus between the state and big business), separating ownership from management, giving labour a voice at the bargaining table, and improving minority shareholder rights.

The best symbol of how administrative guidance went from stoking the Korean industrial economy to reforming it, in the process saving flagship firms from their own worst selves as the entire economy teetered on the brink of bankruptcy, is the 'Big Deal' industrial reorganisation of 1998 which proposed to find the comparative industrial advantage of each conglomerate and then demand that the firms stick to it – and thus Samsung would do electronics but give up making cars, Daewoo would make cars but forget about shipbuilding, Hyundae would make ships and cars, Lucky-Goldstar would get its nose out of semi-conductors, and the like. The end goal was to reduce overinvestment by shrinking the number of firms in a given industry, thus forcing firms to focus on their 'core competence' after years of excess redundant diversification. Kim's reforms sought both to preserve the perceived comparative advantage of Korea's chaebol in world markets, and to break the nexus of state and corporate power, which had gained its sustenance through capital provisioned by the government to the big firms in the form of huge state-mediated, preferentially priced loans, something that had long been the distinguishing characteristic of the Korean model of development.

In January 1998, even before Kim was inaugurated but under the prodding of the International Monetary Fund (IMF) for serious reform of Korean economic practice, Kim Dae Jung met with conglomerate leaders and concluded a major agreement on five key principles of corporate reform, which became known as the 'Big Deal': increased corporate transparency, elimination of cross-debt guarantees by firm subsidiaries, improvement of the capital structure of the firms (a euphemism for the big firms no longer depending on the government for loans), business concentration on core competence areas, and strengthened cooperation with small and medium-sized enterprises. The Big Deal might be agreed upon quickly, but implementing it took the rest of 1998, and a particular sticking point was the state's demand that Lucky-Goldstar (now known simply as LG) give up semi-conductor production (see Weiss, this volume). LG, quite predictably, could not see much difference between what Kim Dae Jung wanted to do to it, and what Chun had done to Kukje. If the legality of the Big Deal becomes an issue, as some expect it to be after Kim Dae Jung's term expires, the contention will likely evolve around the interpretation of administrative guidance, especially its limits under the rule of law. It had not been okay for Chun Doo Hwan to disabuse Mr Yang of his investment and property in Kukje because this went beyond the realm of friendly advice and voluntary compliance. Was it okay for Kim Dae Jung's government to use AG to decide which corporations should produce which products?

In attempting to reform corporate governance in Korea in the current milieu, where civil society is active and quite strong, the state has had to balance between democratic activists (often holding the same values that elsewhere might be called neoliberal, like adherence to the rule of law) and the undemocratic status quo, which is deeply shaped by informal practices (like AG) that gave great power to the state and carry correspondingly little expectation that ordinary people can make any difference in the way the state and the big firms operate. For instance, activist groups like the People's Solidarity for Participatory Democracy demand instant reforms for mandatory cumulative voting (a tool used by minority corporate shareholders to elect their preferred directors) and the introduction of class-action lawsuits into corporate law, which then prompted the government to announce that it would abandon obligating corporations to practise cumulative voting, and pledged that class-action lawsuits would be introduced gradually. It is still unclear, though, whether corporations will actually implement new voting procedures giving small stockholders a voice, and the government fears that if it were immediately to approve class-action lawsuits, the courts would be flooded with petitioners.

In short, in the worst of times Korean administrative guidance has been destructive of the rule of law, involving outright expropriation of property in the name of industrial reorganisation (or just punishing someone who was stingy with political funds, as we saw in the Kukje case), such that Adam Smith's hidden hand materialised as an all too conspicuous mailed fist; in ordinary times it has been the mundane, informal instrument of an intrusive executive power. But does that necessarily negate the value of administrative guidance, which in the best of times was the core architectonic force behind Korea's rapid industrialisation?

In the empyrean of the Hayekian rule of law, administrative guidance should be (at best) no more than the handmaiden of an arm's-length, disinterested third-party justice, and even then it would be better if it simply did the right thing and abolished itself. But perhaps the Japanese precedents we surveyed earlier provide a more realistic roadmap towards how real-world AG can morph into a useful practice constrained by an evolving and ever-stronger form of judicial review or, as in the Korean case, an energised populace. In any case it is better to bark up that tree, than to hope that this manifest, blatant, unambiguously domineering 'hand' will issue its death rattle and disappear quietly into that good night. The alternative of a delayed and dilated euthanasia for Korean administrative guidance looks even better when we grasp that in the aftermath of the 1997 crisis it did in fact become an effective mechanism of reform, the intrusive arm of government that propelled financial restructuring, cleaned up corporate governance, and got economic growth back on track. Perhaps now we can look forward to administrative guidance finding a way to prepare its own deathbed.

More like them: common law 'looks East'

Malaysia is a fascinating case to compare to Korea and Japan, however briefly, given that it long has had a more liberal market and a state based in a common law background that was less interventionist than Japan's (let alone Korea's), yet under its notorious leader Mahathir it developed the aspiration to be more like Japan and Korea (during the so-called 'Look East' strategy), and even though it failed in that effort, it succeeded in destroying its own common law based constitution. How did it do so, and what happened to its British common law tradition? The simple answer is that Mahathir expanded the power of the state and used it first to hamstring and then to demolish the judiciary. Law did not appear to be the 'proxy' for the state or the determinant of the state–market nexus as the LLSV scholars would claim, but quickly fell away before the advance of a powerful state.

The legal basis of pre-colonial Malaya was customary and Islamic law, but it had a far longer period of exposure to British or common law than did many colonies, as British control lasted from 1874 to 1957. The post-independence legal system consisted basically of British law and some elements of Islamic law, which reflected the ethnic balance between Chinese businessmen and other non-Islamic groups, and the majority Malays who believe in Islam. Existing laws and statutory and judicial precedents bear the indelible marks of English common law and equity and what the colonial judges thought was just, fair, reasonable, and equitable. The 1957 Federal constitution was drafted by the British parliamentary draftsmen, broadly based on the Westminster parliamentary model. The judiciary and the entire judicial process operated and is still operating under the profound influence of the English common law and equity, judicial precedents, principles, ideas, and concepts. Even today, venerations to the views, observations, and comments of the British judges is very much prominent in the courts' decisions. The polity had a number of major democratic features, such as regular elections contested by independent parties, a Parliament to which the government was responsive, and a constitutionally independent judiciary (Biddle and Milor 1999: 11). If the organised bar was small, countervailing legal efforts to control the government's growing power were rule-based. Administrative law, as interpreted by the courts, provided rudimentary controls over the government; judicial independence was high; and judges were career appointees and not at that time part of the political majority.

Despite the trappings of democracy, though, the actual limitations on democratic process were many, including the introduction of the Internal Security Act (ISA) in 1960 allowing detention without trial. Following racial riots in 1969, and a temporary suspension of Parliament, authoritarian controls were expanded, but these limitations on Malaysia's democracy were not fatal, and until the 1980s most observers applauded the functioning of its democratic system. The same was true of the economic system, formed in a common law incubator.

As the Malaysian economy began to take off in the 1960s, laws and legal procedures were 'market-allocative' and rule-based. In this period the procedures reflected a rights-based approach to internal government controls, and laws provided for the regulation of various professions (accounting, architecture, engineering, and so on). There was also a mix of state and market-allocative laws to support the government's economic strategy. After the 'Look East' policy began in 1981, however, abuses of public office grew, and the legal system was used extensively to implement policy. More laws conferring discretionary power on the Executive were adopted than in any previous time since Malaysian independence (see, for example, Das 1981: 2).

The Malaysian state frankly adopted the Japanese and Korean model, choosing the same trade-off between economic growth and democracy characteristic of Park Chung Hee's Korea. The policy was anti-Western, and more especially, anti-British. Prime Minister Mahathir pursued an interventionist strategy partially modelled on South Korea's heavy and chemical industries industrial policy of the early 1970s (often called 'the Big Push'), involving close collaboration between the government and big business. At the same time, however, the Malaysia Inc. policy was if anything even more encompassing, with collaborative relations envisioned between public and private sectors in all sectors of the economy, between the differently placed racial groups, and at the state as well as federal levels. What was 'Malaysia Inc' supposed to look like? Let's hearken to the horse's mouth himself: in 1984 Mahathir said:

> the Malaysia Incorporated concept means close and mutually support-
> ive cooperation between the public and private sectors ... The private
> sector must understand national policies, objectives and procedures
> in order to facilitate their dealings with the Government. They must
> appreciate that regulations and procedures are not meant to frustrate
> them but are in fact a means of ensuring orderliness in commerce and
> industry ... The service sections of the Government, the policy and
> lawmakers, have a duty to ensure that no undue hindrance is put in
> the way of the private sector.   (Biddle and Milor 1999: 15)

The Malaysian government established HICOM (Heavy Industries Corporation of Malaysia) to diversify manufacturing activity, increase local linkages, and generate local technological capacity. HICOM, however, suffered significant financial losses, and these, combined with a deterioration in the terms of trade (fuelled by the drop in world prices for major commodities such as petroleum and palm oil) and increasing external debt, alongside a slump in external demand in primary commodities and electronics and curtailed demand for steel, cement, and cars, occasioned a recession lasting from late 1984 until 1987. As a consequence, Malaysia experienced negative growth rates, and investments, both public and private, dropped precipitously. Many of the firms the state had sponsored proved to be inefficient, usually due to cronyism, but also because there were simply too many competing firms in the region (Pillay 2000: 209).

But the economic failure did not stop Mahathir from decisively defeating judicial activism, at the hands of the Executive; basically, the independence of the judiciary was destroyed in a few years in the late 1980s. Let us trace this a little bit. Previously Article 4(1) of the Constitution had proclaimed the Constitution to be supreme, and borrowing from the US model, allocated certain powers, including judicial review,

to the Malaysian courts. Judicial review was also one of the five pil-
lars of the national ideology, called the *Rukunegara*: 'The rule of law is
ensured by the existence of an independent judiciary with powers to
pronounce on the constitutionality and legality or otherwise of executive acts' (Milne and Mauzy 1999: 46).

The year preceding the crippling of the judiciary saw a great deal of
judicial activism, with a number of important decisions going against
the government. For example, in 1986 the judiciary upheld a challenge
against a government expulsion order against a foreign journalist; in
1987 it granted habeas corpus to an ISA detainee; but the upshot of this
judicial activism (or resistance) was that Mahathir, who had encountered no resistance in the cabinet or the Parliament, felt that he faced
resistance only from the judiciary – and so judicial independence had to
go. Mahathir got much assistance from the Parliament, which passed the
Federal Constitution (Amendment) Act of 1988, removing the powers
of the judiciary from the Constitution, deeming instead that they would
be conferred by Parliament through statutory decree. By this Act, the
courts were summarily stripped of the power of judicial review previously granted in the Constitution (Milne and Mauzy 1999: 47).

Observers were understandably shocked that the whole judicial system could be transformed so easily, but Mahathir claimed that he was
merely guarding the prerogatives of the legislature to 'develop the law'.
Or as Mahathir told *Time* magazine: 'If we find out that a Court always
throws us out on its interpretation, if it interprets contrary to why we
made the law, then we will have to find a way of producing a law that
will have to be interpreted according to our wish' (quoted in Khoo 1995:
288). In general, laws which at first blush seemed to undergird the power
of the judiciary and various checks and balances, over time were used to
entrench the executive's power. A legislature which should have been a
main source of resistance to Mahathir's rule, turned out to be the handmaiden of his will in demolishing the courts and removing even as lip
service the Constitution's protection for judicial review. Rule making
in the Executive expanded as its economic activism spread, despite the
significant growth of lawyers in the economy (almost 6,000 advocates
and solicitors by the end of 1995) (Pistor and Wellons 1999: 91).

In short, there is precious little in the Malaysian case to suggest that
the heritage of common law, a carefully crafted democratic Constitution,
or several decades of human experience with the workings of the rule
of law, offered much of an obstacle to an authoritarian reworking of the
system. It seems more likely that Korea, moving out of its authoritarian

path even as it uses the mechanisms of state intervention to do so, comes much closer to democracy and to an effective form of the rule of law than does Malaysia, going in the opposite direction. In any event neither the Korean nor the Malaysian case offers much support for the idea that learning how to act according to the ideal of disinterested third-party rule enforcement will ever be a simple or easy process of hearkening to the scholars and then acting accordingly.

Conclusion: the right institutions

The concern with law and economic governance is part and parcel of the 'second generation reform', which in the words of the President of the World Bank, James Wolfensohn (1999), refers to 'the structure of the right institutions, of the improvement of the administrative, legal, and regulatory functions of the state, addressing the incentives and actions that are required to have private sector development and to develop the institutional capacity for reforms...' First-generation reform had focused on macroeconomic policies designed to make markets work more efficiently – 'pricing, exchange rate and interest rate reforms, tax and expenditure reforms and the establishment of rudimentary market institutions' (Camdessus 1999) – but with the second wave the very structure of law and government, that is, *politics*, came to the fore.

The 1997 financial crisis was the real-world disaster that opened many developing countries up to the ministrations of neoliberal reformers, and it is clear that the World Bank, in particular, has high hopes for how much the second-generation reforms will contribute to economic growth – even to the point of mathematical estimations of how much projected real GDP growth in East Asia for 2000–10 would be attributable to better institutions – understood chiefly as 'new rules' (for a critique of this view, and discussion of the institutions required, in the context of revitalising that development, see Doner and Ramsay, this volume).

This chapter has argued that this new emphasis on rule of law, conceived as an elixir for developing and transitional countries, cannot solve the vexing problems of politics and development. However admirable in its intentions, the new World Bank perspective draws on a peculiarly Anglo-American discourse and experience, generalising on the basis of a set of governmental institutions that are themselves anomalous survivors in the twenty-first century – this state form that Samuel Huntington once called the 'Tudor polity' (Huntington 1968). As the *Federalist Papers* long ago noted, the point of this state form was to disperse and confine political power, to divide it into three branches of government that would check and balance each other, to have the legislators keep an eye on the executive, the local states corral and confine the central government, and the judges watch them all. It was a form of politics suitable to an agrarian economy of yeoman farmers, and as that economy slowly became urban and industrial, no less than Thomas Jefferson condemned this transformation in the name of the pastoral ideals that underlay his conception of American governance. That was more than 200 years ago, of course, and for the past 150 years the central problem was not how to *restrain* power, but how to *create* it in the first place. Ever since, the problem of good governance has been how to comprehend and deal with the large bureaucratic central states that emerged in the context of industrialisation – either to further the growth of industry, as in Germany and Japan, or to rein in the excesses of industrial capitalism, as in the American New Deal.

I think the real problem – the actually existing practical conundrum of good *policy* – is how to find effective tools to realise the substance of arm's-length, third-party governance in the existing context of strong states that may not be 'the right institutions', but happen to be the ones we have to work with in the real world. We have to find ways to achieve the admirable goals of transparency, accountability, and disinterested justice without expecting to mimic a set of institutions developed in the tranquil, bucolic ambience of the eighteenth century; often this will be a matter of creatively utilising those 'wrong institutions' that were the sources of past developmental success, like the heritage of administrative guidance that I have focused on in this chapter. As the contemporary Korean case makes clear, tools of strong state intervention can be an effective expedient to achieve the goals of second-generation reform; Kim Dae Jung has wielded these tools against the big banks and the big chaebol firms, but has also used the state to reform the state (as with the increasing effectiveness of judicial review and prosecutorial activism), and has used the people (in the form of new citizen groups) to pressure the state, all in the name of reform.

My arguments were qualitative and not quantitative, but other scholars have used quantitative methods to arrive at similar conclusions: Kevin Davis and Michael Trebilcock (1999), in a World Bank study, found little evidence of a causal relationship between law and economic development; their empirical studies of the relationship between growth and law in a variety of areas from family to taxation law do not point to causality. The more daunting challenge, they think, is to enhance 'the quality of institutions charged with the responsibility of enacting laws and regulations', and that exclusive or predominant occupation with the court system inappropriately discounts the important role played by government departments and agencies. Both of these points support my arguments about working within the existing governmental systems to increase the influence of the rule of law.

This chapter has pointed to the need to rethink the role of the state in economic reform. It supports the central points of work by Jean-Philippe Platteau (1994), who has argued that strong states are often required to *create* the rule of law, or that in the absence of appropriate private-sector moral or legal norms, a strong state is needed to support economic exchange. State intervention can alter social norms and correct 'trust failure', in his view. My study of the East Asian countries – Korea in particular – shows how better economic governance can be mandated, if not coerced, by the state (in countries with strong state traditions), albeit through means that are informal and discretionary. A second point follows from the first, namely, that legal and institutional reform has to be moored in local experience and know-how, and, preferably, with the help of an energised citizenry. Again Korea showed how the mobilisation of state tools to reform the political economy could be helped by pressure coming from outside, through new participatory political institutions that also help to aggregate local knowledge and thereby help build better institutions.

Part III
Governing globalisation

11　Managing openness in India: the social construction of a globalist narrative

Jalal Alamgir

Why does a state like India continue policies oriented towards economic openness despite unfavourable domestic political and social conditions? Conventional explanations emphasise the role of technology, economic crisis, and the influence of multinational agencies and corporations. In doing so, these accounts conflate the *causes* of economic opening with its maintenance or *continuity*, shifting the agency away from the state and its institutions. Ontologically, in addition, research on globalisation tends to focus on change, whether it is in business practices, technology, social policy, culture, or state capacity. Continuity seems either taken for granted or uninteresting.

It makes sense to separate continuity from either cause or change as a distinct subject of inquiry. There is nothing inherent about a triggering event (cause) that assures policy continuity. In fact, it is the continued management of economic openness – whether it is through active intervention, deniable tacit support, or an explicit hands-off approach – that illustrates most starkly the state's role in promoting globalisation. Works by Eric Helleiner (1994), Ethan Kapstein (1994), Louis Pauly (1997), and Linda Weiss (1998), in this vein, underscore the state's industrial and financial policy interventions. Equally important, but less evident, is the state's effort at constructing an enabling narrative in support of its policies. Policy statements, speeches, publications, debate, academic and professional training, historiography – all of these entail rhetorical exercises that cumulate in creating an environment to either support or discourage cross-platform consensus on openness, or on any other significant policy stance for that matter. A well-formulated narrative allows the state to effectively use the political power of rhetoric, interpretation, emotion, and imagination to reach out to constituents to elicit support for its economic policies.

By examining India's political economy, this chapter argues that the social construction of an enabling narrative is crucial for managing, accepting, and sustaining a set of policies through economic and political changes. India began to open up its economy definitively in mid-1991. The political and economic circumstances were fragile. The finance minister admitted that it would take a 'miracle' to sustain openness in a country as diverse and politicised as India. Between 1991 and 2000, the government in India changed five times, and confronted a steady wave of opposition from social groups, labour, trade associations, nationalists, environmentalists, and intellectuals. Yet successive Indian governments, regardless of party, have affirmed that reversal of outward orientation is 'ruled out'.

The fact that India has persisted with economic openness in spite of its previously ardent inward-looking policies, its factionalism, and egalitarian pressures, indicates an unlikely compromise among key policymakers and institutions. To reach such a compromise, maverick policymakers had to construct and market a narrative that could cast a broad net to muster adequate support for policy continuity. Culling material from India's history, speeches, political writings, and other documentary sources, they promoted a sort of *nationalist globalism*, which stabilised expectations and unified different interests. It contributed to sustaining open-door policies by enabling the state to portray economic openness as compatible with Indian values and the state's international goals. This rationale gave the state crucial room to manoeuvre: It legitimised an active policy role and allowed the state to refute the conventional claim that globalisation had emasculated its economic and social power.

The key emotive appeals of the narrative are an assertion of India's civilisational grandeur, a lament at its recent power position in the world, an urgent need to raise the state's visibility and role in international affairs, and an acute sense of enmity and envy of the state's principal external competitor. The rest of this chapter reviews these facets, with considerable attention to delineating their historical sources. The power of the narrative owes greatly to its historical base, drawing from some of the most revered names and poignant events in Indian intellectual and political chronicles. In its recent application to promoting economic openness, therefore, it could be presented as a storyline congruent with the historical and ideological mainstays of the state itself, creating implicitly a sense of continuity rather than a jarring break from the past. The concluding sections of the chapter describe how policymakers in the nineties evoked the emotive facets of nationalist globalism to capture mass imaginations. The narrative became successful in creating an environment in which maintaining openness seems the right thing to do.

The roots of nationalist globalism: civilisational grandeur

The bedrock of India's nationalist globalism is a belief in the grandeur and international influence of India's civilisation, a creed rooted firmly in the imaginations and convictions of the early nationalist elite. The nationalist project in India was spearheaded by a small elite to whom the British eventually transferred power. Thanks to their formal Western education, most of them were familiar with post-Enlightenment ideas about the modern state and international relations. Their exposure to the West, coupled with prevalent ideational and ideological currents, made the nationalist elite globalist in its outlook. They viewed India as a vast country, rich in resources, an ancient civilisation occupying a prominent geopolitical space. A notion of grandeur, of being or becoming a great power, was an integral part of their anti-colonial nationalist project. In spite of all the attendant problems of postcolonial development, this belief has remained innate in the Indian policymaking elite. Even India's failings were on a grand scale, observed Nehru in his famous speech on the eve of independence.

In the mindset of the early nationalists, reaching out for regional and perhaps global influence was inevitable. Although the nationalist project was pulled towards several divergent polarities – unity versus diversity, secularism versus religiosity, idealism versus realism, globalism versus autarky – it staked a persuasive claim that details and instruments aside, India in the end must play a strong and influential part in world affairs. This, in essence, is the heart of India's globalist narrative. Through examining myths, folklore, art, architecture, rituals, warfare, and written accounts, nationalist historiography imagined an internationally influential civilisation, whose religious and cultural marks extended from Persia in the west to Indonesia in the east. Nationalist orators and writers pointed to the early influence of India on kingdoms in Southeast Asia through the spread of Hinduism and Buddhism, and began to talk about a 'Greater India', based on civilisational kinship. The emigration of a large number of Indian workers to other British colonies in Southeast Asia, Southern and Eastern Africa, the Caribbean, and the Pacific

227

also gave India a concrete presence worldwide. Nationalist strategists recognised that given India's size, 'commanding position in the Indian Ocean', and geopolitical location between the Near East and the Far East, 'India must have a say in all developments affecting Asia' (Prasad 1962: 3–4).

Ideologically this narrative stood opposed to foreign imperialism, and became imbued with powerful doctrines about peace and non-violence. The globalism it espoused was normative. Its international ramifications included support for self-determination, pacifism, non-alignment, and cooperative means for resolving international conflicts. These were considered indigenous values, to be reflected in foreign relations, and disseminated to counter other more confrontational and imperialist norms.

Politics of the Indian National Congress (INC) reflected these ideational and ideological currents. The more radical leaders of the Congress spoke and wrote openly about India's eventual emergence as a major recognised power. One of the most influential leaders, Bal Gangadhar Tilak, wrote a letter to the president of the Peace Conference in 1919, urging for India's admission into the League of Nations:

> With her vast area, enormous resources and a prodigious population she [India] might well aspire to be a leading power in Asia, if not in the world. She could, therefore, be a powerful steward of the League of Nations in the East. (Prasad 1962: 70)

By the 1920s India's normative globalism had become well entrenched within the nationalist movement. The movement itself had gained full momentum by this time. Thanks to the printing press, tales extolling India's glorious past and unified destiny were distributed widely to an enthusiastic audience (Chatterjee 1993: 7). Although the spread of nationalist ideas generated considerable debate, isolationism as a concept did not gain wide currency. Rabindranath Tagore, for instance, questioned at times whether the rising movement of non-cooperation would ultimately mean that India would isolate itself from the rest of the world. Gandhi assured him that, to the contrary, it would send messages of pacifism to other regions, and implied that India's foreign policy would disseminate such values.

Indeed, international interconnectedness seemed inevitable, isolationism seemed ineffective, and a strong foreign policy seemed essential. Theories of capitalism as well as Marxism had begun to highlight, for different reasons, the interconnections among nations and economic players. As a result, it was natural among prominent Indian intellectuals and activists, like Tagore, Tilak, Gandhi, Rammohan Roy and Netaji Subhas Chandra Bose, to espouse cosmopolitan views, even while they advocated a breaching of colonial ties.

Jawaharlal Nehru, educated in the West and impressively aware of prevalent currents of internationalism, was at the centre of both the nationalist project and the Congress. Under his single-handed dominance of India's external relations, globalism became a major objective of the independence struggle. Independence, for him, was 'an opportunity to establish India as a presence on the world stage' (Khilnani 1997: 178). In his view, the image of colonial subjection could be shed by transforming India into a prominent actor in international politics with a splendid, cosmopolitan past and an independent voice. He wrote in 1939:

> A free India, with her vast resources, can be a great service to the world and to humanity. India will always make a difference to the world; fate has marked us for big things. When we fall, we fall low; when we rise, inevitably we play our part in the world drama.
>
> (Quoted in Nayar 1979: 123)

Over the decade following independence, Nehru and his contemporaries revelled in India's potential for grandeur, as evident in numerous speeches and debates in the Parliament and in subsequent policy statements. In a famous debate on foreign policy in the Constituent Assembly in 1947, Nehru remarked:

> India is a great country, great in her resources, great in manpower, great in her potential, in every way. I have little doubt that free India on every plane will play a big part on the world stage, even on the narrowest plane of material power.   (Nehru 1961: 13)

Parliamentary proceedings around that time were peppered with such proclamations about India's power potential and globalist future. India's globalism became a faith: because of its past and its potential, India was bound to play a global role in politics and economics. But it contained contradictions. On one hand, India needed to disseminate around the world its own values, to reproduce the prominent role the civilisation once played in shaping cultures and religions far abroad. Achieving this idealist enterprise, none the less, required a practical, 'realist' stance in everyday international relations, so that India would be recognised as a competent player, not a hapless developing country with utopian dreams.

Instead of picking one over the other, India's foreign policy pursued both. Indian globalism, as a result, was fragmented, practised in multiple domains and pulled in different directions by divergent ideologies. Indian international relations reflected this contradiction. The strategy for India's defence, shaped in large part by Nehru, incorporated a realist framework with idealist goals, a merger that he considered necessary in part because of globalist ambitions. Nehru reasoned that given India's geopolitical position and importance, the world powers would not let any single country conquer or dominate India. The conquest of India would give any one power a disproportionate strategic advantage in the world. So any attempt to dominate India would be balanced by the intervention of other powers. The doctrine of non-alignment supported not only this strategic vision but also India's globalism. As Baldev Raj Nayar pointed out:

> It is precisely India's perception of itself as a potential great power –
> however distant the prospect may seem – combined with the recogni-
> tion of its present weakness [e.g., developmental problems] that led to
> the policy of nonalignment in the first place... Given the perception
> of India's potential, a satellite role was clearly unacceptable.
>
> (Nayar 1979: 122)

This line of thinking, that idealism and realism are complementary for a developing country with globalist ambitions, continued well after independence, and has been stated explicitly by subsequent foreign ministers (Nayar 1979). India saw itself as unique in the world in pioneering a type of foreign policymaking that promoted normative values. What is important to recognise is that the value-orientation or 'idealism' was not utopian; it was instrumental. It was the means to achieve a distinct, independent voice. Like the way India's nationalism, based on non-violent civil disobedience, gave the country respect and renown, its globalism, based on pacifism, non-alignment, cooperation, and democratic self-determination, was to propel India into global prominence. Considered timeless, these values could not be shed from policymaking, for they constituted the persona of India's great, ancient civilisation.

Globalism and 'hegemonic rivalry' with China

The second principal element of India's globalist narrative is the idea of a long-term strategic rivalry with China for regional hegemony. Nehru and his contemporaries realised that the existence of another large civilisation to the north, China, raised the possibility of conflict in the future. The sense of rivalry has evoked feelings of both enmity and envy in Indian policymakers. Although its roots are in British colonial policy and convictions, its present shape is influenced by the experience of a war with China in 1959–62 and the growth of nuclear insecurity since the seventies.

Indian strategists initially envisioned China as an Asian compatriot forging an independent, non-aligned path of the kind India championed. As China began to question the legitimacy of the mutual border, which was an ambiguous colonial artifact to begin with, Indian policy circles began to employ a discourse of hegemonic competition against China. China mounted a full-scale invasion along India's northeastern frontier in October 1962. It routed the Indian army and occupied about 14,000 square miles of what used to be Indian terrain. This experience firmly instilled in Nehru and other policymakers a belief that China was seeking Asian leadership at India's expense, if not by physical domination then certainly by forcing 'a mental surrender' (Hoffman 1990: 217).

Such feelings permeated wider strategic circles as well. Although India lost a large piece of territory, Indian policymakers did not interpret the loss as a dent on India's potential for great power status. Instead, they looked forward and emphasised the need to practise *realpolitik* backed by adequate material strength. This was necessary to engage effectively the other great – and in their view, more aggressive – power, China (Dixit 1998: ch. 4). In *India and the China Crisis*, a detailed study of decisionmaking during the war, Steven Hoffman contends that India's misgivings that China would become an assertive rival were now confirmed and transformed into 'a coherent and long-lasting belief system' (Hoffman 1990: 215).

From the perspective of globalist policymakers, India's only major mistake was an oversight: not having a strong defence – a lapse unpardonable for a state claiming regional hegemony. This was a crucial lesson for the Indian state:

> India had obviously behaved irresponsibly as a major power, devoting to defence a mere 2 per cent of its gross national product ... For India, the real message of the border conflict was that the country's role pretensions were inconsistent with its capabilities.
>
> (Nayar 1979: 140–1)

India's ensuing programme for a coherent strategic and competitive vision was a direct outgrowth of the war with China. It implanted an acute sense of insecurity about China's rising military budget and expanding sphere of influence. Although strategists knew that techno-logical and power projection capabilities were commensurate with In-dia's globalist aspirations, the war ensconced an urgency to aggrandise material power. Not just the staunch nationalists, but a wider spectrum of political interests found common ground in the belief that China posed a real threat to India's future, militarily, politically, and econom-ically. The election manifestoes of all Indian political parties between 1967 and 1972 included an aggressive competitive stance against China (Tharoor 1982: 228–9).

The line of actual control between India and China, established in 1962, has remained to date in an undeclared state of war. India accepted China's ceasefire line as *de facto*, not *de jure*. Because of the uncertainty of the border and insecurity about increasing Chinese assertions in South-east Asia, territorial competition and security continued to be the centre-piece of India's China strategy through Indira Gandhi's leadership in the seventies (Tharoor 1982). Compared to her father, Nehru, Indira adopted a stronger approach towards China, due to Indira's belief in *realpolitik*, rising insurgency in the border areas, China's support of Pakistan, and most importantly, India's growing defence capabilities.

The combustion of globalist ambitions and exigencies arising out of rivalry with China and its allies gave a powerful thrust to India's pro-gramme for big science and prestige weaponry. Just two years after the war, China conducted its first nuclear test at Lop Nor in October 1964. This immediately raised the stakes for India to develop a deterrent. Minoo Masani expressed the fears of many of India's political leaders at that time: 'The Chinese explosion cannot be ignored; it cannot be written off; it cannot be played down; it is of major significance. We are the coun-try for which it has the most immediate importance' (quoted in Ganguly 1999: 152–153). In the wake of this explosion, Lal Bahadur Shastri, India's Prime Minister, tried to obtain security guarantees from other big powers. When that failed, as admitted in the Parliament in 1965, he authorised India's SNEP (subterranean nuclear explosion project) pro-gramme. The project culminated in India's so-called 'peaceful' explosion of 1974. Since then Indian strategic analysts have been repeatedly urg-ing the development of not just prototype but proven nuclear capability, especially since the 1980s when it became clearer that China had been transferring to Pakistan technologies related to nuclear weapons devel-opment. These were major triggers for India's second round of explo-sions in May 1998 (Ganguly 1999: 170) and for Defence Minister George

Fernandes's public identification that China, not Pakistan, was India's 'threat number one' (see, for example, *New York Times*, 5, 12, and 15 May 1998). In view of India's feeling of long-standing rivalry with China, highlighted in strategic writings, policy discourse, and news commentaries, Pratap Mehta remarked after the 1998 tests: 'the surprise is not that these [nuclear] tests occurred but that it took so long for them to occur' (Mehta 1998: 17).

'India's due': from normative claims to material capabilities

Intertwined with civilisational grandeur and insecurity about China is a third element of India's globalist narrative: a feeling of lost glory and neglect. Indian leaders felt that India did not get the respect it deserved as a prominent civilisation. At the same time they resented the fact that China commanded comparatively greater attention from the West. Indian policymakers identified material weakness as the main reason for this apparent neglect.

Historically India's bid for global prominence had been based on an assertion of rights, not capabilities. Nehru and most other early strategists claimed great power status because India, in their view, *deserved* it as an ancient civilisation, the world's largest country in population, the largest democracy, and one of the largest in land area. Especially from the fifties to the eighties, rhetoric in India and in some of its allies abroad evoked this sentiment. A characteristic statement, for instance, is this commentary published in *Pravda* in 1955: 'India is indeed a great power...she should be given one of the first places among the great powers of the world' (quoted in Ray 1986: 39). The tone typically is romanticist: India should be 'given' that status, rather than command it through manifesting its power and capabilities. It was India's due.

Not only features of 'giantism' and grandeur, but moral indignation also was grounds for India's claim to stature: 'The fact that the last several hundred years saw India under alien rule only makes aspirations to the restoration of greatness all the more deeply felt' (Nayar 1979: 122). This is not to say that India's early strategists and writers thought naïvely that such right-based claims would be enough to attain the rank India deserved. They did not, but, primarily because of India's economic weaknesses, they chose to pursue a normative route to globalism rather than one based on material strength.

The scenario began to change after the war and China's nuclear tests. Since the seventies the Indian state has tried to strengthen its pursuit of globalism by emphasising a more visible, independent international role. This effort has ranged from leadership in the Non-Aligned Movement to organising developing countries in different international forums, such as UNCTAD, Group of 77, and the New International Economic Order. India has been trying to raise its capacity as a regional donor, creditor, and mediator. It has been keen to obtain permanent membership in the UN Security Council. Indian diplomats have pointed out that its population was larger than all the permanent members combined, except China. Moreover, as a member it would be a representative of the Third World in global decisionmaking. Indian diplomats also argued that China's inherent status was never questioned by the great powers; only the legitimacy of the regime representing China was periodically in doubt. If China were to have such status, so should India.

Overall, Indian statesmen have been disappointed at the lack of attention from traditional powers, including the United States: 'Everyone in Washington ignores India' (Sieff 1998: 38). The disappointment grew at a time when US policies began to overlook China's political lapses in consideration of its growing military and economic power. C. Raja Mohan, a strategic columnist, asked in 1995: 'Why cannot we be like the Chinese? The effective combination of defiance and dealmaking has been the hallmark of the Chinese approach to the United States.' Raja Mohan urged India to develop economic might as well as declared nuclear capability to achieve the kind of power China enjoyed (quoted in Perkovich 1999: 363).

This, then, was the direction towards which India's globalist discourse was gradually heading after 1962. Aspiration for a global role combined with a perception of neglect pushed the state into emphasising the development of technology-intensive prestige weapons and strategic forces capable of power projection. The desire for power projection, like other quests in India's strategic trajectory, has evolved historically. British strategy for India during colonial rule in the twentieth century had been defensive, since Britain by that time had become a status quo power interested in preservation rather than expansion. India inherited that strategic temperament (Tanham 1992: ch. 2). But the need for power projection was increasingly felt from the sixties onwards. Indian policymakers have assured the public that prestige weapons with the capacity to project offensive power would concretely demonstrate India's capabilities. In hindsight, they were correct.

The need to develop military technology and heavy industry was felt for a long time to enhance national power, evident as early as the 1938 deliberations of the National Planning Committee of Congress (Sondhi 1994: ch. 4). Nehru himself was a firm believer that high technology could catapult India into greater national power and international visibility. From 1947 to 1950, in addition to being Prime Minister and Foreign Minister, Nehru was also the Minister for Scientific Research. He went on to fund a large number of scientific laboratories around the country. The Department of Atomic Energy, from its establishment in 1954, remained under his direct control until his death. The other major figure in establishing India's high technology programme was Homi Bhaba, who led atomic research under the department set up and commanded by Nehru. In many instances he and the other scientists convinced Nehru to allocate greater funds for strategic technologies. As Bhaba justified it: 'No country which wishes to play a leading part in world affairs can afford to neglect pure and long term research' (Sondhi 1994: 61). Although developing weapons was not the main object of India's atomic programme when it began, its goal was to acquire 'complete technological capability', including competence to produce the bomb.

The shifts from a normative to a material path to globalism have not altered the sense of destiny and entitlement in Indian strategic thinking. In the changing mindset of Indian policymakers, India's globalism was still deserved historically, but it was to be achieved through a demonstration of capabilities rather than an assertion of rights. This sense of a material urgency for achieving greatness rhetorically fuelled and justified expenses that would otherwise seem wasteful for one of the poorest countries in the world. It gave deeper significance to the notion of hegemonic rivalry, and portrayed as necessities apparent luxuries such as atomic weapons, missile technology, aircraft carriers, nuclear submarines, and a comprehensive space programme. The narrative of grandeur and competition, already compelling, became even more so, once injected with appeals about neglect and lost glory and later, a confident discourse on capabilities. As Stephen Cohen, a veteran analyst of South Asian security, observed:

> Most Indians, especially those in the Delhi-centered strategic and political community, strongly believe that their country is once again destined to become a great state, one that matches the historical and civilisational accomplishments of the Indian people. This view is encountered at nearly all points along the Indian political spectrum.
>
> (Cohen 2000: 17)

Managing openness rhetorically: the use of nationalist globalism

Since the nineties, the Indian state has utilised all three elements of the globalist narrative – civilisational grandeur, strategic and hegemonic rivalry with China, and the need to assert material capabilities – to support its quest for opening up India's economy. A new government came to power in India in March 1991. Taking a balance of payments crisis as justification, the government announced sweeping changes in economic policy, beginning with an almost 20 per cent currency deval-uation. The policies pursued since then have included several rounds of tariff reduction and currency devaluation, which are standard in-gredients in a recipe for economic openness. Before liberalisation was announced in 1991, Indian peak tariff rate was 300 per cent, the highest in the developing world. Chinese peak tariff rate at that time was 150 per cent. By the end of 1997 China and India had, in numerous successive turns, lowered their average tariffs to 20.1 per cent and 20.3 per cent respectively. India's trade policies have included gradual reduction in the subsidies and tax incentives for export diversification, abolition of licensing, export processing zones, and a liberal foreign currency re-tention system. Towards the middle of the nineties, policymakers gave greater attention to regulatory institutions, such as supervisory authori-ties over capital and financial markets, and legal instruments to facilitate cross-national mergers and acquisitions. There is evidence that much of the policy-set, especially on trade and investment, used cues from the Chinese experience with open-door policies (Alamgir 1999).

What is interesting for our purposes is an examination of the narrative used to rationalise, both internally and externally, India's policies. The first round of currency devaluation in 1991 occasioned separate state-ments by the Finance Minister, Dr Manmohan Singh, and the Governor of the central bank, R. Venkitaramanan. They both explained the deval-uation by pointing to competitive pressures from China in the export market (*The Hindu*, 4 July 1991). The following January the Commerce Minister declared that exports needed to be boosted, in light of stiff com-petition from China as well as from other Asian countries. He cautioned Indian industry that policymakers 'will have to think more radically' (*The Hindu*, 4 January 1991).

The *Economic Survey 1991–92*, one of the major policy statements published by the government, built on this urgency about a poten-tial competitive loss against rivals. It also argued that gaining strength and self-reliance have been the hallmarks of economic policy in India since independence, but added: 'Self-reliance does not mean isolation. We live in a world of great variety – of people, resources, of knowledge and behaviour. It is there for us to cooperate with, trade with, learn from, and contribute to. It is there for us to measure ourselves against' (Government of India 1992: 27). The Finance Minister's subsequent speeches strongly asserted that India had attained the capability to raise international engagement, and must begin to do so. Through the next few years the government continued to employ a narrative urging constituencies to realise a sense of loss, to engage in competition and international benchmarking, towards eventual empowerment and regional hegemony. Disputing apologists of the slow growth rate of India, the finance minister noted: '[T]he world-is-in-a-recession attitude has created in our country a disastrous mindset...If the world is in a recession, why are the Chinese exports booming? In 1973 our level of exports was the same as that of the Chinese. Where are the Chinese today, and where are the Indians?' (Cited in *India Today*, 31 March 1993.) Such feeling of relative loss along with despair about India's position as a great power comes across in official government publications as well as in formal and informal interviews of policymakers. As a key justification of openness, the *Economic Survey 1991–1992* pointed out the success of East Asia. Policy documents kept on emphasising the need to emulate East Asia's, and particularly, China's economic success (see, for example, Government of India 1997: 21).

In addition to government assessments and proclamations, a number of studies that came out in the early nineties (Suri 1992; Paul 1992; Cable 1995 for instance) also identified a loss of India's competitive position to China and other Asian countries. China's stellar performance in the nineties, coupled with its relative gains over India in crucial markets, began to give policymakers, analysts, and many academic researchers a sense of both enmity and envy. As one policymaker stated in an interview: 'China's growth rates put Indian economists to shame. Here was a country that started at the same social and economic level, a country we were boasting we could match in greatness and capabilities. Well, that China just flew past us. We were bystanders' (author interview with Dr Ashok Lahiri, Ministry of Finance, New Delhi, 16 September 1997).

The spate of comparative studies by scholars of all hues added to the urgency, by pointing out, in sometimes heartfelt and other times cynical language, the gains China had made compared to India. Jairam Ramesh

237

noted tersely, 'One visit to East Asia is enough to show just where India is' (cited in *India Today*, 24 May 1999). Achin Vanaik, at the other end of the political spectrum, wrote in his Marxist analysis of India's political economy in the eighties: '[T]he Chinese road to socialism, for all its detours, hiatuses, political drawbacks and indeed, its highly "unsocialist" features, has nevertheless had a far more impressive record than the Indian road to capitalism' (Vanaik 1990: 50). In the end, evidence about China's performance, combined with the globalist narrative that the government successfully re-popularised in India, shattered the alternative belief that openness and export-led growth are suited mostly to special cases and hence not easily applicable to India. The growth rates of China not only matched the earlier growth spurts of the newly industrialising countries (NICs) but also proved sustainable for a giant country. As Jean Drèze and Amartya Sen pointed out:

> China's choice of market-oriented reform and of a policy of integration with the world economy has given those policies a much wider hearing in India than they could have conceivably had on the basis of what had happened in countries that are much smaller and perceived to be quite dissimilar to India: Hong Kong, Taiwan, Singapore, even South Korea. From revolutionary inspiration to reformist passion, China has got India's ear again and again.   (Drèze and Sen 1995: 58)

More recently, China's successful handling of the Asian crisis increased Indian policymakers' confidence in the Chinese model. Indian policymakers were impressed by the fact that China was not affected as deeply as Japan and Korea, which were thought to be strong Asian countries. The Indian Institute of Foreign Trade, however, estimated in a study that possible Chinese devaluation during the Asian crisis would result in a loss of $300 million in exports for India, especially in textiles, clothing, footwear, chemicals, and light engineering goods (*Business Standard*, 12 February 1998).

Indian strategists observed that China's successful coping with the Asian crisis had increased its bargaining power against the United States, which, to them, was a concrete indication of how economic strength can have positive externalities for negotiation in other areas. Some thinkers urged the state to study closely how China coped with the crisis and how others faltered (see, for example, Sanjaya Baru in *Business Standard*, 4 December 1998). From different fronts the pressure to open up, raise international visibility, and emulate China was mounting. There is evidence that significant parts of India's recent external economic policies draw from the earlier Chinese experience with open-door policies (Alamgir 1999). The discourse on India's potential for a global role continued, and added a sense of shame and urgency for Indian policymakers. The words of P. Chidambaram, India's Commerce Minister during the early years of liberalisation, and Finance Minister in the late nineties, reflect this viewpoint: 'I speak for generations of young Indians. We are not happy. We are not proud that smaller countries have outgrown India, but India can become a giant economy in ten years' (cited in *Toronto Star*, 6 April 1995).

The ultimate aim of economic openness, as policymakers convinced their constituencies, was to reverse the loss of competitive position and respect. By invoking a globalist vision, they were able to muster, somewhat paradoxically, a nationalist sentiment in their efforts to market open-economy policies. When they encountered resistance – and there was ample resistance from a variety of industrial, labour, and social interests – spokesmen of the state acknowledged that economic liberalisation would be accompanied by austerity, but that it would be a temporary condition. They promoted austerity as an ancient civilisational virtue, practised by leaders of Indian thought, including Mahatma Gandhi.[1] The other virtue of India's great leaders was said to be globalism and cosmopolitanism. The narrative of nationalist globalism encapsulated both of these elements simultaneously and successfully. In the budget speech to Parliament in 1996, the Finance Minister averred:

> In an interdependent world, *Swadeshi* [self-reliance] must not be interpreted to mean economic isolation but rather self-reliance in building a prosperous India which interacts as an equal with other countries in the world. We seek to build a new India which, in the words of Gandhiji, will be like a house with windows open on all sides; let ideas from all the cultures and civilisations of the world freely flow in; but we must refuse to be blown off our feet by any one of them.
>
> (Government of India 1996: 104)

What captured mass imaginations, all in all, was the prospect of empowerment. Prominent ministers hardly ever lost sight of this goal in their speeches, policy documents, interviews, and debates. As Dr Manmohan Singh stated succinctly, 'India's economic destiny is safe only when India knows how to stand on its own feet, to compete against everyone in the world on an equal footing. That is what we are trying to do' (cited in *Financial Times*, 6 October 1995). Leaders of the state did not simply use the narrative as a marketing ploy. They themselves believed in it, and shaped policies accordingly. They used it assiduously both at home and abroad. This is why the narrative gained both public popularity and political momentum. It is no accident that the 1990s have seen the Indian state increasingly assertive in international strategic discourse. As India was able to increase its international economic power, rhetorically and materially, Indian policymakers tried to shift attention from the fall-outs in the domestic economy to the potential for further international empowerment. Indian diplomats changed their tone for laying out the rationale for India's admittance to the Security Council from a normative to a material basis. Admittance was due not just because it was India's moral right, as argued previously, but because India had become too powerful, economically and militarily, to be neglected. Prime Minister Narasimha Rao echoed this in 1996 when he asserted, 'Our voice is being heard internationally and we are being consulted on every major issue. Our defence might is well known' (*The Hindu*, 26 January 1996). This feeling of empowerment was bolstered after the nuclear explosions, and the political consensus on having a credible strategic weapons arsenal was widespread, as was the threat perception from China. It was boosted significantly from the economic policy reforms in the 1990s. Continuity of reforms, in turn, manifested India's international power potential, and strengthened the nationalist appeal of India's open-economy programme.

Such interconnections between economic, diplomatic, and military logic have been central in sustaining openness in India. From an integrated perspective, the waning of India's civilisational influence and grandeur after independence was a result of inward-looking economic policies. The best way to raise India's visibility as well as its global role, therefore, was to reverse autarky by giving other states an interest in India's future. China, the hegemonic rival, provided Indian policymakers with both a vivid example of such reversal and a strong competitive argument to convince the literate public to persist with openness.

This is not to argue that India's path to liberalisation faithfully reproduces the Chinese path. China's experience with external liberalisation in the early years (1978–90) was not only slow-paced and piecemeal, but much more inconsistent than it has been in the nineties. Such inconsistencies as the stop-go-stop pattern of tariff and forex liberalisation were caused partly by the struggles between the old guard and the reformists and partly by frequent adjustment to trade fluctuations. Indian policymaking displayed less inconsistency. Policymakers in India were able to institute within two years counterparts to the pro-globalisation policies that China had taken thirteen years to establish. From the standpoint of the nationalist-globalist narrative, however, what matters more is the strategic relevance of China's policies to India, rather than the specific nature of the policy path. Although China's military and political goals have been strategically relevant to India since the war, its economic policies gained strategic relevance only from the late eighties, when Indian policymakers began to take stock of China's economic progress and to analyse seriously what it might mean for India's prospects for security and leadership.

The relationship between narrative significance and policy relevance and continuity is neither straightforward nor unidirectional. Indian policymakers took time to realise that India was falling far behind China. Not only did they have to overcome an inclination to see Chinese policies as inapplicable and unworthy, and to be rejected, but they also had to be certain that China's economic success was sustainable. India's liberalisation of trade and investment itself made economically poignant the long-term sense of competition between India and China. In addition to military competition, they now competed in the same pool of exports and financial capital.

Conclusions: the success of nationalist globalism

I have ventured in this chapter to argue that successful management of openness requires not just policy intervention but narrative intervention. Scholars have analysed in depth the policies associated with India's economic liberalisation. This chapter provides some initial observations about the social construction of a narrative to enable the continuity of those policies.

To manage openness, the Indian state has imagined, believed in, subscribed to, and popularised a narrative that may be appropriately termed 'nationalist globalism': the state's intention of playing a world role by increasing its international visibility and material power. Involving elements of civilisational grandeur, a sense of lost glory, and a perceived historical rivalry with China, the narrative helped overcome the ideological compunctions Indian policymakers might have had in switching rapidly from forty years of inward-looking economic policies to an outward orientation.

It is important to observe that the narrative of nationalist globalism was employed by policymakers from diverse platforms. The two mavericks of India's economic programme in the 1990s, Prime Minister

Narasimha Rao and Finance Minister Manmohan Singh, were neither hardcore nationalists nor right-wing capitalists. They were essentially social democrats. Much of their policy rhetoric included populist and social democratic appeal, but the core has remained committed to the principal elements of India's globalism, linked back to the thought of early strategists like Nehru. Globalism imparted a spurt of nationalism and a sense of mission into an economically and strategically lethargic India. Just as significantly, it offered threads of continuity through a period of rapid change.

Although I have focused primarily on examining the narrative that was utilised in the state's efforts to rationalise openness, policy continuity cannot be assured just by marketing a popular narrative. Continuity needs to be entrenched institutionally as well as psychologically. One example of institutional entrenchment is entering into international treaties and organisations, such as MIGA or WTO. Entrenchment is also achieved through creating and strengthening certain domestic institutions. For our purposes, institutional aspects of continuity should be kept in mind particularly because they offset the centrality of approach required by this chapter's narrative analysis. For instance, I have treated the state as a unified entity. Although it has been useful for the present analysis, the actual process of policymaking is more decentralised and haphazard. Policy deliberations within the different institutions seem to include discussions of China's policies, but they are not organised into a coherent, national strategy through a clear-cut process. Usually, various ministries and departments prepare internal analytical reports on competitiveness in different sectors, which are then discussed in the pertinent department, followed by policy response. Although the government, especially the Finance Ministry, has routine and fairly sophisticated ways of monitoring the economy, the push for policies to enhance competitiveness often comes from outside the government. The three major peak industry organisations, Assocham, the Federation of Indian Chambers of Commerce and Industry, and the Confederation of Indian Industry regularly meet with government executives, apprise them of needs to enhance India's competitive position, and obtain promises of policy response.[2] Institutionally dispersed decisionmaking is also a consequence of India's giantism, a function of 'layers of official hierarchy', as John Lewis (1991) would put it. Yet those disparate decisions are informed in no small part by a strategic vision and narrative training centred on globalism and competition, embedded deeply in India's national policy circles. Additional investigation is required to discern the effect of nationalist globalism at a disaggregated level.

From an aggregate standpoint, however, India's efforts at continuity of openness seem to have been stimulated significantly by narrative engagement by the state. Nationalist globalism has been successful as a tool for continuing openness for several reasons. First of all, it integrated different arenas of policymaking, and injected a sense of strategic urgency. A power with globalist aspirations, Indian military strategists realised in the late seventies and early eighties, cannot be defensive and inward looking; it must be capable of projecting its military power well beyond its borders. A similar logic informed India's reformist economic policymakers in the nineties. The multidimensionality assures that the same narrative is applicable in a wide range of policy arenas, which increases its rhetorical and political power and provides the crucial proactive manoeuvrability the state needs to counter the popular opposing view that globalisation enfeebles the state economically and politically.

The perception of China as a hegemonic rival was compelling for India's policymakers precisely because China posed a potential threat across multiple arenas of competition: military, economic, diplomatic, and technological. Rivalry with Pakistan, by contrast, was mostly military. Especially since 1991, Indian policymakers have interpreted China's progress in each of these competitive areas as a possible threat to India, and therefore policy-relevant and publicisable. From their point of view, India's switch to a freer trade and investment regime in 1991 had only introduced additional arenas of competition between these two countries. This, in effect, tied economic competition to security exigencies, and helped policymakers interpret and portray China's economic lead on India as a potential security threat. Security, by the same logic, could be derived out of economic interdependence. As Sanjaya Baru wrote: 'A more open Indian economy is a necessary condition for acquiring a higher profile in the region. Unless India's economic involvement with the region increases, it is unlikely to match the influence of the three Big Powers in the region, namely, the United States, China and Japan' (*Business Standard*, 4 December 1998). The social construction of nationalist globalism, furthermore, provided much-needed historical and intellectual continuity. The founders of Indian nationalism and foreign policy believed that a global presence was inevitable for this slumbering giant. India's leaders longed for a world role, which meant not only material power but also an ability to influence world politics according to values considered indigenous: peace, democracy, self-determination, and non-alignment. Initially India claimed world status as its historic, normative right, and later moved to claim it on the basis of its increasing capabilities. While the increase in military capabilities, especially the ability to project strategic power abroad, was accomplished with a long-term coherent vision, the route to projecting economic power has been more circuitous. The founders of India's open economy, nevertheless, interpreted and presented India's history to portray openness as compatible with its indigenous values and fit for a civilisation that once had a powerful presence across the continent. They also justified their persistence with an open economy in terms of an urgent need to raise material capabilities.

The strong nationalist grounding was pivotal for the success of the narrative. This countered the popular feeling of vulnerability against the power of multinational corporations. Moreover, strategic policymakers, and eventually newspapers, analysts, and academics began to automatically compare India and China along every possible sociopolitical dimension. By itself the juxtaposition of comparative statistics did not mean much – but once rivalry was imagined, it began to convey a sense of relative loss or gain, of enmity and envy. The ultimate aim of strategic policymaking, the narrative claimed, was quintessentially nationalist: the empowerment of the Indian state.

Finally, while it is nationalist, the narrative is simultaneously internationalist. The desire to play a global role is the glue that holds together the diverse interests that the narrative can serve. It elevated the importance of international rivalry relative to domestic political exigencies. Domestic interests that were fundamentally at odds over an open-economy regime none the less found common ground over the need for strategic advancement towards a global role. Policymakers came to believe that, ultimately, it is only through sustained outward openness that India can achieve its globalist aims.

Notes

1. See, for example, the first three post-1991 budget speeches of the Finance Minister.
2. Ms Manashi Roy, Deputy Director General, Confederation of Indian Industry, author's interview, New Delhi, 11 September 1997; Dr Amit Mitra, Secretary General, Federation of Indian Chambers of Commerce and Industry, author's interview; provided written answers to questionnaire, 10 October 1997.

12 Guiding globalisation in East Asia: new roles for old developmental states

Linda Weiss

According to the new mantra of globalisation analysis, states are not 'disappearing' or 'declining' in importance. They are being 'transformed'. Since states are increasingly pressured from below by capital mobility and from above by supranational forms of governance such as the WTO, their traditional hold over economic actors has diminished, their control of the domestic economy has eroded, and their room for manoeuvre in the policy arena has been reduced to the margins. While meant to apply more generally, this view has become increasingly influential in the literature on East Asia's developmental states (DS). It is now widely anticipated that whatever remained of developmental states in the region before the financial turmoil of 1997, the pressures of financial liberalisation as well as the market-opening measures being imposed by the WTO agreements and IMF conditionalities have squeezed out developmental ambitions and eliminated the scope for coordinating economic outcomes in the domestic arena.

This claim is examined in the light of the Korean and Taiwanese experiences. As capitalist developmental states with Japan-style institutions, they are seen to be the most deviant, within the region, from the free-market model and it is the forced retreat of such developmental states from economic governance that now defines the standard view inside and outside the academy. We must ask therefore in what significant ways are developmental states affected by increasing exposure to global markets, and in what respects is state transformation real?

This chapter advances two propositions. First, globalisation impacts on the state, but not necessarily in the restrictive way anticipated by the standard view. Contrary to the idea of globalisation as constraint, the global economy does not preclude a role for national governance, but tends increasingly to demand it. As we shall see in a number of cases – ranging from the management of currency appreciation and industrial restructuring to foreign exchange and investment flows – the challenges of interdependence provide states with both the impetus for action and the room in which to act. The related proposition however is that the ways in which these enabling conditions of globalisation are likely to inform state responses and be actualised in policy outcomes will depend heavily on existing features of the domestic institutional environment. As stable constellations of norms, rules, and organisational arrangements, domestic institutions filter the effects of external pressures and condition responses to them – softening, exaggerating, or neutralising the impacts of openness, as the case may be.

In order to assess the nature and extent of domestic changes and, in particular, to see where the impact of globalisation comes into play, I discuss developments before and after the 1997 financial crisis in Taiwan and Korea – arguably postwar capitalism's two most successful examples of state-guided development, outside of Japan. As such, they offer a fruitful context for appraising globalist claims about state transformation. The discussion reports on research being undertaken for a larger project. Some of these findings are of a more preliminary nature than others (e.g., in some cases, they report on changes that are still in the process of implementation, especially regarding Korea). None the less, the thrust of the evidence to date does indicate that there continues to be considerable scope for state guidance in national economic management and for government–business cooperation, even – or perhaps especially – as economies restructure to meet the new conditions of economic openness. In Taiwan, the state's capacity to coordinate structural change has been enhanced by economic liberalisation; in Korea, where significant dismantling of the developmental state had occurred prior to the Asian crisis, a newly created state agency has been hastening chaebol restructuring and preparing firms to withstand the entry of foreigners; while the government–business nexus has been reconstituted in completely new ways to develop new sectors of the economy.

The analysis is set out in two parts. The first focuses on Korean developments both prior to and since the 1997 financial crisis. It shows how, after a period of considerable state dismantling, the government–business nexus is being reconstituted in ways reminiscent of the early Korean model, and how in post-crisis Korea the state has resumed a key coordinating role in a bid to strengthen the nation's industry and financial sector as increasing openness is forced upon the Korean economy. The section on Taiwan highlights the continuing developmental purposiveness of its decisionmaking elite for whom the persistent threat to national security from China has made state retreat unthinkable. It shows how increasing economic openness has gone hand-in-hand with an enhancement of the state's catalytic role in economic restructuring and its regulatory control of international financial flows. By way of introduction, however, I preface that analysis with a brief overview of the developmental model and its particular evolution in Taiwan and Korea.

Developmental capitalism in Taiwan and Korea

The concept of developmental state means more than a state that is pro-development. As originally conceived and applied to Japan, Korea, and Taiwan (and Singapore) during their high-growth periods, developmental states could be distinguished by their commitment to production-enhancing, growth-oriented priorities; their organisational arrangements (a relatively insulated pilot agency in charge of that transformative project); and institutionalised government–business cooperation (formal and informal links with organised economic actors privileging sectors or industry associations rather than simply individual firms) as the basis for policy input, negotiation, and implementation. In addition to the three fundamentals, one should note the importance of a political system which supports a shared project of economic transformation, where there is elite cohesion over core national goals, and where the economic bureaucracy is given sufficient scope to take initiatives and act effectively (see the contributors to Woo-Cumings 1999; also Weiss 1998: ch. 3).

Thus, transformative goals, a pilot agency, and institutionalised government–business cooperation form the three essential ingredients of any developmental state. In the absence of the first two criteria, the state lacks an insulated coordinating intelligence and is vulnerable to capture by special interests. In the absence of the third, the state lacks the embedded (quasi-corporatist) quality of effective policy design and implementation, and is vulnerable to information blockage and policy failure. I call this institutional set-up 'governed interdependence', which in its most evolved form involves negotiated policymaking under government sponsorship.

Control over key resources such as finance is also very important, but the significance of specific policy tools should not be overstated. While Korea relied more heavily on state-directed credit to increase private-sector investment and create large industrial conglomerates (chaebol) during the high-growth phase (*c.* 1960–80), Taiwan placed more emphasis on tax credits for the private sector and the control of large public enterprises in key sectors of upstream production (such as petrochemicals and steel). Moreover, as the relevant tasks of economic transformation have evolved, so have the instruments for achieving them. This evolution is clearly illustrated in Taiwan where the strong postwar emphasis of the industrial bureaucracy on increasing investment and exports gave way in the 1980s to promoting technological diffusion and continuous upgrading. The success of that shift appears in some respects less marked in Korea, where the state has moved between two extremes: on the one hand, total reliance on financial control in the 1960s and 1970s to achieve its objectives of creating a Korean presence in all the major export industries and, on the other hand, gradual relinquishment of control over financial institutions and state-guided investment in the decade up to 1993. Thus as President Kim Young-Sam led the first all-civilian, democratically elected government that year, the new administration appeared to look more to the free-market ideas of the United States than to Japan for a guide to financial liberalisation.

The politics of that change and its larger consequences (e.g., Korea's increased vulnerability to, and ultimately direct involvement in, financial turmoil) are very important, but quite separate issues which cannot be discussed here. Suffice to note that a key reason for Korea's gradual shift away from state-directed credit and the guided-market model in the decade or so prior to the 1997 financial crisis was not so much a direct response to external pressure being applied by the US administration,[1] as an effort to overcome the contradictions of the Korean model which had resulted in a pronounced stalemate between government and business. We return to this point below.

Since my aim in this chapter is to cover the major globalisation challenges and how state-guided systems have responded to these, I shall not attempt to 'compare' Korea and Taiwan across parallel adjustment episodes. Rather, I shall pay attention to those episodes that have significantly tested state capacities in each national setting. Thus, in the Korean context, I focus in particular on post-crisis reforms which seek to restructure industry and finance in response to market opening measures required by the IMF conditionalities and the WTO Financial

Services Agreement. In Taiwan, where financial crisis was averted, I turn instead to major episodes of industrial restructuring and financial liberalisation – the first in response to world currency movements, the second driven in large part by geopolitical concerns to strengthen Taiwan's international links (and thus bolster its security against mainland aggression).

Korea: relinquishing and retrieving state capacity

A stylised account of the Korean development model as it evolved up to the mid-1980s would highlight the following ingredients: a strong state in command of the financial system; a strategic industrial policy oriented towards closing the technology gap, involving 'disciplined support', i.e., generous benefits in exchange for performance outcomes; subsidised, tightly coordinated investment via the Economic Planning Board (EPB) – the state's pilot agency in charge of national economic management; creation and nurturing of large industrial conglomerates; and rapid structural transformation (e.g., the shift from light to heavy to technology-intensive production).

At least since the early 1990s, Korean developments have seemed to many to herald the retreat of this state-guided model. This is partly because, of all the developmental states, the Korean was the most top-down in approach and thus the most deviant from the free-market model. But it was also in part because, in recent years, the Korean model had become the most contested domestically (both inside and outside the state sector), and thus the most subject to redefinition. The 1997 financial turmoil and subsequent intervention of the IMF have helped reinforce the conviction that state-guided capitalism must give way to the power of global markets. Korea is now seen by many outside observers to have little choice other than to transform its system along neoliberal lines. Under IMF guidance, many believe economic openness is bringing Korean economic management into line with the so-called Washington consensus.

The evidence, we will see, suggests a more complex outcome in which change and continuity go hand-in-hand. For, in the aftermath of the crisis, two patterns stand out. First, major restructuring is under way, but that process is being driven by the state, not the market. Second, increased market opening is taking place alongside extensive re-regulation. But before we turn to current developments, we must begin with the pre-crisis unravelling of the Korean model.

The unravelling of 'Korea Inc.' prior to 1997

For two reasons, the Korean experience seems a misleading gauge of globalisation's transformative powers. First, the very features of the Korean case which brought the state-guided model into contestation and led to its considerable unravelling in that country prior to the Asian crisis are features that are specific to the Korean setting. They concern the deep tensions that issue from interactions between, on the one hand, a strong state given to top-down, often repressive, control and, on the other, huge concentrations of industrial power based on family-centred conglomerates. The contradiction stemmed from the fact that the chaebol, in their continuing quest for diversification and expansion, had become financially 'over-enmeshed' in the DS, while in their structure and ambition they had grown more and more independent of it. It was this contradiction within the Korean model itself that state actors sought to address from the early 1980s onwards, in response to an earlier financial crisis. Two related courses of action remained: restructure the chaebol and the financial system.

Korean efforts to this end were aimed at reducing the state's role in industrial finance, partially liberalising the financial sector to create alternative sources of corporate funding, reducing chaebol business units to core activities, and thus limiting their levels of debt. Accordingly, in the decade prior to the Asian crisis, the key challenge for the DS, at least as state actors approached it in Korea, shifted from that of being guide and 'midwife' (Evans 1995) – helping to bring new projects to fruition – to one of seeking to impede and control the expansionary tendencies of its industrial behemoths. As we shall see, it would take almost two decades and ruinous financial collapse before the state's restructuring efforts would begin to bear fruit.

More to the point, however, significant state dismantling took place *prior* to the crisis, culminating in the 1993 abolition of Korea's pilot agency, the EPB. Dismantling had been driven by reformist-minded bureaucrats who viewed state retreat from industrial finance (and thus industrial policy) as the solution to the government–business impasse. Thus, unlike their Taiwan counterparts who used financial reforms to enhance their coordinating powers, the Koreans approached financial liberalisation as a means of distancing the state from industry. Neoliberal ideas thus gained a stronger foothold among Korea's economic bureaucrats than in either Taiwan or Japan. The reason they did so was largely because such ideas resonated with efforts to overcome a specifically

Korean problem: that of 'developmental blockage', whereby massive business structures were firmly bound to the state, while at the same time increasingly constraining its capacity to discipline those structures. The more the chaebol were financially dependent on state-directed credit, the more the state was bound to protect them against failure.

So, on the eve of the Asian crisis, Korea's state-guided development model had undergone significant unravelling. State withdrawal from industrial policy nevertheless came with its own price, for it left a highly indebted corporate sector free to overextend its financial obligations and to invest in overlapping (oversupplied) sectors. Partial, but ill-conceived financial liberalisation deregulating short-term flows in the first half of the 1990s – a mark of Korea's 'free-market' credentials intended to seal its membership in the OECD – further increased vulnerability to financial turmoil, as the events of 1997 made clear. With its direction uncertain and its domestic institutions weakened, the Korean state proved ill-equipped to manage internationalisation. Dismantling, in short, left Korea more vulnerable to economic turmoil and paved the way for global flows to wreak their havoc.

Corporate restructuring in post-crisis Korea

A rather different, yet equally important, consideration casting doubt on globalisation's role in Korean state dismantling is that even a 'post-developmental' Korea is likely to have more in common with what preceded it than with the neoliberal outcomes of competitive liberalism widely anticipated by globalisation proponents. Current forms of state involvement in industrial restructuring offer support for this proposition, as I shall presently illustrate with reference to aspects of regulatory reform in post-crisis Korea.

Headed by President Kim Dae-Jung, Korea's new administration has declared its intention to drive through corporate restructuring yet maintain the principle of upholding market mechanisms and to refrain from intervening in chaebol affairs. To this end, the state would determine the deadlines and extent of corporate restructuring, but allow the chaebol to decide which business units to retain and release. But deadlines came and went as the chaebol refused to relinquish existing subsidiaries and piled up further debt. By the end of 1998, however, all this would begin to change with the rise of a new reform bureaucracy centred on a single supervisory body, the Financial Supervisory Commission (FSC).

The FSC (rather like the EPB in its prime) is authorised to do much more than regulate the entire financial services industry. Because the FSC can deploy traditional policy mechanisms of credit rationing and refusal, the chaebol are also effectively under its control. The FSC is thus empowered to implement the state's corporate restructuring policy; moreover, its approach seems quite consistent with an earlier model of economic management which had been partially dismantled by the early 1990s. In ways reminiscent of the now defunct EPB, the FSC made clear its intention, in the years following the crisis, to discipline any bank or financial institution that lent to firms not considered viable by the government. By the same token, if the chaebol failed to proceed with corporate restructuring, then no new bank loans would be forthcoming. In this respect, the FSC represents a significant recomposition of state capacity.

With its newly enhanced leverage over the chaebol and a renewed sense of public purpose to put Korea back on track, the state appears at last to have broken through the government–business impasse. Thus the Korean state is leading the drive for industrial restructuring. Corporate restructuring is perceived as critical, not only to national recovery, but also to the nation's ability to meet the key globalisation challenge: that of preparing Korean firms in industry and finance to fend off competition from outsiders as Korean markets are pried open by the WTO and IMF agreements. The strategy, in short, is to streamline the chaebol, using a mix of sanctions and incentives to force them to divest non-core units and consolidate business lines in a series of mergers and acquisitions, and 'swaps' which required certain chaebol to exchange certain operations so as to specialise in particular industry lines. Through these so-called Big Deals, the aim is not only to reduce the high debt-to-equity ratios of the chaebol, but also to create a few lean and highly competitive players in strategic industries, especially in the critical export sectors of automobiles and electronics.

Essentially, the government is seeking to create new streamlined 'national champions' to withstand the entry of foreign multinationals. In order to gain chaebol compliance with such plans, the government has deployed a number of mechanisms, ranging from financial sanctions (credit suspension and forced liquidation) and tax probes to financial incentives (on the role of 'administrative guidance' in achieving economic reform, see Woo-Cumings, this volume). In December 1998, for example, the government cut off LG Semicon's new lines of credit as a punitive measure for its refusal to merge with Hyundai electronics. In

June 1999, the government announced a massive tax probe into the five affiliates of the Hanjin Business Group (Korea's sixth largest conglomerate). The unprecedented tax investigation, employing a 150 strong tax audit team, was widely viewed as a warning to the top five chaebol to maintain their pledge to restructure.

The Hyundai–LG merger is a good example of the state's efforts to create a new national champion. Viewed as the centrepiece of the state's restructuring drive, the union aims to create the world's second-largest producer of DRAM chips, with a global market share of almost 16 per cent (*Korea Times* 25 December 1998). After initially agreeing to merge, however, LG Semicon pulled out when it was proposed that Hyundai take the controlling share. It took the threat of financial sanctions, including the loss of $6.5 billion in loans and a tax probe, before LG finally agreed to the merger, relinquishing management control to Hyundai electronics. The Hyundai–LG merger is regarded as an important turning point for having given momentum to the restructuring process, paving the way for further Big Deals.

For their part, the chaebol have continued to struggle hard against reform – just as they did in the decade prior to the crisis. The main difference in this new phase is that the state now has something it lacked before the financial upheaval: a renewed sense of direction and national purpose and, somewhat paradoxically, the external authority of the IMF under which to pursue its long-sought objectives of corporate reform.

These measures notwithstanding, the extent to which the government remains committed to reform has been frequently questioned. By early 2000, President Kim Dae-Jung's government had eased its demands for compliance from the chaebol and the banking sector in the belief that market forces would drive restructuring onward. Instead, the reform process began to lose momentum and the stockmarket contracted amid rumours of reform stalemate. The response from the Korean authorities was swift and dramatic. The second phase of reforms, initially proposed for implementation in 2001, were to begin immediately. Whereas the first round of reforms had focused on quantity, i.e., forcing commercial banks to meet the Bank for International Settlements (BIS) capital requirements of 8 per cent and businesses to lower their debt-to-equity ratios to below 200 per cent, the second round of reforms focused on quality, i.e., enhancement of management transparency and the improvement of corporate governance structures.

To this end, the state has once again deployed a range of carrot-and-stick measures to coax and prod the chaebol into compliance. For example, it was discovered that a number of conglomerates had been using their so-called 'restructuring coordination bodies' as vehicles for strengthening their control over subsidiaries, by means such as intervening in personnel reshuffles of affiliates. In response, the government moved to dismantle these bodies, provoking a strong but ultimately ineffective backlash from the Federation of Korean Industries (FKI) who called for an immediate halt to the government's 'excessive intervention' in the management affairs of private companies (*Korea Herald*, 26 April 2000). Defending these measures, Lee Yung-Keun, Chairman of the FSC, argued that the chaebol's 'anachronistic activities' were in part a cause of the crisis. and that the government had a responsibility to protect the rights of the people (*Korea Herald*, 27 April 2000). In swift succession, the Korean government announced the launch of major tax probes into the nation's top conglomerates, including Hyundai, Samsung, and LG to determine their involvement in violations of the securities transaction law, put in place to prevent 'the illicit accumulation of wealth by chaebol owners'. The purpose of these audits appears clear enough to corporate Korea, which views them not as routine check-ups, but as yet another form of state pressure to accelerate corporate restructuring (*Korea Herald*, 22 April 2000). By contrast, those who comply with the restructuring guidelines enjoy rather different treatment. Thus, for example, the conglomerates which agree to replace founding family members in management positions with professional executives are offered higher credit ratings.

Evidently then, reform of the corporate sector – a long-held objective of the Korean state – could not have taken place without the assistance of an external impetus, in this case the shock of financial crisis and the authority of the IMF. By the same token, corporate reform also required a capable and determined state. For while the reform of the corporate sector has at times faltered as economic growth in Korea has deteriorated, the overall thrust has been impressive, especially when compared with other countries in the region, a conclusion reiterated by the BIS (BIS 2000: 46–7).

Reregulating the financial sector

A similar story can be told for financial restructuring. The Korean state is reregulating foreign financial institutions and leading a merger drive in the domestic banking sector at the same time as Korean financial markets are being opened up by the WTO and IMF agreements. It is widely understood that IMF conditionalities require greater foreign participation in Korea's domestic banks. Indeed, foreign investors now hold majority shares in five of Korea's eight nationwide commercial banks (Ministry of Finance and Economy 2001). However while the administration lays claim to being strongly committed to a liberalised economy and to foreign investment in every sector, it has not interpreted this to mean an unregulated environment or one that leaves outcomes entirely to the survival of the fittest foreigners. On the contrary, its new focus on 'prudential regulations' aims to reverse earlier damage caused by deregulatory haste. Thus, the state has stepped up regulatory measures to control foreign bank operations.

With regard to foreign bank participation, Korea is of course a signatory to the WTO's Financial Services Agreement (FSA) and must allow foreign financial institutions access to its domestic market. However, the Korean authorities, in common with their counterparts in Japan and Taiwan (see below), have responded to this competitive challenge with a wave of state-sponsored bank mergers aimed at reconsolidating the financial sector. Stronger banks, such as Kookmin and Housing and Commercial, have been urged to merge with weaker banks and the Kim administration has set up a fund to encourage such mergers on a voluntary basis. The importance the state attaches to the creation of national financial champions can be seen in the incentives it offers. One is the government purchase of non-performing loans from merged banks to improve capital adequacy ratios. Another is the permission for merged banks to expand operations into securities underwriting and insurance business, which would pave the way for them to become investment banks (*Korea Herald*, May–June 2000).

The approach is in many respects similar to the first round of financial reforms following the crisis. During that round, the government focused on improving capital ratios by buying bad loans at discount prices and injecting funds into weak but still functioning banks. When sufficient capital could not be raised, the government intervened by closures, forced mergers and, in some instances, nationalisations. According to BIS appraisals, these relatively aggressive interventionist measures proved effective.

With regard to the control of foreign bank operations, the new measures set limits to their financial expansion in the domestic arena by redefining a foreign bank's capital, setting new credit ceilings, and establishing new monitoring mechanisms. The first two measures are aimed at curbing overall domestic lending by foreign banks and reducing the amount of credit they can extend to individual chaebol. The third targets foreign exchange transactions. While removing restrictions on foreign exchange, the new regulations require all banks to submit up to 100 daily on-line reports to the Bank of Korea 'to prove the legitimacy of every single foreign currency transaction in the market' (*Korea Times*, 18 March 1999).

Foreign bank managers may appear perplexed that in Korea liberalisation goes hand-in-hand with re-regulation. But as Steven Vogel's (1996) comparative study of regulatory reform has shown, 'freer markets' generally require 'more rules'. Depending on the ideational and institutional context, the new rules appear less to hasten state disengagement than to maintain its involvement in new and different ways. In post-crisis Korea it is not the state's withdrawal or the constraints placed on intervention that leaps to the eye. Rather, what stands out is the renewal of a long-standing tradition of 'administrative guidance', this time aimed at achieving corporate reform and creating modern national champions fitted to survive economic openness.

State transformation in Korea: the prince who leaps like a frog

Few would argue that little has changed in the Korean political economy, either before or since the crisis. If 'transformation' means a 'major change in the form, appearance, character, disposition, or function',[2] then globalists are right, in some respects at least, to speak of state 'transformation' in post-authoritarian Korea. But the Korean experience of 'state transformation' is not – as transformationalists would expect – a case of the proverbial 'frog being transformed into a prince' (or 'prince into frog', depending on one's perspective). What we find nowadays in Korea seems closer to a prince who leaps like a frog. Moreover, as already intimated, the main drivers of state 'transformation' have been more often domestic than international, and have appeared well in advance of financial opening and the Asian crisis.[3]

Ironically, the impact of the Asian crisis has not been *to disengage* the state from the economy *even further*, as many have anticipated, but rather *to bring it back in* – in a number of new and significant ways. As discussed earlier, under the first all-civilian democratic regime of Kim Young-Sam, the Korean state abandoned what remained of its long-standing industry policy, stepped up financial liberalisation, and dismantled the core agency of its developmental state, the EPB. However, spurred on by the crisis which ravaged its economy in 1997 and keen to diversify its industrial base by encouraging high-technology start-ups the Korean government has been actively leading industry development in a number of new arenas.

Among the most important of the new state-backed initiatives is the development of a venture industry to finance high-technology start-ups (as in Germany), and the creation of a software retail market to support a Korean software industry. In spite of earlier half-hearted efforts to promote venture capital in the 1980s, only after the crisis did the industry begin to boom, inspired by the Silicon Valley experience and boosted by extensive state assistance. Under the 1997 Special Law for the Promotion of Venture Businesses, the state now offers a 10 year programme of tax incentives, exemptions from general corporate laws, R&D support, and state-sponsored funding opportunities. New regulatory measures for venture businesses (VBs) not only facilitate listing on the KOSDAQ (see, e.g., Young 2001) but also increase the availability of venture capital through the creation of joint public–private venture capital companies (Oh 2000). Thus, unlike Silicon Valley, where venture capital grew from market forces, in Korea the industry has emerged from a state initiative. Its centrepiece however is public–private cooperation – a jointly created venture investment fund of about US$900 million. Like the French (as discussed by Loriaux, this volume), the Koreans have abandoned credit activism and policy loans for large industrial corporations, but they have not abandoned financial involvement for developmentalist goals.

The VB promotion polices have begun to bear fruit. By the end of 1999, the number of mostly high-technology VBs in Korea had reached 4,800, exceeding that of Japan (4,700) and Taiwan (1,200). By August 2000, the number exceeded 8,000 and VBs accounted for 8 per cent of total manufacturing firms.

Another developmentally oriented, yet novel, aspect of the state's evolving economic role can be seen in recent moves to create a Korean software industry. The software case is especially interesting in view of the fact that, as a consequence of the pervasive practice of pirating, a consumer market has been virtually non-existent. (An estimated 65 per cent of software in use in Korea is pirated.) The involvement of the state is therefore not only essential, but also welcomed by the industry in order to help create a market for local products.

The thrust of the software industry policy is, once again, public–private partnership. Three features of this relationship deserve high-lighting. First, the Ministry of Information and Communication has

sponsored a consortium of thirty-seven companies, the Software In-
fra Network of Korea (SOFRANO), with which to interact in the policy
arena and to establish a software retail business and distribution network. Second, in conjunction with SOFRANO, it has initiated an Internet
PC project which will greatly expand the number of PCs in circulation
with uniform specifications. The ministry's goal for the project is to
supply some 9 million low-end multimedia PCs in the next three years,
thus bringing more software developers to the industry. Third, it has appointed SOFRANO to operate government projects on its behalf, such as
seeking out and supporting software venture companies, aiding them in
commercialising and marketing their products, and marketing overseas
the software developed in Korea.

Both cases – that of venture capital and especially software – underline
the increasing importance of a collaborative relationship between government and business in joint pursuit of transformative projects. In this
relationship, each party retains its independence, while the government
remains the ultimate arbiter of the rules and goals of interaction in which
information is exchanged, resources are pooled, and tasks shared. Elsewhere I have called this negotiated relationship 'governed interdependence', and analysed its varied and changing forms in Asia and Europe.
Governed interdependence, I have argued, forms one important pillar
of the state's 'transformative capacity' (Weiss 1998; see also Coleman,
this volume). Whilst governed interdependence has definitely waned in
regard to the traditional chaebol-subsidised credit-developmental state
nexus, our sectoral evidence indicates that new forms are continuing to
emerge in post-crisis Korea.

However unclear the outlines of the institutional configuration emerging from new developments such as these, the evidence to date suggests
that it would be unwise to anticipate the emergence of a state expunged
of developmentalist norms and habits. Whether the principal challenges
to a neodevelopmental state like Korea are located in domestic or international processes, the outcomes of regulatory reforms are more likely
to be consistent with pre-existing structures than to overturn them.

Taiwan: globalisation challenges, state capacity enhancement

Turning to Taiwan, I shall focus on a different set of adjustment episodes
in response to three major 'globalisation' challenges since the second half
of the 1980s. The challenges in question can be classified as the need to

adjust to world currency shifts, international financial flows, and the new trading regime under the WTO. This is not to suggest that Korea has not faced similar pressures for adjustment over the years. To reiterate, my purpose is not to compare and contrast these two countries by examining their responses on identical dimensions. Rather, it is to demonstrate the ways in which Korea and Taiwan are 'managing openness' and to appraise the impact of deepening interdependence on the state's transformative capacity.[4] If it is true that Taiwan has none the less been somewhat more open to trade and foreign investment than Korea in recent years, this has much to do with its peculiar diplomatic position and the perceived need to counteract its isolation from world affairs.

Three cases of domestic response to international economic pressures are presented, one highlighting Taiwan's use of industry policy, the others its approach to financial liberalisation. In each case, as we shall see, officials across a range of state agencies – chiefly, the Ministry of Economic Affairs (MOEA), Ministry of Finance (MOF), and the Central Bank of China (CBC) – coordinated responses in order to meet globalisation challenges. Taken together, such efforts illustrate how Taiwan's management of increasing openness has served to maintain and at times enhance domestic capacities.

I begin with some examples of industrial restructuring in Taiwan, undertaken at two different points – the first in the mid-1980s in response to world currency shifts; the second (in the current period), in response to the new trading regime under the WTO. Both give some insights into how, as a small open economy, Taiwan was largely able to avoid becoming embroiled in the financial crisis of 1997 and to maintain a vigorous performance as an exporter of high-technology products. This is in striking contrast to Thailand, for example, which failed to upgrade, became caught in a 'low-technology trap', and piled up balance of payments deficits as its currency rapidly appreciated (see Doner and Ramsay, this volume).

Adjusting to currency appreciation

Taiwan's first major globalisation challenge came in the form of world currency shifts in the 1985–7 period, which rapidly strengthened the NT dollar and made its exports less competitive with those of Southeast Asia's low-cost producers. The Taiwan dollar rose by 28 per cent against the yen and by 40 per cent against the US dollar in this period (cf. Pempel 1999: 68). Taiwan's exports thereby lost a significant element of their competitive edge, posing a serious challenge for both Taiwan business and MOEA officials. Faced with a strongly appreciating currency, officials within the MOEA worked in concert with business associations to press forward a two-pronged strategy: on one hand, the deepening of high technology at home via a national upgrading programme that would shift skills and technology up market in the domestic arena; on the other hand, the relocation of labour-intensive production elsewhere in the region.

This dual response can be explained on one hand by the 'enabling' aspect of globalisation (as discussed at length in Chapter 1) – namely, the pressures on the KMT-led government from smaller producers in traditional sectors (mainly textiles and electronics) set in train by the currency realignments, and by the political incentives that the KMT would derive from helping small firms find lower cost solutions. On the other hand, the upmarket response, which was to fashion a more long-term solution to the currency adjustments (focusing on 'upgrading of technology') can be explained by the institutional structures – the developmental norms and arrangements, such as the state-sponsored agencies around Industrial Technology Research Institute (ITRI), which coordinated Taiwan's high-technology transfer, development, and diffusion. Thus the government did not simply allow market mechanisms to determine outcomes. It deepened involvement to meet both short-term political exigencies and longer-term economic ones.

This process of industrial transformation (and the state capacity that underpins it) is not well captured by standard views of the 'strong state' or 'top-down' development. Government and business have been involved from the outset in Taiwan's upgrading programme. The economic ministry has formed an elaborate network drawn from the industrial bureaux, research institutes, business groups, and industry experts to identify and select sectors, technologies, and products for promotion. Coordination between the Ministry of Economics, the Central Bank, ITRI, and industry helped business and government undertake the deepening of high-technology industry at home, while relocating labour-intensive production offshore. This policy shift became institutionalised as the Statute for Industrial Upgrading (1989) and, with bi-partisan support, subsequently extended for another decade in 1999. It replaced the Statute for Encouraging Industrial Investment. The Upgrading Statute, which provides the most important legal framework for the raising of technological capabilities of Taiwanese firms, laid the institutional foundations for the constant upgrading of skills and technologies in the island's industry.[5] Continuous upgrading, in turn, contributed to higher levels of value-added production, a more advanced technology focus in export sectors, larger export surpluses, and sustained high reserves – all of which served markedly to reduce Taiwan's vulnerability to financial turmoil.[6] Changing world currency markets were therefore central to Taiwan's rethinking of industrial strategy, internationalisation of production, and deepening of high-technology production in the second half of the 1980s.

But the story of adjustment does not rest there. Today it is not world currency movements that are causing concern, but the impact of the WTO, above all on Taiwan's mainland neighbour. The key problem for Taiwan – which is not yet a WTO member – is the threat posed by China moving into Taiwan's markets. Thus, as the world trade regime evolves, we may expect Taiwan's policymakers to maintain rather than abandon this strategic orientation. To see why, we turn to a discussion of the challenges posed by Taiwan's (and especially China's) entry to the WTO.

Managing the impact of the WTO

As Taiwan prepares to join the WTO, the agency charged with enforcing world trade agreements, globalists would predict that the state's capacity to pursue its developmental ambitions and coordinate adaptive change will be seriously constrained, if not eclipsed altogether by the new regime. However, although WTO rules set limits to the forms that state involvement can legitimately take, these are unlikely to be so tight or so rigid as to rule out all transformative action, as the evidence presented below would indicate.

While admission to the WTO will require tariff reductions that will impact negatively on Taiwan's domestically oriented sectors (in particular, home appliances and agriculture), this is regarded in policymaking circles as an unavoidable but acceptable cost. Of far greater concern for Taiwan's policymakers is the adjustment required by Taiwan's high-technology industry as a result of China's admission to the WTO and the further increase in foreign investment that it will stimulate on the mainland. Officials anticipate that China will, as a consequence, move rapidly into Taiwan's PC product markets. The response from Taiwan is once again to mobilise public purpose and government–business innovation networks to drive through a new round of technological upgrading. MOEA officials now define the challenge as that of moving towards a 'post-PC' era. So they have introduced new programmes to shift industry's focus from personal computers to more technologically sophisticated IT products such as CD-ROMs, DVDs, and LCDs, in addition to developing the biotechnology industry.

In each case of adjustment – in the 1980s and again at the turn of the century – the external challenge has been met with a similar response: a national strategy to coordinate rapid upgrading of products. And, in each case, the state has used a mix of tax incentives and subsidised public–private R&D networks led by ITRI, the state agency driving the island's high-technology push, as the main instruments of Taiwan's upgrading strategy. Such networks have been generally based on a 50–50 contribution from government and firms.

But how will the WTO rules impact on Taiwan's adjustment strategy once it joins the world trade body? WTO rules now require that government subsidies be removed wherever they discriminate against foreign companies, if the practices are considered trade distorting. Will this consequently put an end to Taiwan's transformative ambitions and thus its effectiveness in moving up the technology ladder? The answer appears to be contrary to expectations and suggests that there is considerable scope for national governance, even within the existing framework of the WTO. This allows for a significant number of non-actionable subsidies which do not attract WTO discipline and cannot be subject to complaints by other members, such as licensing requirements and the adoption of measures to promote technology transfer.

In the longer run, however, the viability of state support schemes more generally may depend on the way in which a state approaches industry support in order to achieve its objectives. In Taiwan, for instance, as revenues have become increasingly constrained by the new demands of democratisation, government has gradually shifted more of the costs of industry policy to industry itself. Thus, where government funds are outlaid to assist firms to acquire new capabilities, these must be reimbursed once the technology has been commercialised and sales achieved. The key point is that since the Taiwan approach is one in which the 'subsidy' element virtually disappears – industry eventually pays for its own subsidies! – it would be most unlikely to infringe WTO rules, should these become much more restrictive in the future. So industry restructuring may continue to depend on good governance rather than being left to the market. Such examples would suggest that states with transformative ambitions and capabilities like Taiwan can still find ample scope within the existing framework to nurture, preserve, or strengthen national enterprise, whether in preparation for entry to the WTO or beyond.[7]

Regulating international financial flows

Our final example of adjustment concerns financial markets – an area of the global economy perceived to be the most testing for states, especially small states like Taiwan. It is widely believed that when states liberalise the financial sector and open their capital account, they more or less relinquish the tools for national economic management. Not only do they have little control over how much capital flows in, or at what rates it can be purchased, but they also have little control over what the capital is used for. Some studies, however, have found that regulatory reforms, in certain settings, offer up new tools of economic management and investment strategy.[8]

This idea is nicely illustrated in the case of financial liberalisation in Taiwan, a carefully staged process running from the second half of the 1980s to the early 1990s. In 1993, Taiwan's monetary authorities embarked on a second round of capital market opening. In that year, the CBC expanded access for Taiwanese firms to the overseas corporate bond market. But, in doing so, it used the new regulatory arrangements to reinforce rather than relinquish coordinating powers. The authorities deployed the new rules in order to favour *productive* investment by Taiwanese firms, while guarding against foreign exchange speculation (a regulation still in place) (personal interview, Central Bank of China, Taipei, June 1999). Under these regulations, Taiwanese firms are allowed to issue corporate bonds overseas and to remit the proceeds to Taiwan in NT dollars on condition that the funds be invested in a long-term project for new plant or plant expansion. Financial regulators have thereby used the reforms simultaneously to guard against sudden inflows disrupting money markets (in particular, the risk that inflows would be used to speculate against the currency) and to enhance the state's developmental capacity. This experience illustrates an important point that globalist arguments overlook, namely, that even when a state agency appears to be acting in a strictly liberalising and 'regulatory' capacity, there is 'in principle' no reason why the outcome of that process should constrain or narrow the state's room for policy manoeuvre. Depending on their traditional approach and outlook, national authorities may use the new rules they devise in order to enhance the state's transformative powers and to achieve developmental outcomes.

The carefully phased opening of its capital account since the late 1980s and the granting of emergency powers of intervention to the Central Bank in the event of destabilisation encapsulate Taiwan's 'modernisation-with-developmental-prudence' approach. The way Taiwan has regulated foreign exchange both before and since the Asian crisis provides an insight into the overall strategy, which I have referred to elsewhere as 'managed openness' (Weiss 1999b). In Taiwan there are no restrictions in principle on foreign exchange. The foreign exchange market is an open one, but the transactions are closely supervised. Both local and foreign banks are subject to extensive reporting requirements to account for all such transactions. Indeed the CBC encourages self-regulation by making requests for forex depend on a bank's previous record of dealings (personal interview, CBC, Taipei, June 1999). Foreign banks like Citibank may be free to indulge in daily foreign exchange transactions, but they cannot avoid reporting such operations to the authorities. 'Freer markets, more rules' – to repeat Vogel's paradoxical formulation – thus has strong resonance for the international banking community in Taiwan as well as Korea.

Whether states will seek to use regulatory controls in this way is likely to depend on pre-existing regime orientations, priorities, and institutional arrangements in the country in question. In Korea's case, as we saw earlier, the crisis and financial collapse have discredited the idea that financial liberalisation by itself – that is, without careful reregulation – can bring benefits. Korea is thus rebuilding capabilities that it had previously sought to dismantle in favour of more market-oriented solutions to the government–business impasse. In Taiwan's case, persistent geopolitical pressures have preserved public purpose and encouraged a more consistently managed approach to the process of global integration, especially in finance. Exposed to a constant security threat from the mainland, for Taiwan the possibility of financial destabilisation remains ever-present (vividly illustrated by the nine-month missile crisis in 1995–6 which precipitated a run on the currency resulting in a $17 billion depletion of Taiwan's reserves). It is this geopolitical pressure that remains paramount in the routine calculations of Taiwan's financial authorities – not necessarily in an overt way but as part of the background assumptions of the political and bureaucratic elite. Diplomatic isolation and cross-straits relations have served to reinforce state purpose, preserving the developmental orientation. Even the unusually large foreign reserves – reflecting strong capacity to upgrade and maintain trade surpluses – are related to this external impulse, for the reserves offer a security blanket in the event of economic instability.

Moreover, as Taiwan is not a member of the IMF or the World Bank, it cannot rely on support from these institutions in the event of a serious financial threat. Accordingly, the Executive Yuan in September 1999 approved draft regulations to establish a stabilisation fund designed specifically to cope with serious market fluctuations. As these sorts of considerations help to explain, when the MOF and CBC approached the task of financial liberalisation from the late 1980s onwards – in contrast to officials in pre-crisis Korea, as we saw earlier – they did so with a view to enhancing the state's powers of coordination, not effecting state retreat.

Opening the stock exchange to foreign investors has also involved a similar degree of care and caution. Indeed, from Taiwan's point of view, the most significant aspect of its impending accession to the WTO is the Financial Services Agreement, implemented in March 1999, which requires, *inter alia*, removing restrictions on foreign investment in the local stock exchange.[9] For Taiwan's monetary authorities, the dilemma has been that of how to allow free access to local equities, yet ensure against losing control. As of 1 January 2000, Taiwan had phased out all remaining barriers to foreign investment in listed stocks. But the groundwork for market opening has been carefully prepared over a lengthy period. There is little doubt, for example, that the state has purposefully refrained from introducing a capital gains tax in order to encourage a strong local market for equities. Whatever the precise mix of factors, by the late 1990s, the tax-free incentive had helped to produce a very vigorous domestic market. Indeed, so strong is local participation in Taiwan equities (exceeding 96 per cent of capitalisation) – ostensibly 'crowding out' foreign ownership – that officials felt sufficiently confident to remove, ahead of the deadline, the remaining barriers to foreign entry agreed with the WTO. Capital opening, in short, is not expected to alter this ownership structure to any significant degree (personal interviews, CBC, Taipei, June 1999).

Several other 'market governing' measures are relevant to the overall argument that, in new ways, the challenges of openness have reaffirmed, at times even enhanced, the state's role in coordinating change. One should at least note a similarity with Korea in the way Taiwan's government (and one could add Japan's) is openly urging mergers in the financial sector in response to the FSA. The consolidation of the domestic banking industry before WTO accession is seen as particularly critical in Taiwan, where market saturation in the domestic banking industry since liberalisation in 1991 has led to declining returns on assets ever since (*Taiwan Economic News*, 17 February 2000).

Under a new Financial Merger and Acquisition law, the state is therefore promoting national firms capable of withstanding competition from foreign firms in banking, insurance, and securities. The first merger to take place under these new laws was announced by the Ministry of Finance in December 1999, involving the Bank of Taiwan, the Land Bank of Taiwan, and the Central Trust of China. This merger will create the largest bank on the island, with total assets of US$117.41 billion and a combined net asset value of US$8.4 billion, making it the world's forty-sixth largest bank in net asset value terms. Plans for six more mergers have since been announced (*Taiwan Economic News*, 30 December 1999).

The developmental intent behind the push for mergers is clear in Central Bank Governor Fai-nan Perng's statement that 'we aim not just to provide a Wimbledon tennis court for foreigners, we also want to field our own players'. As the Japanese – preoccupied with their own Big Bang – were wont to remind the world, financial liberalisation should not become a Wimbledon-style contest where the foreigners repeatedly took all the prizes. The drive for consolidation, using tax and other incentives, has been one way of countering that possibility; in this way, increasing openness has opened up yet another arena for state action.

The experience of Taiwan demonstrates that in spite of extensive liberalisation (not to mention full-fledged democratisation), developmentalism[10] remains relatively robust at the turn of the century. International and domestic constraints notwithstanding, the state centred on Taipei retains both a key role in defining financial and industrial strategy and a capacity for effective implementation.

Conclusion

The retreat, eclipse, or withering away of the developmental state and its transformation into a different kind of beast has been a widely anticipated outcome in search of a single compelling cause – 'globalisation' being only the latest in a strong line-up of potential assassins. The evidence reported here gives us reason to doubt the decline and transformation thesis, at least in its current form. Neither the experience of Korea nor that of Taiwan offers support for the view that the scope for policy choice or the role for a central coordinating intelligence like the state have been whittled away under conditions of increased openness and interdependence.

At the very least, the findings reported here give us pause to consider ways in which the character of international competition and global markets may actually reaffirm, renew, or recompose state capacities. The approach of Taiwan to financial liberalisation both before and after the region's financial crisis, together with Korea's post-crisis reforms, lend weight to the proposition that increasing openness is compatible with the strengthening of national governance. The new rules of increased market opening can be deployed to bolster developmental purpose.

The Korean and Taiwanese experiences are but two cases. And two swallows do not make a summer. Nonetheless, they are significant swallows, both increasingly exposed to the larger international economy and subject to its dictums, one recently sustaining significant damage from the impact of global flows. Increasing openness notwithstanding, the state would appear to have ample room to move in both the financial and industrial strategy arenas. Rather than shrinking under the grip of external constraints, a more plausible conclusion would seem to be that industrial policy is constantly shifting in character and focus. In part this is because, under conditions of interdependence, upgrading the industrial economy can never be a one-off event, but has to be a continuous process, even in the developed democracies. Thus, in some respects, examples of which we have seen in Taiwan and most recently in Korea (but which extend well beyond there), increased exposure to global markets makes the state's infrastructural and coordinating role more, not less, important.

Most important, where economic actors are well organised and under pressure from international competitors, they may end up inviting, rather than rejecting, state involvement in a shared transformative project. Indeed, rather than driving a wedge between government and business, meeting the challenges of openness may serve to strengthen public–private cooperation (a point developed in more theoretical terms in the Introduction to this volume).

Whether we continue to call the current configurations in Korea and Taiwan 'developmental' or something else, the important point to extract from the evidence is that in internationalising their economies, these two countries, though in somewhat different ways, are undergoing a process of 'adaptive' rather than 'transformative' institutional change – that is, change that is consistent with, rather than overturning, what went before.[11] The fact that Taiwan's approach has been more consistent and robust than Korea's – where significant dismantling occurred prior to (and arguably contributed to) the financial collapse – owes much to the greater strength and persistence of geopolitical pressures. For in contrast with Korea, Taiwan's security environment continues to be marked by a persistent and credible threat in combination with diplomatic isolation and uncertain allies.

With or without those pressures, however, institutional and ideational diversity are likely to persist, even if in newly modified form. Thus we need to take seriously the idea that change within particular politicoeconomic systems is less likely to override or negate the past than to take its cue from pre-existing norms and arrangements, even while embracing the new. This idea has been variously encapsulated in notions of 'path dependency', 'institutional legacy', 'feedback effects', and systemic 'tightness of fit'.[12]

While such concepts give some sense of the tenacity of pre-existing arrangements and the difficulty of systemic change in 'normal' times, we seem to lack the appropriate tools to conceptualise modifications that result in *adaptive* rather than the more thoroughgoing *transformative* change. What, for example, should we call a developmental state that has in some ways toned down its industrial and financial activism, perhaps restructured certain internal arrangements, and redefined its catch-up goals – yet remains distinctively different from its neoliberal Anglo-American counterparts? In greater or lesser degree, changes of this nature can be identified in all four neodevelopmental states – Korea, Japan, Taiwan, and Singapore. Should we therefore conclude that the developmental state and, with it, government–business coordinated capitalism, are terminated? Or should we rather seek to encapsulate its modifications – the 'post-developmental' state – in new ways, which capture the idea of adaptive change and hybrid outcomes (represented in the Korean case, as we saw, in the idea of the 'prince who leaps like a frog'). The latter task, though more challenging, seems more in step with reality.

There is a larger lesson to be drawn from the cases analysed here. While globalisation is having an impact on states, we should neither overstate its importance among the contending pressures on governing institutions, nor oversell its capacity constraining tendency. There is after all no such thing as uniformity of impact or unmediated adjustment to market pressures. All adjustments to economic openness require new laws, regulations, and policies, and this is where the character of the existing domestic regulatory and institutional context comes into play. In the cases presented here, one can see the impact of openness being mediated through national arrangements designed to shape engagement with the global arena (such as the local equities market in Taiwan being closely nurtured in conjunction with carefully phased opening to foreign investment). This is a less expected, but surely more plausible, outcome than the widely canvassed idea of the tightly 'constrained' or extensively 'transformed' state. It shows that institutions equipped with the relevant sense of purpose and capacities can guide the impact of globalisation – much as they guided the process of development in the first developmental state phase.

Notes

1. For example, most 'pressure' coming from the US aimed at gaining access to Korean markets for American financial institutions, not at capital account opening. (The latter agenda appears to have been pursued independently by the IMF.) Ironically, Korea remained protective on market access, while opening its capital account to short-term inflows, sending the freshly deregulated banking system (borrowing short, lending long) spinning out of control.
2. A composite definition from the Oxford and Webster's Dictionaries.
3. For a more detailed critique of the 'external pressures' argument, see Elizabeth Thurbon (2002).
4. By 'transformative capacity', I refer to historically embedded orientations and institutional arrangements which enable the state 'to adapt to external shocks and pressures by generating new means of governing the process of industrial change'. Critical to that outcome is not only the Weberian character of the bureaucracy (as elaborated by Evans 1995), but also the organisation of economic actors and the nature of linkages between the state bureaucracies and the economic sectors (Weiss 1998: 8; ch. 3).
5. On the nature and effectiveness of the guided development of high-technology capabilities of East Asian firms, including Taiwan's, see Mathews and Cho (1999).
6. For the comparative evidence and development of this argument, as applied to the Asian crisis, see Weiss (1999c).
7. It has been argued that many industry support schemes such as fiscal concessions, investment incentives, government–business partnerships, and R&D subsidies (which are typical of the East Asian development strategy) can be designed in such a way that they are permissible under WTO rules (Morrissey and Rai 1995).
8. See, for example, Vogel (1996).
9. The FSA, covering banking, insurance, securities, asset management and financial information, seeks to remove restrictions on the entry and access of all foreign financial enterprises to the local market.
10. I define 'developmentalism' as a project for economic transformation expressed as a set of institutionalised norms regarding state priorities and

13 Governing global finance: financial derivatives, liberal states, and transformative capacity

William D. Coleman

The creation and spectacular growth of global, over-the-counter derivatives markets pose a very stern challenge to traditional modes of regulation by nation-states of financial markets. These markets are truly global in that they transcend borders. In fact, derivatives are financial instruments whose very purpose is to take some of the financial risks out of investing across borders. Many derivatives markets do not fall within the jurisdiction of one nation-state alone, but are the potential responsibility of any number of nation-states. Moreover, a relatively small number of complex, global financial services firms dominate these markets, while being active in most of the principal financial centres of the developed and developing world.

Prudential supervision and regulation of these firms and markets thus pose a singular challenge for any given nation-state. If that state is capable only of supervising and regulating the activities of the given global firm within its own territory, it will have a very partial, and arguably, inadequate view of the financial health of that firm. What is more, the nation-state might worry that if its supervision and regulation were to appear too demanding to a given number of global firms, they might simply transfer aspects of their business to another financial centre where the regulatory touch was more to their liking. The signing and execution of over-the-counter derivatives contracts can be physically located in any number of places.

This chapter investigates how two nation-states, the United Kingdom and the US, have responded to the challenge of global derivatives markets. These two states provide an interesting comparison because historically they approached the supervision and regulation of financial markets in contrasting ways (Coleman 1996). The US regulatory style relied on formal, statutory arrangements managed by independent, expert, bureaucratic agencies. In contrast, the UK preferred a more informal approach focused on self-regulation and collegial relationships between financial services firms and supervisory authorities. The comparison also provides a window on regulatory competition because New York and London are the two largest centres in the world for derivatives activity.

Our analysis of responses to this challenge relies heavily on the notion of transformative capacity developed by Weiss (1998). She argues that variations in transformative capacity across states help explain why some states are more successful than others in steering economic adjustment. Crucial to transformative capacity is the nature of the linkages between governments and economic sectors. Weiss (1998: 15–16) stresses that states are not unitary and monolithic structures, but 'organisational complexes whose various "parts" represent different ages, functions and (at times) orientations' (Weiss 1998: 15–16). Strategies for adjustment and change are formulated and implemented not by the state alone but through policy linkages between relevant bureaucratic agencies and sectoral actors. Weiss (1998: 38) describes this type of negotiating relationship as 'governed interdependence'. State actors and industry representatives retain their autonomy, but negotiate and then agree to work towards broader goals set and monitored by state actors. As Weiss (1998: 39) argues:

> Of central importance is the state's ability to use its autonomy to consult and to elicit consensus and cooperation from the private sector ... Through its linkages with key economic groupings, the state can extract and exchange vital information with producers, stimulate private-sector participation in key policy areas, and mobilise a greater level of industry collaboration in advancing national strategy.

Several factors are conducive to the kind of partnership at the centre of such capacity. The state actors involved must have adequate expertise and a capacity to coordinate activities among themselves when necessary. The interest associations representing the firms in the sector must have sufficiently encompassing domains so that they can speak for the large majority of the firms (Weiss 1998: 60). Finally, negotiations between state actors and industry representatives must be institutionalised and regular rather than *ad hoc* and spasmodic.

When examined in light of these conditions, the prospect of having the 'governed interdependence' to meet the derivatives challenge is higher in the UK than in the US. Although both countries have central banks and other state actors with expertise, responsibilities for relevant financial markets and firms are shared among a greater number of agencies in the US. These agencies have a long history of competing with one another for 'turf' rather than coordinating their efforts. Mirroring these divisions between the state actors is an interest associational system whose members often work to buttress their particular corresponding state actor, thereby reinforcing the cleavages within the state. Finally, the more informal, self-regulatory approach to supervision and regulation in the UK operated on the basis of regular, institutionalised relationships between large financial services firms and the Bank of England. In contrast, the more formal approach to rule-making in the US tended to lead to rather *ad hoc*, often adversarial relationships between industry representatives and state actors.

This difference in transformative capacity appears to have had several effects. The UK was able to draw up an approach to the oversight of derivatives markets that is both inclusive of the key players and accepted by them. The US has not agreed fully upon an approach, leaving some key market actors largely unsupervised. Second, to the degree to which the US has developed an approach to supervision, it resembles more the informal, self-regulatory approach favoured in London than the usual, statutory, and formal American style. This similarity raises the question whether the very global character of these markets and of their key players restricts the freedom of states to follow policy styles consistent with domestic institutional arrangements. Already before either state had developed a supervisory strategy, the market players themselves had set up a nascent 'private regime' (Cutler, Haufler and Porter 1999: ch. 1) at the global level to organise market behaviour. This private regime was to expand in scope and complexity during the 1990s. Simultaneously, nation-states came to collaborate increasingly at the global level in an attempt to develop common approaches to supervision and regulation of derivatives. By the turn of the century, the private regime coexisted with some supranational agreements on information sharing and remarkably similar national approaches to supervision and regulation.

This argument is developed in several steps. First, I provide some elementary definitions of derivatives, noting the difference between those traded on exchanges from those sold over-the-counter. With these definitions in mind, I then explain how derivatives create financial risk, thereby inviting state regulation. The second section examines, in turn, the responses of the UK and the US to these challenges, using the prism of transformative capacity. The third section reviews the development of a private regime and the associated intergovernmental arrangements put in place at the global level by nation-states. The chapter concludes with an analysis of the implications of the argument for an understanding of the role of states in the face of globalisation.

Derivatives, globalisation, and risk
Types of derivatives

A derivative is a financial instrument consisting of a contractual agreement between two or more parties that has a value to the contracting parties and an independent value on the open market (Singher 1995: 1401). The value on the open market depends on the value of the underlying payments based on named assets, ratios, or indices committed to by the contracting parties. This value, in turn, is *derived* from the performance of the named assets, ratios, or indices depending on the terms of the contract. Thus as the value of the contractual payments rises or falls depending on the value of the underlying asset, rate, or index, so too does the value of the derivatives contract. This layering and changeability of values of derivatives contracts give them an uncommon measure of complexity. In fact, this complexity is sufficiently high that investment firms and banks hire persons with Ph.D. degrees in mathematics or physics as well as financial economics to analyse the products.

Although the range of derivative products is now extensive, this chapter focuses on the four most common types of contracts that account for most of the business activity: forwards, futures, options, and swaps. A *forward contract* involves an agreement between two parties to buy or sell an asset at a specified future time (the delivery date) for a specified price. For example, suppose an American automobile manufacturer knew that it would need to buy machine tools from a German firm worth 200 million Euros in three months' time. It might then contract with a bank to buy Euros in three months at a fixed exchange rate with the US dollar. From the company's point of view, the contract provides stability for future financial planning, reduces the risk of loss from adverse price changes in the exchange rate, and thus reduces the cost of doing business (Romano 1996: 7). For the counterparty, the contract provides a guaranteed sale, plus the possibility of making additional profit depending on the performance of exchange rates over the three-month period.

Forwards contracts have a long history in agriculture where, for example, grain merchants would contract with grain companies or cooperatives for deferred delivery of a given commodity at a price agreed to in advance. Financial forwards became useful hedges against currency instability after the collapse of the Bretton Woods system, which resulted in a significant increase in the volatility of exchange rates. In being private contracts between two (or more) counterparties, forwards are said to be sold 'over-the-counter' and thus are called OTC derivatives.

A *futures contract* is a standardised forward contract, that is, an obligation to buy or sell a specified asset at a specified future date for a specified price. No money changes hands until maturity. The standardisation of futures contracts makes them readily transferable to third parties and thus suitable to be traded publicly on exchanges. Futures are written on a wide variety of physical commodities and financial assets including agricultural products, precious metals and natural resources, foreign currencies, and interest rates. The Chicago Board of Trade (CBT) introduced the first financial futures contract in 1975 (Romano 1996: 12). Since that date, financial futures have grown exponentially in response both to volatilities in interest and exchange rates. The value of investments in financial futures now dwarfs the value of futures based on physical assets.

An *option* is a contract that gives the owner the right to buy or sell an asset at a specified price on or before a specified future date. As Romano (1996: 40) notes, option contracts date from Phoenician and Roman contracts on the delivery of goods by ship. Traded options have been available since the eighteenth century in the US. Options create a right, but not an obligation, to buy, thus differentiating them from forward and futures contracts. The Chicago Board Options Exchange, a division of the CBT, introduced the first options traded on an organised exchange – stock options – in the mid-1970s. Options traded on exchanges today cover such assets as stocks, stock indices, currencies, government bonds, and futures contracts. Similar to futures markets, options on financial futures dwarf all other contracts. Like forwards, options may take the form of private contracts between counterparties (OTC contracts) or they may be traded publicly on exchanges.

Finally, a *swap* is a contract between two counterparties to exchange a series of cash flows over time. The contract specifies the currencies to be exchanged, the rate of interest applicable, the payment timetable, and various ancillary issues related to the relationship between counterparties. The usual swaps are on interest rates or exchange rates. Thus, the most common interest rate swap, termed the 'vanilla swap', involves one counterparty agreeing to make fixed interest rate payments to the other counterparty who makes floating rate payments in return. In this respect, a swap might be seen as a portfolio of forward contracts (Romano 1996: 49). Like forwards, swaps are customised contracts that are traded over the counter and not on exchanges.

Swap contracts originated in loan agreements started in the UK in the 1970s that were designed to help the counterparties avoid government controls on foreign exchange transactions. The US securities firm, Salomon Brothers, designed the first currency swap in 1979 for IBM and the World Bank. Interest rate swaps began in 1981, and were first publicised in a transaction by Deutsche Bank in 1982 (Romano 1996: 50). More recently, commodity and equity swaps have become available. Similar to the other three basic types of derivatives, the growth in the value of swaps has exploded since their introduction in the late 1970s and early 1980s.

Derivatives and globalisation

Although there are important differences between each of these four basic types of derivative instruments, they share one property in common: they help interested actors to hedge price risk. They do so by transferring (for a price) the cost of bearing the risk from one party, who wishes to minimise exposure to risk, to another party who is willing to assume that exposure in order to make a profit. This need to hedge prices in financial markets is a direct response to changes in the international monetary and financial systems. As the monetary system has moved away from fixed exchange rates and the financial system has featured more open markets permitting significant fluctuations in interest rates, the risks associated with foreign exchange and interest rate volatility have escalated. Governmental and corporate actors have responded to this volatility by using derivatives to protect themselves from undue fluctuations in prices. Other financial actors have seen opportunities for profit through speculating on the likely changes in foreign exchange and interest rates as well as equities by buying and selling derivatives contracts. Speculators play an essential role in derivatives markets, because the demand of government and corporate actors for hedging is not always met by hedgers on the other side of the market.

Although financial derivatives are barely two decades old, their growth has been nothing short of spectacular. Reliable statistics on their growth only became available in the mid-1990s when the Euro-Currency Standing Committee (renamed the Committee on the Global Financial System in 1999) of the Group of 10 Central Bank Governors at the Bank for International Settlements (BIS) became concerned with the rising levels of risk exposure of global banks active in the derivatives field. The notional values have doubled from $47 trillion in 1995 to over $94 trillion in June 2000 (BIS 1998a, 2000). Counterparty credit risk has risen more slowly, but still is over $2 trillion. In addition, the notional amounts traded over-the-counter have continued to rise relative to those traded on futures and options exchanges.

Global OTC activity is distributed across a variety of financial centres. In the late 1990s, the site of the largest value of OTC transactions was London (UK), followed by the United States and Japan. Based on 1998 figures, activity in West European countries accounts for close to one-half of OTC transactions in terms of value (BIS 1998b: Table C-3). The picture shifts when one examines the location of exchange-traded derivatives. Here the US remains the strongest player, with the three largest US exchanges accounting for 40.9 per cent of world volume. The largest European exchanges accounted for 30.1 per cent of volume in 1998.

Not only then are derivatives a response to changes in the international monetary system and to the liberalisation of capital markets, but also they are globalising in their own right. The new markets created over the past twenty years are global in scope. As the Group of 30 (1997: 6) notes, sophisticated firms like pension funds, insurance companies, and banks are able 'to raise or invest funds, exchange currencies, or change the attributes of assets around the globe and around the clock'. Such large institutional investors have come to dominate financial markets and seek to allocate their assets across a global range of investment options.

To play in the global derivatives markets, firms need a global presence, high levels of technical expertise and sophisticated information and communication systems to manage risks on a global scale. Integrated global financial firms with extremely complex financial and corporate structures have come to dominate these markets (Group of 30 1997: 7). In its review of derivatives, the USGAO (1994: 36) notes that eight US bank dealers accounted for 56 per cent of worldwide notional/contract amounts of interest rate and currency swaps. Within the US, the top seven domestic banks' derivatives dealers accounted for 90 per cent of all US banks' derivatives activity. Similarly, when securities firms are examined, the top five firms accounted for 87 per cent of notional/contract amounts. Concentration appears to be lower for higher-volume, lower-risk derivatives than for lower-volume, higher-risk products.

Derivatives and risk

Preliminary to examining the response of nation-states to the growth of financial derivatives, it is important to understand the challenges for governments arising from the types of risks created. We outline these challenges by examining, in turn, four types of risk associated with the buying and selling of derivatives.

Credit risk refers to the risk that a trading partner might not fulfill its obligations in full on a given due date or at any time thereafter. However, unlike in banking and securities markets, credit risk for derivatives is *not* equal to the principal amount of the trade, but to the cost of replacing the contract if the counterparty defaults. Assessing credit risk for derivatives poses additional difficulties because risks can be transformed in complex ways much more quickly than is customary for banking and securities contracts due to shifts in the value of the respective underlying asset (Dale 1996: 15). Rapid changes in the value of derivatives contracts, which, in turn, change the degree of exposure to credit risk by counterparties daily, if not hourly, complicate risk assessment further. Credit risk is a much more serious problem for OTC derivatives than it is for exchange-traded contracts. Exchange-traded derivatives benefit from various safeguards that do not exist for OTC contracts (Dale 1996: ch. 6).

Market risk refers to risks to an institution's financial condition that result from negative changes in price levels of exchange rates, interest rate instruments, equities, commodities, and securities. The breakdown of the fixed exchange rate international monetary system, the resulting vast expansion in foreign exchange trading, the impact of unstable exchange rates on interest rates, and the trading of derivatives, securities, and commodities in a number of linked markets have all added to the levels of market risk. Of course, many derivatives such as commodity futures or interest rate swaps have been designed explicitly to reduce such market risks. Even so, they do not return financial firms to anything like the *status quo ante* of the early 1960s.

The principal complicating factor for market risk is its measurement. An accurate measurement requires the use of modern computer systems and software that rely on highly advanced mathematical, statistical, and database techniques. Finding an accurate evaluation is so difficult because values are influenced by many different factors. A portfolio of foreign exchange options, for example, will be affected by changes in exchange rates, interest rates, and the length of time before the options expire (USGAO 1994: 60). Again, these complications are particularly pronounced for OTC derivatives where the lack of centralised markets makes it difficult to assess prices. Dealers in OTC derivatives need highly sophisticated computer models to assess a product's value. Even when the market risk of derivative products is measured, the total market risk of a firm may still be unclear. Because derivatives are used in hedging other assets and liabilities, firms must assess the risk of both types of positions to effectively determine market risk.

Legal risk refers to the risk that a transaction proves unenforceable in law or because of inadequate documentation. These risks arise from such phenomena as different legal conditions being placed on netting arrangements in distinct jurisdictions, variations in bankruptcy procedures, distinct privileges given to government-owned entities in some states, and the legality of various complex derivatives transactions in given markets. Once again, this risk is particularly important for OTC transactions. Being private contracts between counterparties, if something were to go wrong and the contract were to be unenforceable in the country of one of the counterparties, the other counterparty could face a serious loss.

Systemic risk refers to the risk of a sudden unanticipated event that would damage the financial system to such an extent that economic activity in the wider economy would suffer (Group of 30 1997: 3). The concentration of global markets' activity in the hands of a relatively small number of global financial services firms raises concerns about systemic risk. For example, the outright collapse of a single, very large global conglomerate might trigger a financial shock because other large firms are likely to be directly exposed to the damaged firm. The former general manager of the Bank for International Settlements, Alexandre Lamfalussy has noted: 'the phenomenal growth of derivatives and associated trading techniques has reduced the transparency of market participants' balance sheets and has obscured the transmission of disturbances across market institutions ... Market participants may not be in a position to impose the necessary discipline on financial institutions to prevent the risk of the build-up of systemic problems' (cited in Dale 1996: 156).

Summary

Possible failures to protect against credit, market, and legal risk raise the likelihood of systemic risk, thereby constituting the principal challenge faced by nation-states. Systemic risk being actualised may be more likely in global OTC derivatives markets for several reasons. First, large global banks dominate these markets. 'Given the close interrelation between banks in many derivatives deals and the role of banks in the payment system and financial intermediation, the failure of banks can have major effects on the entire economy' (Steinherr 1998: 217). Furthermore, with these banks being global players, the world economy becomes a possible victim. Second, there is a high degree of concentration in these markets, a characteristic that increases the likelihood of contagion from one global firm to another. These large, but few, players have assumed a high number of financial positions with one another. What is more, these positions are highly leveraged; the replacement cost to total asset ratio is very high (Steinherr 1998: 222). Consequently, it is also likely that a crisis experienced by one firm in this select group could trigger difficulties throughout the group. As these key global banks ran into difficulties, the effects would be felt quickly in respective domestic financial services systems, triggering runs on deposit and investor insurance facilities. Third, the constant turnover in derivatives contracts means that such a crisis could happen very rapidly. Due to the increased linkages between financial markets across borders, turbulence in one area of the world could then spread very quickly to other areas (Steinherr 1998: 223).

State capacity and derivatives markets

The growth of global OTC derivatives markets poses a stiff challenge because determining the risks being incurred is complex, thereby increasing the likelihood that states will be unable to perceive the threat of systemic risk in time. We investigate how states meet this challenge by examining their actions in the two principal centres for these markets: the UK and the US. In carrying out this analysis, we develop the following arguments. How well states meet the challenge of globalisation is affected critically by their pre-existing institutional arrangements and thus their transformative capacity. We demonstrate that the UK dealt more expeditiously and more comprehensively with the OTC derivatives challenge than did the US. Second, the global character of the challenge is such that what one of these states (the US) chooses to do is affected by the choices of the other (the UK). In this respect, the higher adaptability of the UK may be constraining the US to behave somewhat differently than one might expect, based on past experience. Third, the *global* character of the OTC challenge dictates that states cannot address the challenge acting autonomously from one another. The growth of OTC derivatives markets has sparked a significant expansion of inter-governmental collaboration at the global level. This pooling of political power, however, remains somewhat of a weak match for the private authority constituted by the global banks and securities houses dominant in the markets. Consequently, a private regime has come to occupy an important place in the emerging arrangements for governance of global OTC derivatives markets.

These arguments are developed in two steps. First, we examine how the UK and the US have been responding to the globalisation challenge. This analysis is anchored on an evaluation of the transformative capacity available from pre-existing institutional arrangements in the two countries. In a subsequent section of the chapter, the nature of intergovernmental arrangements at the global level is presented along with an analysis of the role of private authority in governance of global OTC markets.

The United Kingdom

Generally speaking, politics in the UK is society centred, with broad disputes being resolved in an adversarial Parliament. Power is diffused to various independent centres of power where the vast majority of decisions are taken in an incremental fashion in reaction to events in society. When it has come to decisions relating to governance of financial markets, the general business culture in Britain has favoured keeping as much of this decisionmaking as possible in the private realm. The Anglo-Saxon liberal tradition encouraged a certain scepticism about the government's competence in business affairs. Government should remain at arm's length, acting only in times of crisis when called upon by business. For financial services, this business culture translated into an ideology supporting 'practitioner-based self-regulation'. It was assumed that only insiders would fully understand how markets work and how to keep a watch on practitioners. It followed that regulation should feature practitioners themselves in a prominent role.

When UK policy on financial markets was reformed through the Financial Services Act in 1986, this philosophy translated into a policy framework that differed in two key respects from that in the US:

all firms, without exception, were supervised and state responsibilities for such oversight were concentrated, rather than divided and over-lapping. The government's new oversight agency, the Securities and Investments Board (SIB), was set up as a private institution with public powers, unlike the US Securities and Exchange Commission (SEC), a statutory body. The new Act collected under its umbrella the sale of stocks and bonds, life insurance, collective investment schemes, and all other investment businesses. In contrast, each of these tended to be regulated under separate statutes in the US. The central concept of the Act was authorisation: any firm engaged in an investment business would need to be authorised by a recognised agency. The government concluded that they could retain some of the traditional practitioner-based oversight by having the authorisation function delegated to self-regulatory organisations staffed and funded by, and accountable to, practitioners.

The structure of the Act itself predisposed policymakers to look broadly at financial services, fully expecting that many of the various services would come to be offered by large financial conglomerates. Any person dealing in, arranging dealings in, managing, or advising on 'investments' is carrying on an 'investment business' and must be either authorised or exempted under the Act. This definition included both exchange-traded and OTC derivatives.

When the 1986 Act was fully implemented and the framework for wholesale markets was in place, the UK had transformed its system of state-finance relations into a more formal, corporatist structure. Although generally speaking this structure was more fragmented than that found in such continental European states as France and Germany, it did provide a basis for regular, informal discussions and consultation between major corporate actors, their interest associations, and the core agencies involved: the Bank of England and SIB. In this respect, it resembled Weiss's notion of 'governed interdependence' that was capable of responding quickly to the OTC derivatives challenge.

Section 43 of the Act, however, exempted wholesale markets in sterling, foreign exchange, and bullion from SIB authority. In November 1986, the Bank of England established a Wholesale Markets Supervision Division to supervise these itself. The Bank argued successfully that these wholesale markets served 'professionals', and could be overseen using an even less intrusive, more collegial approach. The Bank moved to develop a capital adequacy test for each type of firm and an informal, voluntary code of conduct.

Over the course of the following decade, the UK took further steps to concentrate authority in its supervisory and regulatory system in order to take account of the scope of businesses being engaged in by large, financial services corporations. In 1991, it arranged for the merger of two of its self-regulatory organisations, the Securities Association and the Association of Futures Brokers and Dealers into one Self Regulatory Organisation (SRO), the Securities and Futures Authority. Most importantly, at the end of the decade, the government created a new comprehensive supervisory authority, the Financial Services Authority (FSA), which combined the responsibilities for securities markets held by SIB with those for banking carried out by the Bank of England. In essence, then, the FSA has under one roof the powers divided among the SEC, the Federal Reserve, the Comptroller of the Currency, the Federal Deposit Insurance Corporation, the National Credit Union Administration, and the Commodity Futures Trading Commission in the US.

In 1999, the new FSA produced a revised version of the Bank of England's 'grey paper' outlining the rules for businesses exempted under Section 43 of the 1986 Act. All dealers in the familiar types of derivatives contracts – futures, options, forwards, and swaps – were included. Such OTC dealers and brokers were expected to be large 'professional' firms. They had to abide by the London Code of Conduct, a set of rules drawn up earlier by the Bank of England in consultation with the firms, and to contribute to a compensation scheme for protecting investors from failures (FSA 1999). If the firm at issue was a large bank or securities firm, it would remain supervised by its 'lead regulator' and the grey paper rules would apply only to the units dealing with wholesale markets.

These arrangements ensured that every OTC derivatives dealer operating in London, whether independently or as part of a financial conglomerate, was supervised, albeit lightly and under non-statutory rules. Such supervision was expected to cover problems dealing with credit and market risk. The unified framework put in place for financial conglomerates was expected to equip the relevant authorities to deal with any problems related to systemic risk.

The United States of America

US political culture has always frowned upon the concentration of power. Power is divided between the President and the Congress, between the courts and the President, and among agencies of the executive branch. Behind this separation of power lies the notion that authority must be dispersed in order to produce good government and to avoid the abuse of power. Thus, when it comes to financial services policy, Congress has divided responsibility among several committees. The Senate Banking Committee had separate sub-committees for banking and for securities regulation. In the House of Representatives, the Banking Committee had jurisdiction over banking activities only. Securities regulation fell under the ambit of the Energy and Commerce Committee, with the exception of futures and options, which were the responsibility of the Agriculture Committee. Securities, futures, and options, and banking industry lobbyists thus each had their own particular 'homes' for interest group pressure politics.

Within the executive branch, the Office of the Comptroller of the Currency in the Treasury Department is joined by several 'independent' regulatory agencies: the Federal Reserve Board, the Federal Deposit Insurance Corporation, the National Credit Union Administration, the Commodity Futures Trading Commission (CFTC), and the Securities and Exchange Commission (SEC). The notion of an 'independent' agency is broadly consistent with the idea of dividing rather than concentrating power. If there are lines of accountability, they will flow both to the President and the Congress; having two, often competing, superiors often reinforces independence rather than weakening it. These organisations are headed by a commission or board rather than by a single person. The collective nature of their leadership enables them to play both judicial and policymaking roles. As 'independent' agencies, these organisations are expected to be more resistant to political pressures. Their existence often rests on the assumption that regulation is a complex and highly technical activity where a body of experts is needed to make policy and to arbitrate disputes. This assumption differs fundamentally from the British view that practitioners or market actors themselves are the principal repositories of expertise and thus that self-regulation is the better form of governance.

Finally, the combination of statutory law plus strong, independent regulatory agencies creates an environment for a legalistic policy style. According to Hoberg (1993), legalism becomes more likely when formal administrative procedures dominate with widespread access to information and rights to participate for all affected interests, when interest groups support regulations and are willing and able to challenge these in the courts, and when government duties are clearly defined and are enforceable in court. Each of these conditions is met in financial services. Accordingly, the US system is much more disposed to favour formal, statutory state regulation over the more informal, less statutory, and more practitioner-based self-regulation in the British system.

This fragmentation of authority when joined to highly pluralistic policy networks does not furnish the US policy system with strong transformative capacity. There are poorly developed coordinating arrangements between the various competing centres of authority in the executive branch. The financial services associational system is rent with competitive divisions, showing virtually no integrating structures that control competition for members or for the ear of political authorities (Coleman 1996: ch. 3). Both political authorities and private sector actors espouse a philosophy of policymaking that assumes a strong boundary between state and civil society and that would seem contrary to the 'governed interdependence' Weiss views as central to transformative capacity. This assumption manifests itself in legislation like the Federal Advisory Committee Act, which precludes much of the informal consultation that takes place in other countries like the UK. The Act rules out much of the informal, ongoing negotiations between business and the state required for anticipatory adjustment to international pressures and shocks.

This absence of transformative capacity hampered US policymakers in devising strategies for the governance of OTC derivatives. It also left the door open to an eventual approach to governance that departed significantly from the usual US approach of formal, statutory state regulation. This surprising development has its origins in the complex division of responsibilities among agencies in the financial services field. Generally speaking, the SEC had authority over securities trading and securities markets and the CFTC over futures trading and futures markets. Amendments to the Commodities Exchange Act in 1974 expanded the definition of a commodity to the point where it included virtually anything, including a security. In 1975, the CFTC approved a Chicago Board of Trade application to trade futures on Government National Mortgage Association pass-through mortgage-backed securities (USGAO 2000: 5). The SEC immediately cried foul, arguing that securities fell within its jurisdiction, while the CFTC countered saying that futures fell into its jurisdiction. What to do then with a financial instrument that was both a security and a future?

As financial innovations continued to emerge in the 1980s and early 1990s, with many of them blurring the distinction between securities and futures, the disputes between the two agencies continued (Moore 1994: 443; Benson 1991: 5). The first of these conflicts was eventually resolved in 1982 in an accord between the SEC and the CFTC (the Shad–Johnson Jurisdictional Accord) that was subsequently ratified by Congress. The Accord gave the SEC jurisdiction over securities-based options while the CFTC oversaw securities-based futures, and options on futures.

Essentially untouched by the Accord, however, were many OTC derivatives. Consistent with its formal, statutory approach, the US did not permit trading of many of these instruments, unless it took place on a regulated exchange. Under pressure from the banks and other large firms who feared these rules would ensure much OTC derivatives business would slip away to London, the CFTC indicated in 1989 that it would take no action to regulate certain swap transactions (Moore 1994: 461). Banks continued to press Congress over the loss of market share in OTC derivatives because of the growing internationalisation of futures trading. In 1992, Congress responded by passing the Futures Trading Practices Act exempting qualified swaps transactions from the Commodities Exchange Act. The CFTC followed up in 1993 by issuing the Swaps Exemption.

Despite these steps, at least two key problems remained. The 1992 Act, the terms of the Commodities Exchange Act and the interpretation of its mandate by the CFTC created legal uncertainties about future regulation of OTC derivatives markets in the US. It was not clear to market participants whether the CFTC might still decide to intervene to regulate the swaps markets. Market players also feared that increased use of computer technology for OTC transactions might be construed by the CFTC as operating an electronic exchange and thus be deemed subject to CFTC regulation. In the words of the President's Working Group on Financial Markets (1999: 6): 'These concerns force financial institutions to evaluate legal risks when developing new instruments and new risk-management initiatives and have the potential to reduce the flexibility and competitiveness of US financial markets.'

Second, the principal players in OTC markets are affiliates of banks regulated by the OCC and the Federal Reserve Board, broker-dealers regulated by the SEC, and futures commission merchants (FCM) by the CFTC. Some broker-dealers and FCMs have set up separate affiliates for OTC business as a further step to avoid regulation. Since the CFTC and the SEC regulate markets rather than individual firms, the activities of these separate affiliates are essentially unregulated. In its 1994 report on derivatives, the USGAO noted this gap and signalled its concern. The five major broker-dealers and the three largest insurance firms in this group accounted for about 30 per cent of US OTC dealers' total volume (USGAO 1994: 11). The USGAO and many members of Congress worried that this regulatory 'gap' might provide an opening for systemic risk, because these unregistered affiliates often held large positions in OTC derivatives markets. Some of these large positions were placed with still another unregulated group of firms, hedge funds. Regulators simply did not have access to this information, a factor that added to the severity of the systemic crisis created by the near collapse of a very large hedge fund in 1998, Long Term Capital Management (LTCM) (USGAO 1999: 4).

Moves in Congress and recommendations by the USGAO to bring these firms under some form of regulation were resisted by the Federal Reserve and the SEC, as well as by the industry. All argued that these firms were large and sophisticated and that the markets themselves would discipline their activities. They also reiterated the argument made by the President's Working Group on Financial Markets (1999): any attempt to regulate these firms or OTC derivatives activity more generally would disadvantage US firms in global markets. The lighter touch available in London appeared to dissuade US policymakers from following their long-standing, statutory, formal approach to regulation. Moreover, a small, but economically significant, group of firms was able to escape direct supervision and regulation. Compared to the UK where all firms are supervised, the US is conceivably less well placed to deal with systemic risk arising from global OTC markets.[1]

Global governance initiatives

In his comments to a symposium on derivatives and risk organised by the Group of 30 in 1993, William McDonough (1993: 17), then President of the Federal Reserve Bank of New York, noted, 'given the global nature of derivatives markets, only a global approach to these issues will succeed in the end'. In their assessment of the growth of 'private authority' in the international realm, Cutler, Haufler, and Porter (1999: 3) note, however, that working out such a global approach is by no means easy: governments have difficulty cooperating in the international realm and many of them are unwilling to extend their rule-making capacity beyond the nation-state. Both of these factors are relevant to the governance of OTC derivatives. The attempts by governments to cooperate have been complicated by the very complexity of the issues involved, particularly when it comes to disclosure and transparency. Moreover, as the US and UK case studies above indicate, governments are uncertain about how far they should regulate OTC derivative markets. As the special arrangements in the UK indicate and as the unwillingness to extend the usual formal, statutory approach in the US suggests, on the one side they believe that global financial services corporations should govern themselves. They expect that the harsh realities of competition in global markets will provide the discipline firms need to minimise their risk exposure. On the other side, they are very cognisant of increasing systemic risk. For their part, global firms resist regulation and have moved to set up a private governance arrangement.

Cutler *et al.* (1999: 13) define a 'private regime' as 'an integrated complex of formal and informal institutions that is a source of governance for an economic area as a whole'. They add (1999: 14) that these regimes are created by negotiation and interaction among firms within a given issue area, and generally incorporate a number of business associations, both national and international. This type of arrangement for OTC derivatives began to take shape in 1984 when a group of dealers frustrated with the amount of time it was taking to negotiate a new derivatives contract got together in New York and formed the International Swap Dealers Association (since renamed the International Swaps and Derivatives Association (ISDA)). They began immediately to work on the task of standardising swap documentation (Golden 1994: 18). The association was chartered in 1985 and has grown to include 450 members from 37 countries on five continents. Headquartered in New York City, ISDA also has offices in London, Tokyo, and Singapore.

The association defines its mission to be the promotion of practices conducive to the efficient conduct of business, the development of sound risk management practices, and fostering high standards of commercial conduct. It has pursued these objectives by first providing a Code of Standard Wording Assumptions and Provisions for Swaps. This code has evolved into the preparation of a Master Agreement for swaps transactions. This initial step of preparing a Master Agreement taken in 1988 has been followed by a complex series of additional agreements and supplementary documentation that cover bond options, commodity and energy transactions, credit derivatives, equity derivatives, and foreign exchange and currency derivatives. Governments now accept ISDA documentation as standard practice in the industry.

The activities of other associations have gradually supplemented the work of the ISDA. The Emerging Markets Traders Association (EMTA) has prepared its own Master Agreement for emerging markets derivatives transactions (McGrath 1994: 21). Many optional provisions and choices under the ISDA agreement were not easily adapted to the customs and practices of emerging markets traders (Chamberlain and Saunders 1994: 32). Noting the problem of managing risks across different financial product types and various industry master agreements, a group of associations created a Cross-Party Master Agreement in 2000.[2] This step was a partial response to a June 1999 report on improving counterparty risk management practices by the Counterparty Risk Management Policy Group, an alliance of twelve major globally active commercial and investment banks. Finally, the Futures Industry Association (FIA), the representative body of the derivatives sector in the US, worked out a series of recommendations on 'financial integrity' in 1995. Derivatives firms also agreed in 1995 upon a 'Framework for Voluntary Oversight' of their own activities that is relevant to credit and operational risk.

Complementing these self-regulatory actions taken by the derivatives firms themselves is an emerging intergovernmental consensus on risk management that devolves primary responsibility to the global firm itself. The change in philosophy on the part of governmental authorities was evident in documents released by the Basel Committee on Banking Supervision (BCBS) at the Bank for International Settlements (BIS) in 1995 in response to criticisms of its initial proposals to control market risk. In the past, banking supervisors, for example, could examine quarterly reports on banking assets and liabilities and draw some preliminary conclusions on the financial health of the firm. Alan Greenspan (1996: 35) has noted, however, that this approach is no longer feasible. 'A generation ago a month-old bank balance sheet was a reasonable approximation of the current state of an institution. Today, for some banks, day-old balance sheets are on the edge of obsolescence. In the twenty-first century that will be true of most banks.'

In response to these changing conditions, financial services supervisors have decided that it is more effective to rely on firms' own risk management information systems to protect against losses. Hence their activities are focusing increasingly on firms' internal procedures rather than on after-the-fact results summarised on balance sheets. In response to this changed situation, the Group of 30 (1997: 12) has urged global financial institutions themselves to take the lead in developing risk assessment frameworks. The Basle Committee has welcomed this advice and has begun to work closely with financial services firms on risk management protocols. Its approach is to identify 'best practice' and to publicise these widely. Reflecting a certain faith in market discipline, it believes that the markets will reward those firms whose practices are up-to-date and come closest to these ideal types (Padoa-Schioppa 1997).

These risk management practices will only be effective, however, if two conditions hold: the risks incurred by given firms are transparent and disclosed and there is a sharing of information between respective national supervisors on the activities of these global firms. Governments and the industry have taken some initial steps in both of these areas. Governments have put increasing pressure on the industry to develop common accounting standards for derivatives transactions. Similarly, in developing a revised capital adequacy standard for banks that takes account of market risk, the BCBS has sought to encourage common practices for treating derivatives on and off the balance sheets of global banks.

The idiosyncratic and private character of OTC derivatives contracts has also meant that virtually no one knew how much activity was occurring in these markets. Transparency and disclosure do require some sense of the overall importance of this business and the relative market shares of key global institutions. Beginning in the early 1990s, the BCBS and later the International Organisation of Securities Commissions (IOSCO) began to work on this problem. The Euro-Currency Standing Committee at the BIS encouraged the development of harmonised methods for collecting information on derivatives activity. With these harmonised methods, the BIS was able to publish a first survey of activity in OTC financial markets in 1996 (BIS-BCBS 1996). Subsequently, it has begun a series of regular statistical publications, including semi-annual statistics on positions in the global OTC derivatives market and annual surveys of disclosures about trading and derivatives activities of banks and securities firms. With better knowledge and understanding of the extent of the activities of global firms, the BCBS and the Technical Committee of IOSCO have been able to publish recommendations for public disclosure of trading and derivatives activities (BIS-BCBS 1999). Government supervisors and central banks assume that such disclosure will permit market discipline to keep global firms' derivatives business within acceptable levels of risk.

The collapse of Barings Bank PLC in 1995 following huge losses in derivatives markets incurred by a rogue trader in Hong Kong alerted governments to an additional problem. Mechanisms for the sharing of information on the activities of global firms were inadequate. In May 1995, representatives of regulatory authorities in sixteen countries responsible for supervising the world's derivatives markets met at the invitation of the SIB and CFTC in Windsor, England. In the Windsor Declaration that came out of this meeting, the parties agreed to increase cooperation among themselves, to develop procedures for sharing information, and to devise an approach for cooperation in emergencies. The Technical Committee of IOSCO assumed responsibility for follow-up actions to the Declaration.

Simultaneously, the industry itself working through the FIA convened a Global Task Force on Financial Integrity in March 1995 in response to the collapse of Barings. It included representatives of major international exchanges and clearinghouses, brokers/intermediaries (including futures commission merchants and other brokers) and customers from the following seventeen jurisdictions: Australia, Belgium, Canada, France, Germany, Hong Kong, Italy, Japan, the Netherlands, New Zealand, Norway, Singapore, South Africa, Spain, Sweden, the United Kingdom, and the United States. Out of this task force, futures exchanges and clearing organisations developed a trigger-based agreement whereby the occurrence of certain agreed-upon triggering events affecting an exchange member's financial resources or positions will prompt the sharing of information. On 15 March 1996, forty-nine futures exchanges and clearing organisations initially signed the related Memorandum of Understanding in Boca Raton, Florida at the same time as the signing of a companion regulatory declaration by fourteen futures regulators.

Conclusion

The analysis in this study of the rather similar American and British supervisory approaches to the challenge of global derivatives markets suggests two possible explanations for this outcome. A first explanation might focus on the competition between financial centres in the global marketplace. London and New York are the two leading sites for the business of OTC derivatives. Drawing on its higher level of transformative capacity, the British state was able to fashion a 'light' regulatory and supervisory approach for dealing with risks in these markets. Seeing themselves in competition with the United Kingdom as a financial centre, US policymakers sought consciously to avoid the subsumption of OTC derivatives activity under its existing regulatory structures. The CFTC exemption for selected OTC derivatives, the tolerance for a number of unsupervised affiliates of broker-dealers and FCMs working in OTC markets, and the reluctance to reform existing institutional arrangements to permit a single supervisory authority all exemplify somewhat special treatment for the supervision of OTC derivatives markets and of the firms active in those markets. Consistently, policymakers justified these exemptions by invoking a need to remain 'competitive' in global markets. Given the size of these markets in London, this invocation certainly implied that a measure of regulatory competition exists between the UK and US.

A competing explanation might focus upon the global character of OTC derivatives markets themselves as a principal factor. The transcendence of national borders by these markets, their dominance by complex, global financial services corporations, and the development of a base of private authority organised by these firms all might be seen as leaving nation-states relatively little room for distinctive responses. Differences in regulatory approaches could compromise, if not completely undermine, nation-states' capacity to understand levels of risk in the global financial system. An inadequate understanding in this regard would hamper efforts to fashion agreements on information sharing and the collection of data on exposures. Without the capacity to share information and to view levels of exposure on a global scale, nation-states would be faced with the possibility of being unable to have early warning on unacceptable levels of credit, market, and legal risk. In the absence of this early warning capacity, the likelihood, in turn, of systemic risk rises as well. In this explanation, competition between states is replaced by the need of states to cooperate efficiently.

At this stage of study, it is difficult to say which of these two explanations is the more credible. In fact, both might be credible with states competing to host global banks, while needing to cooperate if any system of governance is to be possible.

Notes

1. An analysis of the near collapse and rescue of the hedge fund, Long Term Capital Management in 1998 would provide support for this conclusion. Such an analysis would be complex and would be more appropriately carried out in a separate paper.
2. The Bond Market Association, the British Bankers Association, EMTA, the Foreign Exchange Committee, the International Primary Market Association, ISDA, the Japan Securities Dealers Association, and the London Investment Banking Association.

14 Is the state being 'transformed' by globalisation?

Linda Weiss

It is time to revisit the orienting questions of this volume and to consider how far our answers take forward the debate on globalisation and the state. What do the pressures of global capitalism imply for the state's ability to govern the domestic economy? How does increasing economic openness affect the institutional capacities and policies of the world's governing authorities? The chapters in this book have been concerned to draw out the implications of interdependence for the capacity of policymaking authorities at the centre of national structures of governance. Three objectives inform their analyses. The first has been to appraise the impact of globalisation, in its various manifestations, on the state's capacity to provide social protection and industrial governance. A further aim has been to specify the institutional conditions under which states are more or less able to mediate such impacts effectively. A final objective has been to elucidate how far, and in what ways, domestic political institutions, in performing that mediating role, are themselves being transformed.

Below we outline the three broad conclusions of the book on these issues, the questions raised for further research, and the way in which the perspective of this volume can help to advance the globalisation–state debate. Our three general conclusions concern: (1) the impact of globalisation on national governance; (2) the institutional conditions which blunt or sharpen the effects of interdependence; and (3) the impact of globalisation on institutional change. They structure the discussion that follows.

Linda Weiss

The impacts of globalisation on governance – room to move

To the extent that the 'straitjacketed state' hypothesis captures the policy spirit of the age, one would expect to find evidence of a clear tendency in one or more of the following arenas: a diminishing capacity to extract revenue over time; a declining propensity to engage in social spending; and a waning ability to promote industry and trade. While the chapters in this book do find globalisation impacting in ways unanticipated by globalists (as we shall see shortly), they find no compelling evidence of the capacity-reducing *tendency* indicated. Rather, most of the book's chapters reveal a surprisingly broad area for action left to states seeking to promote wealth creation and social protection.

Taxation

In matters of taxation, the findings are in important ways uncongenial to the constrained state thesis. In the developed democracies, discussed by Hobson, average tax burdens have grown and expenditure has risen by 20 per cent and 23 per cent respectively over the period of rising interdependence (1965–99). If this is unexpected, so too is the finding that the tax burden on capital has grown, with increases of 52 per cent, somewhat outpacing labour tax increases of 44 per cent. Where nominal corporate rates came down, governments found scope to protect revenues by 'broadening the base' – for example, by reducing tax concessions. Moreover, only four out of twenty OECD countries reduced their average company tax burdens (two very marginally) in the 1995–7 period, compared with the base of 1970–4. Tellingly, all but one of the 'tax cutters' belonged to the Anglo-Saxon group of low-taxing nations (Weiss 2001: 11). It is true that states generally do not treat the corporate sector as a 'cash cow', historically extracting a relatively small share of their total revenue from corporate taxes (today ranging anywhere from c. 2 per cent to 15 per cent). But this structural restraint remains more or less stable and is not a product of rising interdependence. If there is a significant constraint from globalisation, it is not in the direction expected. States have *increased* direct tax yields, but at the price of a partial loss of progressivity in personal income tax, by squeezing middle-income earners. Hence, as Hobson concludes, not a race to the bottom, but 'to the middle'.

It is too obvious to belabour the point that there are limits to the state's extraction capacities; less obvious is that those limits are negotiated domestically. Thus, aggregate tax burdens continue to vary cross-nationally, quite significantly, in accordance with the structure of political and economic institutions, in particular, variations in the strength of labour organisation and party dominance in parliament, examined by Swank in his analysis of welfare states (on the institutional basis of the tax burden, see also Steinmo and Tolbert 1998).

Social welfare

The findings on social welfare tell a similar tale of scope for political choice within domestic constraints. While all developed welfare states have experienced rollbacks in benefit levels, eligibility restrictions, and cost controls, including neoliberal reforms of health and social services, none the less total welfare effort (public social expenditure as a share of national income) has not declined in the period of high globalisation. Indeed, as with taxation, welfare behaviour has varied in important ways across different groups of nations. Thus, as elaborated later, Swank found that increases in international capital movements were associated with quite different spending outcomes linked to distinctive institutional patterns. Slight spending *declines* in some welfare states (i.e., in liberal market economies) have thus been offset by either the *maintenance* or moderate *expansion* of welfare commitments in others (i.e., in coordinated market economies). As these labels imply, the outcomes are linked to distinctive programmatic *norms* (regarding the value of either universalistic or means-tested benefits) and structures of economic and political *organisation* (i.e., the extent to which the former aggregates and the latter offers broad representation of interests resistant to welfare retrenchment).

Thus in the developed democracies the state's fiscal behaviour over the past three decades or more of 'rising globalisation' has not been consistent with the idea of an eroding tax base undermining welfare policy – in short, an all out 'race to the bottom'. This in no way contradicts the fact that income inequality has risen in *some* nations, and that it may in part be associated with globalisation (cf. Quinn 1997). The key point is that while some aspects of globalisation may contribute to rising income inequality, this impact varies cross-nationally, appearing stronger in liberal market economies (notably, the US, New Zealand, and Britain), and weaker in the coordinated market economies (notably Scandinavia) (cf. Galbraith 2001). While more systematic research should clarify the relationship between globalisation and income inequality – and while redistribution is not the only or even the most effective response (cf. Boix

1998) – these patterned differences are precisely what Swank's institutional perspective on welfare state reform would lead one to expect. Thus, in coordinated market economies, with highly organised economic actors and inclusive polities, states are embedded in extensive social infrastructures and face potentially strong resistance to retrenchment. Under these conditions, states tend to maintain or expand their welfare effort, producing lower levels of inequality and poverty (see, e.g., Schmidt, in press: Fig. 2.1).

Industrial governance

Turning to our third broad sphere of state activity, that of industrial governance, a recurring argument is that in a world of mobile capital and international agreements, all states, even those which may have long been involved in promoting economic upgrading, have had to withdraw from industry and trade policy – in short, from any action that smacks of protecting, nurturing, or promoting one's economic advantage. If this is not because of an incompatibility with WTO rules, then it is argued to be due to its sheer futility – tantamount to watering one's own garden in a world where the plants can relocate. Yet our findings show that the state's capacity for industrial policy is not waning with increased interdependence. States continue to foster new growth sectors, subsidise technological innovation and upgrading, invest in infrastructure, finance education and training, including active labour market policies, and regulate industry and finance in distinctive ways to buttress national competitiveness – all in stark contrast to the predictions of the constrained state view.

While the tools of industrial policy often undergo change as circumstances alter, states constantly adapt their instruments to the new tasks. Thus, for example, the Koreans have abandoned directed credit, central to their postwar growth strategy, but they have not withdrawn from transformative projects. Drawing on a range of instruments, old and new, the state remains essential to everything from the restructuring of the chaebol and financial sector to the creation of a venture capital industry and retail market for Korean software (Weiss, this volume). The Japanese, on the other hand, continue to find ways of structuring competition in order to achieve their long-held goals of increased investment and technological upgrading (Tilton, this volume). Even more significant in overturning expectations, as the global race in high technology intensifies, the German state has abandoned its relative passivity in industrial policy in favour of strategic initiatives in the biotechnology and venture capital industries (Lehrer 2000). At the same time, states have not stood by idly after signing up to the WTO's market-opening measures. Thus, neodevelopmentalism continues to involve the state as a pivotal force in Taiwan's technological strategy as an industrial latecomer, constantly moving upscale in IT in the bid to remain ahead of its mainland neighbour (Weiss, this volume; cf. Amsden and Chu, in press). In the banking industry as well, state sponsorship of M&As (via regulatory and tax incentives) has become the favoured tool of both the Europeans (especially France and Germany) and the Asians (notably, Taiwan, Korea, and Japan) – all seeking ways to strengthen their financial sectors as foreign competitors prepare to take advantage of the WTO's market access agreements (see, for example, *Taiwan Headlines*, 11 October 2000; *Business Korea*, January 2001: 14–18).

While we need much more systematic research for the developed democracies, the chapters on regulatory reform and competitive strategy are significant for at least two reasons. First, they indicate that states are just as important as ever in making interdependence possible (Alamgir; Zhu), and in ensuring that global financial markets work rather than self-destruct (Coleman). Moreover, states are just as central as ever in sponsoring new industry sectors (Weiss), even – or especially – in less developed contexts where these initiatives may be blocked (Doner and Ramsay).

Second, they show that states constantly adapt their policy tools, using a mix of old and new instruments (Woo-Cumings) – from tax laws and national competition prizes to venture capital funds – to achieve their policy goals. Among the old instruments, Woo-Cumings observes that administrative guidance – otherwise known as bureaucratic discretion 'to make, interpret and enforce detailed rules of economic behaviour' – has been modified to function entirely for national goals. No longer used in despotic ways (e.g., to dispossess a corporate rebel or political enemy of the President), administrative guidance has become a mechanism of reform 'to propel financial restructuring and clean up corporate governance'.

At the newer end of the 'instruments' spectrum, one of the most important is the public–private 'partnership' which develops as governments extend and deepen ties with organised economic actors to pursue transformative projects (Coleman; Weiss; Tilton; Doner and Ramsay). In many cases, the competitive pressures of global markets encourage producers to enter into such networks. Such relationships of 'governed interdependence', as argued elsewhere (Weiss 1998), and as a number of the chapters in this book have shown in distinctive ways, are the stuff of transformative capacity in today's states.

The larger point is not that macroeconomic constraints do not exist, but rather that the debate needs to move beyond this level. In many respects they are less important for tackling the contemporary problems of competitiveness, joblessness, and economic stagnation, for these are structural rather than cyclical problems. The near total preoccupation in the globalisation debate with the state's growing inability to pursue Keynesian techniques of demand management has obscured the fact that of greater importance for a country's overall economic performance is the ability to improve the level and the quality of the production system, especially the supply of technology and knowledge skills, via support for education and training, innovation and technological upgrading. These so-called supply-side policies seek to induce structural changes rather than simply manage cyclical outcomes (Boix 1998). These areas are vital to both economic *and* social outcomes; moreover, these are areas in which policy choices are real and, in turn, make a real difference.

The cumulative evidence presented in these pages thus weighs against accepting a purely 'constrained state' view. The chapters on taxation, social expenditure, and competitive strategies lead us to conclude that, *however much globalisation throws real constraints in the way of state activity, most notably in the macroeconomic arena, it also allows states sufficient room to move, and thus to act consonant with their social policy and economic upgrading objectives.*

To make sense of the counterevidence we therefore need to add an extra dimension to the globalisation dynamic. Like the proverbial sword, globalisation appears double-edged: not merely constraining, but also enabling. Enablement implies that in the face of relatively similar globalisation pressures, there are countervailing pressures on governments and, often, political incentives, to intervene. We therefore explain the state's room for manoeuvre in terms of the dual logics of global capitalism – not simply constraining, but also enabling policy choice by virtue of the pressures felt by particular social constituencies, the corresponding demands they place on governments, and the political incentives for policy responses.

Clearly, the strength of these enabling pressures and the corresponding policy responses called for will vary in part according to the *kind and level of interdependence* involved. Thus, low-wage imports will have different social and economic consequences (and therefore different policy implications) than those stemming, say, from the loss of export markets to producers in low-wage countries. Not all forms of interdependence are equally constricting. Historically, high trade interdependence in small European states has been met by strong welfare services and active labour market policies; high FDI dependence in Asia (e.g., Singapore and Hong Kong) has seen containment of social welfare spending and greater emphasis on subsidised production-related services (housing, transport, and education). Hence, in discussing 'globalisation's' impacts we need to disaggregate different aspects of 'interdependence' since these have different implications for social groups, compensatory demands, and policy responses (see, e.g., Burgoon: 2001).

But, more importantly, enabling pressures and policy responses will vary according to the *kind of institutional framework* in a given country. Both Britain and Germany, for example, have relatively similar levels of trade integration, at 53 per cent and 57 per cent respectively (based on the share of exports and imports in GDP for 1999), but the welfare retrenchment politics and outcomes in each case diverge. In short, *not all states move in the same way in the room that they have*. The different moves that states make, whether in taxing, spending, or competitive strategy, lead to a consideration of the institutional underpinnings of state reponses.

Institutional mediation of the global

Our second set of conclusions turns on the issue of institutional mediation. In this respect, the present book expands on earlier efforts to theorise in a substantive manner the ways in which institutions mediate the impacts of interdependence in the domestic arena. In doing so, this collection goes somewhat beyond existing efforts in specifying the conditions that loosen or tighten the pressures of economic interdependence in specific issue areas.

Institutional conditions that blunt or sharpen impacts of interdependence

Whether institutions intensify or soften the constraints on economic governance and policy autonomy will depend on their normative and organisational configuration in the specific issue area in question. Consider the examples of trade competition and welfare retrenchment pressures discussed in this volume.

In the context of trade competition, where the challenge is posed to upgrade production and technology (see Doner and Ramsay; and

Weiss), the constraints of interdependence are tightened when the administrative structures, normative orientations of the governing elite, and government–business linkages, combine to block an adequate response. As discussed by Doner and Ramsay, Thailand's failure to upgrade production in the face of mounting trade competition from low-cost producers in its export markets, both before and since the regional financial crisis, offers a convincing illustration of the conditions under which domestic institutions restrict the state's room for managing the challenges of openness.

In understanding what lies behind the failure to upgrade technologically, Thailand's political institutions – specifically, the constellation of norms, rules, and organisational arrangements – tell the tale. A major piece of the puzzle is the normative orientation of the Thai technocratic elite, traditionally prioritising macroeconomic stability and inclined to view sectoral intervention with suspicion. Key components of Thailand's political institutions have also deteriorated in the 1990s, with government downsizing, bureaucratic brain drain to the private sector and cabinet instability, including frequent ministerial changes – all of which have contributed to a loss of expertise, cohesion and stability among the policymaking elite. Other institutional weaknesses persist, including fragmentation of key state agencies, which undermine technical training efforts, and the extreme fragility of public–private sector linkages, which exacerbates the upgrading problem by offering few incentives for industry to engage productively with the state. Add to this combination the state's programmatic structures for industry, which have prevented the emergence of alternative sources of upgrading, and you have an institutional picture almost diametrically the opposite of Taiwan's, with its developmentally oriented elite, cohesive market-driven state agencies, well-organised industry sectors, and systematic public–private linkages.

In Taiwan's case, changing world currency markets compromised its monetary policy autonomy, but, as Weiss shows, they also served as an important stimulus to Taiwan's rethinking of industrial strategy, which focused on deepening high-technology production in the second half of the 1980s. Since the unifying values and concerns of the political elite have been strongly oriented by developmental norms and sustained by national security concerns, the objectives of industrial upgrading became enshrined in government policy. In stark contrast with Thailand, in Taiwan, the norms of state guidance of the national economy, the programmatic rules which reward upgrading of skills and technology, the technology diffusion agencies, and the cooperative public–private arrangements for coordinating technological change have enabled governments to secure continuous improvement of the production structure and thus deliver adjustment policies relatively effectively.

Efforts to meet globalisation challenges in Taiwan have thereby served to enhance rather than diminish domestic capacities. By contrast, Thailand has become trapped at the lower end of technology, jeopardising its ability to sustain development. In this context, existing institutions narrow the state's room for manoeuvre and transform potential opportunities from openness into threats. This leads to the more general conclusion, argued by Doner and Ramsay, that the new developmental problems are 'institution intensive' – requiring not simply clearer rules and regulations, but stronger states, robust private organisations, and public–private sector linkages: in short, the arrangements that facilitate governed interdependence – regular information sharing, mutual monitoring, and so on. It is therefore with some irony that they conclude that whatever pressures for 'convergence' globalisation imposes, these are towards enhanced local institutional capacities, and consequently well beyond the 'neoliberal institutionalism' (with its emphasis on 'getting the rules right') that currently informs World Bank thinking (even if this is an improvement on the old prescription of 'getting the prices right').

Turning from trade competition to pressures for welfare retrenchment in the context of rising financial interdependence, we find another set of contrasting outcomes that can be traced to the different normative and organisational features of institutions. An explanation of the divergent responses in liberal and coordinated market economies involves an analysis not only of programmatic structures (e.g., whether benefits are 'means tested' or 'universalistic'), which shape or reproduce normative orientations towards the welfare state in different settings. It also entails analysis of the organisational configuration within the economic and political arenas, for this structures both the aggregation and representation of interests. Thus, as Swank shows, where there is fragmented interest organisation, a majoritarian electoral system, and means-tested benefits – typical of liberal market systems – pressures for welfare retrenchment in the context of increasing interdependence are sharpened. Consequently, in these institutional settings, welfare reform tends to lean towards contraction rather than expenditure maintenance or expansion. Conversely, where there are encompassing interest representational systems, inclusive electoral institutions and universalistic welfare programmes (typical of coordinated market systems), pressures for retrenchment are neutralised.

As these cases of failed and successful upgrading, on one hand, and welfare maintenance and reduction on the other, demonstrate, *both the normative and organisational configuration of institutions play a key role in conditioning the way states respond to globalisation pressures, enlarging or reducing their room to move as the case may be.*

The mediating power of social norms

However, one recurring question raised by the analyses in this book is the extent to which the embeddedness of social norms, specifically those orienting major power actors, may, in the long run, be more important than organisational configurations. The mediating power of social norms – even in the apparent absence of specific state involvement – should not be underestimated. This is the message of Loriaux's account of the limits to French financial liberalisation. While 'systemic' factors in the international political economy (chiefly, a change in foreign economic policy by a hegemonic US which set off a chain of events) have compelled France to liberalise its financial system and abandon investment coordination, French ideas of *étatisme*, developmentalism, and economic nationalism persist. However, they persist *outside* the institutions of state intervention that once housed them. The important point is that, as a set of normative orientations or shared cultural values, they continue to shape investment practices in French private firms sensitive to long-term development and national economic interests, due to the pervasive presence of an elite that shares a common education, language, socialisation, and self-confidence. Thus behind the changing nature of *étatist* institutions and developmentalist tools lies the apparent permanence of a developmentalist culture. For in France the institutions that count nowadays are not the ones that produce subsidies or channel capital to investment, but the elite state educational institutions that socialise political and economic elites, produce shared norms, link French CEOs into the Grands Corps de L'État, and safeguard the tradition of developmentalism.

The implication is that shared norms can mediate the impacts of globalisation. In spite of financial liberalisation and the demise of investment coordination by French technocrats, the strength of nationalist values that unify the French political and business elite softens the prospects of exit by French institutional investors, thus somewhat reducing the nation's vulnerability to global financial movements.

The distinctive orientations of American and Japanese authorities towards the regulation of their telecommunications sectors, examined by Tilton, offer another important example of the ways in which normative structures (though not only these) mediate policy responses. In Japan, strongly pro-competitive ideas have held less sway among political leaders and bureaucrats than the concrete developmental goals of increased investment and improved technology. Such normative differences – sometimes identified in terms of consumer-oriented versus producer-oriented political economies – have enabled the major Japanese carrier in telecommunications to wield more policy clout than its US counterpart, where social and legal norms stemming from the anti-trust aims of the Sherman Act have long underpinned the formation of a strongly pro-competitive and consumerist ethos at public and private levels.

The key point is that if Japan adopts a more restrained stance on competition, this cannot be convincingly traced to a weaker state capacity than in the United States, but rather to differences in the normative structures that inform such capacities. While the ability to aggressively promote competition depends on the state's goal-setting autonomy, as Levi-Faur argues in his historical comparison between 'hard state' Europe and 'soft state' Latin America, state autonomy does not necessarily bring about that competitive result. For this outcome must depend in some important measure on the entrenched values that orient the administrative and political elite regarding such things as the fundamental purpose of economic activity. While the US approach achieves lower prices and wider use of internet technology at the cost of lower profits and investment, the Japanese support business structures that will achieve their developmental goals of more rapid investment and technology development, even if this means less competition and higher prices. As the US–Japan comparison suggests, without the normative structures, state autonomy (and indeed state capacity) is like a train without the tracks.

Elite cohesion, institutional persistence, and change

As these observations imply, the existence of elite cohesion is an important factor often sidelined in discussions of institutional change. It therefore deserves some emphasis in this context. We might even venture that elite cohesion is key to understanding institutional stability and change – a proposition that emerges throughout, rather than being fully developed in, this volume. Whether institutional change is likely to occur in line with globalist expectations – for example, enabling state transformation and the creation of liberal-market institutions – will be strongly influenced by the extent to which elites divide or cohere around core goals.[1] The evidence for this proposition surfaces in a number of the chapters.

Thus, in a novel analysis of how India managed to stay the course of openness against most unlikely odds, Jalal Alamgir shows how India's political elites remained united on the need to pursue economic openness, succeeding in sustaining major policy reform. What remained vital to this outcome was the strength of shared values regarding India's security, identity, and historic role, combined with a growing apprehension that China constitutes an increasingly strategic threat. The Indian elite thus succeeded in constructing a coherent and compelling narrative that convinced the literate public that India's future lay with economic opening. In this respect, shared values and the construction of a compelling public discourse provided the state elite with crucial room to manoeuvre.

Loriaux's fresh look at the state of French *étatisme* since financial liberalisation, referred to above, similarly highlights the enduring importance of shared norms among elites – this time from business and government. Moreover, this may have important consequences for French capitalism. For, as mentioned, even though credit activism ended some time ago, the ideas of stateness and the values of *étatisme* have not. They have simply re-emerged in the private sector where business elites share the same normative presumptions about French interests and the state's role in the economy as do their colleagues in the state bureaucracy. Thus Loriaux shows how certain normative and organisational features of the French state and of the government–business relationship have carried over into the liberalised post-*dirigiste* economy.

Whether the elite is divided or cohesive matters theoretically for at least two reasons. First, consensus over core goals may contribute to institutional stability since it implies less need for side payments to earn supporters, hence relatively stable power relations, and therefore few incentives to break the mould. Under certain conditions, it may also smooth the way for institutional change should elites decide, for whatever reason, that this would preserve or increase domestic legitimacy or international support (as Taiwan leaders sought to do in managing the transition from authoritarianism in the mid-1980s). On the other hand, the absence of elite unity for the same reason encourages the growth of distributive coalitions and diverts resources, which may, at least in new or developing states, inhibit the process of institution building (Waldner 1998).

Second, elite cohesion may enable greater insulation from both domestic and external pressures. Differences in the extent of elite cohesion that Weiss observes (in Chapter 12) contribute much to an explanation of why changes to the developmental state have been so much more pronounced in pre-crisis Korea than in Taiwan where the strength of a much more persistent and credible threat to national security has preserved elite unity over core economic goals. Intensifying ideological and political division (at both bureaucratic and political levels) left Korean governments much more exposed than the Taiwanese to external pressures for change. Conversely, the strength of shared values among French political and business elites, suggests Loriaux, may plausibly orient French business to seek more strength through 'voice' rather than 'exit'.

Future work on institutional change (as well as major policy shifts) must therefore pay close attention to the sources and extent of elite cohesion. As such examples imply, the mechanisms for elite cohesion vary cross-nationally and one important research question this raises is whether and in what ways some of these mechanisms are more vulnerable to globalisation. For instance, is elite cohesion in France less fragile than that of other developmental states because of its dependence on socialisation into an elite culture via *domestic* institutions, rather than on the shared perceptions of vulnerability that spring from *geopolitics* and the structure of *international* relations? From a slightly different perspective, can the Indian elite – galvanised to cooperate on market opening by great power rivalry and an affront to national dignity – turn their newly won unity and narrative skills to the more demanding tasks of capacity building for the globalisation challenges ahead? If elite cohesion can offer a buffer against external threats, then understanding more about the variety of domestic mechanisms that work either to reinforce, or weaken it, offers a fruitful area for research.

In drawing out the ways in which institutions matter, it may appear that the international system has little or no domestic impact. Indeed, a question raised in the chapters by Swank and Ramesh on welfare states is whether in fact it is institutions or interdependence which explains the observed effects. Both Swank and Ramesh make the case that it is the character of domestic institutions that matter. However, we may not need to choose between them, since there would seem to be much more complementarity than conflict.

Institutions versus interdependence?

There is indeed substantial research to support the interdependence or international system argument, which shows that trade openness generally correlates with growth in government spending (Boix 1998; Rodrik 1998; Garrett 1998a). Indeed, the group of states which maintain welfare generosity – Swank's 'social democratic' states – are for the most part the so-called 'small states' of northern Europe with high trade interdependence, made famous by Peter Katzenstein (1985). They are 'small' because of their vulnerability rather than size *per se*. Perceived vulnerability to changing international markets, argued Katzenstein, helped historically to forge a distinctive institutional structure based on an ideology of social partnership and corporatist style arrangements. (Is the corporatist effect of trade interdependence on small states an early version of the current spread of governed interdependence in response to competition in global markets, as discussed below?) Thus openness (*qua* trade interdependence) matters historically in shaping the institutional trajectory. But once the institutions are in place they take on an importance of their own. Does this mean that declining levels of interdependence would lead European states to adjust their welfare models? Conversely, would countries with relatively low levels of trade interdependence, either because of market size or protectionist policies (e.g., the United States, Britain, Australia) be likely to adjust their welfare models as interdependence and vulnerability *increased significantly*? The answer to both questions seems clear: nations would indeed adjust to changes in their external environment – but would do so via their existing institutional structures. It would be wrong then to juxtapose the institutional argument with the international system one, for they are complementary rather than competing.

Yet, if interdependence really matters, one might ask why then is Singapore – highly integrated economically and vulnerable to global markets – apparently such a 'mean' version of a small state (not only compared with Europe, but also with current welfare growth in Taiwan and Korea)? Ramesh argues that it is not interdependence that drives social spending in East Asia, but the institutions of competitive politics, which is why welfare spending is growing in democratic Korea and Taiwan but not in oligarchic Singapore. It would seem that the new democracies create political incentives to offer forms of social security, which are not in any direct way 'compensating' for openness.

So, is openness of little account in shaping East Asian policy? The answer may depend on how one disaggregates 'interdependence'. Taking this tack shows that Singapore differs from the European small state norm in being strongly dependent on FDI.[2] This raises the question as to whether high FDI dependence may give rise to different perceptions of vulnerability from those based on trade alone and, accordingly, whether this carries different implications for social compensation. Singapore, for example, places more emphasis on social infrastructure and certain services in its public spending (e.g., subsidised housing, transport, and education), than on transfers such as high-cost pensions, which are funded out of compulsory savings (the Central Provident Fund). Is there a correlation between this type of interdependence (FDI) and the pattern of domestic compensation, in the same way found for trade dependency in the small European states? Such questions deserve more systematic investigation, suggesting a fruitful line of enquiry for future research, especially into other countries with FDI-driven development, notably in East Asia and Eastern Europe.

More generally, however, there is ample evidence that a persistent and heightened exposure to international system pressures (in the form of high levels of either economic instability or military threat) has served to institutionalise perceptions of vulnerability, along with ideas of social partnership (Sweden), economic nationalism (Japan, Korea, Taiwan), and *étatisme* (France). In the present context, this raises the question of whether we can expect institutional structures in the developed democracies to become rather more like the small state pattern – taking on some of its social partnership, corporatist, and coordinated market attributes – as the vulnerabilities of interdependence increase; or whether, instead, existing institutions will act as fetters that impede such adjustment.

While the idea of 'convergence' has fascinated scholars at least since Marx, it has become something of an overworked concept. Take the case of Japan: through one lens, Japan has apparently been converging on the West ever since the famous Iwakura Mission of the nineteenth century diligently set about the task of 'institutional transfer'. Through another lens, it has evolved a highly distinctive social system. Both perspectives are right: 'same, same, but different'. So let us apply the lesson to contemporary developments: thus, the fact that the bureaucracy has toned down the more 'statist' features of administrative guidance that governed business–bureaucrat relations in the recent past, as noted by

Woo-Cumings, does not mean a rush headlong into the arm's-length regulatory stance favoured (but not always practised) by the Americans.

We believe, then, that – for reasons not only evident from the preceding discussion but also amply discussed in existing studies (cf. Hall and Soskice 2000; Kitschelt *et al.*, 1999; Berger and Dore 1996) – outright convergence, whether at the macro- or micro-institutional level, should not be anticipated. To the extent that interdependence is producing pressures for domestic change, a *more plausible scenario is the emergence of different forms of cooperation, alliance, and social partnership between political and economic actors (business, government, and labour) in specific areas that are especially vulnerable to major systemic risk or instability.* Such alliances may take different forms – for example, be more or less formal, more or less intensively interactive, more or less extensive in reach and aims. As interdependence presses for such alliances, domestic structures put their stamp on that process, aiding or hindering as the case may be. Thus: same, same, but different. To consider these points in more detail, let us turn to our third main conclusion.

Impacts of globalisation on institutional change
State power: from statism to governed interdependence
The debate about globalisation's impact on governance has clearly moved forward since radical globalists first began to proclaim the end or decline of the nation-state. In recent years, as the introduction to this volume made clear, mainstream or moderate globalists have distanced themselves from the 'endist' claims of the radicals. Instead they contend that the state remains firmly in place, but that it is rather undergoing a 'hollowing out' or 'profound transformation' of its powers as its policymaking capacities steadily shrink in the domestic arena, and as they get distributed to other power actors at home and abroad (Held *et al.*, 1999: 442–4; Rosenau 2000: 186; Hirst and Thompson 1996: 183–94). To what extent then have domestic political institutions, in mediating the effects of interdependence, undergone radical transformation, as many globalists contend? Is the state transformation thesis on track?

This book offers a different perspective on the globalisation– governance relationship. On the question of state transformation, we conclude that *the main institutional impact of global markets is a tendency to weaken statist forms of rule and to encourage, domestically, the growth of various forms of 'governed interdependence'*. This latter entails a variety of public–private partnerships and alliances, policy networks, information exchange, and self-regulation under the state's goal-setting auspices. In contemporary political economies, governed interdependence may be viewed as the obverse of statism, much as infrastructural power – as Michael Mann (1984) has argued in a broader historical perspective – came to be the obverse of despotic power (in the transition from pre-industrial to modern states). In both cases, state–society relations become closer and more negotiated in character as states seek to achieve their goals. Infrastructural power is a defining characteristic of all modern states, with their territorial reach, their penetrative and extractive capacities. Governed interdependence is a more specialised version of infrastructural power, vital to the state's transformative capacity in a variety of economic arenas (Weiss 1998: ch. 2). The claim is not that governed interdependence (GI) has generally supplanted statist and liberal pluralist state–society relations. Rather, the claim is that GI is a *tendency* of globalisation, and that to the extent that it is emerging in different national settings and sectors, it provides states with a new or increased transformative capacity.

What evidence do we have of its growth? One way in which the growth of governed interdependence (hence changes in transformative capacity) can be observed in settings both European and Asian is by means of the state building or extending its links with domestic power actors – both vertically and horizontally, as William Coleman (2002) has shown for France in the context of agricultural policy, and as Mark Lehrer (2000) has demonstrated for Germany with regard to high technology and its financing. Similar developments have been analysed in the case of neodevelopmental states in East Asia where the state's success in coordinating more complex industrial upgrading in the context of increasing openness has come to rely more heavily on participation of organised business in the policy process (Weiss 1998: ch. 3; Amsden and Chu, forthcoming). There is evidence in other arenas as well that states may interact more closely with organised power actors – NGOs, MNCs, business associations and so forth – in order to enhance their policy effectiveness in an era of growing complexity (on financial institutions, and central–local government relations, see chapters by Coleman and Zhu, respectively). As Tim Dunne (1999: 26–7) observes with regard to transnational organisations, states are increasingly involving NGOs in the formulation of public policy in ways that increase their capacity to shape outcomes. Thus states may not control their territory in quite the *same* way as in the past, but this is not to say that their control is less *consequential* or *effective*.

Indeed, from Asia to Europe, GI has become a catalyst for nurturing new growth sectors and supportive services, from biotechnology and retail software to information technology hardware and venture capital (e.g., in Germany, Korea, Taiwan, and France), as well as for regenerating older ones (e.g., in French agriculture). Governed interdependence has even emerged in the United States as national authorities abandon their legalistic, arm's-length approach in order to regulate global derivatives markets, both nationally and internationally (Coleman).

Another important way in which shifts in state capacity have occurred is by means of states forging new, or extending existing, relationships with other states. Constraints transformationalists are inclined to view cooperative alliances of this kind as evidence of a 'loss of sovereignty' – the EU experience being, ironically, the (regional) example most favoured to illustrate such a (global) trend. But more complex views of European cooperation recognise how such alliances can extend territorial reach and thus enhance national capacity (Mann 1993; Ikenberry 1995; Weiss 1999a; Schmidt, in press).

While the evidence assembled here and elsewhere offers firm ground for positing governed interdependence as a tendency associated with globalisation, we need more studies to determine the robustness of this conclusion. Is it, for example, more likely to emerge in certain sectors and markets rather than others, in some countries more than others? In short, what are the conditions encouraging its growth?

We suggest that globalisation is the common denominator that is driving the development of GI. However, as already made clear, globalisation needs to be disaggregated, so that future research should consider both the character of global markets and the character of international competition. Where either of these conditions are met, yet GI does not take hold (to be discussed below), then we should consider also the character of existing domestic institutions, which may block desired change.

Specifying the conditions of state power transformation under globalisation

What conditions determine whether globalisation leads to increased infrastructural power in industrialising states (e.g., China) or governed interdependence in the developed democracies (e.g., the United States, Germany, Korea)? We hypothesise that among the most important conditions for state power transformation in the direction of increased infrastructural power or forms of governed interdependence, two are obvious contenders: the character of global markets and the character of the competitive problem. But, as we will see, where these conditions do not produce the outcomes in question, we must consider a third possibility – the character of domestic institutions.

The character of global markets

In genuinely global markets characterised by strong systemic risk, especially where the risk is clearly perceived by regulators (as in the case of Long Term Capital Management – in the United States), one may hypothesise that the greater the systemic risk, the stronger the pressure for public–private cooperation and information exchange in regulating markets. A critical case in this regard is the experience of the United States in regulating the market for global derivatives. Since the latter is the most genuinely 'globalised' of markets, it offers a highly significant case for appraising globalisation's impact. Its significance can be seen in two other respects. First, being truly global in operation, derivatives pose a very high systemic risk. Second, the United States' traditional approach to financial market regulation is in direct contradistinction to that of governed interdependence.

Thus, to the extent that regulatory convergence is occurring in derivatives markets, it is not in the expected direction, but rather convergence on a form of governed interdependence – as the US moves closer to the more informal regulatory approach of the UK. In the UK, the system of state–finance relations has evolved into a corporatist structure in which the major corporate actors, their interest associations, and the core public agencies (Bank of England and SIB) engage in regular consultation and informal exchange. The result is the transformation of an arm's-length, formal, legalistic regulatory relationship to one based on closer collaboration for shared objectives, through information exchange and government-sponsored self-monitoring. This is the case of the US regulatory response to derivatives examined by Coleman.

Coleman asks whether this unexpected shift is due to the nature of the competition (American fear of losing out to the British who are strong in derivatives trading), or to the global character of derivatives markets (which poses the fear of systemic risk, and which present arrangements do little to assuage). He wonders whether the global character of the market restricts the freedom to follow policy styles consistent with domestic institutional arrangements.

It is none the less possible to embrace the idea of change without resorting to notions of globalisation imposing generalised convergence.

Thus, one might propose as an alternative hypothesis that the more globalised the market, and the greater the systemic risk, or perceived risk to national security, the greater the incentives for a GI response. Thus, GI will not be institutionally all-pervasive, but will be more likely to emerge in areas with these characteristics.

Of course there are earlier parallels in America's formation of public–private partnerships in agriculture and high technology, which support the hypothesis (e.g., the formation of Sematech in 1987 to relaunch the US semiconductor industry). This and similar high-technology initiatives have meant the overthrow of an arm's-length approach to industrial change, and the embracing of GI. And such cases have been impelled by fear of losing out to the Japanese, legitimated in the strategic language of a threat to national security.

So, it would seem that a hegemon like the United States is prepared to adjust its regulatory approach (orientation and arrangements) in particular sectors, under quite specific conditions: whenever systemic risk (or the national security threat) is sufficiently large (and perceived to be so), and when the advantages of current institutional arrangements have been tested and found wanting. Conversely, in markets with little systemic risk (or external competition) – for example, in US telecommunications, as examined by Tilton – one may expect preservation of an arm's-length regulatory style (hence, unlike financial derivatives, no attempted emulation of the Japanese approach, which allows for more bargaining and interdependence between regulators and corporate actors.)

In the case of financial derivatives, then, we see genuinely globalised markets with the greatest potential for system destabilisation apparently moving the US federal authorities away from their traditional institutional approach. In this particular context, state power as authoritatively ordered regulation at a distance is giving way to a more negotiated form that elicits private-sector cooperation and information exchange – in short, what we have earlier identified as a form of 'governed interdependence'.

The character of the competitive problem

At the opposite end of the political economy spectrum, the Chinese experience offers a different variation on the power transformation tendency. Although on a much greater scale, and in response to a different set of challenges, it runs in a similar direction to that noted for the US.

As a transitional, newly industrialising economy, China's problem has been how to strengthen the market economy in preparation for increased opening. In the process, there has been a clear shift from an 'absolute', highly statist form of rule to one based on increased infrastructural power, negotiated rule, and capacity for selective intervention. Tianbiao Zhu shows how economic opening, both in trade and investment, has played a critical role in transforming the powers of the Chinese state. While it has contributed to a decline in absolute power based on centralised resource control and central planning, it has also acted as a stimulus to the development of new capacities. In particular, the Chinese central state has reconfigured central–local relations to emphasise tighter cooperation in order to more effectively manage national–global relations. As a result, state authorities have also established new capacities to engage in *selective* industrial promotion, both at central and local levels. Thus, the process of managing economic opening has neither reduced nor strengthened state powers. Rather, it has weakened the 'absolute' powers of the state in a communist centrally controlled economic system (via increased power sharing with local governing bodies), and correspondingly contributed to a strengthening of its infrastructural capacities (via increased administrative ability to extract taxes and to coordinate industrial upgrading in particular sectors). In sum, the Chinese case shows how *globalisation tends to blunt highly statist forms of rule* (and dirigisme too, in the case of France), *while sharpening the importance of negotiated forms of power that potentially enhance transformative capacity.*

While these cases exemplify developments at each end of the political economy spectrum, others, like Germany and the neodevelopmentalist states of Taiwan and Korea (discussed earlier) are creatively adapting old forms of GI to new problems – chiefly competitive problems in product markets – in everything from IT hardware and software to biotechnology and venture capital formation (Weiss, Chapter 12, this volume).

While the global integration of financial markets poses problems of systemic risk, competition in product markets generates a different set of pressures for the adjustment of domestic structures. Two questions arise for further research. How can such pressures of interdependence be identified and weighted cross-nationally – for example, via trade balances, the composition of intra-industry trade, the presence of export rivals, and so forth? Moreover, under what conditions do such pressures transmogrify into the perception of vulnerability that call forth new institutional and policy responses? While there has been much work conducted in this vein on welfare states, namely the relationship between trade interdependence and domestic structures, we know a great deal less about such relationships in the sphere of industrial governance. While this volume goes some way towards identifying what interdependence pressures mean for, and the conditions for change in, both developing countries and developed democracies, we need more systematic research in both areas.

Such research should take into account a final set of considerations. Where interdependence pressures are strong but GI is stalled, we should look to a third possibility – the character of domestic institutions. The case of Thailand, illustrated earlier, and discussed in a different context below, is an example of the institutional conditions under which globalisation is least likely to lead to institutional adaptation.

The character of existing domestic institutions

The combination of strong interdependence pressures and stalled institutional adaptation indicates that neither the global character of markets, nor the nature of the competitive problem *per se* are sufficient conditions to explain whether or not state power changes will occur in the direction observed in this book. In such cases, much would appear to depend also on the character of existing institutions. For these help not only to blunt or heighten perceptions of vulnerability, but also to stifle or mobilise the political energies necessary for relevant action.

The Thai case of stalled upgrading indicates that the pressures of interdependence may be necessary but not sufficient to bring about change. The problem of competing with lower cost producers at similar or more advanced technology levels – for example, China – provides a strong impetus for the upgrading programmes that depend on public–private cooperation. Thailand's upgrading challenge is, as Doner and Ramsay argue, 'institution intensive', but we have seen why – beset by bureaucratic weakness, elite division, fragile public–private linkages – it lacks the ingredients for that outcome. For in spite of the intensification of public–private linkages since the financial crisis, consistent incentives for collaboration have been absent. In Korea and Taiwan, on the other hand, existing institutional conditions – strong developmental ambitions, producer-oriented norms, well-organised business sectors, the state as independent goal-setter – have paved the way for more effective public–private cooperation for shared projects.

Thus we find that globalisation stimulates changes in domestic structures of governance, but in ways that may enhance as well as restrict state capacity in particular arenas. We propose that whether the changes become capacity constricting or enhancing – intensive or superficial – depends to a large degree on the prevailing norms and state–society linkages in the domestic environment. This applies to developing and developed countries alike. Thailand, like France, lost an effective mechanism for investment coordination when it liberalised its financial sector; since then, it has failed to build the institutional capacities to manage the new challenges of openness. While French reforms, though for very different reasons, also undid financial links between firms and the state, the consequences have been quite different. The 'statist' cloak has worn thin: the state's role as creator and coordinator of national champions has waned. This supports the general argument. But one is inclined to ask: what has emerged in the place of statism? In the arena of industrial governance, argues Loriaux, French *étatisme* survives as a kind of culture that continues to orient investment practices of the business elite in the absence of intervention. Of course, complete elite cohesion may be dysfunctional for the emergence of GI since it offers no independent perspective from which to establish the rules of the game or monitor performance – that is, the 'governed' element in GI; hence the tendency of French 'developmentalism' to collapse into 'rescues for the ailing' (Hall 1986). So, is France a case of stalled GI or one in which this power shift is now under way? Again, the answer appears to be sector specific, as new forms of government–business coordinated change are being documented in a number of sectors, from agriculture (Coleman 2002) to high-technology start-ups (Cieply 2001).

Is the state being 'transformed' by global markets?

Finally, then, we return to the larger theoretical point advanced in this analysis: namely, that globalisation does indeed impact on national governance and its domestic structures, but the impact is not *only*, or even *generally*, constraining. Rather, the impact is just as likely to be enabling – in particular, enabling the emergence of governed interdependence. For, under certain conditions – which, in a first approximation, we have sought to specify here as the basis for a new research agenda – globalisation also stimulates the expansion of governing capacities through both the transformation of public–private sector relations and the growth of new policy networks. Understanding and elaborating the conditions under which globalisation has this effect should be the subject of future research.

Thus, in offering a fresh perspective on the globalisation–state relationship, this book anticipates and helps to account for a different kind of change from the one projected by current globalisation theory. To the extent that globalisation 'transforms' the state (or at least important *parts* of this polymorphous beast), the most important change identified in this book is the transformation from absolute, *dirigiste*, statist, or rigidly arm's-length types of rule (China at the 'absolute' end of the spectrum in non-democracies, France and the United States at the 'statist' and arm's-length ends respectively in the developed democracies), to one based on either increased infrastructural state power (China) or new forms of governed interdependence.

This contrasts markedly with the conclusions of the constraints-transformationalist literature on globalisation and governance. For the latter, these new policy networks – between states and other power actors in the domestic and international arenas – are supposed to illustrate the 'transformation' (read 'power dilution') and 'hollowing out' of the state. This conclusion, however, seems somewhat hollow itself, being based less on substantive evidence than on zero-sum reasoning.

While this whole area offers many an opportunity for new projects, in so far as much of the research remains to be done, the starting point should be clear. For however pervasive the new state–society relations and policy networks turn out to be, the power-sharing arrangements that such networks tend to imply do not mean a *reduced*, or less important role for the state. In many respects they reflect the real growth ('transformation'?) in powers and responsibilities that states have come to acquire in an increasingly interdependent era. In the domestic arena, the new state–society 'synergy' often created by such arrangements – to use Peter Evans' language – means that a 'capable and involved state' is the necessary prerequisite for civil society groups to act effectively (1997: 74; see also Levy on France, 1999: 10–11).

It is difficult to offer serious appraisal of the state transformation thesis because few of its claims are systematically laid out. At times it looks more like a dispute about terms and definitions (e.g., 'sovereignty') than about substantive, testable propositions. Big claims about state transformation lead one to expect changes of a qualitative-institutional kind, when what transformationalists often have in mind is either *policy* change (sometimes incorrectly characterised as generalised 'retreat from welfare'); or changes in policy *instruments* (e.g., as a result of financial liberalisation removing certain kinds of controls for influencing investment); or changes in policy and regulatory *networks* (as states extend

316

existing links or fashion new ones with other power actors inside and outside the state). In this volume, however, sustained analysis of such changes at both the domestic and international levels has offered up quite a different story in which state powers (*qua* 'transformative capacities'), while sometimes blocked or restrained by domestic institutions, are more often than not being sustained or enhanced in new forms in response to globalisation. So, is the state being 'transformed' by global markets and international competition? We say, yes, indeed. In unexpected ways, certainly.

Notes

1. For a similar argument that the making and the future of the European Monetary System is an elite-level phenomenon, depending on the maintenance of a shared system of beliefs, see Kathleen McNamara (1998: 175).
2. Singapore's dependence on FDI over the period 1995–8 (measured in terms of FDI inflows as a percentage of GDP) was nearly double that of Sweden's, which had the highest FDI dependence of all the European small states.

References

Achara, Pongvutitham 1999 Business textile education to be upgraded, *The Nation* (5 October) (World Wide Web edition).

Adema, Willem 1999, *Net Social Expenditure*, Labour Market and Social Policy Occasional Paper No. 39, Paris: Organisation for Economic Cooperation and Development.

Alamgir, Jalal 1999, India's trade and investment policy: the influence of strategic rivalry with China, *Issues and Studies* 35, 3: 105–33.

Alderson, Arthur S. and Nielson, François (in press), Globalization and the great U-turn: income inequality trends in 16 OECD Countries, *American Journal of Sociology*.

Amenta, Edwin and Carruthers, Bruce G. 1988, The formative years of US social spending policies: theories of the welfare state and the American states during the great depression, *American Sociological Review* 53: 661–78.

Amsden, Alice and Chu, Wan-wen (in press), *Second Mover Advantage: Latecomer Upscaling in Taiwan*, Cambridge, MA: MIT Press.

Anantaraman, Venkataraman 1990, *Singapore's Industrial Relations System*, Singapore: McGraw-Hill.

Andersen, Arthur 1997, *Review of Business Taxation*, Canberra: AGPS.

Anek, Laothamatas 1988, Business and politics in Thailand: new patterns of influence, *Asian Survey* 28 (April): 451–70.

Anglade, Christina and Fortin, Carlos 1985, *The State and Capital Accumulation in Latin America*, London: Macmillan.

Aron, Janine 2000, Growth and institutions: a review of the evidence, *The World Bank Research Observer* 15: 99–135.

Asian Development Bank 1999, *Key Indicators of Developing Asian and Pacific Countries 1999*, Oxford University Press.

Aufderheide, Patricia 1999, *Communications Policy and the Public Interest: The Telecommunications Act of 1996*, New York: The Guildford Press.

Bahl, Roy W. 1998, China: evaluating the impact of intergovernmental fiscal reform, in R. M. Bird and F. Vaillancourt (eds.) *Fiscal Decentralisation in Developing Countries*, Cambridge University Press.

Bairoch, Paul 1996, Globalisation myths and realities: one century of external trade and foreign investment, in Robert Boyer and Daniel Drache (eds.) *States Against Markets: The Limits of Globalization*, New York: Routledge.

Bank for International Settlements (BIS), Basel Committee on Banking Supervision (BCBS) 1996, *Survey of Disclosures about Trading and Derivatives Activities of Banks and Securities Firms 1996*, Basle: BIS.

1998a, *The Global Derivatives Market at end June 1998*, Basle: BIS.

1998b, *Central Bank Survey of Foreign Exchange and Derivatives Market Activity 1998*, Basle: BIS.

Bank for International Settlements 2000a, *70th Annual Report*, Switzerland: BIS.

2000b, *The Global OTC Derivatives Market Continues to Grow*, Basle: BIS.

BIS-BCBS 1999, *Recommendations for Public Disclosure of the Trading and Derivatives Activities of Banks and Securities Firms*, Basle: BIS.

Bates, Robert and Da-Hsiang Donald Lien 1985, A note on taxation, development and representative government, *Politics and Society* 14: 53–70.

Baumgartner, Frank R. and Jones, Bryan D. 1991, Agenda dynamics and policy subsystems, *Journal of Politics* 53: 1044–74.

Bennett, Alfred 1895, *The Telephonic Systems of the Continent of Europe*, London: Longmans, Green and Co.

Benson, John D. 1991, Ending the turf wars: support for a CFTC/SEC consolidation, *Villanova Law Review* 42: 1–21.

Berger, Suzanne 1981, Lame ducks and national champions: industrial policy in the Fifth Republic, in S. Hoffmann and W. G. Andrews (eds.) *The Fifth Republic at Twenty*, Brockport, NY: SUNY Press.

Berger, Suzanne and Dore, Ronald. 1996, *National Diversity and Global Capitalism*, Ithaca, NY: Cornell University Press.

Bernstein, Lisa 1992, Opting out of the legal system: extralegal contractual relations in the diamond industry, *Journal of Legal Studies* 21: 115– 57.

Bhagwati, Jagdish 1998, The design of Indian development, in I. J. Ahluwalia and I. M. D. Little (eds.) *India's Economic Reforms and Development: Essays for Manmohan Singh*, Oxford University Press.

2000, *The Wind of the Hundred Days*, Cambridge, MA: MIT Press.

Biddle, Jesse and Milor, Verdat 1999, *Consultative mechanisms and economic governance in Malaysia*, Occasional Paper No. 38, Private Sector Development Department: World Bank.

Blecher, Marc 1991, Developmental state, entrepreneurial state: the political economy of socialist reform in Xinji municipality and Guanghan county, in G. White (ed.) *The Chinese State in the Era of Economic Reform*, London: Macmillan Press.

Boix, Carles 1998, *Political Parties, Growth and Equality: Conservative and Social Democratc Economic Strategies in the World Economy*, Cambridge University Press.

Boyer, Robert and Drache, Daniel 1996, *States Against Markets: The Limits of Globalization*, New York: Routledge.

Breslin, Shaun 1999, The politics of Chinese trade and the Asian financial crises: questioning the wisdom of export-led growth, *Third World Quarterly* 20: 1179–99.

Brimble, Peter 1995, Adoption and impact of new technologies in Thailand: a firm-level analysis, Prepared for the UN University Institute for New Technologies, Bangkok.

Burgoon, Brian 2001, Globalization and welfare compensation: disentangling the ties that bind, *International Organization* 55: 509–51.

Burki, Shahik Javed and Perry, Guillermo E. 1998, *Institutions Matter: Beyond the Washington Consensus*, Washington, DC: World Bank Latin American and Caribbean Studies.

Busaba, Sivasomboon and Cholada, Ingsrisawang 1998, Analysts: many other textile firms to fall, *Bangkok Post*, 18 July.

Busrin, Treerapongpichit 1999, Garment industry gets US help, *Bangkok Post*, 3 September.

Byrd, William A. and Gelb, Alan 1990, Why industrialise? The incentives for rural community governments, in W. A. Byrd and Q. Lin (eds.) *China's Rural Industry: Structure, Development, and Reform*, Oxford University Press.

Cable, Vincent 1995, Indian liberalization and the private sector, in R. Cassen and V. Joshi (eds.) *India: The Future of Economic Reform*, Oxford University Press.

Camdessus, Michel 1999, Second generation reforms: reflections and new challenges. Opening Remarks to IMF Conference on Second Generation Reforms, 8 November.

Cameron, David 1978, The expansion of the public economy: a comparative analysis, *American Political Science Review* 72: 1243–61.

Camilleri, Joseph A. and Falk, James 1992, *The End of Sovereignty?*, London: Aldershot.

Carlile, Lonny E. 1998, The politics of administrative reform, in M. Tilton and L. E. Carlile (eds.) *Is Japan Really Changing Its Ways? Regulatory Reform and the Japanese Economy*, Washington, DC: The Brookings Institution Press.

Caron, François 1981, *Histoire Économique de la France, XIXe–XXe Siècles*, Paris: Armand Colin.

Carruthers, Bruce 2000, Institutionalizing creative destruction: predictable and transparent bankruptcy law in the wake of the East Asian financial crisis, in Meredith Woo-Cumings (ed.) *Neoliberalism and Institutional Reform in East Asia*. Ithaca, NY: Cornell University Press.

Castles, Francis 1996, Needs-based strategies of social protection in Australia and New Zealand, in Gøsta Esping Andersen (ed.) *Welfare States in Transition: National Adaptations in Global Economies*, Thousand Oaks, CA: Sage.

Cerny, Philip 1990, *The Changing Architecture of Politics*, London: Sage.

   1994, The dynamics of financial globalization: technology, market structure and policy response, *Policy Sciences* 27: 319–42.

   1996, International finance and the erosion of state policy capacity, in P. Gummett (ed.) *Globalisation and Public Policy*, Brookfield, VT: Edward Elgar.

Chalmers, Ian 1992, *Weakening state controls and ideological change in Singapore: the emergence of local capital as a political force*, Working Paper No 13, Perth: Murdoch University: Asia Research Centre.

Chalongphob Sussangkarn 1997, Thailand: looking ahead to 2020 in light of global and regional changes, *TDRI Quarterly Review* 12: 3–14.

Chamberlain, Michael M. and Saunders, Robert H. 1994, EMTA's master agreement for emerging market debt, *International Financial Law Review* 13: 14–15.

Chan, Steve, Clark, Cal and Lam, Danny (eds.) 1998, *Beyond The Developmental State: East Asia's Political Economies Reconsidered*, New York: St. Martin's Press.

Chandler, Clay 2000, *Washington Post Foreign Service*, 13 July: H01.

Chang, Ha-Joon 1994, *The Political Economy of Industrial Policy*, New York: St. Martin's Press.

 2000, Breaking the mould: an institutionalist political economy alternative to the neo-liberal theory of the market and the state. Unpublished Paper, Faculty of Economics and Politics: University of Cambridge.

Chatterjee, Partha 1993, *The Nation and its Fragments: Colonial and Postcolonial Histories*, Princeton University Press.

Chen, Kang 1991, The failure of recentralisation in China: interplays among enterprises, local government, and the center, in A. L. Hillman (ed.) *Markets and Politicians: Politicized Economic Choice*, Boston: Kluwer Academic Publishers.

Cheung, Peter Tsan-yin 1994, The case of Guangdong in central–provincial relations, in Hao and Zhimin (eds.) *Changing Central–Local Relations in China: Reform and State Capacity*, Oxford: Westview Press.

Chin, Tom Yee Huei 1990, Old age and social security in Taiwan: a study in policy and planning, Ph.D. Thesis: University of Edinburgh.

Christensen, Scott Robert 1993, Coalitions and collective choice: the politics of institutional change in Thai agriculture, Ph.D. Thesis: University of Wisconsin-Madison.

Cieply, Sylive 2001, Bridging capital gaps to promote innovation in France, *Industry and Innovation* 8: 159–78.

Claessens, Stijn, Simeon Djankov, and Klapper, Leora 1999, *Resolution of Corporate Distress: evidence from East Asia's financial crisis*, Working Paper No. 2133, The World Bank.

Clague, Christopher 1997, The new institutional economics and economic development, in Clague (ed.) *Institutions and Economic Development*, Boston: Johns Hopkins University Press.

Clark, Ian 1999, *Globalisation and International Relations Theory*, Oxford University Press.

Clifford, Mark L. 1994, *Troubled Tiger*, New York: M. E. Sharpe.

Cohen, Benjamin J. 1996, Phoenix risen: the resurrection of global finance, *World Politics* 48: 269–96.

 2000, Money in a globalised world, in Ngaire Woods (ed.) *The Political Economy of Globalisation*, London: Macmillan.

Cohen, Jeffrey 1992, *The Politics of Telecommunications Regulation: The States and the Divestitures of AT&T*, New York: M. E. Sharpe.

Cohen, Stephen P. 2000, Why did India 'go nuclear'?, in R. G. C. Thomas and A. Gupta (eds.) *India's Nuclear Security*, Boulder: Lynne Rienner.

Colaco, Francis X. 1998, Thailand's international competitiveness: a framework for increased productivity, Paper presented at the conference on Thailand's Dynamic Economic Recovery and Competitiveness, Bangkok, 20–21 May.

Coleman, William D. 1996, *Financial Services, Globalisation and Domestic Policy Change: A Comparison of North America and the European Union*, Basingstoke: Macmillan.

2002, State power, transformative capacity and adapting to globalization: an analysis of French agricultural policy, 1960–2000, *Journal of European Public Policy* 9 (in press).

Collier, Ruth and Collier, David 1991, *Shaping The Political Arena*, Princeton University Press.

Cox, Robert 1997, Economic globalization and the limits to liberal democracy, in McGrew (ed.) *The Transformation of Democracy?*, Malden: Polity Press.

Cox, Robert W. (ed.) 1996, *Approaches to World Order*, Cambridge University Press.

Crandall, Robert W. and Waverman, Leonard 1995, *Talk Is Cheap: The Promise of Regulatory Reform in the North American Telecommunications*, Washington, DC: The Brookings Institution.

Crane, Alan 2000, Price falls are worrying long-distance operators, *Financial Times Telecommunications Survey*, 15 Nov.: II.

Crispin, Shawn 2000a, Out of the driver's seat, *Far Eastern Economic Review*, 17 August: 46.

2000b, E-commerce emasculated, *Far Eastern Economic Review*, 21 September: 26–9.

2001, Election trade-off, *Far Eastern Economic Review*, 28 December: 16–18.

Cumings, Bruce 1999, The genealogy of the developmental state, in Meredith Woo-Cumings (ed.) *The Developmental State*, Ithaca, NY: Cornell University Press.

Cutler, A. C., Haufler, V., and Porter, T. 1999, Private authority and global governance, in Cutler, Haufler, and Porter (eds.) *Private Authority in International Affairs*, State University of New York Press.

Dale, Richard 1996, *Risk and Regulation in Global Securities Markets*, London: John Wiley.

Das, C. V. 1981, Administrative law and the citizen, *CLJ* 1; http://www.cljlaw.com/articles/1981.html

Davis, Kevin and Trebilcock, Michael J. 1999, What role do legal institutions play in development? Paper Prepared for the International Monetary Fund's Conference on Second Generation Reforms, Washington, DC, 8–9 November.

Derthick, Martha and Quirk, Paul J. 1985, *The Politics of Deregulation*, Washington, DC: The Brookings Institution.

Deyo, Frederick C. 1981, *Dependent Development and Industrial Order: An Asian Case Study*, New York: Praeger.

1989, *Beneath the Miracle: Labor Subordination in the New Asian Industrialism*, Berkeley: University of California Press.

1992, The political economy of social policy formation: East Asia's newly industrialised countries, in R. P. Appelbaum and J. Henderson (eds.) *States and Development in the Asian Pacific Region*, Newbury Park CA: Sage.

Deyo, Fredrick and Doner, Richard F. 2001, Dynamic flexibility and sectoral governance in the Thai auto industry: the enclave problem, in Deyo, Doner and E. Hershberg (eds.) *The Challenge of Flexible Production in East Asia*, Boulder: Rowman and Littlefield.

DGBAS 2000, *Statistical Yearbook of the Republic of China 1999*, Taipei: Director General of Budget, Accounting and Statistics.

Dicken, Peter 1998, *Global Shift: Transforming the World Economy*, 3rd edn, London: Paul Chapman Publishing.

Dixit, J. N. 1998, *Across Borders: Fifty Years of India's Foreign Policy*, New Delhi: Picus.

Doner, Richard F. 1991, *Driving a Bargain: Automobile Industrialisation and Japanese Firms in Southeast Asia*, University of California Press.

2001, Institutions and the Tasks of Economic Upgrading, paper prepared for 2001 Annual Meeting of the American Political Science Association, San Francisco, 30 August–2 September.

Doner, Richard and Hawes, Gary 1995, The political economy of growth in East Asia, in M. Dorraj (ed.) *The Changing Context of Third World Political Economy*, London: Lynne Reiner.

Doner, Richard and Ramsay, Ansil 1993, Postimperialism and development in Thailand, *World Development* 21: 691–704.

1997, Competitive clientelism and economic governance: the case of Thailand, in Sylvia Maxfield and Benn Ross Schneider (eds.) *Business and the State in Developing Countries*, Ithaca: Cornell University Press.

2000, Rent-seeking and economic development in Thailand, in M. H. Khan and K. S. Jomo (eds.) *Rents, Rent-Seeking and Economic Development: Theory and Evidence in Asia*, Cambridge University Press.

Doner, Richard and Ross Schneider, Ben 2000, *The new institutional economics, business associations and development*, Discussion Paper 110/2000, Geneva: International Institute for Labor Studies.

Drèze, Jean and Sen, Amartya 1995, *India: Economic Development and Social Opportunity*, Oxford University Press.

Dungey, Mardi, 1999, Decomposing exchange rate volatility around the Pacific Rim, *Journal of Asian Economics* 10: 525–35.

Dunne, Tim 1999, The spectre of globalization, *Indiana Journal of Global Legal Studies* 7: 17–33.

Ebbinghaus, Bernhard (2001), When labour and capital collide: the varieties of welfare capitalism and early retirement in Europe, Japan, and the USA, in B. Ebbinghaus and P. Manow (eds.).

Ebbinghaus, Bernhard and Manow, Philip (2001), Introduction: studying varieties of welfare capitalism, in B. Ebbinghaus and P. Manow (eds.).

Ebbinghaus, Bernhard and Manow, Philip (eds.) (2001), *Varieties of Welfare Capitalism: Social Policy and Political Economy in Europe, Japan, and the USA*, London: Routledge.

Economides, Nicholas 1998, U.S. Telecommunications today, *Business-Economics* 33: 7–13.

ECRI (European Credit Research Institute) 2000, Consumer credit in the European Union, *ECRI Research Report No. 1*, ECRI: Belgium.

Esping-Andersen, Gøsta 1990, *Three Worlds of Welfare Capitalism*, London: Polity Press.

1996, Welfare states without work: the impasse of labour shedding and familialism in Continental European social policy, in Esping Andersen (ed.) *Welfare States in Transition*, Thousand Oaks, CA: Sage.

1997, Hybrid or unique?: The Japanese welfare state between Europe and America, *Journal of European Social Policy* 7: 179–89.

Evans, Peter 1995, *Embedded Autonomy: States and Industrial Transformation*, Princeton University Press.

1997, The eclipse of the state? Reflections on stateness in an era of globalisation, *World Politics* 50: 62–87.

Evans, Peter and Chang, Ha-Joon 2000, The role of institutions in economic change, Paper prepared for the meeting of the 'Other Canon' group, Oslo, 15–16 August.

Falk, Richard A. 1997, State of siege: will globalisation win out? *International Affairs* 73: 123–36.

Felker, Gregory 1997, *Upwardly global? The State, Business and MNCs in Malaysia and Thailand's Technological Transformation. The Politics of Technology Development – State, Business, and Multinationals in Malaysia and Thailand*, Ph.D. Thesis: Princeton University.

Felker, Greg and Jomo, K. S. 1999, New approaches to investment policy in the ASEAN-4, Paper presented at the Asian Development Bank Institute Second Anniversary Workshop on Development Paradigms, Tokyo, 4 December.

Financial Services Authority (FSA) 1999, *The Regulation of the Wholesale Cash and Derivative Markets: 'The Grey Paper'*, London: FSA.

Findlay, Christopher and Watson, Andrew 1997, Economic growth and trade dependency in China, in D. S. G. Goodman and G. Segal (eds.) *China Rising: Nationalism and Interdependence*, New York: Routledge.

Flora, Peter and Heidenheimer, Arnold J. (eds.) 1981, *The Development of Welfare States in Europe and America*, New Brunswick, NJ: Transaction Books.

Fransman, Martin 1996, Comment: the future of Japanese telecommunications policy, *Telecommunications Policy* 20: 83–8.

Frieden, Jefffrey and Rogowski, Ronald 1996, The impact of the international economy on national policies: an analytical overview, in R. Keohane and

H. Milner (eds.), *Internationalisation and Domestic Politics*, Cambridge University Press.

Friedman, Thomas 1999, *The Lexus and the Olive Tree: Understanding Globalisation*, New York: Farrar, Strauss and Giroux.

Fūke Hideaki, 1999, *Jōhō tsūshin sangyō no kōzō to kisei kanwa: nichibei hikaku kenkyū* [Structural Change and Deregulation in the Telecommunications Industry: A Comparative Study of Japan, the USA and the UK], Tokyo: NTT Shuppan.

Galbraith, James K. 2001, Globalisation fails to make the money go around, *Sydney Morning Herald*, 26 July.

Ganghof, Steffen 2001, Global markets, national tax systems, and domestic politics: re-balancing efficiency and equity in open states' income taxation, *MPIfG Discussion Paper 01/9*, Cologne: Max Planck Institute for the Study of Societies. www.mpi-fg-koeln.mpg.de/pu/discpapers_en.html

Ganguly, Sumit 1999, India's pathway to Pokhran II: the prospects and sources of New Delhi's nuclear weapons program, *International Security* 23: 148–77.

Garrett, Geoffrey 1998a, Global markets and national policies: collision course or virtuous circle?, *International Organisation* 52: 787–824.

1998b, *Partisan Politics in a Global Economy*, Cambridge University Press.

2000a, The causes of globalization, *Comparative Political Studies* 33: 941–91.

2000b, Globalisation and national autonomy, in N. Woods (ed.).

Garrett, Geoffrey and Lange, Peter 1991, Political responses to interdependence: what's 'Left' for the Left?, *International Organization* 45: 539–64.

1995, Internationalization, institutions, and political change, *International Organization* 49: 627–55.

1996, Internationalisation and domestic politics: an introduction, in Keohane and Milner (eds.).

Garrett, Geoffrey and Mitchell, Deborah 2001, Globalisation and the welfare state: income transfers in the advanced industrialised democracies, 1965–1990, *European Journal of Political Research* 39: 145–77.

Gereffi, Gary and Tam, Tony 1998, Industrial upgrading and organisational chains, International Conference on Business Transformation and Social Change in East Asia, Institute of East Asian Societies and Economics, Tunghai University, Taiwan, 22–23 May.

Gill, Stephen and Law, David 1988, *The Global Political Economy*, Boston: Johns Hopkins University Press.

1998a, Internal and external constraints egalitarian policies, in D. Baker, G. Epstein, and R. Pollin *Globalisation and Progressive Economic Policy*, Cambridge University Press.

1998b, Social democracy and full employment, *New Left Review* 211: 33–55.

Golden, Jeffrey B. 1994, Setting standards in the evolution of swap documentation, *International Financial Law Review* 13: 18–19.

Goodman, Roger and White, Gordon 1998, Welfare orientalism and the search for an East Asian welfare model, in Goodman, White and H.-J. Kwon (eds.)

References

The East Asian Welfare Model: Welfare Orientalism and the State, London: Routledge.

Gore, Charles 2000a, The rise and fall of the Washington consensus as a paradigm for developing countries, *World Development* 28: 789–804.

Gore, Lance L. P. 2000b, A meltdown with 'Chinese characteristics'?, in R. Robison, M. Beeson, K. Jayasuriya and H.-R. Kim (eds.) *Politics and Markets in the Wake of the Asian Crisis*, London and New York: Routledge.

Gough, Ian, Bradshaw, J., Ditch, J., Eardley, T., and Whiteford, P. 1997, Social assistance in OECD countries, *Journal of European Social Policy* 7: 17–43.

Gourevtich, Peter 1986, *Politics in Hard Times: Comparative Responses to International Economic Crises*, Ithaca, NY: Cornell University Press.

Government of India 1992, *Economic Survey 1991–92*, New Delhi: Government of India, Ministry of Finance.

1996, *Speech of Shri Manmohan Singh, Minister of Finance, Introducing the Budget for the Year 1996–97*, New Delhi: Government of India, Ministry of Finance.

1997, *Economic Survey 1995–96*, New Delhi: Government of India, Ministry of Finance.

Greenspan, Alan 1996, Presentation, in U. Cartellieri and A. Greenspan (eds.) *Global Risk Management*, Washington: Group of 30.

Grofman, Bernard, Lee, Sung-Chul, Winckler, Edwin A., and Woodall, Brian (eds.) 1999, *Elections in Japan, Korea, and Taiwan Under the Single Non-Transferable Vote: The Comparative Study of an Embedded Institution*, University of Michigan Press.

Group of 30 1993, *Derivatives: Practices and Principles*, Washington, DC: Group of 30.

1997, *Global Institutions, National Supervision and Systemic Risk*, Washington, DC: Group of 30.

Haggard, Stephan 1994, Business, politics and policy in Northeast and Southeast Asia, in A. MacIntyre (ed.) *Business and Government in Industrialising Asia*, Sydney: Allen and Unwin.

1997, Democratic institutions, economic policy, and development, in C. Clague (ed) *Institutions and Economic Development*, Boston: Johns Hopkins University Press.

Haley, John O. 1986, Administrative guidance versus formal regulation: resolving the paradox of industrial policy, in G. R. Saxonhouse and K. Yamamura (eds.) *Law and Trade Issues of the Japanese Economy: American and Japanese Perspectives*, University of Washington Press.

Hall, Peter A. 1986, *Governing the Economy: The Politics of State Intervention in Britain and France*, Cambridge: Polity Press.

1989, *The Political Power of Economic Ideas: Keynesianism across Nations*, Princeton University Press.

1997, The role of interests, institutions, and ideas in the comparative political economy of the industrialised nations, in M. I. Lichbach and A. S. Zucherman (eds.) *Comparative Politics*, Cambridge University Press.

Hall, Peter A. and Soskice, David 2001, An introduction to varieties of capitalism, in Hall and Soskice (eds.) *Varieties of Capitalism: The Institutional Foundations of Comparative Advantage*, Oxford University Press.

Hall, Peter A. and Taylor, Rosemary C. R. 1994, Political science and the four new institutionalisms, Paper presented at a conference on What Is Institutionalism Now?, College Park: University of Maryland, 14–15 October.

1996: Political science and the three new institutionalisms, *Political Studies* 44: 936–57.

Hallerberg, Mark and Basinger, Scott 1998, Internationalization and changes in tax policy in OECD countries: the importance of domestic veto players, *Comparative Political Studies* 31: 321–52.

Hancke, Bob and Amable, Bruno 2001, Innovation and industrial renewal in France in comparative perspective, *Industry and Innovation* 8: 113–34.

Handley, Paul 1997, More of the same: politics and business, 1987–96, in K. Hewison (ed.) *Political Change in Thailand: Democracy and Participation*, London: Routledge.

Hashimoto, Kiminobu 1963, The rule of law: some aspects of judicial review of administrative action, in A. T. von Mehren (ed.) *Law in Japan*, Cambridge, MA: Harvard University Press.

Hausman, Jerry A. and Sidak, Gregory J. 1999, A consumer-welfare approach to the mandatory unbundling of telecommunications networks, *The Yale Law Journal*, 109: 417–505.

Hayward, Jack 1986, *The State and the Market Economy: Industrial Patriotism and Economic Intervention in France*, New York University Press.

Held, David and McGrew, Anthony 1998, The end of the old order? Globalisation and the prospects for world order, *Review of International Studies*, Special Issue 217–43.

Held, David and McGrew, Anthony (eds.) 2000 *The Global Transformations Reader*, Cambridge: Polity Press.

Held, David, McGrew, Anthony, Goldblatt, David, and Perraton, Jonathan 1999, *Global Transformations: Politics, Economics and Culture*, Cambridge: Polity Press.

Helleiner, Eric 1994, *States and the Emergence of Global Finance: From Bretton Woods to the 1990s*, Ithaca, NY: Cornell University Press.

1995, Explaining the globalisation of financial markets: bringing states back in, *Review of International Political Economy* 2: 315–41.

Helliwell, John F. 1998, *How Much Do National Borders Matter?* Washington, DC: Brookings Institution.

Hicks, Alexander 1999, *Social Democracy and Welfare Capitalism*, Ithaca, NY: Cornell University Press.

Hicks, Alexander and Kenworthy, Lane 1998, Cooperation and political economic performance in affluent democratic capitalism, *American Journal of Sociology* 103: 1631–72.

Hirst, Paul and Thompson, Grahame 1996, *Globalisation in Question: The International Economy and the Possibilities of Governance*, Cambridge: Polity Press.

327

Hoberg, George 1993, Environmental policy: alternative styles, in M. M. Atkinson (ed.) *Governing Canada*, Toronto: HBJ Holt.

Hobson, John M. 1997, *The Wealth of States*, Cambridge University Press.

2000, *The State and International Relations*, Cambridge University Press.

Hobson, John M. and Ramesh, M. 2002, Globalisation makes of states what states make of it: between agency and structure in the state/globalisation debate, *New Political Economy* 7: 5–22.

Hoffmann, Steven A. 1990, *India and the China Crisis*, University of California Press.

Holcombe A. N. 1911, *Public Ownership of Telephones on the Continent of Europe*, Cambridge, MA: Harvard University Press.

Holliday, Ian 2000, Productivist welfare capitalism: social policy in East Asia, *Political Studies* 48: 706–23.

Holton, Robert J. 1998, *Globalisation and the Nation-State*, London: Macmillan.

Hong, Joon-Hyung 1999, The rule of law and its acceptance in Asia: a view from Korea, *Asia Perspectives* 2: 11–18.

Horsman, Mathew and Marshall, Andres 1994, *After the Nation State*, London: HarperCollins.

Howlett, Michael and Ramesh, M. 1998, Policy subsystem configurations and policy change: operationalizing the postpositivist analysis of the politics of the policy process, *Policy Studies Journal* 26: 466–81.

Huang, Yasheng 1996, *Inflation and Investment Controls in China: The Political Economy of Central–Local Relations During the Reform Era*, Cambridge University Press.

Huber, Evelyne and Stephens, John D. 1998, Internationalisation and the social democratic welfare model: crises and future prospects, *Comparative Political Studies* 33: 353–97.

2001, *Development and Crisis of Advanced Welfare States: Partisan Policies in Global Markets*, University of Chicago Press.

Hulsink, William 1999: *Privatisation and Liberalisation in European Telecommunications: Comparing Britain, the Netherlands, and France*, London: Routledge.

Huntington, Samuel P. 1968, *Political Order in Changing Societies*, New Haven, London: Yale University Press.

Hussain, Athar and Stern, Nicholas 1991, Effective demand, enterprise reforms and public finance in China, *Economic Policy* 12: 141–86.

Hutchcroft, Paul 1998, *Booty Capitalism: The Politics of Banking in the Philippines*, Ithaca, NY: Cornell University Press.

Hyug, Baeg Im 1992, State, labor and capital in the consolidation of democracy, in H. Y. Lee and D.-J. Chang (eds.) *Political Authority and Economic Exchange in Korea*, Seoul: Oruem.

Ikenberry, John G. 1993, Creating yesterday's new world order: Keynesian 'New Thinking' and the Anglo-American Postwar Settlement, in J. Goldstein and R. O. Keohane (eds.) *Ideas and Foreign Policy: Beliefs, Institutions and Political Change*, Ithaca, NY: Cornell University Press.

1995, Funk de siècle: impasses of Western industrial society at century's end, *Millennium* 24: 113–26.

Itada, Shogo 2001, Competition in Japan's telecommunications sector: challenges for the Japan Fair Trade Commission, Speech given in Washington, DC, 11 October 2001.

Iyori, Hiroshi and Uesugi, Akinori 1983, *The Antimonopoly Laws of Japan*, New York: Legal Publications Antitrust Bulletin.

Jackson, Karl D. 1999, Introduction: the roots of the crisis, in Jackson (ed.) *Asian Contagion: The Causes and Consequences of a Financial Crisis*, Boulder: Westview Press.

Jansen, Karel 1997, *External Finance in Thailand's Development: An Interpretation of Thailand's Growth Boom*, New York: St. Martin's Press.

Johnson, Chalmers 1982, *MITI and the Japanese Miracle: The Growth of Industrial Policy, 1925–1975*, Stanford University Press.

1984, The institutional foundations of Japanese industrial policy, *California Management Review* 27: 59–69.

1989, MITI, MPT, and the telecom wars: how Japan makes policy for high technology, in C. Johnson, L. Tyson, and J. Zysman (eds.) *Politics and Productivity: How Japan's Development Strategy Works*, Cambridge: Ballinger.

Joo, Jaehuyn 1999, Explaining social policy adoption in South Korea: the cases of the Medical Insurance Law and the Minimum Wage Law, *Journal of Social Policy* 28: 387–412.

Jowitt, Kenneth 1978, *The Leninist Response to National Dependency*, Institute of International Studies, University of California Press.

Kalyvas, Stathis 1994, Hegemony breakdown: the collapse of nationalisation in Britain and France, *Politics and Society* 22: 316–48.

Kaplinsky, Raphael 1999, Spreading the gains from globalisation: what can be learned from value chain analysis?, *IDS Working Paper 110*, Brighton: University of Sussex.

Kapstein, Ethan 1994, *Governing the Global Economy: International Finance and the State*, Cambridge, MA: Harvard University Press.

Katzenstein, Peter J. 1978, Domestic and international forces and strategies of foreign economic policy, in Katzenstein (ed.) *Between Power and Plenty*, University of Wisconsin Press.

1983, The small European states in the international economy: economic dependence and corporatist policies, in J. G. Ruggie (ed.) *The Antinomies of Interdependence*, New York: Columbia University Press.

1985, *Small States in World Markets*, Ithaca, NY: Cornell University Press.

1996a, *Cultural Norms and National Security*, Ithaca, NY: Cornell University Press.

Katzenstein, Peter J. (ed.) 1996b, *The Culture of National Security*, New York: Columbia University Press.

Keohane, Robert and Milner, Helen (eds.) 1996, *Internationalisation and Domestic Politics*, Cambridge University Press.

Keohane, Robert, and Nye, Joseph S. Jr 2000, Globalisation: What's new? What's not? (And so what?), *Foreign Policy* Spring: 106–17.

Khilnani, Sunil 1997, *The Idea of India*, London: Hamish Hamilton.

Khoo, Boo Teil 1995, *Paradoxes of Mahathirism*, Oxford University Press.

Kim, Joon-Hyung 1997, Economic policy-making in Korea: Policy change in turbulent times, Ph.D. Thesis, Washington: The George Washington University.

King, Desmond and Wood, Stewart 1999, The political economy of neoliberalism: Britain and the United States in the 1980s, in Kitschelt *et al.* (eds.).

Kingdon, John W. 1984, *Agendas, Alternatives and Public Policies*, Boston: Little, Brown and Company.

Kitschelt, Herbert, Lange, Peter, Marks, Gary, and Stephens, John (eds.) 1999, *Continuity and Change in Contemporary Capitalism*, Cambridge University Press.

Krasner, Stephen D. 1995, Power politics, institutions and transnational relations, in Risse-Kappen (ed.).

   1999, *Sovereignty: Organized Hypocrisy*, Princeton University Press.

Ku, Yeun-wen 1997, *Welfare Capitalism in Taiwan: The State, Economy and Social Policy*, London: Macmillan.

Kurzer, Paulette 1993, *Business and Banking: Political Change and Economic Integration in Western Europe*, Ithaca, NY: Cornell University Press.

Kwon, Huck Ju 1997, Beyond European welfare regimes: comparative perspectives on East Asian welfare systems, *Journal of Social Policy* 26: 467–84.

   1998, *The Welfare State in Korea: The Politics of Legitimation*, London: Macmillan.

La Porta, Rafael, Lopez-de-Silanes, Florencio, Shleifer, Andrei, and Vishny, Robert W. 1998, Law and finance, *Journal of Political Economy* 106: 1113–55.

   1999, The quality of government, *Journal of Law, Economics, and Organisation* 15: 222–79.

   2000, Investor protection and corporate governance, *Journal of Financial Economics*, 58: 3–27.

Lall, Sanjaya 1998, Thailand's manufacturing sector: the current crisis and export competitiveness, Paper presented at the conference on Thailand's Dynamic Economic Recovery and Competitiveness, Bangkok, 20–21 May.

Lan, Dingxiang and Cao, Bangying 2000, Guoyou qiye de zhanluexing gaizu [The strategic re-organisation of SOEs], *Jingji Tizhi Gaige* [Reform of Economic System] January.

Laothamatas, Anek 1998, *Business Associations and the New Political Economy of Thailand: From Bureaucratic Polity to Liberal Corporatism*, Boulder: Westview Press.

Lardy, Nicholas R. 1992, *Foreign Trade and Economic Reform in China, 1978–1990*, Cambridge University Press.

   1994, *China in the World Economy*, Washington, DC: Institute for International Economics.

1999, China and the Asian financial contagion, in K. D. Jackson (ed.) *Asian Contagion: The Causes and Consequences of a Financial Crisis*, Boulder: Westview Press.

Lauridsen, Laurids 2000, Industrial policies, political institutions and industrial development in Thailand, 1959–91, Working Paper No. 21, Denmark: Roskilde University.

Lee, Pak K. 2000, Into the trap of strengthening state capacity? China's tax-assignment reform, *China Quarterly* 164: 1007–24.

Lee, Sungkyun 1997, A comparative study of welfare programs for old age income security in Korea and Taiwan, Ph.D. Thesis, Madison: University of Wisconsin.

Lehrer, Mark 2000, Has Germany finally fixed its high-tech problem? The recent boom in German technology-based entrepreneurship, *California Management Review* 42: 89–107.

Levi, Margaret 1990, A logic of institutional change, in K. S. Cook and M. Levi (eds.) *The Limits of Rationality*, University of Chicago Press.

Levi-Faur, David 1998, The competition state as a neomercantilist state: restructuring global telecommunications, *Journal of Socio-Economics* 27: 655–85.

1999a, The governance of competition: the interplay of technology, economics, and politics in the making of the European Union's electricity and telecom regimes, *Journal of Public Policy* 19: 137–69.

1999b, The governance of international telecommunications competition: cross-international study of international policy regimes, *Competition and Change* 4: 1–28.

Levy, Jonah 1999, *Tocqueville's Revenge: State, Society, and Economy in Contemporary France*, Cambridge, MA: Harvard University Press.

Lewis, John P. 1991, Some consequences of giantism: the case of India, *World Politics* 43: 367–89.

Li, Jian 1996, The reform of China's foreign trade regime, in W. Cai, M. G. Smith, and X. Xianquan (eds.) *China and the World Trade Organisation: Requirements, Realities, and Resolution*, Ottawa: The Centre for Trade Policy and Law.

Lieberthal, Kenneth and Oksenberg, Michel 1988, *Policy Making in China: Leaders, Structures, and Processes*, Princeton University Press.

Lincoln, Edward 2001, *Arthritic Japan: The Slow Pace of Economic Reform*, Washington, DC: Brookings Institution Press.

Liu, Alan P. 1992, The 'Wenzhou model' of development and China's modernisation, *Asian Survey* 32: 696–771.

Liu, Hong 1994, Industrial relations in the four newly industrializing countries in East Asia (Korea, Taiwan, Singapore, Hong Kong, China), Ph.D. Thesis, Chicago: University of Illinois.

Loriaux, Michael 1991, *France After Hegemony: International Change and Financial Reform*, Ithaca, NY: Cornell University Press.

1999, Myth and moral ambition: France as a developmental state, in Woo-Cumings (ed.).

References

Mahoney, Paul G. 1999, The common law and economic growth: Hayek might be right, *Transition* 10: 28–9.

Malviya, Gopalji 1998, The Sino-Indian security environment: inadequate responses from New Delhi, in S. Mansingh (ed.) *Indian and Chinese Foreign Policies in Comparative Perspective*, New Delhi: Radiant.

Mann, Michael 1993, *The Sources of Social Power*, Cambridge University Press.

1994, The autonomous power of the state: its origins, mechanisms and results, *Archives Européenne de Sociologie* 25: 185–213.

1997, Has globalisation ended the rise and rise of the nation-state?, *Review of International Political Economy* 4: 472–96.

Manow, Philip 1998, Welfare state building and coordinated capitalism in Japan and Germany, paper presented at the Conference on Varieties of Capitalism, Max Planck Institute for the Study of Societies, 11–13 June.

Manow, Philip and Seils, Eric 1999, Globalisation and the welfare state: Germany, Typescript, Cologne: Max Planck Institute.

Manzetti, L. (ed.) 2000, *Regulatory Policy in Latin America: Post-Privatisation Realities*, Coral Gables: North-South Center Press.

March, James G. and Olsen, Johan P. 1984, The new institutionalism: organisational factors in political life, *American Political Science Review* 78: 738–49.

1989, *Rediscovering Institutions*, New York: The Free Press.

Martin, Philippe 1997, The exchange rate policy of the Euro: a matter of size? *Discussion Paper No. 1646*, London: Centre for Economic Policy Research (CEPR).

Mathews, John A. and Cho, Dong-Sung 1999, *Tiger Technology: The Creation of a Semiconductor Industry in East Asia*, Cambridge University Press.

Maxfield, Sylvia and Ross Schneider, Ben (eds.) 1997, *Business and the State in Developing Countries*, Ithaca, NY: Cornell University Press.

McArthur, John H. and Scott, Bruce R. 1969, *Industrial Planning in France*, Boston Division of Research, Graduate School of Business Administration: Harvard University.

McDonough, William J. 1993, A regulatory perspective on derivatives, in J. A. Leach, W. McDonough, D. Mullins, and B. Quinn (eds.) *Global Derivatives: Public Sector Responses*, Washington, DC: Group of 30.

McGrath, John 1994, Derivatives under global scrutiny, *International Financial Law Review* 13: 20–1.

McKendrick, David, Doner, Richard F., and Haggard, Stephan 2000: *From Silicon Valley to Singapore: Location and Competitive Advantage in the Hard Disk Drive Industry*, Stanford University Press.

McKenzie, Richard and Lee, Dwight 1991, *Quicksilver Capital: How the Rapid Movement of Wealth Has Changed the World*, New York: The Free Press.

McKeown, Timothy J. 1999, The global economy, post-Fordism, and trade policy in advanced capitalist states, in J. D. Stephens, H. Kitschelt, P. Lange, and G. Marks (eds.) *Change and Continuity in Contemporary Capitalism*. Cambridge University Press.

McKibbin, Warwick and Tang, K. K. 1998, The global economic impacts of trade and financial reform in China, *Working Papers in Trade and Development No. 8/98*, Department of Economics, Research School of Pacific and Asian Studies: Canberra: Australian National University.

McNamara, Kathleen 1998, *The Currency of Ideas: Monetary Politics in the European Union*, Ithaca, NY: Cornell University Press.

Mehta, Pratap Bhanu 1998, Exploding myths, *The New Republic* 218: 17–18.

Merryman, John H., Clark, David S., and Haley, John (eds.) 1994, *The Civil Law Tradition: Europe, Latin America, and East Asia*, Charlottesville: Michie Company.

Messere, Ken 1998, An overview, in Messere (ed.) *The Tax System in Industrialised Countries*, Oxford University Press.

Meyer, Alan D. 1982, Adapting to environmental jolts, *Administrative Science Quarterly* 27: 515–37.

Milne, R. S. and Mauzy, Diane 1999, *Malaysian Politics Under Mahathir*, London and New York: Routledge.

Milner, Helen 1993, The assumption of anarchy in international relations theory: a critique, in D. A. Baldwin (ed.) *Neorealism and Neoliberalism*, New York: Columbia University Press.

1997, *Interests, Institutions and Information: Domestic Politics and International Relations*, Princeton University Press.

Ministry of Finance and Economy 2001, *Beyond the Financial Crisis, a Resilient Korean Economy: Korea's Achievements and Future Tasks*, Ministry of Finance and Economy.

Ministry of International Trade and Industry 2000, *Tsūshō hakusho* [Trade and industry white paper], Tokyo: MITI.

Ministry of Posts and Telecommunications 2000, *Outline of the Telecommunications Business in Japan*, Tokyo: MPT.

Mo, Jongryon and Moon, Chung-In 1998, Democracy and the origins of the 1997 Korean economic crisis, in Jongryon and Moon (eds.) *Democracy and the Korean Economy*, Stanford: Hoover Institution Press.

Mody, Ashoka 1998, Industrial policy after the East Asian crisis: from 'outward-orientation' to new internal capabilities? Unpublished Manuscript, World Bank, 15 November.

Molano, Walter 1997, *The Logic of Privatisation: The Case of Telecommunications in the Southern Cone of Latin America*, London: Greenwood Press.

Montesquieu, Baron de 1748, *The Spirit of the Laws*.

Montinola, Gabriella, Qian, Yingyi, and Weingast, Barry R. 1996, Federalism, Chinese style: the political basis for economic success, *World Politics* 48: 50–81.

Moon, Chung-in and Prasad, Rashemi 1998, Networks, politics and institutions, in S. Chan, C. Clark, and D. Lam (eds.) *Beyond the Developmental State: East Asia's Political Economies Reconsidered*, New York: St. Martin's Press.

Moore, Paul M. 1994, The role of regulation: case study of the emerging regulation of derivative products, in *Securities Regulation: Issues and Perspectives, Queen's Annual Business Law Symposium*, Carswell: Scarborough.

References

Moore, Thomas G. 1996, China as a latecomer: toward a global logic of the open policy, *Journal of Contemporary China* 5: 187–208.

1999, China and globalisation, *Asian Perspective* 23: 65–95.

Morrissey, O. and Rai, G. 1995, The GATT Agreement on Trade Related Investment Measures: implications for the developing countries and their relationships with TNCs, *Journal of Development Studies* 31: 702–24.

Mosley, Layna 2000, Room to move: international financial markets and national welfare states, *International Organization* 54: 737–73.

Muscat, Robert 1994, *The Fifth Tiger: A Study of Thai Development Policy*, New York: M. E. Sharpe.

Nadvi, Kalid 1999, Collective efficiency and collective failure, *World Development* 27: 1605–26.

Nareerat, Wiriyapong 2000, Divisions on policy clouds the future, *Nation*, 28 September.

Nattapong Thongpakde, Pupahavesa, W., and Pussarangsi, B., 1994, Thailand, in S. D. Meyanathan (ed.), *Industrial Structure and the Development of Small and Medium Enterprise Linkages*, EDI Seminar Series, Washinghton, DC: World Bank.

Naughton, Barry 1992, Implications of the state monopoly over industry and its relaxation, *Modern China* 18: 15–41.

1996, *Growing Out of the Plan: Chinese Economic Reform, 1978–1993*, Cambridge University Press.

1999, China: domestic restructuring and a new role in Asia, in T. J. Pempel (ed.) *The Politics of the Asian Economic Crisis*, Ithaca, NY: Cornell University Press.

Nayar, Baldev Raj 1979, A world role: the dialectics of purpose and power, in J. W. Mellor (ed.) *India: A Rising Middle Power*, Boulder: Westview Press.

Nehru, Jawaharlal 1961, *India's Foreign Policy: Selected Speeches, September 1946–April 1961*, New Delhi: Government of India, Ministry of Information and Broadcasting.

Noam, Eli 1992, *Telecommunications in Europe*. Oxford University Press.

1997, *Telecommunications in Western Asia and the Middle East*, Oxford University Press.

1998, *Telecommunications in Latin America*, Oxford University Press.

1999, *Telecommunications in Africa*, Oxford University Press.

Noam, Eli, Komatsuzaki, Seisuke, and Conn, Douglas A. (eds.) 1994, *Telecommunications in the Pacific Basin*, Oxford University Press.

Noble, Gregory 1998, *Collective Action in East Asia: How Ruling Parties Shape Industrial Policy*, Ithaca, NY: Cornell University Press.

Nolan, Peter and Wang, Xiaoqiang 1999, Beyond privatisation: institutional innovation and growth in China's large state-owned enterprises, *World Development* 27: 169–200.

Nordlinger, A. Eric 1981, *On the Autonomy of the Democratic State*, Cambridge, MA: Harvard University Press.

1987, Taking the state seriously, in M. Weiner and S. P. Huntington (eds.) *Understanding Political Development*, Boston: Little & Brown.

North, Douglass C. 1981, *Structure and Change in Economic History*, New York: Norton.

1990, *Institutions, Institutional Change and Economic Performance*, Cambridge University Press.

Ockey, James 1994, Political parties, factions, and corruption in Thailand, *Modern Asian Studies* 28: 251–77.

OECD 1990, *Taxation and International Capital Flows*, Paris: OECD.

1995, *The OECD Jobs Study*, Paris: OECD.

1996, *International Capital Market Statistics*, Paris: OECD.

1998, *Harmful Tax Competition*, Paris: OECD.

2000a, *OECD in Figures*, Paris: OECD.

2000b, OECD Internet price comparison 2000: 40 hours basket, http://www.oecd.org/dsti/sti/it/cm/states/isp-40hrs.htm, 17 Oct. 2000.

Oh, Sekyung 2000, The Korean venture capital industry: present and future, Paper presented at the international symposium on financial reforms and venture business in Korea, The Korea Institute of Finance and Center for International Development, Harvard University.

Ohmae, Kenichi 1995, *The End of the Nation State*, London: HarperCollins.

Ohnesorge, John K. M. 1999, "Ratch"eting up the anti-corruption drive: could a look at recent history cure a case of theory-determinism?, *Connecticut Journal of Law* 14: 101–7.

Oi, Jean C. 1989, *State and Peasant in Contemporary China: The Political Economy of Village Government*, Berkeley: University of California Press.

1992, Fiscal reform and the economic foundations of local state corporatism in China, *World Politics* 45: 99–126.

1999, *Rural China Takes Off: Institutional Foundations of Economic Reform*, Berkeley: University of California Press.

Owens, J. 1990, Tax reform in OECD countries: objectives and achievements, in *Taxation and International Capital Flows – A symposium of OECD and non-OECD countries*, Paris: OECD.

Pack, Howard and Westphal, Larry E. 1986, Industrial strategy and technological change: theory versus reality, *Journal of Development Studies* 22: 87–128.

Padoa-Schioppa, Tomaso 1997, Market-friendly regulation of banks: an international perspective, in D. Duwendag (ed.) *Szenarien der Europäischen Währungsunion und der Bankenregulierung*, Berlin: Duncker and Humblot.

Paopongsakorn, Nipon and Fuller, Belinda 1997, Thailand's industrial development experience from the economic system perspective: open politics and industrial activism, in T. Yanagihara and S. Sambommatsu (eds.) *East Asian Development Experience: Economic System Approach and its Applicability*, Tokyo: Institute of Developing Economies.

Park, Byung Hyun 1990, The development of social welfare institutions in East Asia: case studies of Japan, Korea, and People's Republic of China, DSW thesis: University of Pennsylvania.

Park, Chan-Ung 1997, Institutional legacies and state power: the first state health insurance movements in Great Britain, the United States, and Korea, Ph.D. Thesis: University of Chicago.

Pasuk, Ponpaichit and Baker, Chris 1998, *Thailand's Boom and Bust*, Chiangmai: Silkworm Books.

Patat, Jean-Pierre and Lutfalla, Michel 1986, *Histoire Monétaire de la France au XXe Siècle*, Paris: Économica.

Paul, S. 1992, *India's Exports: New Imperatives and Newer Vistas*, New Delhi: Commonwealth Publishers.

Pauly, Louis 1995, Capital mobility, state autonomy, and political legitimacy, *Journal of International Affairs* 48: 369–88.

  1997, *Who Elected the Bankers? Surveillance and Control in the World Economy*, Ithaca, NY: Cornell University Press.

Pearson, Margaret M. 1991, The erosion of controls over foreign capital in China, 1979–1988: having their cake and eating it too?, *Modern China* 17: 112–50.

  1997, *China's New Business Elite: The Political Consequences of Economic Reform*, University of California Press.

Pei, Minxin 1998, Democratisation in the greater China region, *Access Asian Review* 1: 2.

Pempel, T. J. 1998, *Regime Shift*, Ithaca, NY: Cornell University Press.

  1999, Regional ups, regional downs: the politics of the East Asian economic crisis, in Pempel (ed.) *The Politics of the Asian Economic Crisis*, Ithaca, NY: Cornell University Press.

Perez, Sofia 1998, *Banking on Privilege: The Politics of Spanish Financial Reform*, Ithaca, NY: Cornell University Press.

Perkovich, George 1999, *India's Nuclear Bomb: The Impact on Global Proliferation*, University of California Press.

Peters, Hans J. 1998, Thailand's trade and infrastructure, Paper presented to Conference on Thailand's Dynamic Economic Recovery and Competitiveness, Bangkok, 20–21 May.

Petit, Pascal 1989, Expansionary policies in a restrictive world: the case of France, in P. Guerrieri and P. C. Padoan (eds.) *The Political Economy of European Integration*, New York: Harvester Wheatsheaf.

Petit, Pascal, and Soete, Luc 1998, *Globalization in search of a future*, Working Paper No. 9819, Paris: CEPREMAP.

Petrazzini, Ben 1995, *The Political Economy of Telecommunications Reform in Developing Countries: Privatisation and Liberalisation in Comparative Perspective*, London: Praeger.

Pierson, Paul 1994, *Dismantling the Welfare State: Reagan, Thatcher and the Politics of Retrenchment in Britain and the United States*, Cambridge University Press.

Pierson, Paul (ed.) 2001, *The New Politics of the Welfare State*, Oxford University Press.

Pillay, Subramaniam S. 2000, The Malay model: governance, economic management and the future of the development state, in F.-J. Richter (ed.) *The*

East Asian Development Model: Economic Growth, Institutional Failure and the Aftermath of the Crisis, New York: St. Martin's Press.

Pistor, Katharina and Wellons, Philip A. 1999, *The Role of Law and Legal Institutions in Asian Economic Development: 1960–1995*, Oxford University Press and the Asian Development Bank.

Platteau, Jean-Philippe 1994, Behind the market stage where real societies exist – part II: the role of moral norms, *Journal of Development Studies* 30: 753–817.

Poapongsakorn, Nipon and Tonguthai, Pawadee 1998, Technological capability building and the sustainability of export success in Thailand's textile and electronics industries, in D. Ernst, T. Ganistsos, and L. Mytelka (eds.) *Technological Capabilities and Export Success in Asia*, London and New York: Routledge.

Pontusson, Jonas 1992, *The Limits of Social Democracy: Investment Politics in Sweden*, Ithaca, NY: Cornell University Press.

Ponvutitham, Achara 1999, Textile exporters urged to focus on the supply chain, *The Nation*, 28 May.

Powell, Walter and DiMaggio, Paul 1991, *The New Institutionalism in Organisational Analysis*, University of Chicago Press.

Prakash, Asseem and Hart, Jeffery A. (eds.), 2000, *Copying with Globalization*, London and New York: Routledge.

Prasad, Bimla 1962, *The Origins of Indian Foreign Policy: Indian National Congress and World Affairs 1885–1947*, Calcutta: Bookland.

President's Working Group on Financial Markets 1999, *Over-the-Counter Derivatives and the Commodity Exchange Act*, Washington: PWGFM.

Prieger, James 1998, Universal service and the Telecommunications Act of 1996, *Telecommunications Policy* 22: 57–72.

Przeworski, Adam and Teune, Henry 1970, *The Logic of Comparative Social Inquiry*, Florida: Robert E. Krieger.

Quinn, Dennis 1997, The correlates of change in international financial regulation, *American Political Science Review* 91: 531–49.

Quinn, Dennis and Inclan, Carla 1997, The origins of financial openness: a study of current and capital account liberalization, *American Journal of Political Science* 41: 771–814.

Rajan, Raghuram G. and Zingales, Luigi 2000, The great reversals: the politics of financial development in the 20th century, NBER Working Paper No. w8178.

Ramesh, M. 1995, Social security in South Korea and Singapore: explaining the differences, *Social Policy and Administration* 30: 228–40.

2000, The politics of social security in Singapore, *The Pacific Review* 13: 243–56.

Ramesh, M. with Asher, Mukul 2000, *Welfare Capitalism in Southeast Asia: Social Security, Health, and Education Policies in Indonesia, Malaysia, the Philippines, Singapore, and Thailand*, Basingstoke: Macmillan.

Ramsay, Ansil 1987, The political economy of sugar in Thailand, *Pacific Affairs* 60: 248–70.

References

Ray, Hemen 1986, *Sino-Soviet Conflict Over India*, New Delhi: Abhinav Publications.

Reich, Robert 1991, *The Work of Nations*, New York: A. A. Knopf.

Rhodes, Martin 2001, The political economy of social pacts: competitive corporatism and European welfare reform, in Pierson (ed.) *The New Politics of the Welfare State*, Oxford University Press.

Risse-Kappen, Thomas (ed.) 1995, *Bringing Transnational Relations Back In*, Cambridge University Press.

Ritchie, Bryan 2001, Political economy of technical intellectual capital formation, Ph.D. diss., Emory University, Department of Political Science.

Roberts, Dan 2000, Big spenders face debt hangover as mood changes, *Financial Times Telecommunications Survey*, 15 November: I, II.

Rock, Michael 2000, Thailand's old bureaucratic polity and its new semi-democracy, in M. H. Khan and K. S. Jomo (eds.) *Rents, Rent-Seeking and Economic Development: Theory and Evidence in Asia*, Cambridge University Press.

Rodan, Garry (ed.) 1996, *Political Oppositions in Industrialising Asia*, London: Routledge.

Rodan, Garry 1997, Singapore in 1996: extended election fever, *Asian Survey* 37: 175–80.

Rodrik, Dani 1997a, *Has Globalisation Gone Too Far?*, Washington, DC: Institute for International Economics.

1997b, TFPG controversies, institutions, and economic performance in East Asia, NBER Working Paper 5914, February.

1998, Why do more open economies have bigger governments?, *Journal of Political Economy* 106: 997–1032.

2000a, How far will international economic integration go?, *Journal of Economic Perspectives* 14: 177–86.

2000b, Development strategies for the next century, Paper presented at the conference on Developing Economies in the 21st Century, Institute for Developing Economies, 26–27 January.

Romano, Roberta 1996, A thumbnail sketch of derivative securities and their regulation, *Maryland Law Review* 55: 1–83.

Rosanvallon, Pierre 1992, *L'État en France de 1789 à nos jours*, Paris: Seuil.

Rosen, Daniel H. 1999, *Behind the Open Door: Foreign Enterprises in the Chinese Marketplace*, Washington, DC: Institute for International Economics.

Rosenau, James N. 2000, Governance in a globalizing world, in Held and McGrew (eds.) *The Global Transformations Reader*, Cambridge: Polity Press.

Ruding Committee 1992, *Report of the Committee of Independent Experts on Company Taxation*, Brussels: Commission of the European Community.

Rueda, David and Pontusson, Jonas 2000, Wage inequality and varieties of capitalism, *World Politics* 52: 350–83.

Ruggie, John Gerard 1982: International regimes, transactions, and change: embedded liberalism in the postwar economic order, *International Organisation* 36: 379–415.

1994, Trade, protectionism, and the future of welfare capitalism, *Journal of International Affairs* 48: 1–11.

Sandholtz, Wayne 1998, The emergence of a supranational telecommunications regime, in W. Sandholtz and A. Stone Sweet (eds.) *European Integration and Supranational Governance*, Oxford University Press.

Schaberg, Mark 1999, Globalization and financial systems: policies for the new environment, in D. Baker, G. Epstein, and R. Pollin (eds.) *Globalization and Progressive Economic Policy*, Cambridge University Press.

Scharpf, Fritz W. 2000a, Institutions in comparative policy research, *Comparative Political Studies* 33: 762–90.

2000b, The viability of advanced welfare states in the international economy, vulnerabilities and options, *Journal of European Public Policy* 7: 190–228.

Schmidt, Susanne K. 1997, Sterile debates and dubious generalisations: European integration theory tested by telecommunications and electricity, *Journal of Public Policy* 16: 233–71.

Schmidt, Vivienne A. 1995, The new world order, incorporated: the rise of business and the decline of the nation-state, *Daedalus* 124: 75–106.

1996, *From State to the Market: The Transformation of French Business under Mitterrand*, Cambridge University Press.

(in press), *The Futures of Capitalism: European Pathways to Adjustment*, Oxford University Press.

Schmitter, Phillipe C. 1982, Reflections on where the theory of neo-corporatism has gone and where the praxis of neo-corporatism may be going, in G. Lehmbruch and P. Schmitter (eds.) *Patterns of Corporatist Policy Making*, London: Sage.

Schneider, Volker and Vedel, Thierry 1999, Franco-German relations in telecommunications, in D. Webber (ed.) *The Franco-German Relationship in the European Union*, London: Routledge.

Schneider, Volker, Dang-Nguyen, Godefroy, and Werle, Raymund 1994, Corporate actor networks in European policy-making: harmonizing telecommunications policy, *Journal of Common Market Studies* 32: 473–98.

Scholte, Jan Aart 1997, Global capitalism and the state, *International Affairs* 73: 427–52.

2000, *Globalisation: A Critical Introduction*, London & New York: Macmillan.

Schwartz, Frank J. 1998, *Advice and Consent: The Politics of Consultation in Japan*, Cambridge University Press.

Schwartz, Herman 2000a, *States and Markets: The Emergence of a Global Economy*, London and New York: Macmillan.

2000b, Internationalisation and two liberal welfare states: Australia and New Zealand, in F. W. Scharpf and V. A. Schmidt (eds.) *From Vulnerability to Competitiveness: Welfare and Work in the Open Economy* (volume 2), Oxford University Press.

Seifu Kisei Nado To Kyōsō Seisaku Ni Kansuru Kenkyūkai [Study Group on Government Regulations and Competition Policy] 2000, *Denki tsūshin jigyō bunya ni okeru kyōsō seisaku jō no kadai (kōeki jigyō bunya ni okeru kisei kanwa to kyōsō seisaku, chūkan hōkoku*) [Issues regarding competition policy in the field of telecommunications: interim report on regulatory reform and competition policy in the public utilities sector], Report 11.2-00–003, 082-47-B, June.

Sevilla, Ramon C. and Soonthornthada, Kusol 2000, *SME Policy in Thailand: Vision and Challenges*, Institute for Population and Social Research, Thailand: Mahidon University.

Sharman, Jason C. 2001, International tax competition, regulative norms and confounding Pareto, Unpublished Paper, Government & International Relations, University of Sydney.

Shihata, Ibrahim F. I. 1991, The World Bank and 'governance' issues in its borrowing members, in F. Tschofen and A. R. Parra (eds.) *The World Bank in a Changing World*, Dordrecht: Martinus Nijhoff.

Shin, Dong-Myeon 2000, Financial crisis and social security: the paradox of South Korea, *International Security Review* 53: 83–107.

Shin, Eui Hang 1999, Social change, political elections, and the middle class in Korea, *East Asia* 17: 2828–60.

Shirk, Susan 1993, *The Political Logic of Economic Reform in China*, University of California Press.

1994, *How China Opened its Door: The Political Success of the PRC's Foreign Trade and Investment Reforms*, Washington, DC: The Brookings Institution.

1996, Internationalisation and China's economic reform, in Keohane and Milner (eds.).

Shue, Vivienne 1988, *The Reach of the State: Sketches of the Chinese Body Politic*, Stanford University Press.

Shue, Vivienne and Blecher, Marc 1999, Into leather: state-led development and the private sector in Xinji, Unpublished Paper, Cornell University.

Siamwalla, Ammar. 2000. Anatomy of the Thai economic crisis, in P. C. Warr (ed.) *Thailand Beyond the Crisis*, London: Routledge.

Sieff, Martin 1998, Passage to India, *National Review* 50: 36–8.

Sikkink, Kathryn 1991, *Ideas and Institutions: Developmentalism in Brazil and Argentina*, Ithaca, NY: Cornell University Press.

Simmons, Beth A. 1999, The internationalization of capital, in J. D. Stephens, H. Kitschelt, P. Lange, and G. Marks (eds.) *Change and Continuity in Contemporary Capitalism*, Cambridge University Press.

Singapore Department of Statistics 2001, *Yearbook of Statistics, Singapore, 2000*, Singapore: Singapore Department of Statistics.

Singher, Thomas 1995, Regulating derivatives: does transnational regulatory cooperation offer a viable alternative to congressional action? *Fordham International Law Journal* 18: 1397–472.

Skocpol, Theda 1985, Bringing the state back in: strategies of analysis in current research, in P. Evans, D. Rueschemeyer and T. Skocpol (eds.) *Bringing the State Back In*, Cambridge University Press.

Smith, Adam 1976, *An Inquiry into the Nature and Causes of the Wealth of Nations*, Oxford: Clarendon Press.

Smyth, Russell 1998, Recent developments in rural enterprise reform in China: achievements, problems, and prospects, *Asian Survey* 38: 784–800.

2000, Should China be promoting large-scale enterprises and enterprise groups?, *World Development* 28: 721–7.

So, Alvin Y. and Hua, Shiping 1992, Democracy as an antisystemic movement in Taiwan, Hong Kong, and China: a world systems analysis, *Sociological Perspectives* 35: 385–404.

Sombat Champathong 1998, The textile industry, *Bangkok Bank Monthly Review*, http://www.bbl.co.th/research/junindust1.htm

Somporn Thapanachai 1997, Companies invest heavily to modernize technology to bring competitiveness, *Bangkok Post*, 5 May.

2001, Thailand strives to be a fashion center, *Bangkok Post*, 15 January.

Sondhi, Sunil 1994, *Science, Technology and India's Foreign Policy*, Delhi: Anamika Prakashan.

Song, Sang-Hyun 1996a, Role of judges in Korea, in Song (ed.) *Korean Law in the Global Economy*, Seoul: Bak Yong Sa.

1996b, Administrative action, guidance and discretion, in Song (ed.) *Korean Law in the Global Economy*, Seoul: Bak Yong Sa.

Sorensen, Georg 1999, Sovereignty: change and continuity in a fundamental institution, *Political Studies* 47: 590–604.

Soskice, David 1990, Wage determination: the changing role of institutions in advanced industrial societies, *Oxford Review of Economic Policy* 6: 36–61.

1999, Divergent production regimes: coordinated and uncoordinated market economies in the 1980s and 1990s, in Kitschelt *et al.* (eds.).

SSB (State Statistic Bureau, China) 1991, 1998, 2000, *Zhongguo tongji nianjian* [Almanac of China's Economy], Beijing: Chinese Statistical Publishing House.

Starling, Jay D. 1975, The use of systems constructs in simplifying organized social complexity, in T. La Porte (ed.) *Organized Social Complexity: Challenge to Politics and Policy*, Princeton University Press.

Steinherr, Alfred 1998, *Derivatives: The Wild Beast of Finance*, Chichester: John Wiley & Sons.

Steinmo, Sven 1993, *Democracy and Taxation*, New Haven, CT: Yale University Press.

Steinmo, Sven, Thelen, Kathleen, and Longstreth, Frank 1992, *Structuring Politics*, Cambridge University Press.

Steinmo, Sven and Tolbert, Caroline 1998, Do institutions really matter? Taxation in industrialized democracies, *Comparative Political Studies* 31: 165–87.

Stephens, John D. 1979, *The Transition from Capitalism to Socialism*, Atlantic Highlands, NJ: Humanities Press.

1996, The Scandinavian welfare states: achievements, crises, and prospects. in Esping Andersen (ed.) *Welfare States in Transition*, Thousand Oaks, CA: Sage.

Strange, Susan 1996, *The Retreat of the State: The Diffusion of Power in the World Economy*, Cambridge University Press.

References

Suleiman, Ezra 1974, *Politics, Power, and Bureaucracy in France: The Administrative Elite*, Princeton University Press.

1978, *Elites in French Society*, Princeton University Press.

Suri, Kamla 1992, *India's Economy and the World*, New Delhi: Vikas.

Swank, Duane 1998, Funding the welfare state: global capital and the taxation of business in advanced market economies, *Political Studies* 46: 671–91.

2000, Globalisation, democratic institutions, and policy change in European welfare states: the corporatist conservative cases, Paper presented at Annual Meeting of the American Political Science Association, Washington, DC, 31 August – 3 September.

2001, Political institutions and welfare state restructuring: the impact of institutions on social policy change in developed democracies, in Pierson (ed.).

2002, *Global Capital, Political Institutions, and Policy Change in Developed Welfare States*, Cambridge University Press.

Swank, Duane and Martin, Cathie Jo 2001, Employers and the welfare state: the political economic organisation of firms and social policy in contemporary capitalist democracies, *Comparative Political Studies* 34: 889–923.

Takayanagi, Kenzo 1963, A century of innovation: the development of Japanese law, 1868–1961, in von Mehren (ed.) *Law in Japan*, Cambridge, MA: Harvard University Press.

Tang, Wen-Hui Anna 1997, Explaining Social Policy In Taiwan Since 1949: State, Politics, And Gender, Ph.D. Thesis: Cambridge, MA: Harvard University.

Tanham, George 1992, *Indian Strategic Thought*, Chicago, IL: Rand.

Tanzi, Vito and Schuknecht, Ludger 2000, *Public Spending in the Twentieth Century*, Cambridge University Press.

Telecommunications Act of 1996, *Pub. L. No 104, preamble, 110 State, 56*, cited in Hausman and Sidak, 1999.

Tharoor, Shashi 1982, *Reasons of State: Political Development and India's Foreign Policy Under Indira Gandhi 1966–1977*, Delhi: Vikas.

Thatcher, Mark 1999, *The Politics of Telecommunications*, Oxford University Press.

Thelen, Kathleen 1999, Historical institutionalism in comparative politics, *Annual Review of Political Science* 2: 369–404.

Thelen, Kathleen and Kume, Ikuo 1999, The effects of globalisation on labor revisited: lessons from Germany and Japan, *Politics and Society* 27: 477–505.

Thurbon, Eizabeth 2002, Ideational inconsistency and institutional inertia: why financial liberalization in Korea went horribly wrong, Unpublished Manuscript, Department of Government and International Relations, University of Sydney.

Tilly, Charles 1975, *The Formation of National States in Western Europe*, Princeton University Press.

Tilly, R. 1992, An overview on the role of the large German banks up to 1914, in Y. Cassis (ed.) *Finance and Financiers in European History, 1880–1960*, Cambridge University Press.

342

Tilton, Mark 1996, *Restrained Trade: Cartels in Japan's Basic Materials Industries,* Ithaca, NY: Cornell University Press.

1998, Regulatory reform and market opening in Japan, in Tilton and L. E. Carlile (eds.) *Is Japan Really Changing its Ways? Regulatory Reform and the Japanese Economy,* Washington, DC: The Brookings Institution.

Tsuruta, Toshimasa 1997, *Kisei kanwa: shijō no kasseika to dokkinhō* [Regulatory reform: the Antimonopoly Law and the vitalization of the market], Tokyo: Chikuma Shinsho.

Unger, Danny 1998, *Building Social Capital in Thailand: Fibers, Finance and Infrastructure,* Cambridge University Press.

Unger, Jonathan and Chan, Anita 1995, China, corporatism, and the East Asian model, *Australian Journal of Chinese Affairs* 33: 29–53.

United Nations 1996, *World Investment Directory,* New York and Geneva: United Nations.

UNCTAD 2000, *World Investment Report,* New York and Geneva: United Nations.

United Nations Development Programme (UNDP) 2000, *Human Development Report 2000,* Oxford University Press.

United States Trade Representative 2000, United States comment on MPT Study Group LRIC Model for Interconnectio, http://www.ustr.government/new/dftcmnt.html, 3 March.

Upham, Frank K. 2001, Ideology, experience, and the rule of law in developing societies, in M. Woo-Cumings (ed.), *Neoliberalism and Institutional Reform in East Asia,* Ithaca, NY: Cornell University Press.

USGAO (United States General Accounting Office) 1994, *Financial Derivatives: Actions Needed to Protect the Financial System,* Washington: USGAO.

1999, *Long Term Capital Management: Regulators Need to Focus Greater Attention on Systemic Risk,* Washington: USGAO.

2000, *CFTC and SEC: Issues Related to the Shad-Johnson Jurisdictional Accord,* Washington: USGAO.

Vanaik, Achin 1990, *The Painful Transition: Bourgeois Democracy in India,* London: Verso.

Visser, Jelle and Hemerijck, Anton 1997, *A Dutch Miracle? Job Growth, Welfare Reform, and Corporatism in the Netherlands,* Amsterdam: University of Amsterdam Press.

Vogel, Stephen K. 1996, *Freer Markets, More Rules: Regulatory Reform in Advanced Industrial Countries,* Ithaca, NY: Cornell University Press.

2000, Creating competition in Japan's telecommunications market, friendship commission public policy series, *Japan Information Access Project Working Paper,* http://www.nmjc.org/jiap, 3 May (Revised 19 May 2000).

2001, The crisis of German and Japanese capitalism: stalled on the road to the liberal market model, *Comparative Political Studies* 34: 1103–34.

Wachtel, Howard M. 2000, Tobin and other global taxes, *Review of International Political Economy* 7: 335–52.

Wade, Robert 1990, *Governing the Market: Economic Theory and the Role of Government in East Asian Industrialisation,* Princeton University Press.

1996, Globalisation and its limits: reports of the death of the national economy are greatly exaggerated, in Berger and Dore (eds.).

Waldner, David 1998, *State Building and Late Development*, Ithaca, NY: Cornell University Press.

Wallerstein, Michael 1999, Wage-setting institutions and pay inequality in advanced industrial societies, *American Journal of Political Science* 43: 649–80.

Wallerstein, Michael, Golden, Miriam, and Lange, Peter 1997, Unions, employers' associations, and wage-setting institutions in Northern and Central Europe, 1950–1992, *Industrial and Labor Relations Review* 50: 379–401.

Waltz, Kenneth N. 1979, *Theory of International Politics*, New York: McGraw Hill.

Wang, Shaoguang 1997, China's 1994 fiscal reform, *Asian Survey* 37: 801–17.

Wang, Shaoguang and Hu, Angang 1994, *Zhongguo guojia nengli baogao* [A Report on Chinese State Capacity], Oxford University Press.

Watson, Laura 1998, Labor relations and the law in South Korea, *Pacific Rim Law and Policy Journal* 7: 229–47.

Webb, Michael 1998, Global markets and state power: explaining the limited impact of international tax competition, Paper presented at conference on Globalizaton and its Discontents, Vancouver: Simon Fraser University, 23–24 July.

Weir, Margaret 1992, Ideas and the politics of bounded innovation, in Steinmo, Thelen and Longstreth (eds.).

Weiss, Linda 1998, *The Myth of the Powerless State*, Ithaca, NY: Cornell University Press.

1999a, Globalisation and national governance: antinomy or interdependence?, *Review of International Studies* 25: 59–88.

1999b, Managed openness: beyond neoliberal globalism, *New Left Review* 238: 126–40.

1999c, State power and the Asian crisis, *New Political Economy* 4: 317–42.

2001, Does size matter less when domestic institutions count?, Paper presented to the Conference on Small States in World Markets – Fifteen Years Later, Gothenburg, Sweden, 27–29 September.

Wellenius, Bjorn 2000, Regulating the telecommunications sector: the experience of Latin America, in L. Manzetti (ed.).

West, James M. 1998, Kukje and beyond: constitutionalism and the market, *Seggye honbop yongu [World Constitutional Law Review]* 3: 321–51.

Western, Bruce 1997, *Between Class and Market*, Princeton University Press.

Westphal, Larry E., Kritayakirana, Kopr, Petchsuwan, Kosal, Sutabutr, Harit, and Yuthavong, Yongyuth 1990, The development of technological capability in manufacturing: a macroscopic approach to policy research, in R. Evenson and G. Ranis (eds.) *Science and Technology: Lessons for Development Policy*, Boulder: Westview Press.

Wichit Sirithaveeporn 1998, Tariff changes win approval, *Bangkok Post*, 7 May.

Williamson, John B. 2000, Social security privatisation: lessons from the United Kingdom, Working Paper 2000–10, Center for Retirement Research, Chestnut Hill, MA: Boston College.

Wilsford, David 1994, Path dependency, or why history makes it difficult but not impossible to reform health care systems in a big way, *Journal of Public Policy* 14: 251–84.

Wolfensohn, James 1999, Keynote Address at the IMF Conference on Second Generation Reforms, Washington, DC, 8 November.

Woo, Jung-en (Meredith Woo-Cumings) 1991, *Race to the Swift: State and Finance in Korean Industrialisation*, New York: Columbia University Press.

Woo-Cumings, Meredith (ed.) 1999, *The Developmental State*, Ithaca, NY: Cornell University Press.

Woods, Ngaire (ed.) 2000, *The Political Economy of Globalisation*, London: Macmillan.

World Bank 1993, *The East Asian Miracle: Economic Growth and Public Policy*, Oxford University Press (for the World Bank).

2000a, *Thailand Economic Monitor*, June.

2000b, *Thailand Economic Monitor*, December.

2002, *World Development Report*, New York: Oxford University Press.

WTO 2001, *Annual Report 2001*, Geneva: WTO.

Xu, Fengxian *et al.* 1993, Sunan moshi de xin fazhan [New developments of Sunan Model], *Jingji Yanjiu* [Economic Research Journal] 2.

Young, Cheol Jeong 2001: Korea: venture businesses, venture capital and KOSDAQ, *International Financial Law Review*: 85–7. Supplement.

Young, Michael 1984, Judicial review of administrative guidance: governmentally encouraged consensual dispute resolution in Japan, *Columbia Law Review* 84: 923–83.

Yuwadee, Tunyasiri 2000. Economic ministries to be revamped, *Bangkok Post*, 28 May (World Wide Web edition).

Ziegler, Dominic 2000, China survey, *The Economist*, 8 April.

Ziegler, Nicholas 1997, *Governing Ideas: Strategies for Innovation in France and Germany*, Ithaca, NY: Cornell University Press.

Zweig, David 1995, 'Developmental communities' on China's coast: the impact of trade, investment, and transnational alliances, *Comparative Politics* 27: 253–74.

Zysman, John 1983, *Governments, Markets and Growth*, Ithaca, NY: Cornell University Press.

1996, The myth of a 'global economy': enduring national foundations and emerging regional realities, *New Political Economy* 1: 157–84.

Index

capitalism
  developmental capitalism in Taiwan
    and Korea 247–8
  erosion of national 3
  global, and domestic economies 293
  varieties of, and social welfare reform
    73–8
CFTC (Commodity Futures Trading
  Commission) 284, 285, 286, 291
Chicago Board Options Exchange 275
Chicago Board of Trade (CBT) 275, 285
Chidambaram, P. 239
Chile, telecommunications liberalisation
  169, 170
China 142–59
  and the Asian financial crisis 154, 238
  banking system 151–2, 155
  cadre control system 154
  central–local relations in 150–4, 158
  civil service 157
  closed economy in 143, 147
  compared with developmental states in
    Northeast Asia 142, 158
  development of state capacity 157–9
  economic growth 142
  economic openness 142–3
    and the decline of the old form of
      state power 144–9
    and the rise of new state capacities
      149–57, 312–13, 316
  FDI 142, 146, 154
  financial reforms 155
  fiscal reforms 153
  and India's economic policies 236,
    237–8, 240–1
  India's hegemonic rivalry with 230–3,
    243, 244
  inflation 148, 151–2
  and the Multi-Fibre Agreement (MFA)
    134
  nuclear tests 232–3
  rural collective enterprises 147
  Special Economic Zones (SEZs) 145–6,
    151
  state-owned enterprises (SOEs) 144,
    147, 149, 155–7
  and Taiwan 142, 158, 260–1
  township and village enterprises (TVEs)
    147, 149–50
  trade 145, 146, 154, 237
  and WTO membership 18, 142, 143, 150,
    155
  see also Taiwan
Chun Doo Hwan 211, 212–13
CIT *see* corporate income taxes (CIT)

civil law *see* common law and civil law
civil service
  China 157
  France (*Grands Corps de l'État*) 107, 112,
    113, 114, 119, 302
  Thailand 132
clientism in Thailand 129
Clifford, Mark 213
Cohen, Stephen 235
Coleman, William 18, 25, 310, 311
collective bargaining, and welfare states
  65, 67, 74–5
Commodity Futures Trading Commission
  (CFTC) 284, 285, 286, 291
common law and civil law
  in East Asia 200–1, 202–6
  LLSV arguments concerning 201, 202–6,
    216
  in Malaysia 201, 216–17, 219–20
competitive liberalism
  and economic interdependence of states
    1
  and the logics of globalisation 6
competitive trade and industry strategies
  26
conservative welfare states *see* corporatist
  (conservative) welfare states
constraints view of globalisation 3–4, 5–15,
  26, 29–30
  beyond measurement 14–15
  delimiting the constraints 10–12
  and domestic institutions 21
  and fiscal policymaking 56
  measuring interdependence 12–15
  standard view 5–10
  and transformationalism 7, 10, 310, 315,
    316
convergence 307
coordinated markets, and the logics of
  globalisation 6
corporate governance, and common and
  civil law countries 204
corporate income taxes (CIT), and OECD
  fiscal policy 41, 45–7, 48, 49–52, 55,
  294
corporatist (conservative) welfare states
  61–2, 65, 78–9
  and collective bargaining 74–5
  in East Asia 92, 98
  effects of international capital mobility
    on 77, 78
  and political institutions 72
  and production regimes 67
  and welfare retrenchment 69–70
  and 'welfare without work' 75, 80

CAMBRIDGE STUDIES IN INTERNATIONAL RELATIONS

360